Fruits Basket™

Volume 7

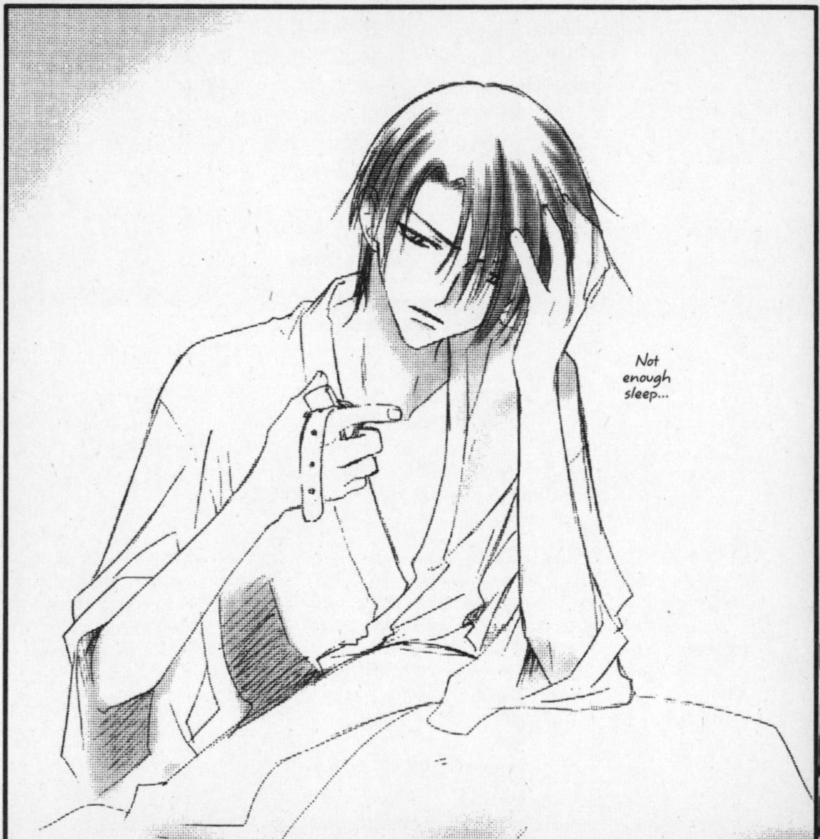
Not enough sleep...

Natsuki Takaya

Fruits Basket Vol. 7
Created by Natsuki Takaya

Translation - Alethea Nibley and Athena Nibley
English Adaptation - Jake Forbes
Contributing Writer - Adam Arnold
Copy Editor - Peter Ahlstrom
Retouch and Lettering - Deron Bennett
Production Artist - Jason Milligan
Cover Design - Gary Shum

Editor - Paul Morrissey
Digital Imaging Manager - Chris Buford
Pre-Press Manager - Antonio DePietro
Production Managers - Jennifer Miller and Mutsumi Miyazaki
Art Director - Matt Alford
Managing Editor - Jill Freshney
VP of Production - Ron Klamert
Editor-in-Chief - Mike Kiley
President and C.O.O. - John Parker
Publisher and C.E.O. - Stuart Levy

A  Manga

TOKYOPOP Inc.
5900 Wilshire Blvd. Suite 2000
Los Angeles, CA 90036

E-mail: info@TOKYOPOP.com
Come visit us online at www.TOKYOPOP.com

FRUITS BASKET Vol. 7 by Natsuki Takaya
© 2001 Natsuki Takaya. All rights reserved.
st published in Japan in 2001 by HAKUSENSHA, INC., Tokyo
English language translation rights in the
United States of America and Canada arranged with
HAKUSENSHA, INC., Tokyo through
Tuttle-Mori Agency Inc., Tokyo
English text copyright © 2005 TOKYOPOP Inc.

All rights reserved. No portion of this book may be
reproduced or transmitted in any form or by any means
without written permission from the copyright holders.
This manga is a work of fiction. Any resemblance to
actual events or locales or persons, living or dead, is
entirely coincidental.

ISBN: 1-59532-402-X

First TOKYOPOP printing: February 2005
10 9 8 7 6 5 4 3 2 1
Printed in the USA

Fruits Basket™

Volume 7

By
Natsuki Takaya

TOKYOPOP®

HAMBURG // LONDON // LOS ANGELES // TOKYO

Fruits Basket™

Table of Contents

STORY SO FAR...

Hello, I'm Tohru Honda and I have come to know a terrible secret. After the death of my mother, I was living by myself in a tent, when the Sohma family took me in. I soon learned that the Sohma family lives with a curse! Each family member is possessed by the vengeful spirit of an animal from the Chinese Zodiac. Whenever one of them becomes weak or is hugged by a member of the opposite sex, they change into their Zodiac animal!

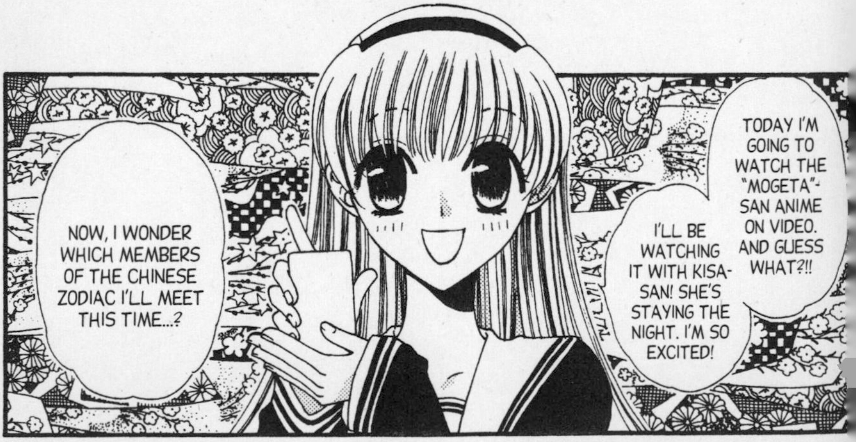
TODAY I'M GOING TO WATCH THE "MOGETA"-SAN ANIME ON VIDEO. AND GUESS WHAT?!!
I'LL BE WATCHING IT WITH KISA-SAN! SHE'S STAYING THE NIGHT. I'M SO EXCITED!
NOW, I WONDER WHICH MEMBERS OF THE CHINESE ZODIAC I'LL MEET THIS TIME...?

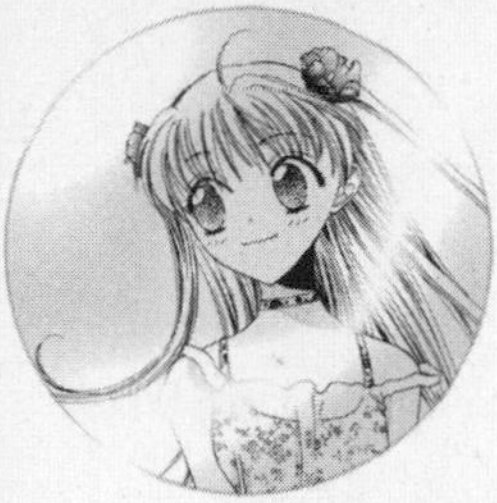

Tohru Honda

The ever-optimistic hero of our story. An orphan, she now lives in Shigure's house, along with Yuki and Kyo, and is the only person outside of the family who knows the Sohma family's curse.

Yuki Sohma, the Rat

Soft-spoken. Self-esteem issues. At school he's called "Prince Yuki."

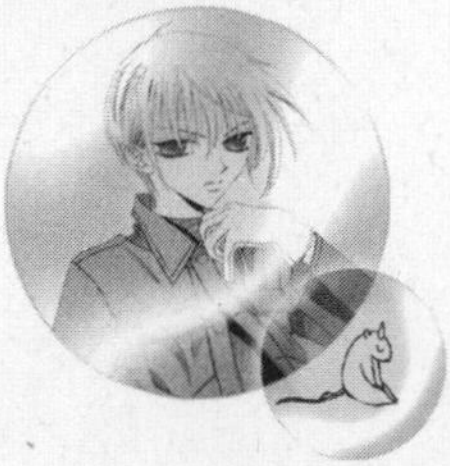

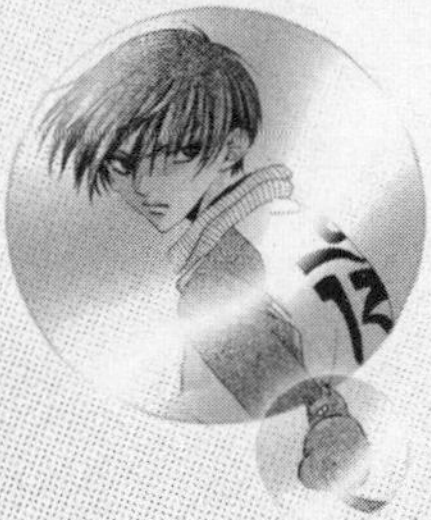

Kyo Sohma, the Cat

The Cat who was left out of the Zodiac. Hates Yuki, leeks and miso. But mostly Yuki.

Mabudachi Trio

Shigure Sohma, the Dog

Enigmatic, mischievous and a little perverted. A popular novelist.

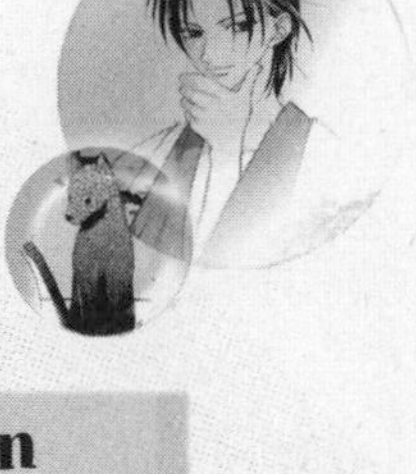

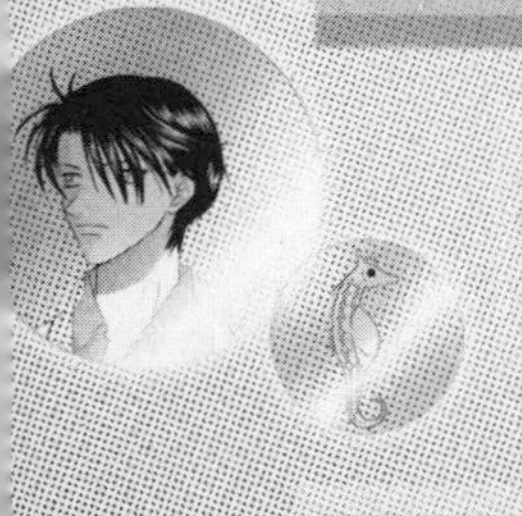

Hatori Sohma, the Dragon

Family doctor to the Sohmas. Only thing he can't cure is his broken heart.

Ayame Sohma, the Snake

Yuki's older brother. A proud and playful drama queen…er, king. Runs a costume shop.

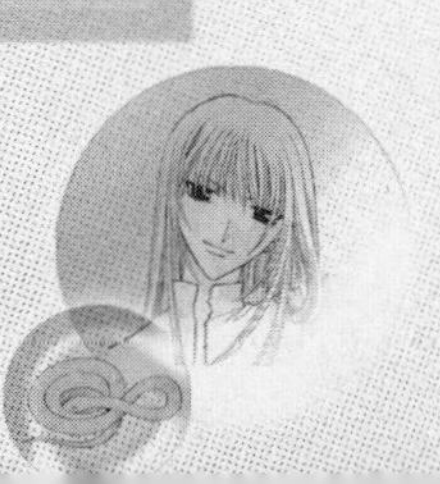

Fruits Basket Characters

Kagura Sohma, the Boar

Bashful, yet headstrong. Determined to marry Kyo, even if it kills him.

Momiji Sohma, the Rabbit

Half-German. He's older than he looks. Mother rejected him because of the Sohma curse.

Hatsuharu Sohma, the Ox

The nicest of guys, except when he goes "Black." Then you'd better watch out.

Akito Sohma

The head of the Sohma clan. A dark figure of many secrets. Treated with fear and reverence.

Tohru's Best Friends

Saki Hanajima

"Hana-chan." Can sense people's "waves." Goth demeanor scares her classmates.

Arisa Uotani

"Uo-chan." A tough-talking "Yankee" who looks out for her friends.

Kisa Sohma, the Tiger

Kisa became shy and self-conscious due to constant teasing by her classmates. Yuki, who has similar insecurities, feels particularly close to Kisa.

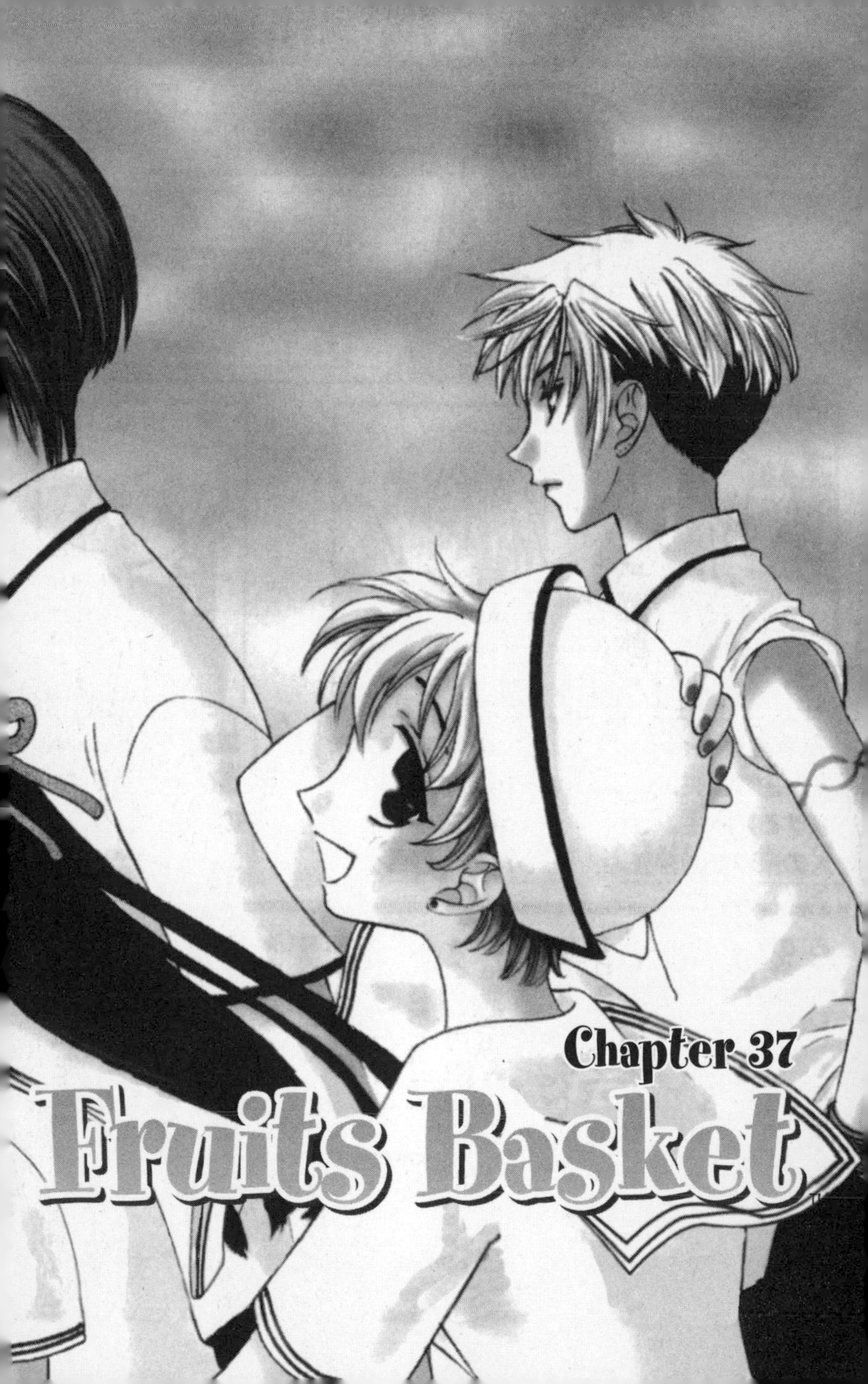
Chapter 37
Fruits Basket

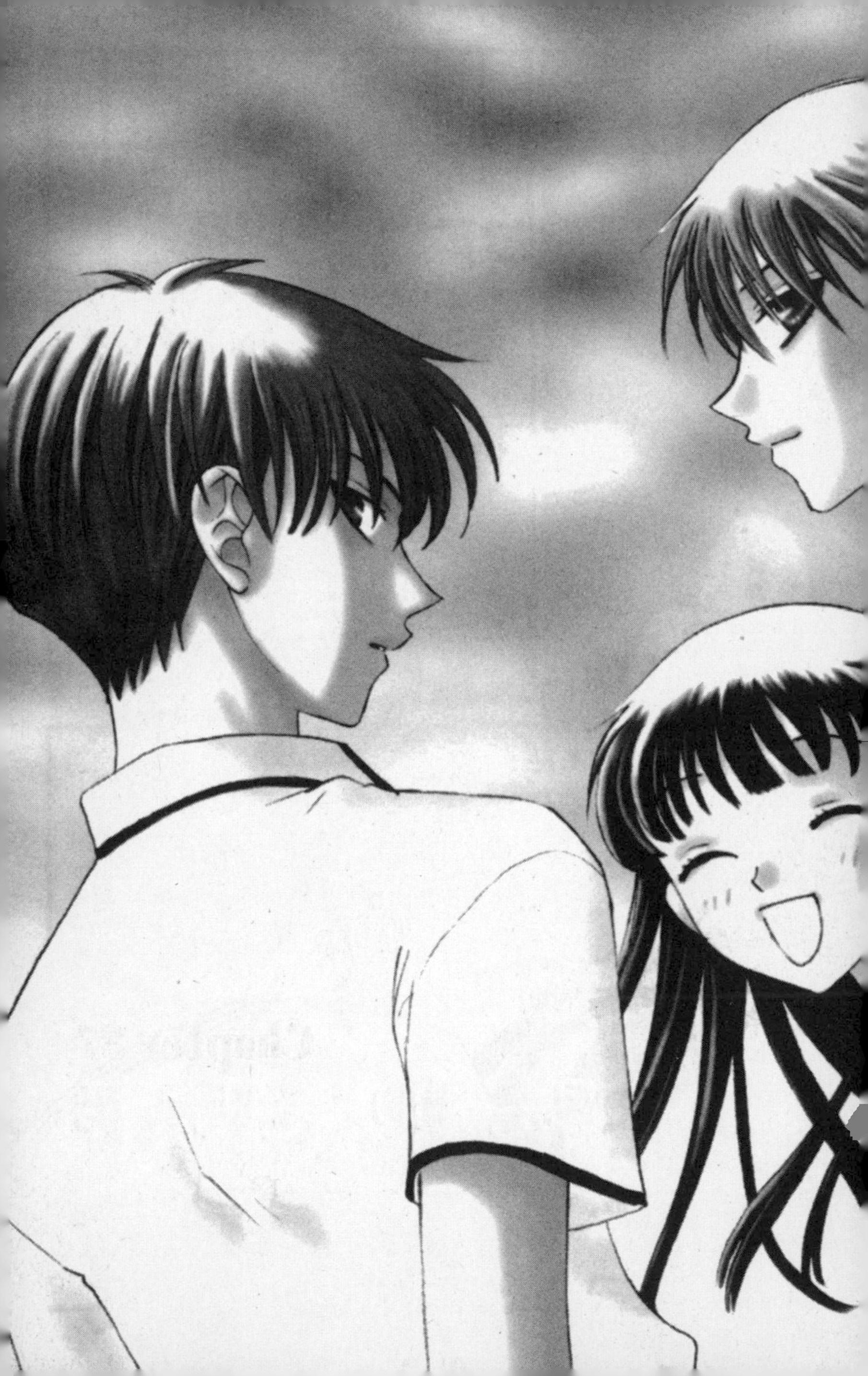

ULTRA-SPECIAL BONUS BLAH, BLAH, BLAH

Please don't think too much about Mogeta. Seriously. Just go with it. Takaya just drew it because she felt like it.

Today is the day, once again. Yes it's true! Ari's taking a walk with Mogeta!

(Aritamis Donpanina Taios is long, so it's always abbreviated)

Today is the day, and you know he can't lose! That mysterious creature, Mogeta!*

Sometimes--well, rarely--when they remember--they fight scaaaary enemies.

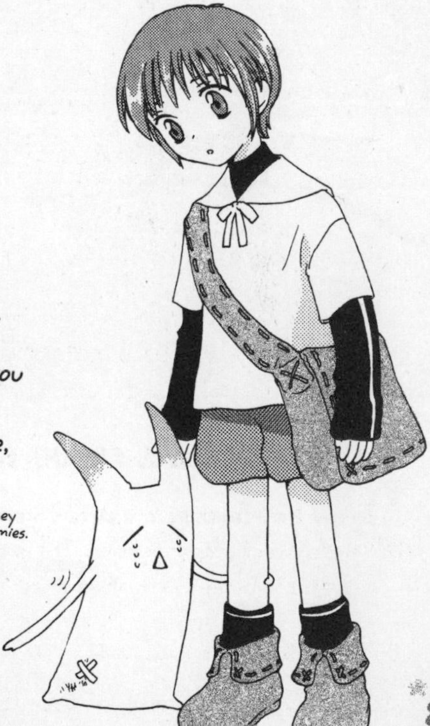

Today's enemy

*This is the Mogeta anime theme song...more or less...

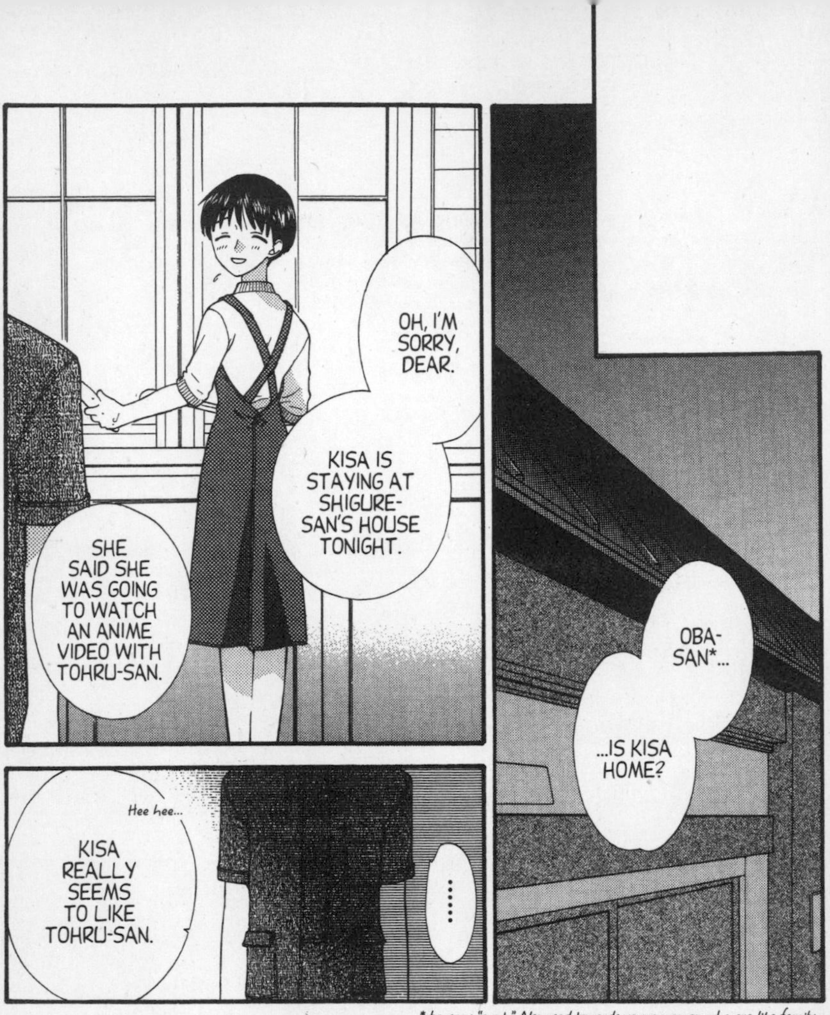
OBA-SAN*...
...IS KISA HOME?
OH, I'M SORRY, DEAR.
KISA IS STAYING AT SHIGURE-SAN'S HOUSE TONIGHT.
SHE SAID SHE WAS GOING TO WATCH AN ANIME VIDEO WITH TOHRU-SAN.
Hee hee...
KISA REALLY SEEMS TO LIKE TOHRU-SAN.
......

*oba-san: "aunt." Also used towards young women who are like family.

ULTRA-SPECIAL BLAH, BLAH, BLAH, 1

I had hay fever before a few years back, but this time my nose won't stop running. It's a real problem. Where on earth does all that snot come from? Sigh...

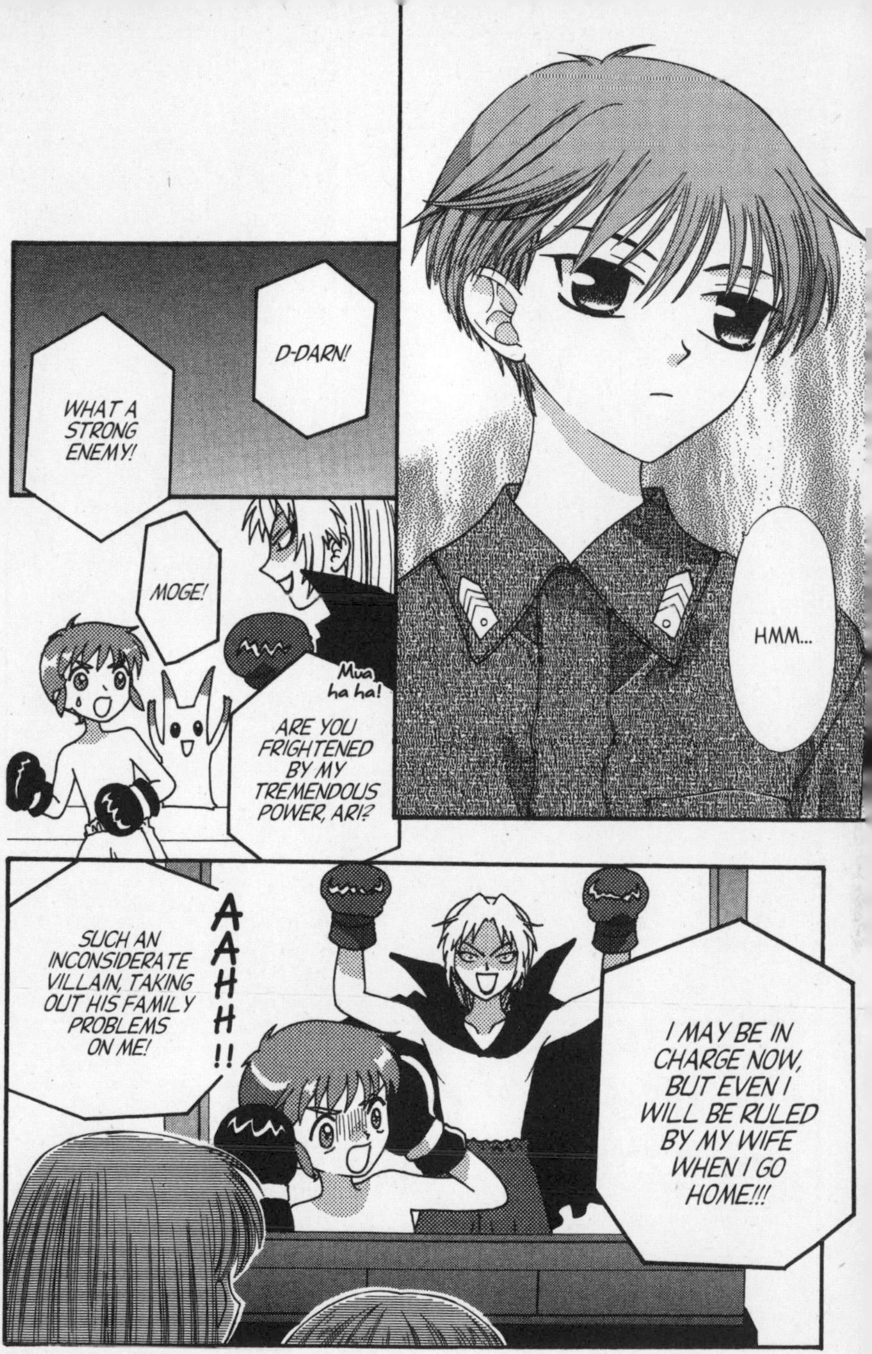
HMM...
D-DARN!
WHAT A STRONG ENEMY!
Mua ha ha!
ARE YOU FRIGHTENED BY MY TREMENDOUS POWER, ARI?
MOGE!
I MAY BE IN CHARGE NOW, BUT EVEN I WILL BE RULED BY MY WIFE WHEN I GO HOME!!!
AAHH!!
SUCH AN INCONSIDERATE VILLAIN, TAKING OUT HIS FAMILY PROBLEMS ON ME!

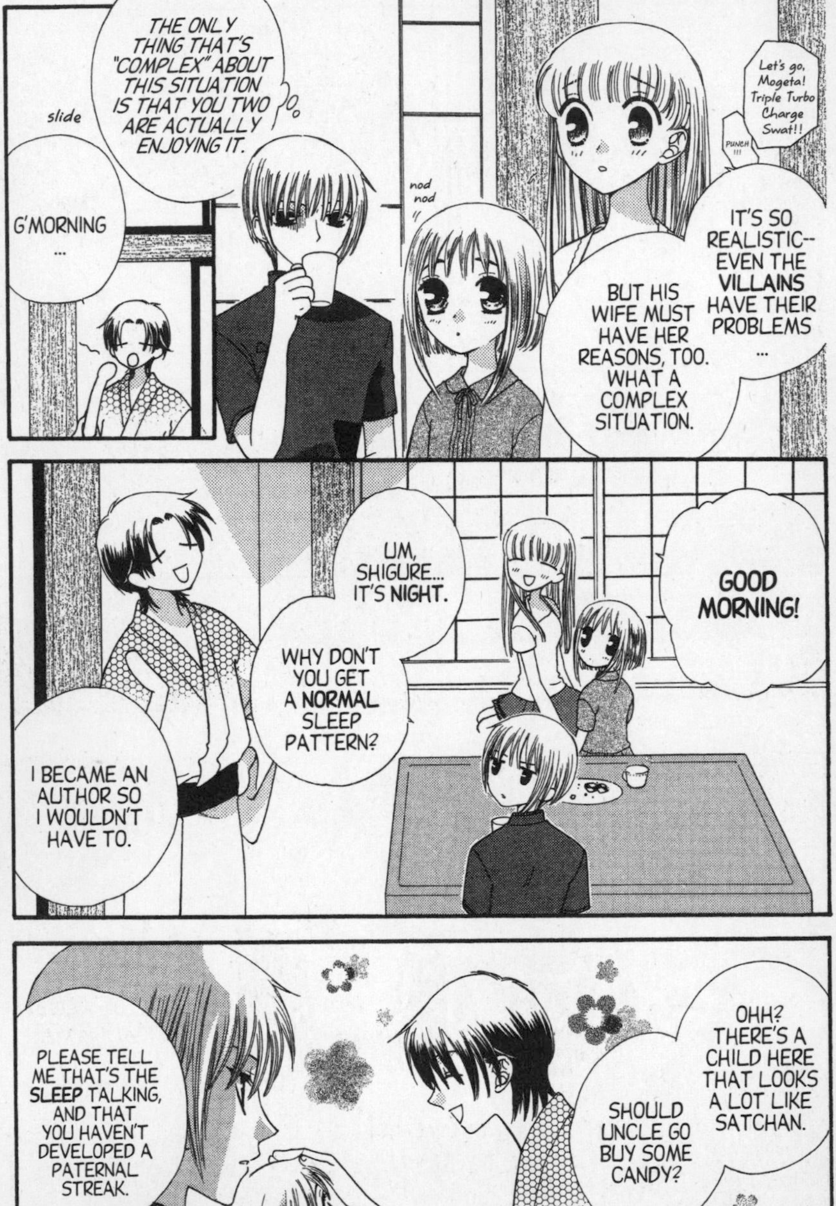
Let's go, Mogeta! Triple Turbo Charge Swat!!
PUNCH!!!
IT'S SO REALISTIC-- EVEN THE VILLAINS HAVE THEIR PROBLEMS ...
BUT HIS WIFE MUST HAVE HER REASONS, TOO. WHAT A COMPLEX SITUATION.
nod nod
THE ONLY THING THAT'S "COMPLEX" ABOUT THIS SITUATION IS THAT YOU TWO ARE ACTUALLY ENJOYING IT.
slide
G'MORNING ...
GOOD MORNING!
UM, SHIGURE... IT'S NIGHT.
WHY DON'T YOU GET A NORMAL SLEEP PATTERN?
I BECAME AN AUTHOR SO I WOULDN'T HAVE TO.
OHH? THERE'S A CHILD HERE THAT LOOKS A LOT LIKE SATCHAN.
SHOULD UNCLE GO BUY SOME CANDY?
PLEASE TELL ME THAT'S THE SLEEP TALKING, AND THAT YOU HAVEN'T DEVELOPED A PATERNAL STREAK.

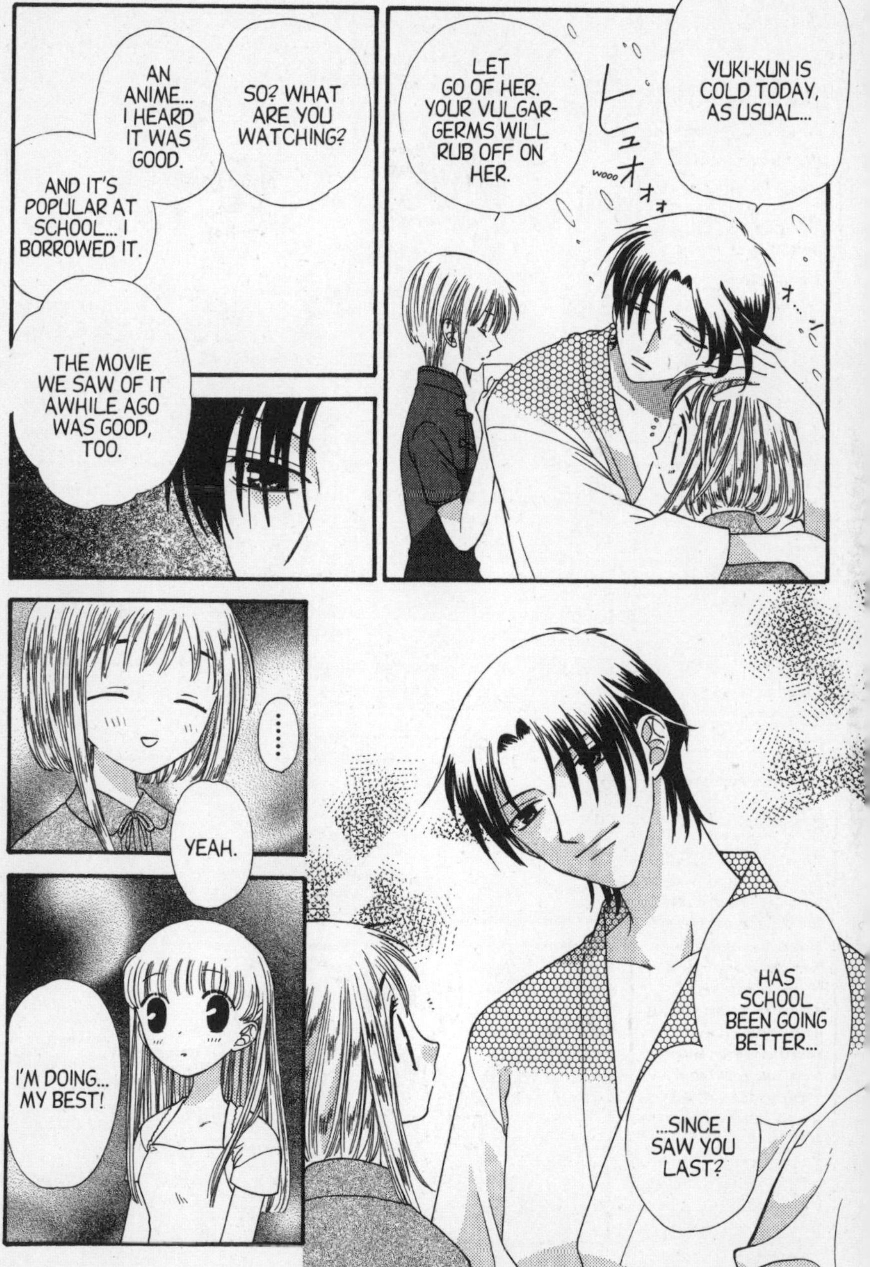
YUKI-KUN IS COLD TODAY, AS USUAL...
ヒュオォ
wooo
LET GO OF HER. YOUR VULGAR-GERMS WILL RUB OFF ON HER.
オ...ォ
SO? WHAT ARE YOU WATCHING?
AN ANIME... I HEARD IT WAS GOOD.
AND IT'S POPULAR AT SCHOOL... I BORROWED IT.
THE MOVIE WE SAW OF IT AWHILE AGO WAS GOOD, TOO.
HAS SCHOOL BEEN GOING BETTER...
...SINCE I SAW YOU LAST?
......
YEAH.
I'M DOING... MY BEST!

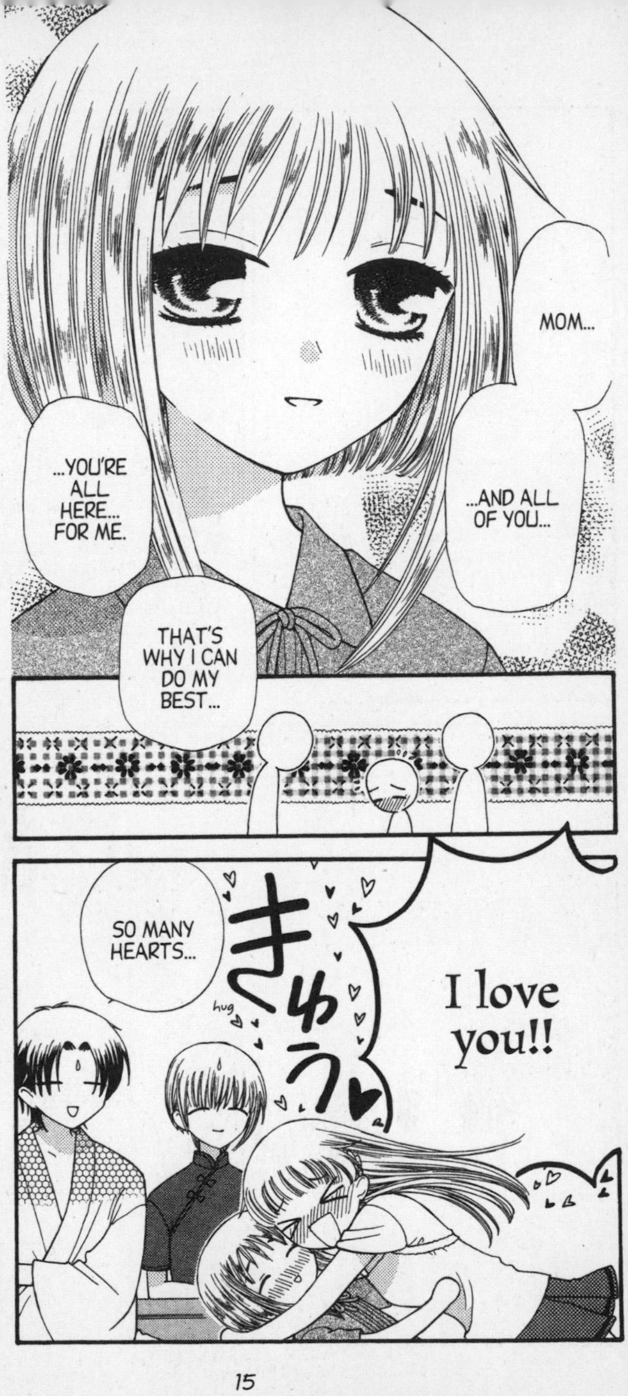
MOM...
...AND ALL OF YOU...
...YOU'RE ALL HERE... FOR ME.
THAT'S WHY I CAN DO MY BEST...
きゅう♥
I love you!!
hug
SO MANY HEARTS...

Fruits Basket 7: Part 1

Hajimemashite and Konnichiwa. Natsuki Takaya reporting for duty. You've waited a long time, and here it is--volume 7! It's Hatori, this time. Goodness, it took a long time for me to recover fully; I apologize. I think there **may** have been people waiting for a Hatori cover... Were there? (I feel bad having to ask.) Anyway, Furuba has returned, so please enjoy it.

Editor's note: While Takaya-sensei was working on **Furuba** vol. 6, she sustained a serious injury to her drawing hand that caused the series to go on hiatus in Japan. (She mentions her hand in a vol. 6 sidebar). Fortunately, it was a speedy recovery and after a delay on Vol. 7, Takaya-sensei was able to return to the work she loves.

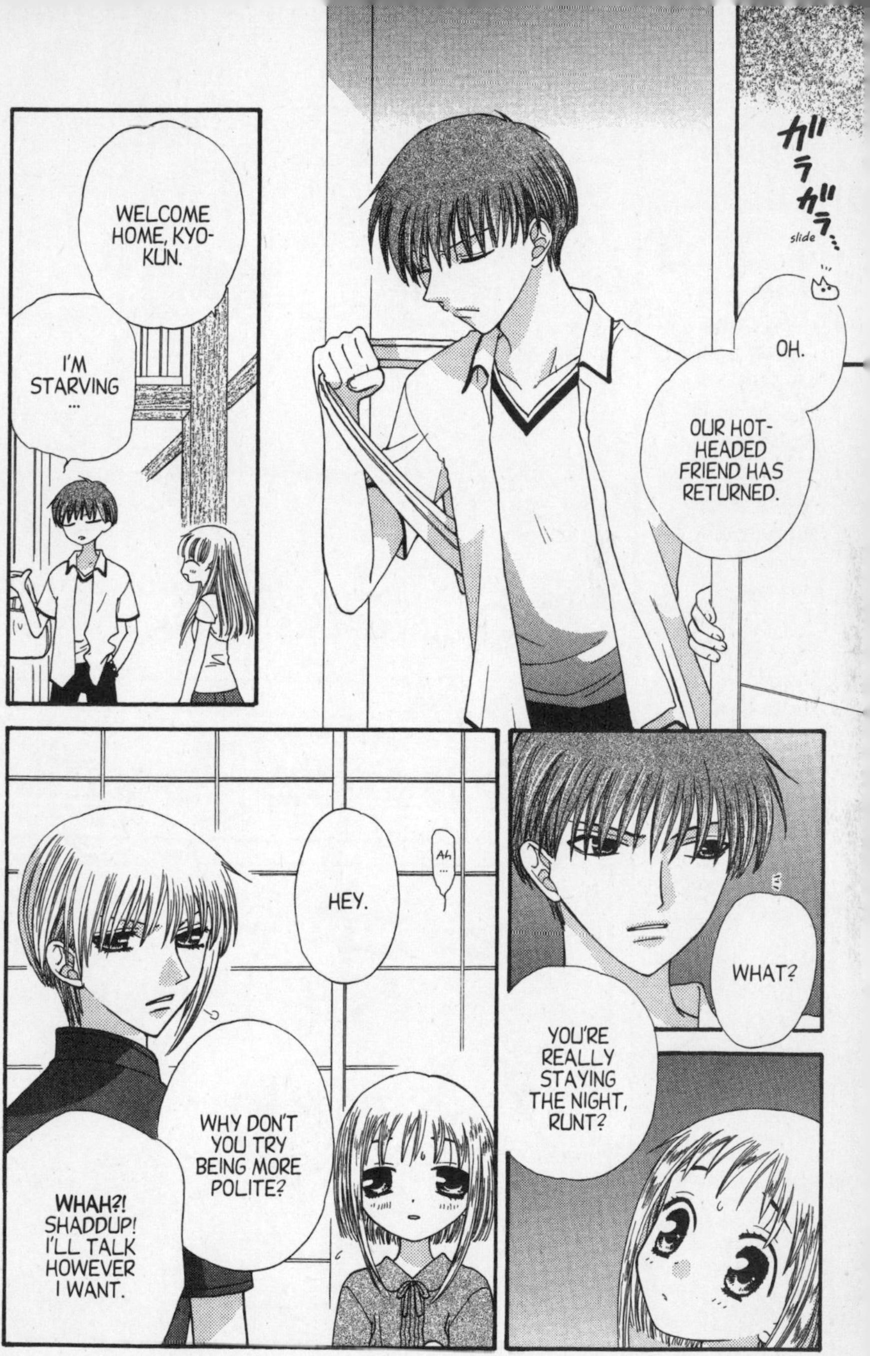
ガラガラ
slide
OH.
OUR HOT-HEADED FRIEND HAS RETURNED.
WELCOME HOME, KYO-KUN.
I'M STARVING ...
WHAT?
YOU'RE REALLY STAYING THE NIGHT, RUNT?
HEY.
Ah ...
WHY DON'T YOU TRY BEING MORE POLITE?
WHAH?! SHADDUP! I'LL TALK HOWEVER I WANT.

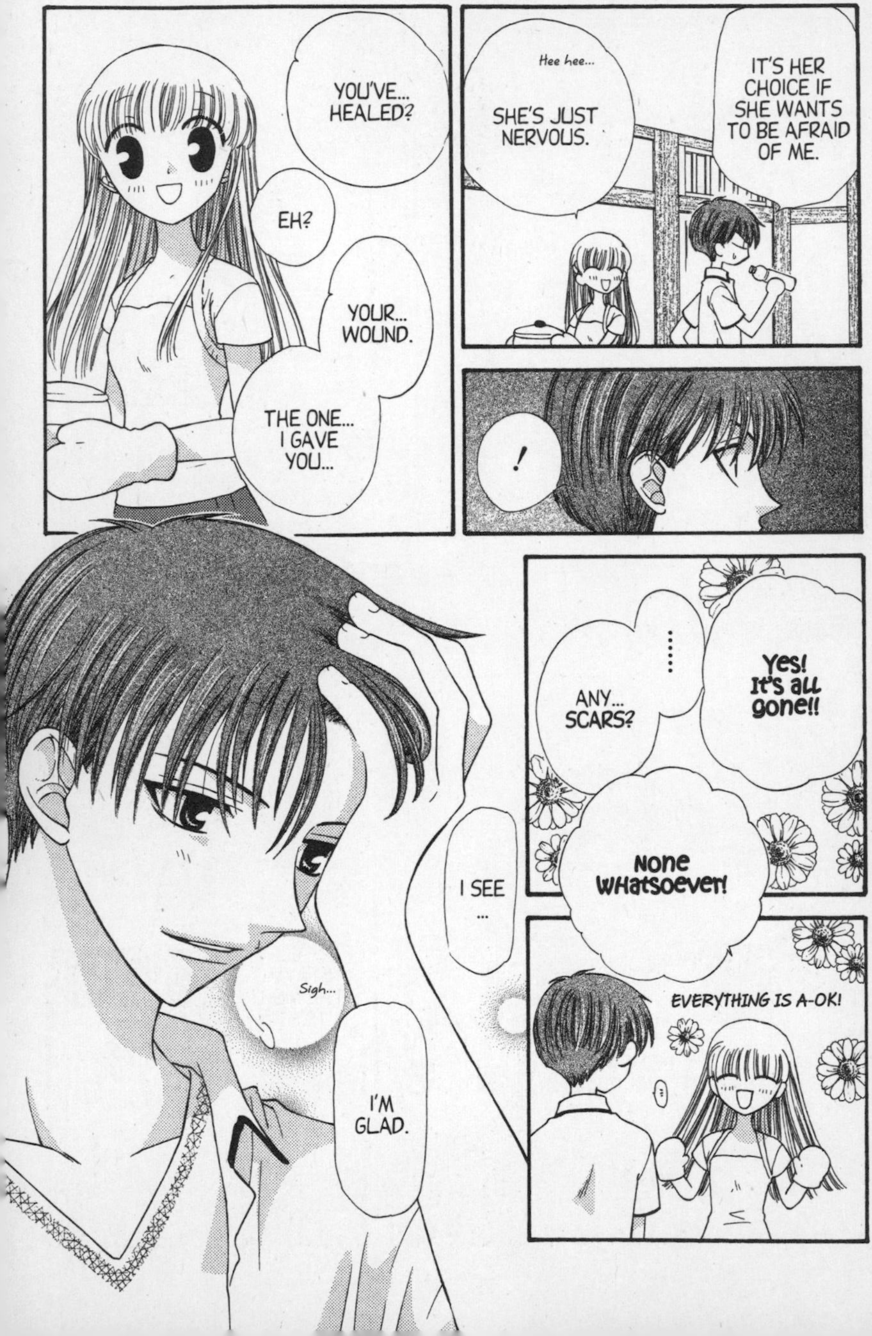

IT'S HER CHOICE IF SHE WANTS TO BE AFRAID OF ME.
Hee hee...
SHE'S JUST NERVOUS.
!
YOU'VE... HEALED?
EH?
YOUR... WOUND.
THE ONE... I GAVE YOU...
Yes! It's all gone!!
......
ANY... SCARS?
None whatsoever!
EVERYTHING IS A-OK!
I SEE ...
Sigh...
I'M GLAD.

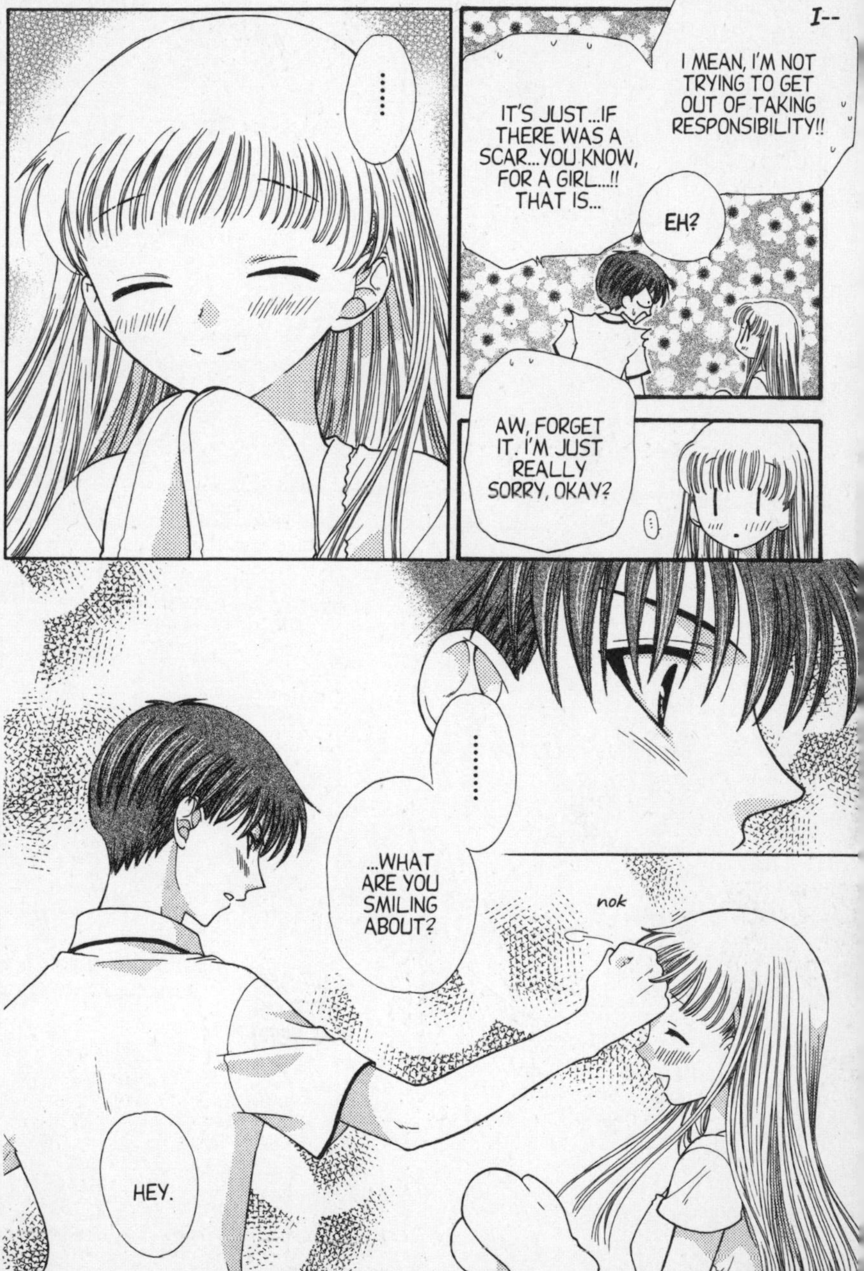
I--
I MEAN, I'M NOT TRYING TO GET OUT OF TAKING RESPONSIBILITY!!
IT'S JUST...IF THERE WAS A SCAR...YOU KNOW, FOR A GIRL...!! THAT IS...
EH?
AW, FORGET IT. I'M JUST REALLY SORRY, OKAY?
...
......
......
...WHAT ARE YOU SMILING ABOUT?
nok
HEY.

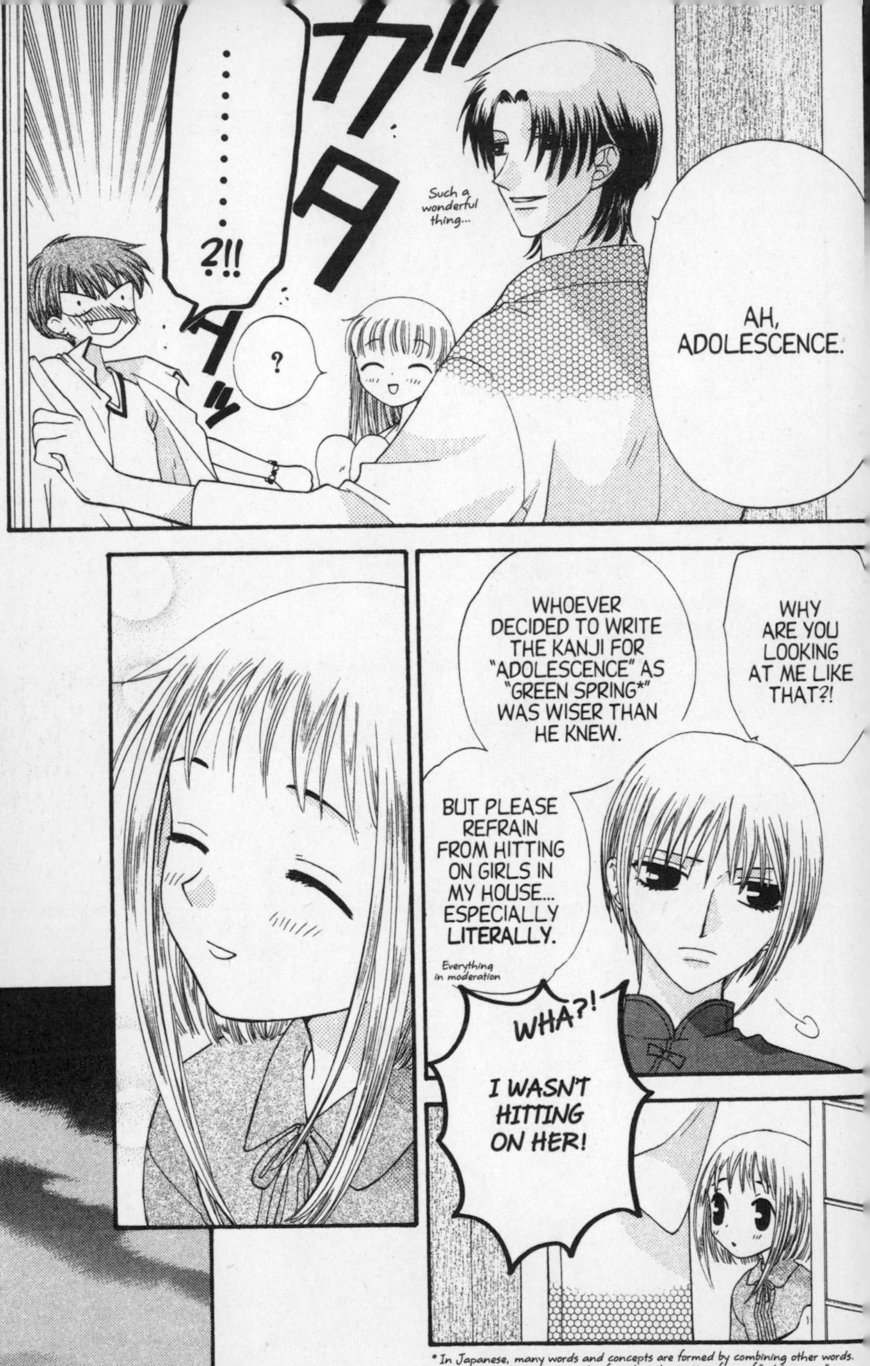
AH, ADOLESCENCE.
Such a wonderful thing...
ガタッ
......?!!
?
WHY ARE YOU LOOKING AT ME LIKE THAT?!
WHOEVER DECIDED TO WRITE THE KANJI FOR "ADOLESCENCE" AS "GREEN SPRING*" WAS WISER THAN HE KNEW.
BUT PLEASE REFRAIN FROM HITTING ON GIRLS IN MY HOUSE... ESPECIALLY LITERALLY.
Everything in moderation
WHA?!
I WASN'T HITTING ON HER!

* In Japanese, many words and concepts are formed by combining other words. Shigure is commenting on the fact that the written form of "adolescence" is formed by combining the written words for "green" and "spring."

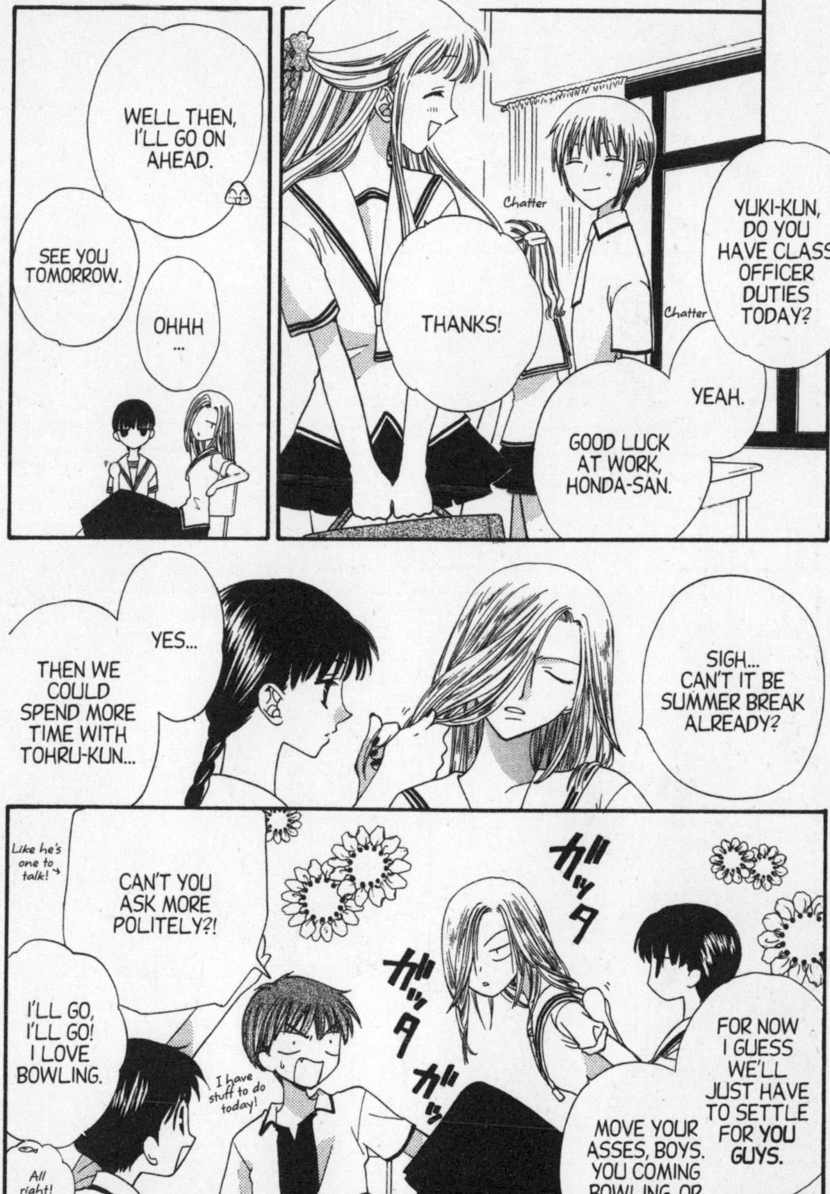
YUKI-KUN, DO YOU HAVE CLASS OFFICER DUTIES TODAY?
Chatter
YEAH.
Chatter
GOOD LUCK AT WORK, HONDA-SAN.
THANKS!
WELL THEN, I'LL GO ON AHEAD.
SEE YOU TOMORROW.
OHHH ...
SIGH... CAN'T IT BE SUMMER BREAK ALREADY?
YES...
THEN WE COULD SPEND MORE TIME WITH TOHRU-KUN...
ガッタ
ガッタ
ガッ
FOR NOW I GUESS WE'LL JUST HAVE TO SETTLE FOR YOU GUYS.
MOVE YOUR ASSES, BOYS. YOU COMING BOWLING, OR WHAT?
I have stuff to do today!
CAN'T YOU ASK MORE POLITELY?!
Like he's one to talk!
I'LL GO, I'LL GO! I LOVE BOWLING.
All right! Come on!

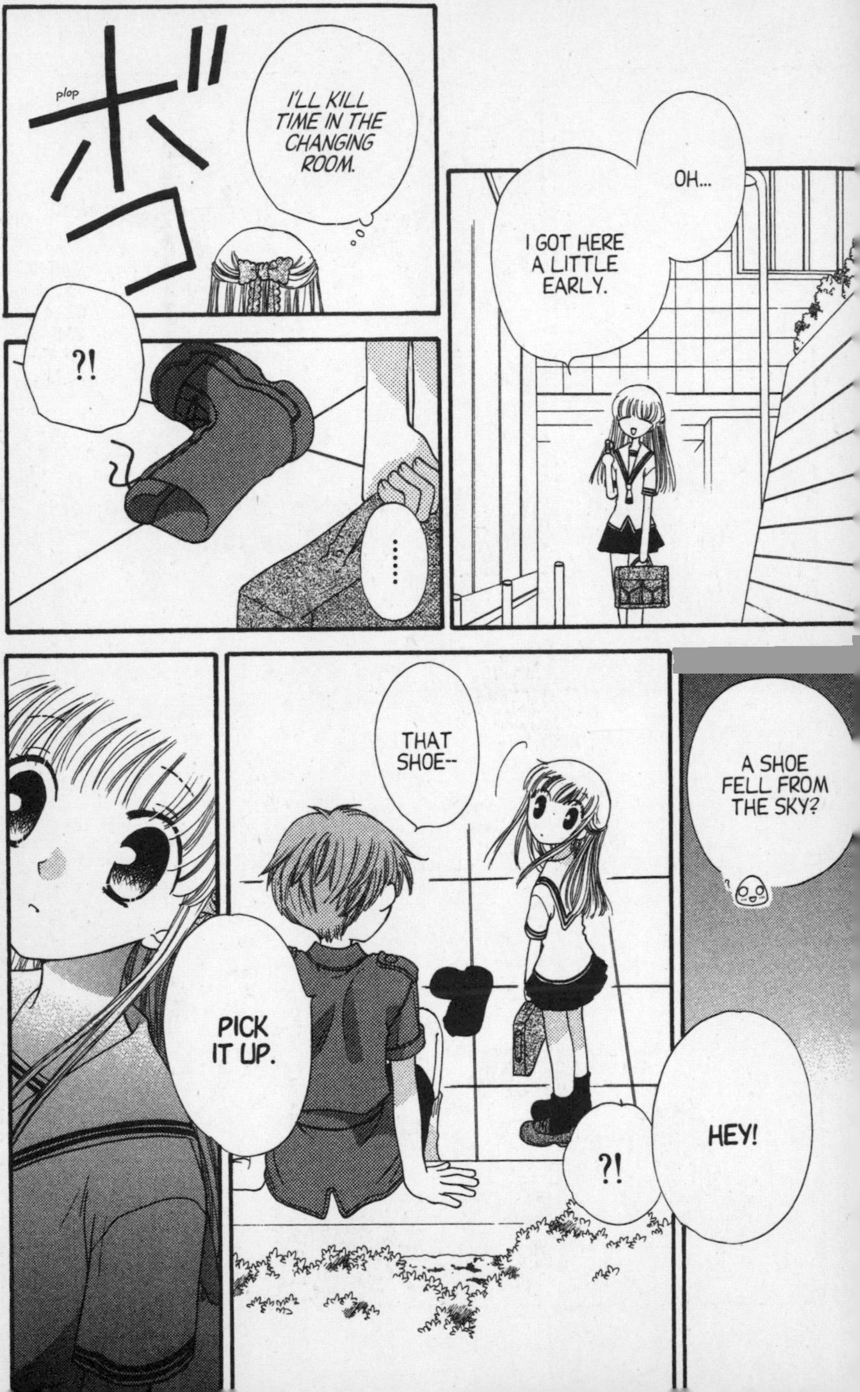
OH...
I GOT HERE A LITTLE EARLY.
I'LL KILL TIME IN THE CHANGING ROOM.
plop
?!
......
A SHOE FELL FROM THE SKY?
HEY!
?!
THAT SHOE--
PICK IT UP.

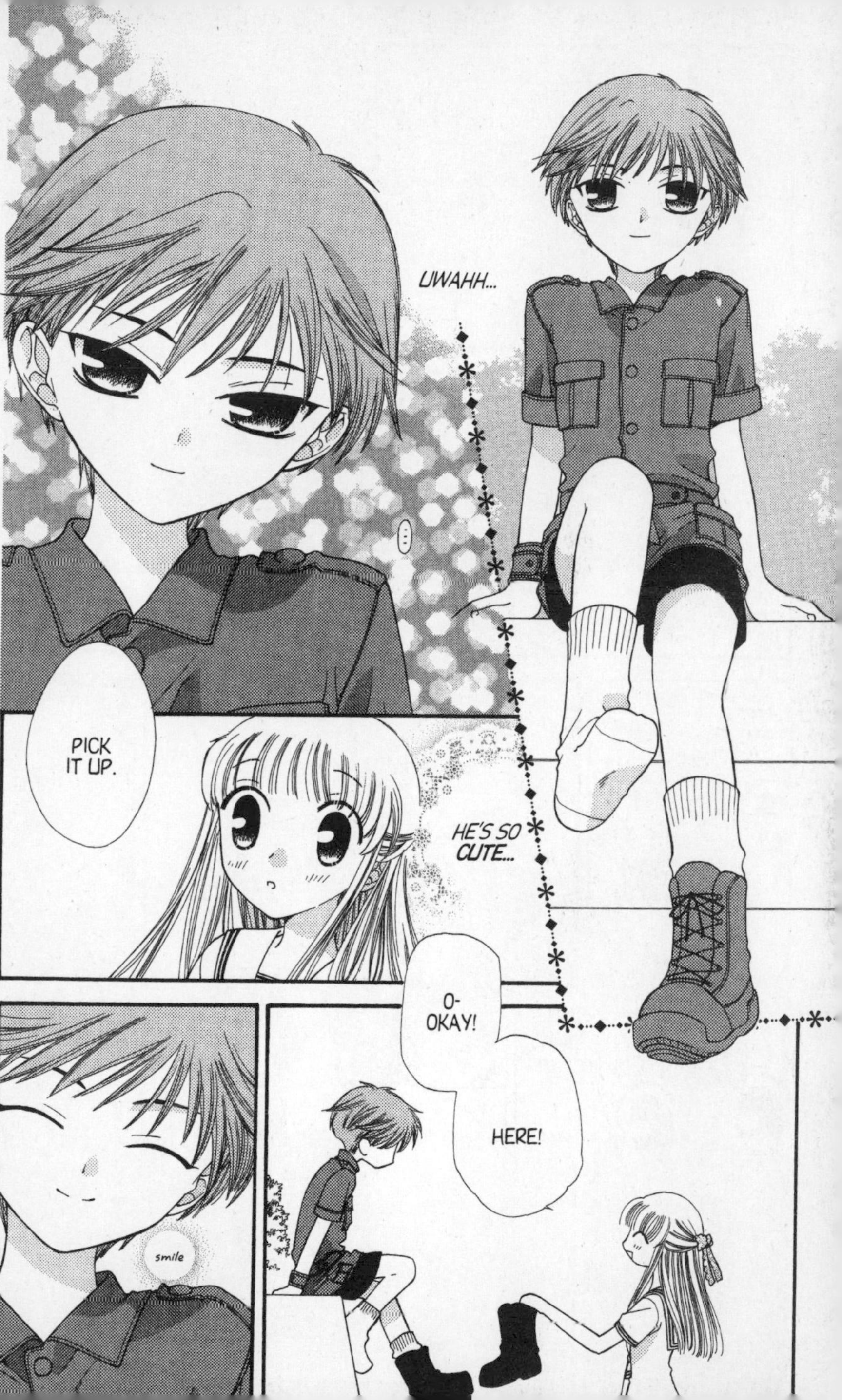
UWAHH...
HE'S SO CUTE...
...
PICK IT UP.
O-OKAY!
HERE!
smile

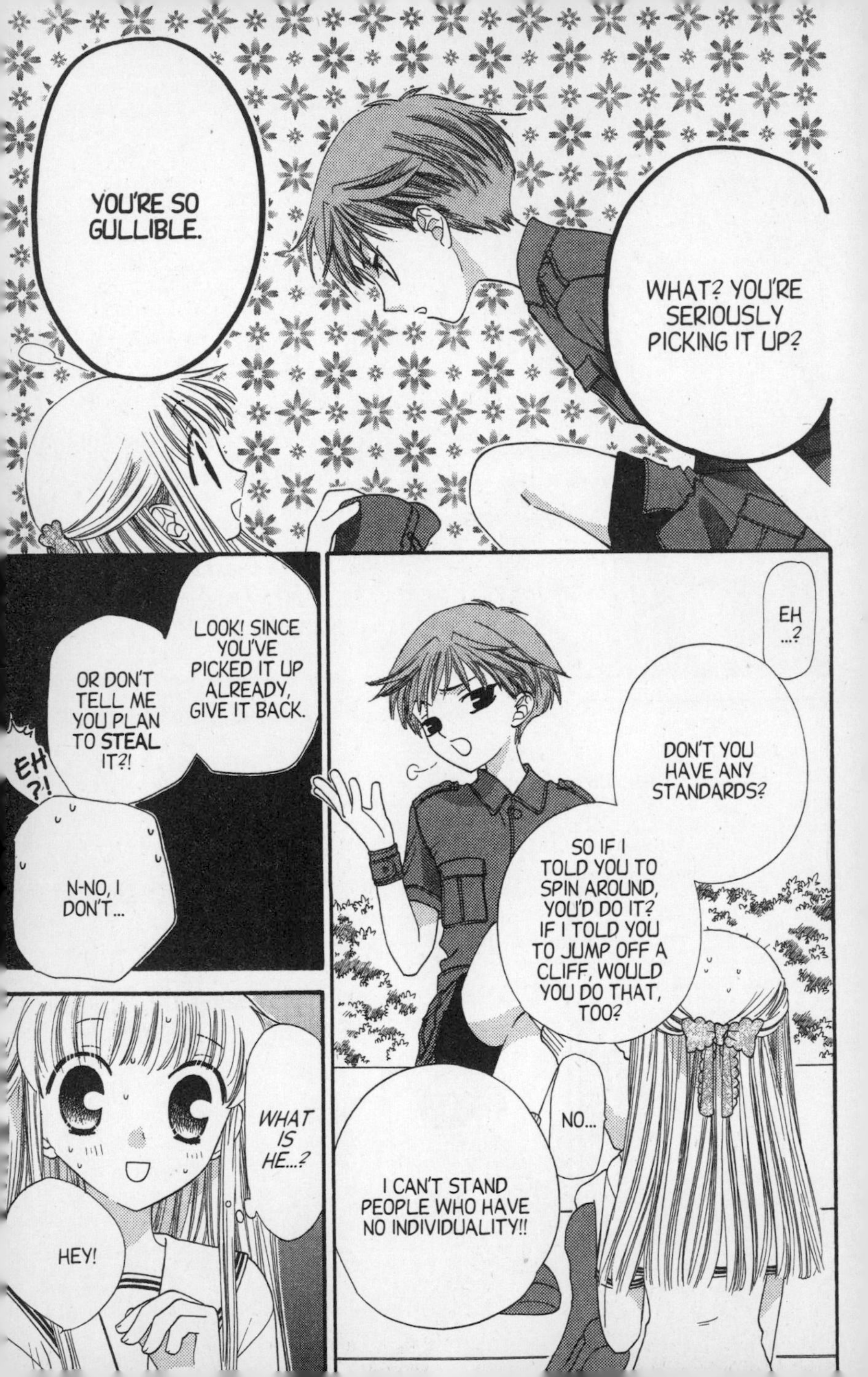
WHAT? YOU'RE SERIOUSLY PICKING IT UP?
YOU'RE SO GULLIBLE.
EH ...?
DON'T YOU HAVE ANY STANDARDS?
SO IF I TOLD YOU TO SPIN AROUND, YOU'D DO IT? IF I TOLD YOU TO JUMP OFF A CLIFF, WOULD YOU DO THAT, TOO?
NO...
I CAN'T STAND PEOPLE WHO HAVE NO INDIVIDUALITY!!
LOOK! SINCE YOU'VE PICKED IT UP ALREADY, GIVE IT BACK.
OR DON'T TELL ME YOU PLAN TO **STEAL** IT?!
EH?!
N-NO, I DON'T...
WHAT IS HE...?
HEY!

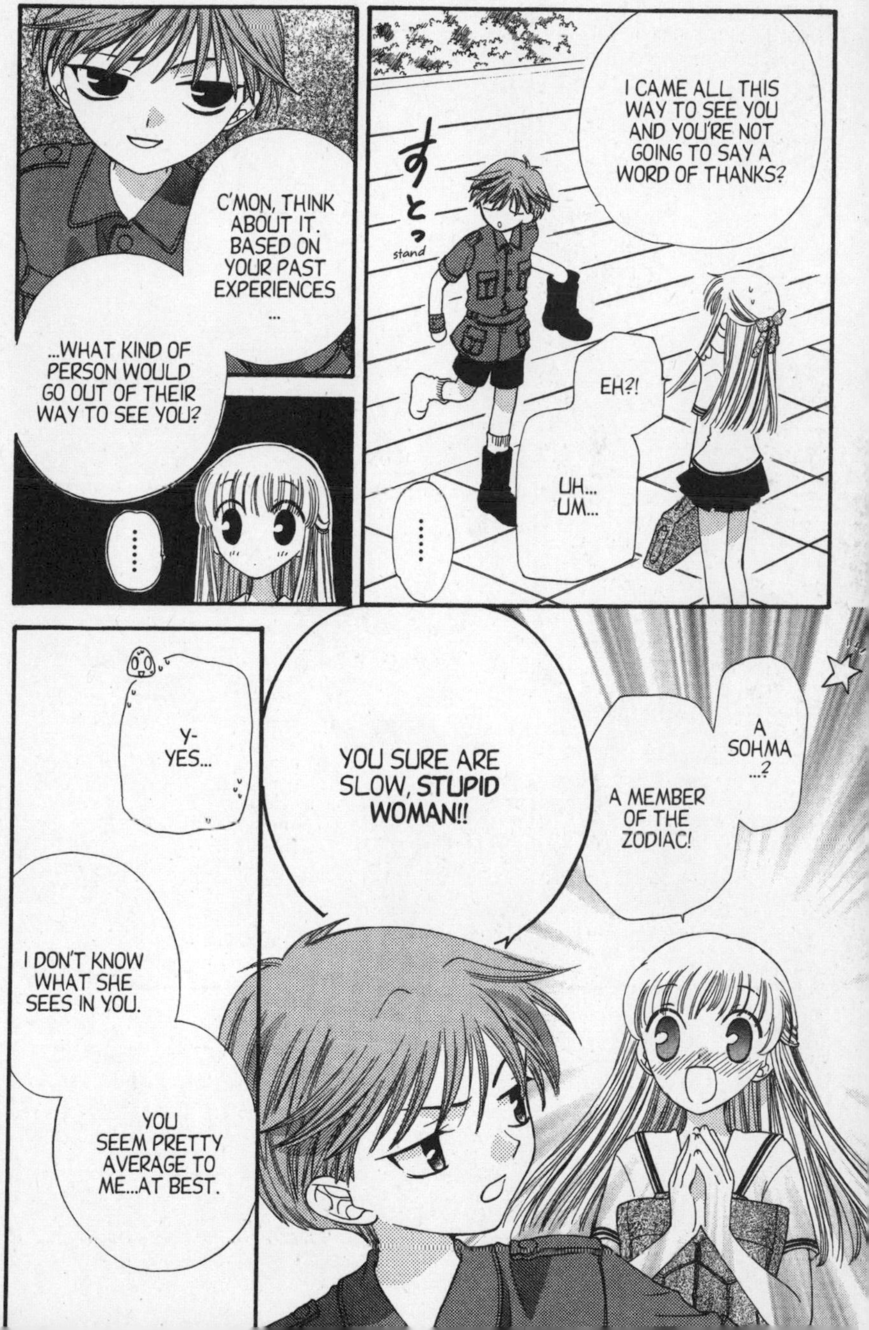
I CAME ALL THIS WAY TO SEE YOU AND YOU'RE NOT GOING TO SAY A WORD OF THANKS?
すとっ
stand
EH?!
UH... UM...
......
C'MON, THINK ABOUT IT. BASED ON YOUR PAST EXPERIENCES ...
...WHAT KIND OF PERSON WOULD GO OUT OF THEIR WAY TO SEE YOU?
......
A SOHMA ...?
A MEMBER OF THE ZODIAC!
YOU SURE ARE SLOW, STUPID WOMAN!!
Y- YES...
I DON'T KNOW WHAT SHE SEES IN YOU.
YOU SEEM PRETTY AVERAGE TO ME...AT BEST.

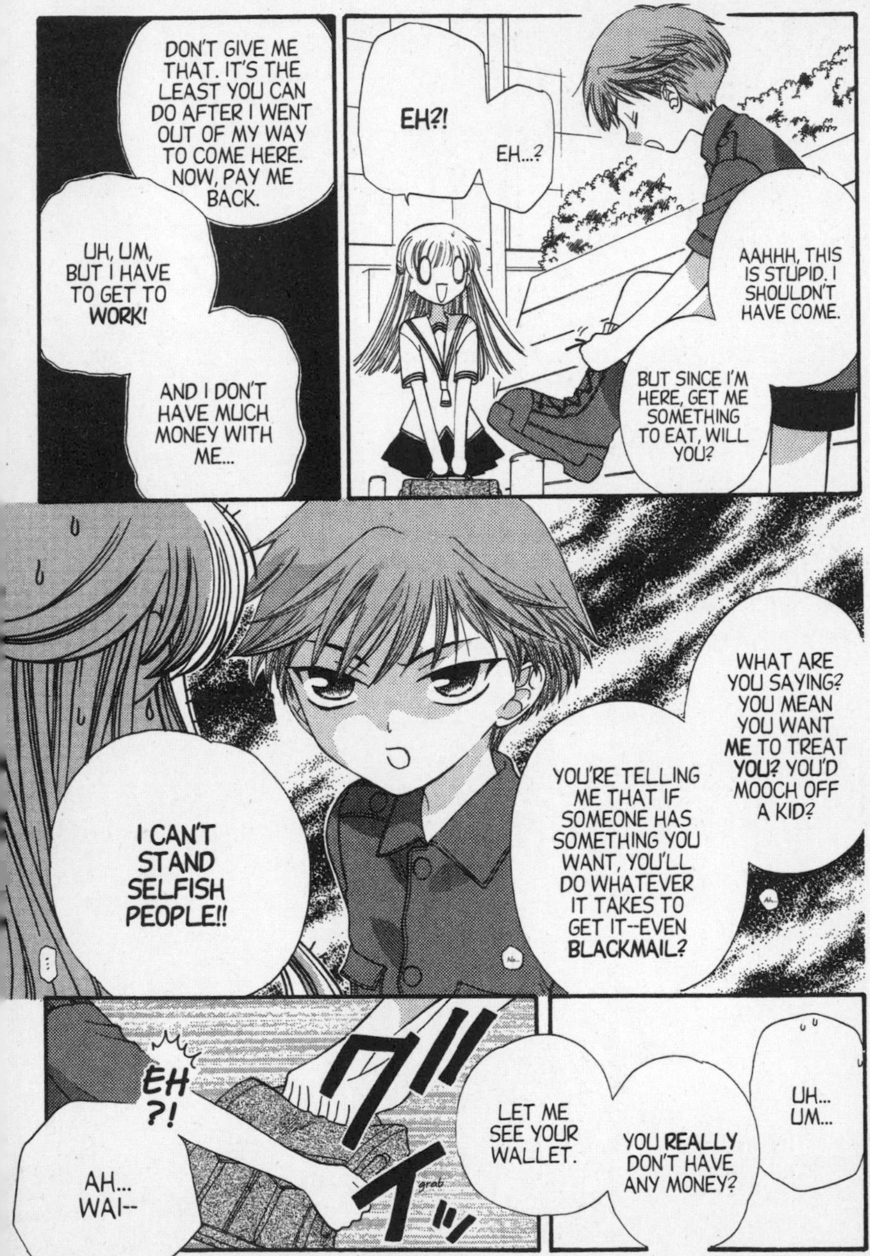
AAHHH, THIS IS STUPID. I SHOULDN'T HAVE COME.
BUT SINCE I'M HERE, GET ME SOMETHING TO EAT, WILL YOU?
EH...?
EH?!
DON'T GIVE ME THAT. IT'S THE LEAST YOU CAN DO AFTER I WENT OUT OF MY WAY TO COME HERE. NOW, PAY ME BACK.
UH, UM, BUT I HAVE TO GET TO WORK!
AND I DON'T HAVE MUCH MONEY WITH ME...
WHAT ARE YOU SAYING? YOU MEAN YOU WANT ME TO TREAT YOU? YOU'D MOOCH OFF A KID?
YOU'RE TELLING ME THAT IF SOMEONE HAS SOMETHING YOU WANT, YOU'LL DO WHATEVER IT TAKES TO GET IT--EVEN BLACKMAIL?
I CAN'T STAND SELFISH PEOPLE!!
...
UH... UM...
YOU REALLY DON'T HAVE ANY MONEY?
LET ME SEE YOUR WALLET.
grab
EH?!
AH... WAI--

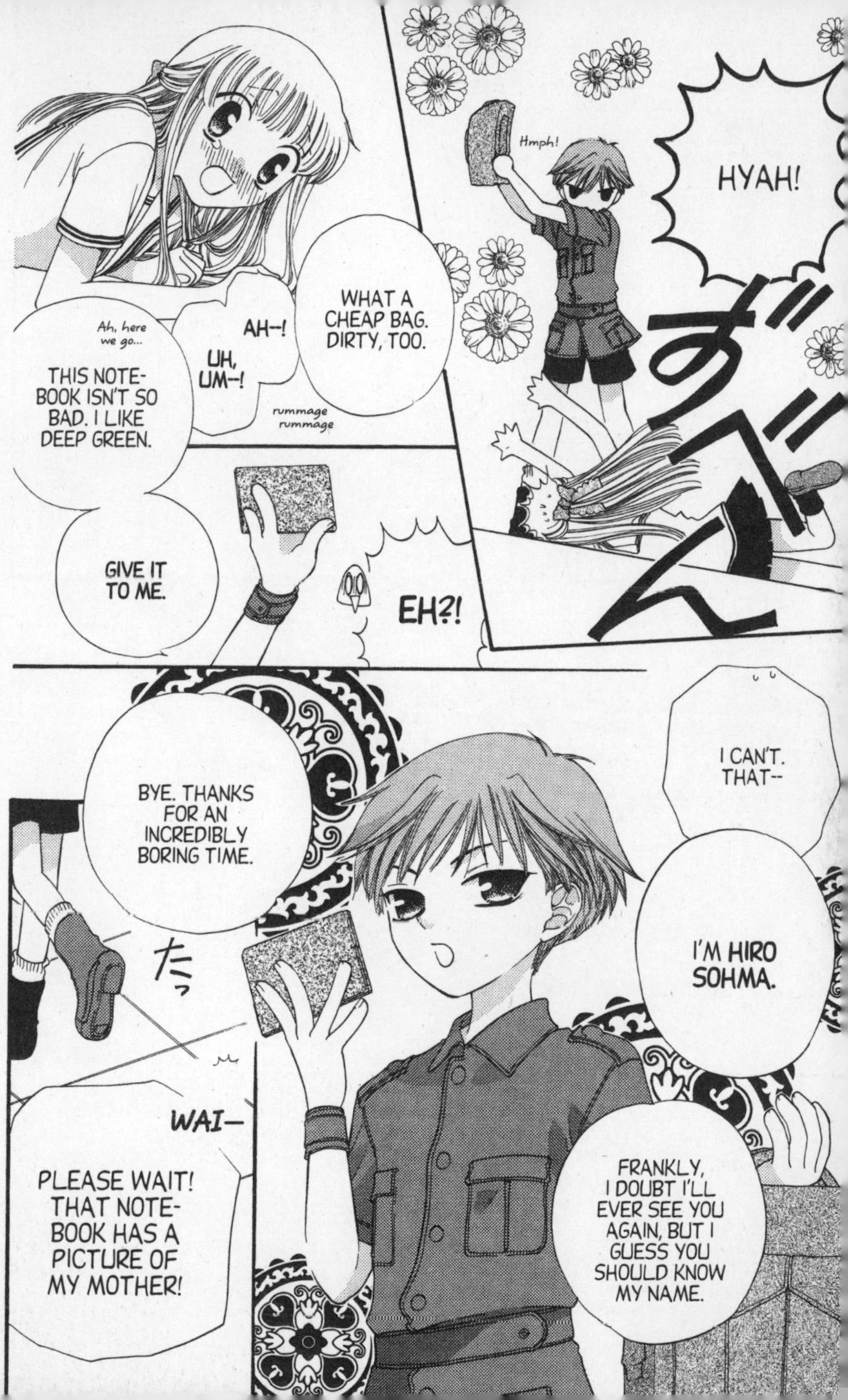
HYAH!
Hmph!
WHAT A CHEAP BAG. DIRTY, TOO.
AH--!
UH, UM--!
rummage rummage
Ah, here we go...
THIS NOTE-BOOK ISN'T SO BAD. I LIKE DEEP GREEN.
GIVE IT TO ME.
EH?!
I CAN'T. THAT--
I'M HIRO SOHMA.
FRANKLY, I DOUBT I'LL EVER SEE YOU AGAIN, BUT I GUESS YOU SHOULD KNOW MY NAME.
BYE. THANKS FOR AN INCREDIBLY BORING TIME.
WAI—
PLEASE WAIT! THAT NOTE-BOOK HAS A PICTURE OF MY MOTHER!

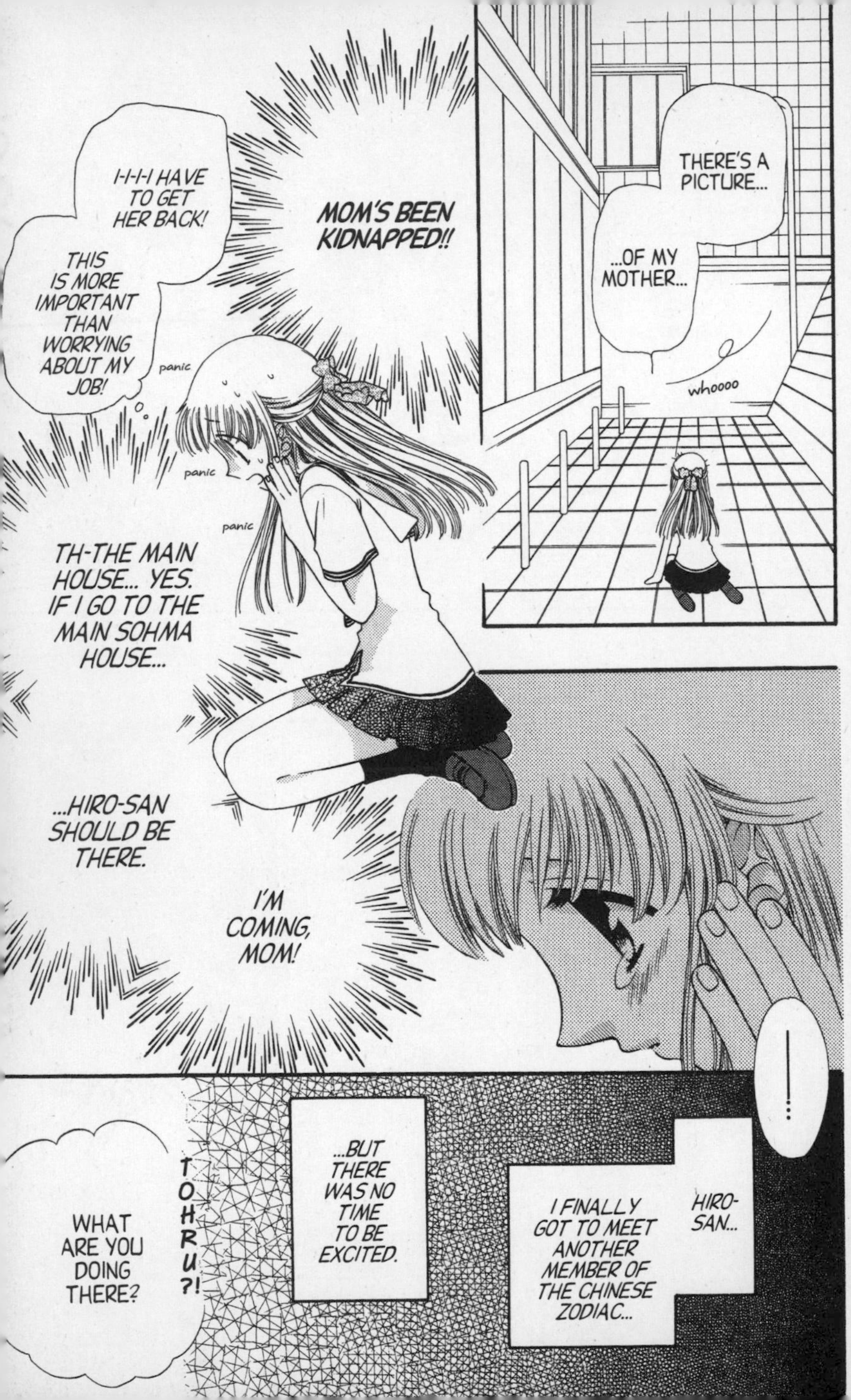
THERE'S A PICTURE...
...OF MY MOTHER...
whoooo
!
MOM'S BEEN KIDNAPPED!!
I-I-I-I HAVE TO GET HER BACK!
THIS IS MORE IMPORTANT THAN WORRYING ABOUT MY JOB!
panic
panic
panic
TH-THE MAIN HOUSE... YES. IF I GO TO THE MAIN SOHMA HOUSE...
...HIRO-SAN SHOULD BE THERE.
I'M COMING, MOM!
HIRO-SAN...
I FINALLY GOT TO MEET ANOTHER MEMBER OF THE CHINESE ZODIAC...
...BUT THERE WAS NO TIME TO BE EXCITED.
TOHRU?!
WHAT ARE YOU DOING THERE?

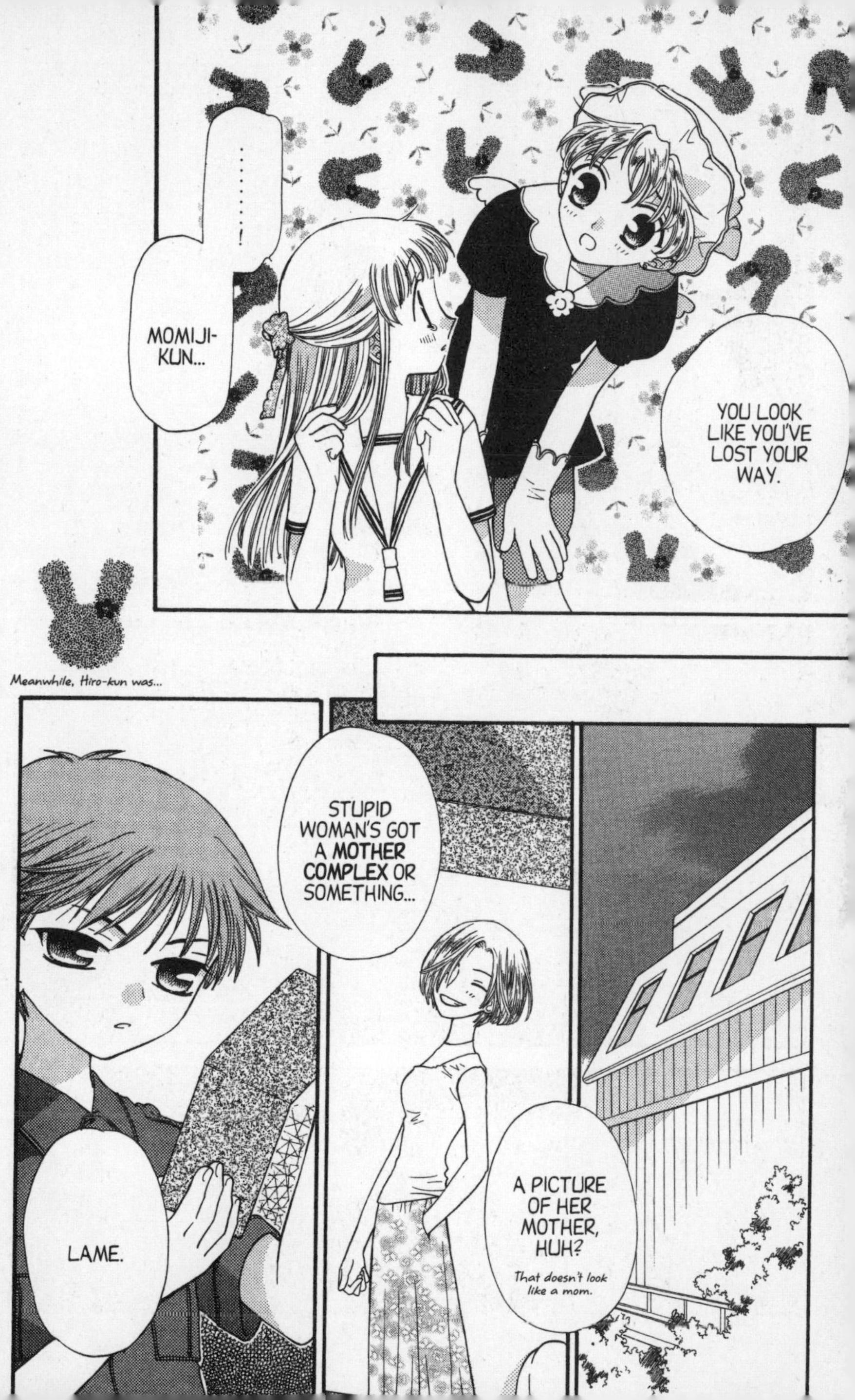
YOU LOOK LIKE YOU'VE LOST YOUR WAY.
......!
MOMIJI-KUN...
Meanwhile, Hiro-kun was...
A PICTURE OF HER MOTHER, HUH?
That doesn't look like a mom.
STUPID WOMAN'S GOT A MOTHER COMPLEX OR SOMETHING...
LAME.

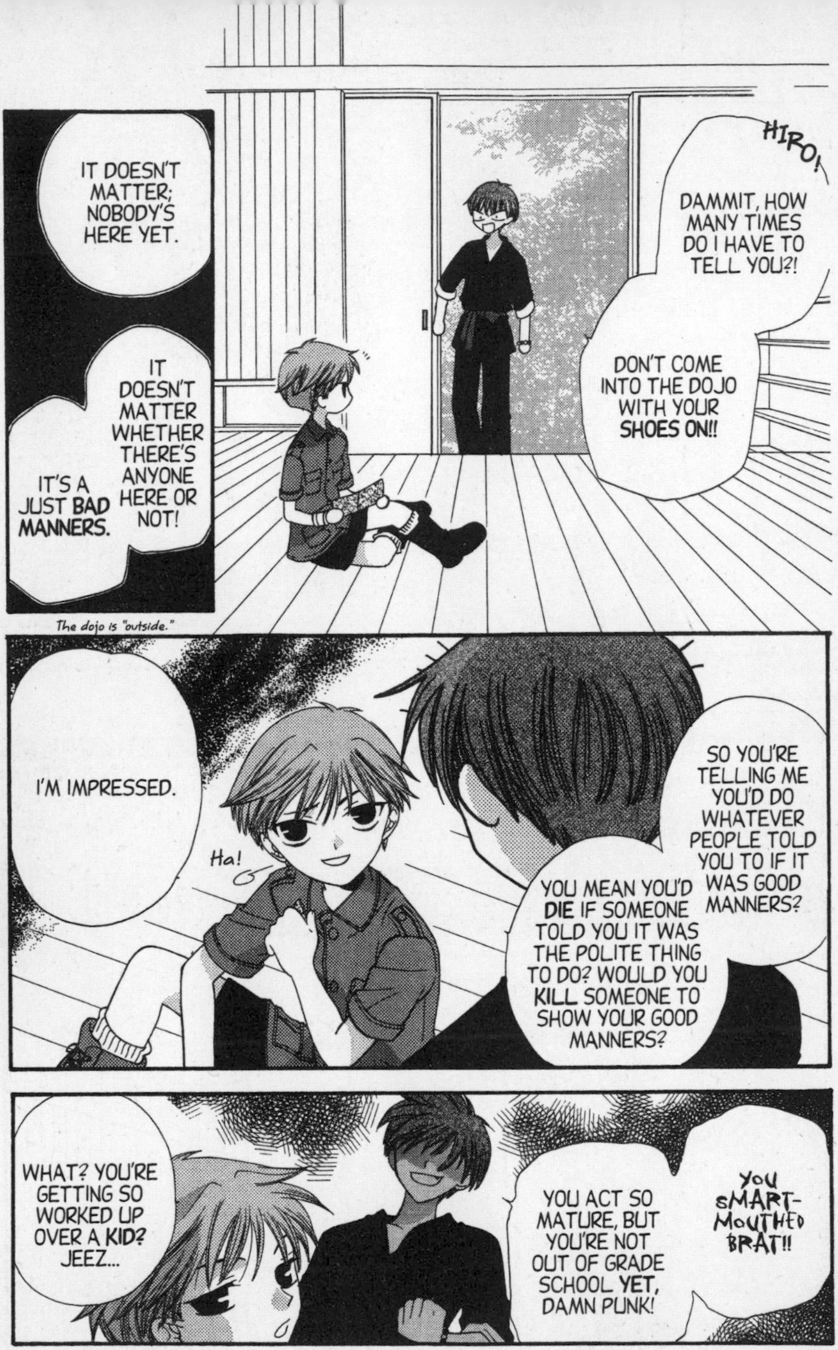
HIRO!
DAMMIT, HOW MANY TIMES DO I HAVE TO TELL YOU?!
DON'T COME INTO THE DOJO WITH YOUR **SHOES ON!!**
IT DOESN'T MATTER; NOBODY'S HERE YET.
IT DOESN'T MATTER WHETHER THERE'S ANYONE HERE OR NOT!
IT'S A JUST **BAD MANNERS.**
The dojo is "outside."
SO YOU'RE TELLING ME YOU'D DO WHATEVER PEOPLE TOLD YOU TO IF IT WAS GOOD MANNERS?
YOU MEAN YOU'D **DIE** IF SOMEONE TOLD YOU IT WAS THE POLITE THING TO DO? WOULD YOU **KILL** SOMEONE TO SHOW YOUR GOOD MANNERS?
I'M IMPRESSED.
Ha!
YOU SMART-MOUTHED BRAT!!
YOU ACT SO MATURE, BUT YOU'RE NOT OUT OF GRADE SCHOOL **YET**, DAMN PUNK!
WHAT? YOU'RE GETTING SO WORKED UP OVER A **KID?** JEEZ...

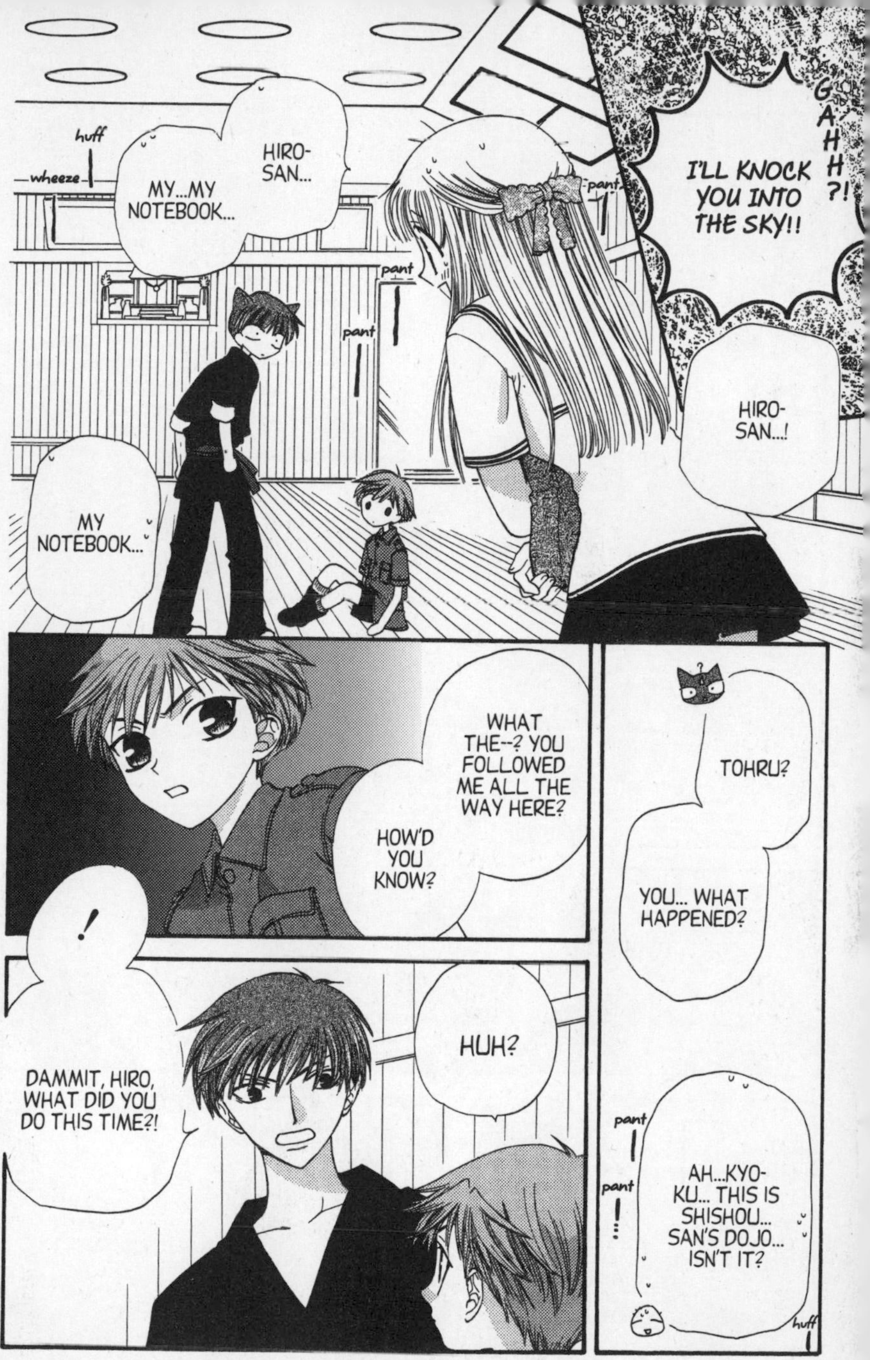
GAHH?!
I'LL KNOCK YOU INTO THE SKY!!
HIRO-SAN...!
pant
pant
pant
HIRO-SAN...
MY...MY NOTEBOOK...
huff
wheeze
MY NOTEBOOK...
TOHRU?
YOU... WHAT HAPPENED?
AH...KYO-KU... THIS IS SHISHOU... SAN'S DOJO... ISN'T IT?
pant
pant
huff
WHAT THE--? YOU FOLLOWED ME ALL THE WAY HERE?
HOW'D YOU KNOW?
HUH?
!
DAMMIT, HIRO, WHAT DID YOU DO THIS TIME?!

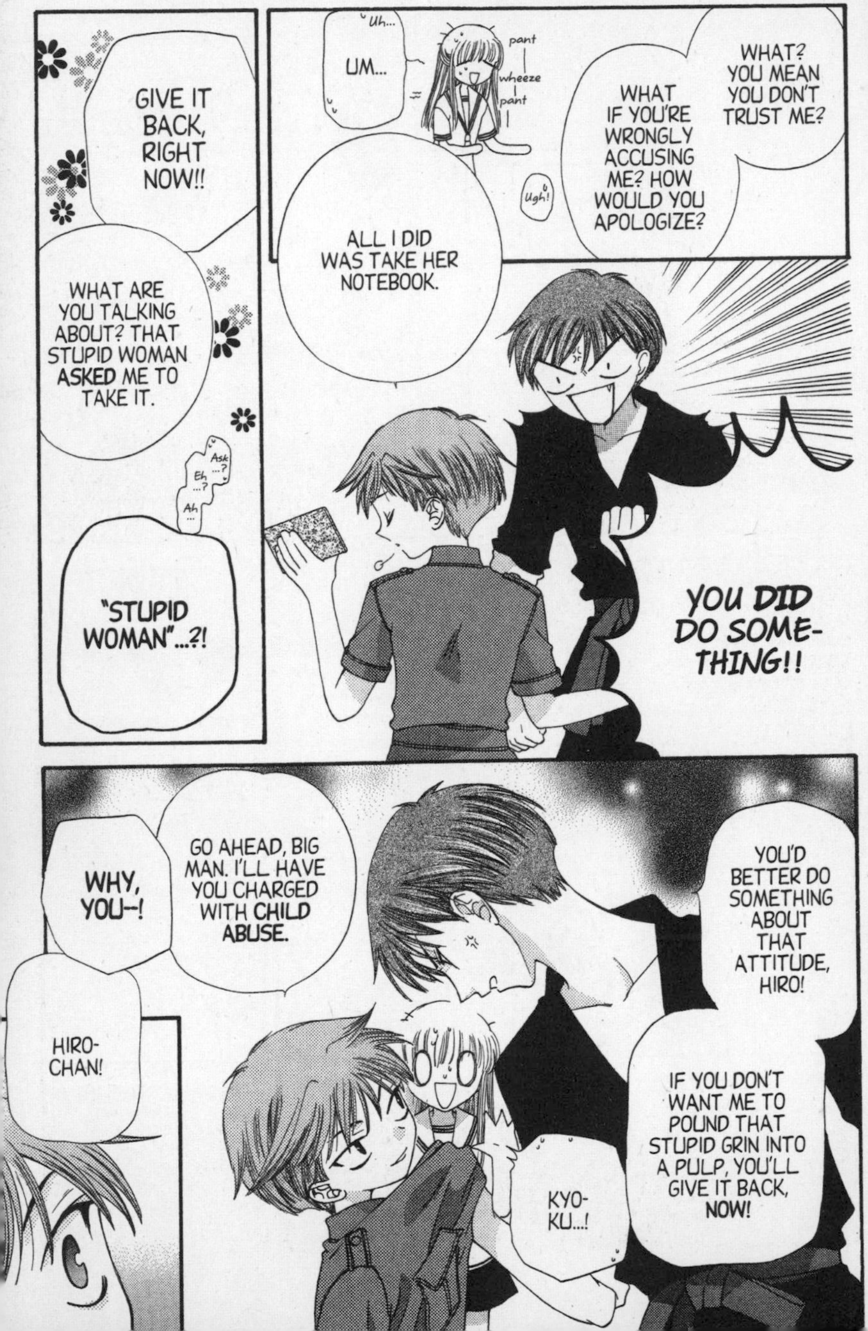
WHAT? YOU MEAN YOU DON'T TRUST ME?
WHAT IF YOU'RE WRONGLY ACCUSING ME? HOW WOULD YOU APOLOGIZE?
Ugh!
pant wheeze pant
Uh...
UM...
ALL I DID WAS TAKE HER NOTEBOOK.
YOU DID DO SOME-THING!!
GIVE IT BACK, RIGHT NOW!!
WHAT ARE YOU TALKING ABOUT? THAT STUPID WOMAN ASKED ME TO TAKE IT.
Ask ...?
Eh ...?
Ah ...
"STUPID WOMAN"...?!
YOU'D BETTER DO SOMETHING ABOUT THAT ATTITUDE, HIRO!
GO AHEAD, BIG MAN. I'LL HAVE YOU CHARGED WITH CHILD ABUSE.
WHY, YOU--!
IF YOU DON'T WANT ME TO POUND THAT STUPID GRIN INTO A PULP, YOU'LL GIVE IT BACK, NOW!
KYO-KU...!
HIRO-CHAN!

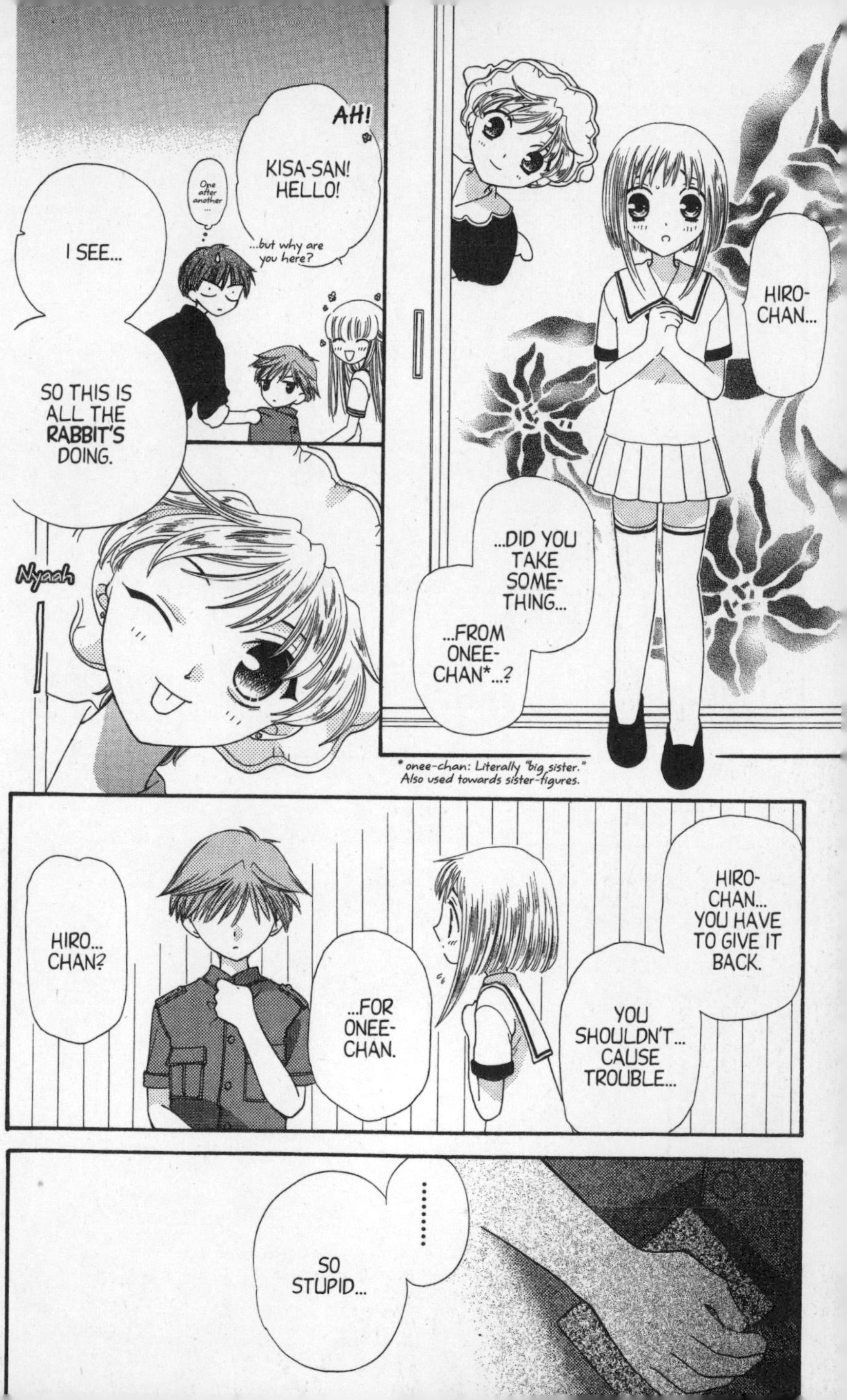
HIRO-CHAN...
...DID YOU TAKE SOME-THING...
...FROM ONEE-CHAN*...?
AH!
KISA-SAN! HELLO!
...but why are you here?
One after another...
I SEE...
SO THIS IS ALL THE RABBIT'S DOING.
Nyaah
HIRO-CHAN... YOU HAVE TO GIVE IT BACK.
YOU SHOULDN'T... CAUSE TROUBLE...
...FOR ONEE-CHAN.
HIRO... CHAN?
......
SO STUPID...

* onee-chan: Literally "big sister." Also used towards sister-figures.

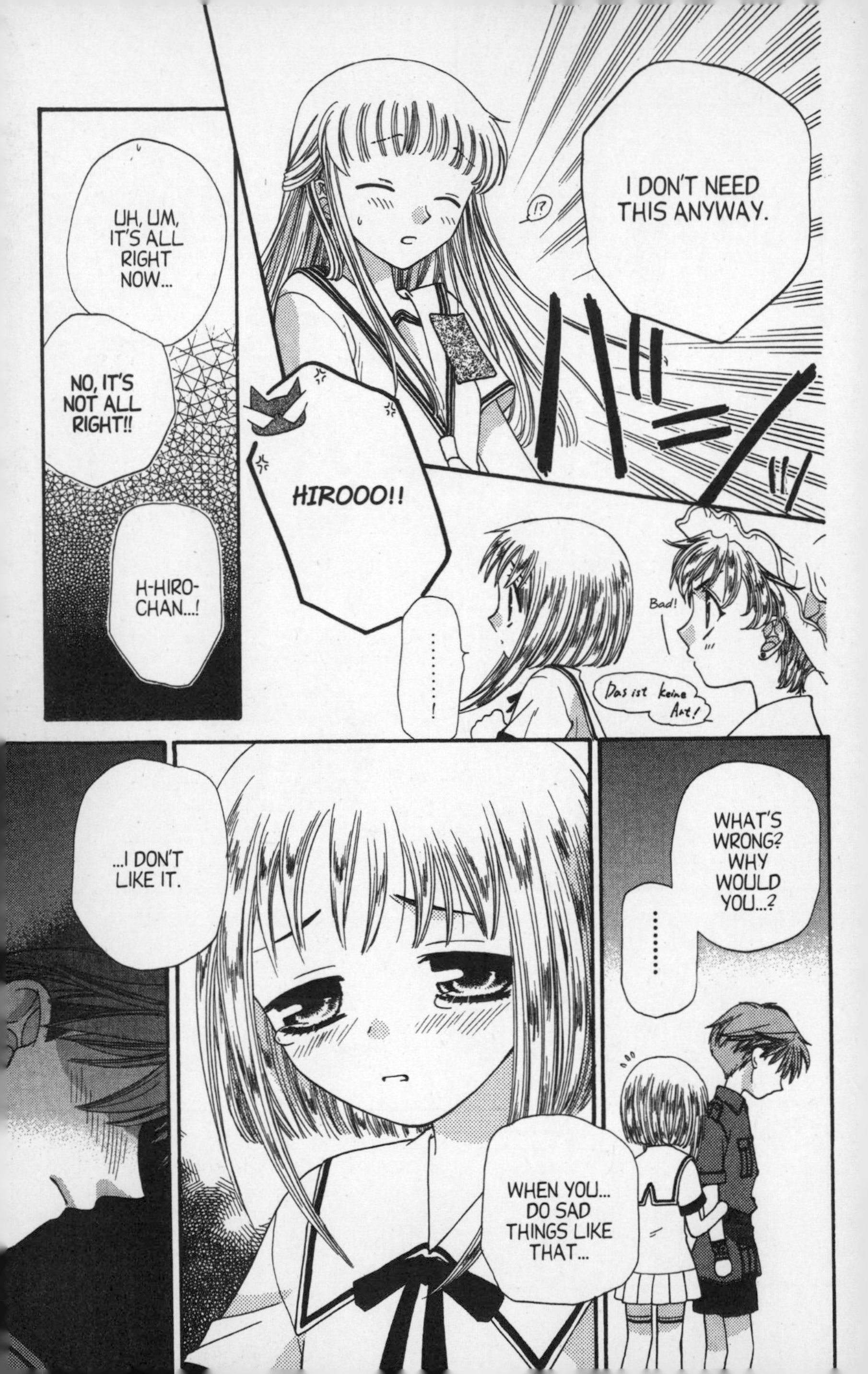
!?
I DON'T NEED THIS ANYWAY.
HIROOO!!
Bad!
Das ist keine Art!
......!
UH, UM, IT'S ALL RIGHT NOW...
NO, IT'S NOT ALL RIGHT!!
H-HIRO-CHAN...!
WHAT'S WRONG? WHY WOULD YOU...?
......
WHEN YOU... DO SAD THINGS LIKE THAT...
...I DON'T LIKE IT.

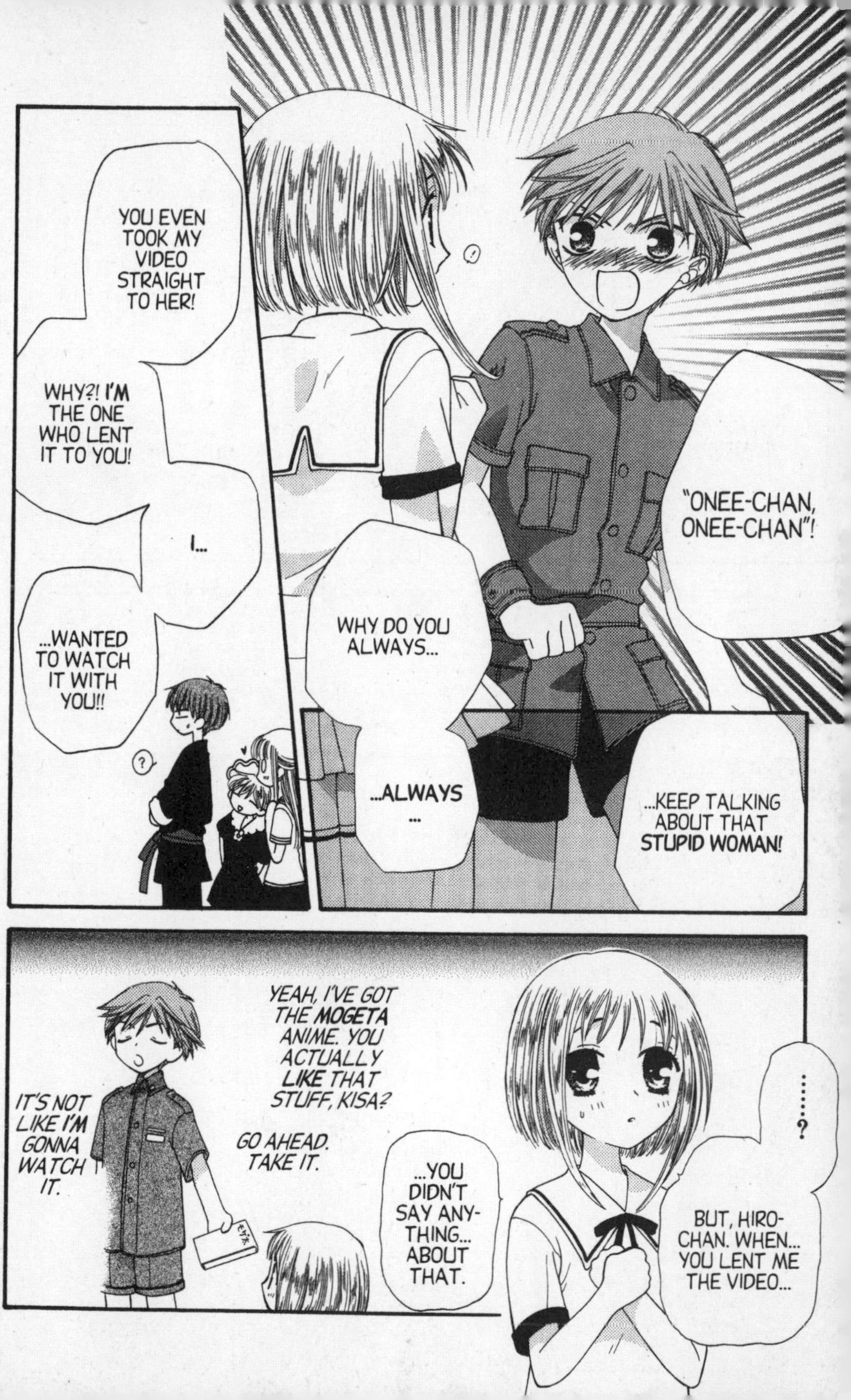

"ONEE-CHAN, ONEE-CHAN"!
WHY DO YOU ALWAYS...
...ALWAYS ...
...KEEP TALKING ABOUT THAT **STUPID WOMAN!**
YOU EVEN TOOK MY VIDEO STRAIGHT TO HER!
WHY?! I'M THE ONE WHO LENT IT TO YOU!
I...
...WANTED TO WATCH IT WITH YOU!!
......?
BUT, HIRO-CHAN. WHEN... YOU LENT ME THE VIDEO...
...YOU DIDN'T SAY ANYTHING... ABOUT THAT.
YEAH, I'VE GOT THE **MOGETA** ANIME. YOU ACTUALLY **LIKE** THAT STUFF, KISA?
GO AHEAD. TAKE IT.
IT'S NOT LIKE **I'M** GONNA WATCH IT.

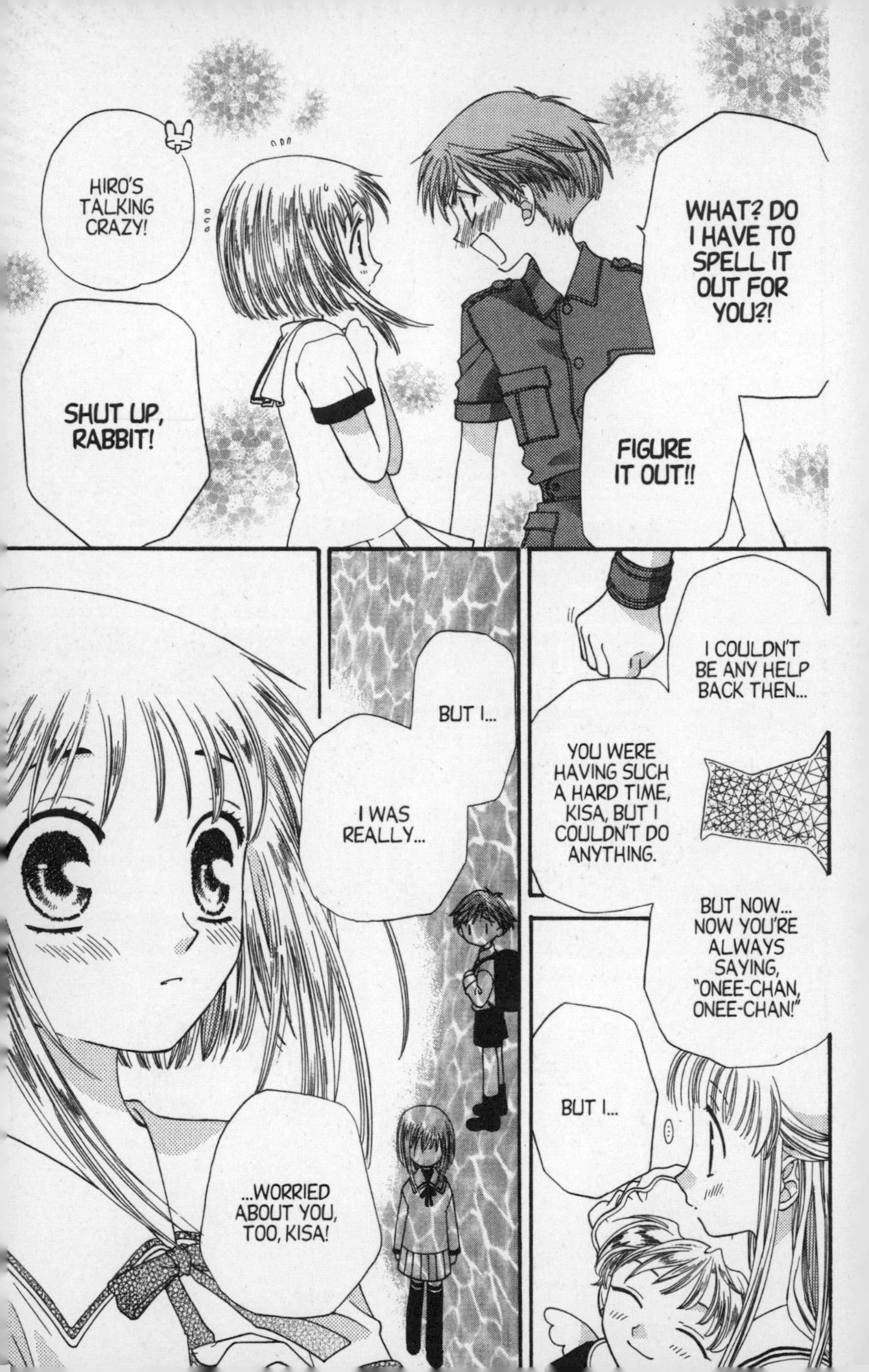

WHAT? DO I HAVE TO SPELL IT OUT FOR YOU?!
FIGURE IT OUT!!
HIRO'S TALKING CRAZY!
SHUT UP, RABBIT!
I COULDN'T BE ANY HELP BACK THEN...
YOU WERE HAVING SUCH A HARD TIME, KISA, BUT I COULDN'T DO ANYTHING.
BUT NOW... NOW YOU'RE ALWAYS SAYING, "ONEE-CHAN, ONEE-CHAN!"
BUT I...
BUT I...
I WAS REALLY...
...WORRIED ABOUT YOU, TOO, KISA!

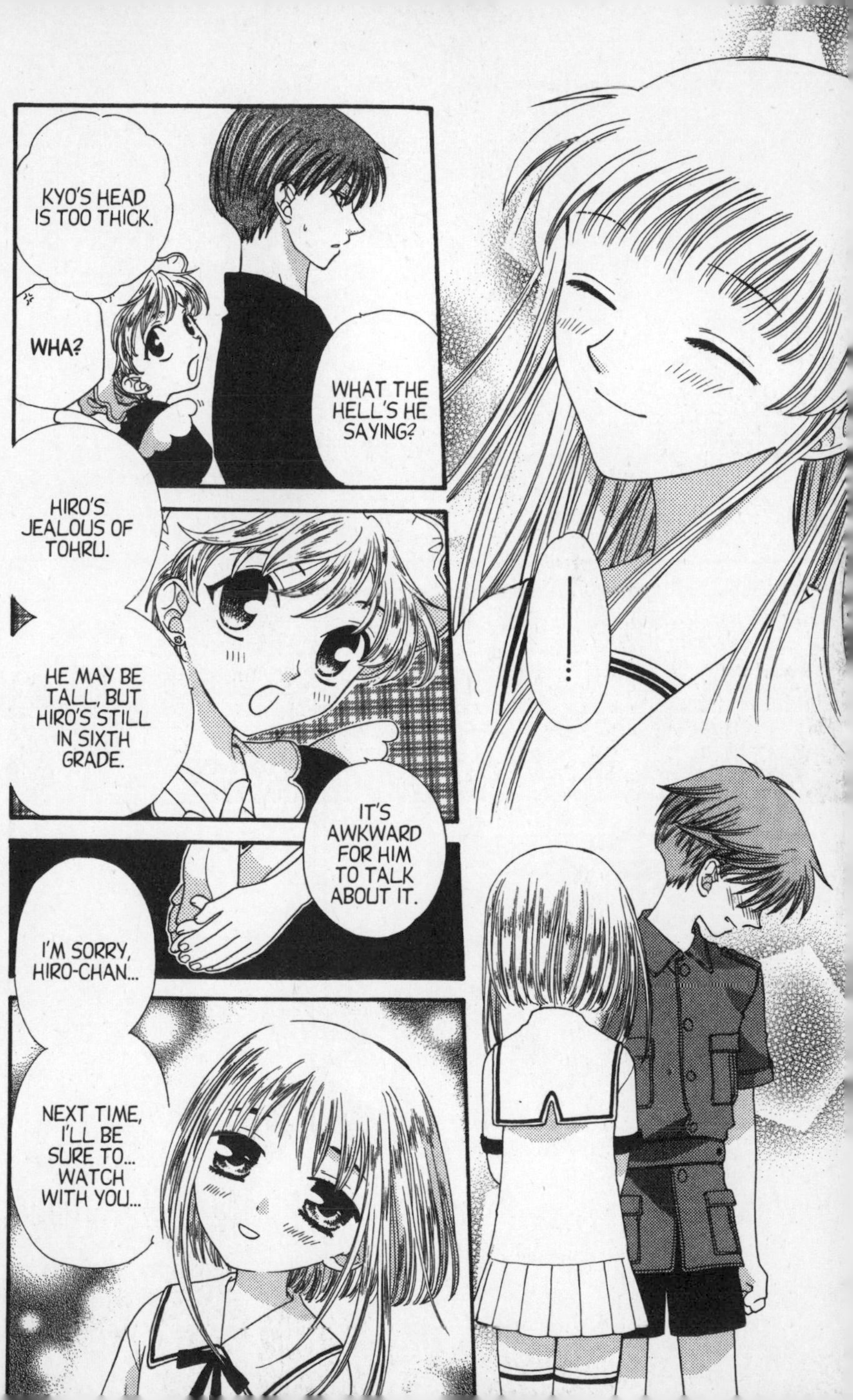
......!
KYO'S HEAD IS TOO THICK.
WHAT THE HELL'S HE SAYING?
WHA?
HIRO'S JEALOUS OF TOHRU.
HE MAY BE TALL, BUT HIRO'S STILL IN SIXTH GRADE.
IT'S AWKWARD FOR HIM TO TALK ABOUT IT.
I'M SORRY, HIRO-CHAN...
NEXT TIME, I'LL BE SURE TO... WATCH WITH YOU...

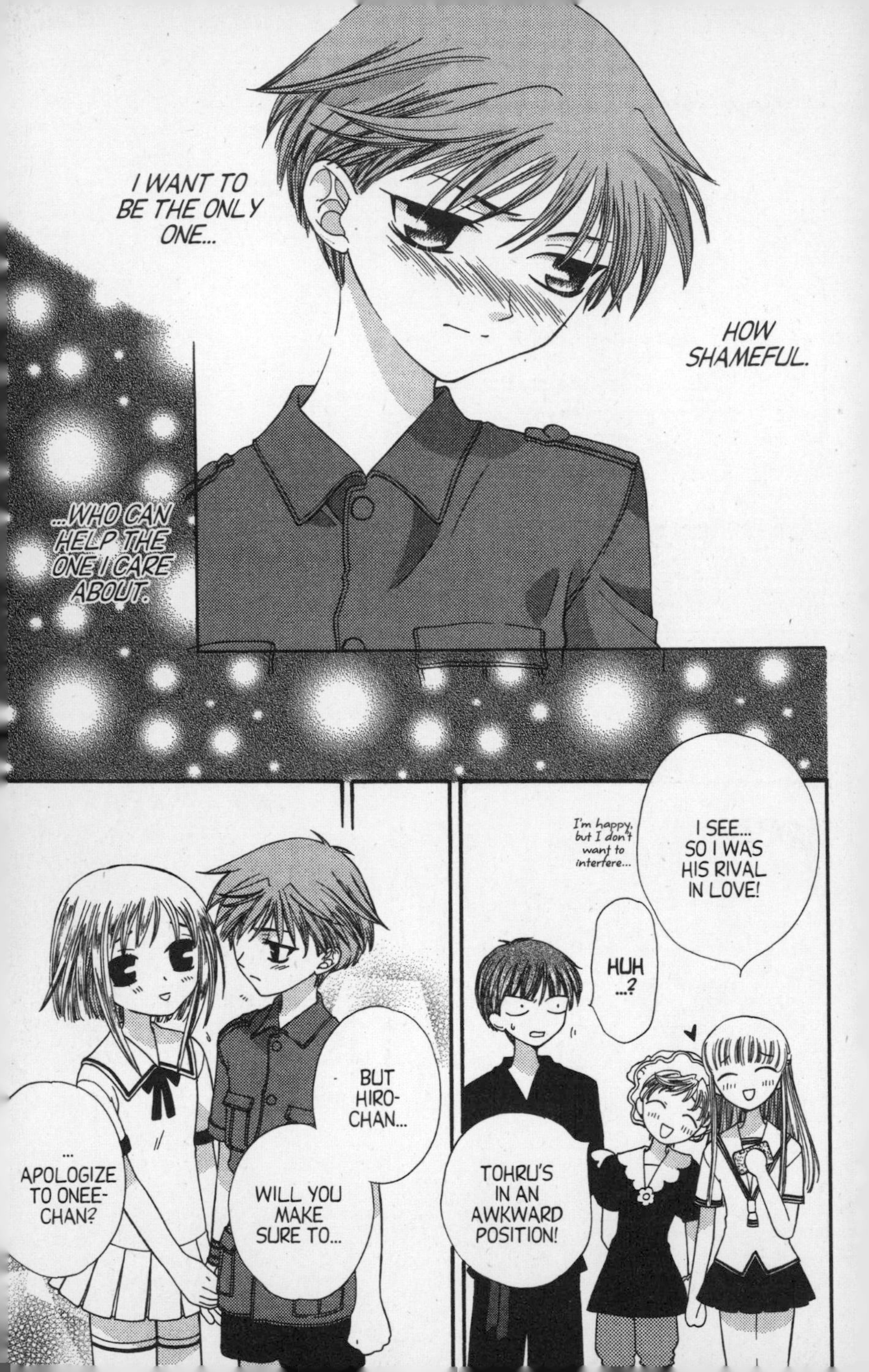
I WANT TO BE THE ONLY ONE...
...WHO CAN HELP THE ONE I CARE ABOUT.
HOW SHAMEFUL.
I SEE... SO I WAS HIS RIVAL IN LOVE!
I'm happy, but I don't want to interfere...
HUH ...?
TOHRU'S IN AN AWKWARD POSITION!
BUT HIRO-CHAN...
WILL YOU MAKE SURE TO...
... APOLOGIZE TO ONEE-CHAN?

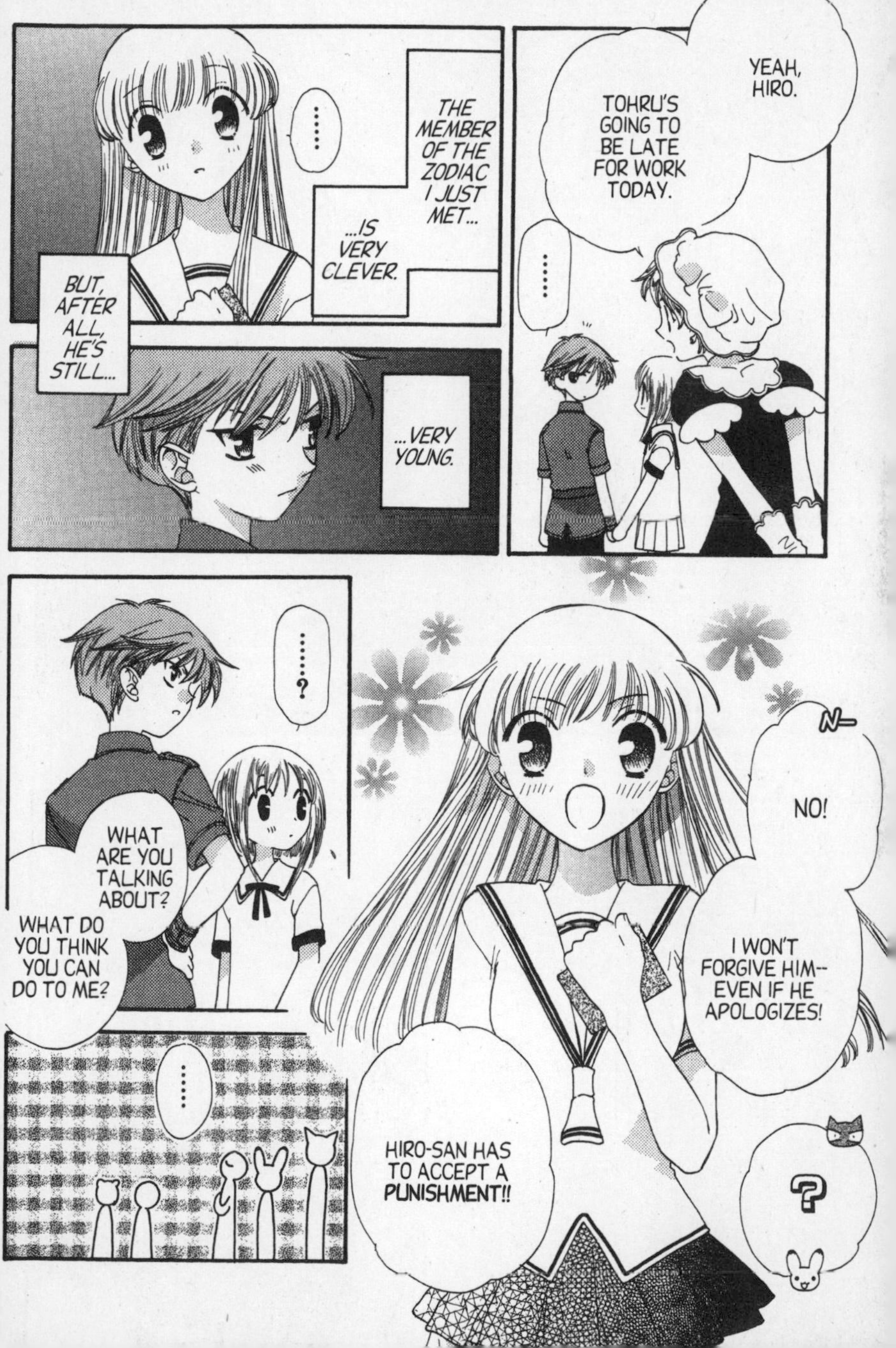
YEAH, HIRO.
TOHRU'S GOING TO BE LATE FOR WORK TODAY.
......
THE MEMBER OF THE ZODIAC I JUST MET...
...IS VERY CLEVER.
......
BUT, AFTER ALL, HE'S STILL...
...VERY YOUNG.
N—
NO!
I WON'T FORGIVE HIM-- EVEN IF HE APOLOGIZES!
HIRO-SAN HAS TO ACCEPT A **PUNISHMENT**!!
?
......?
WHAT ARE YOU TALKING ABOUT?
WHAT DO YOU THINK YOU CAN DO TO ME?
......

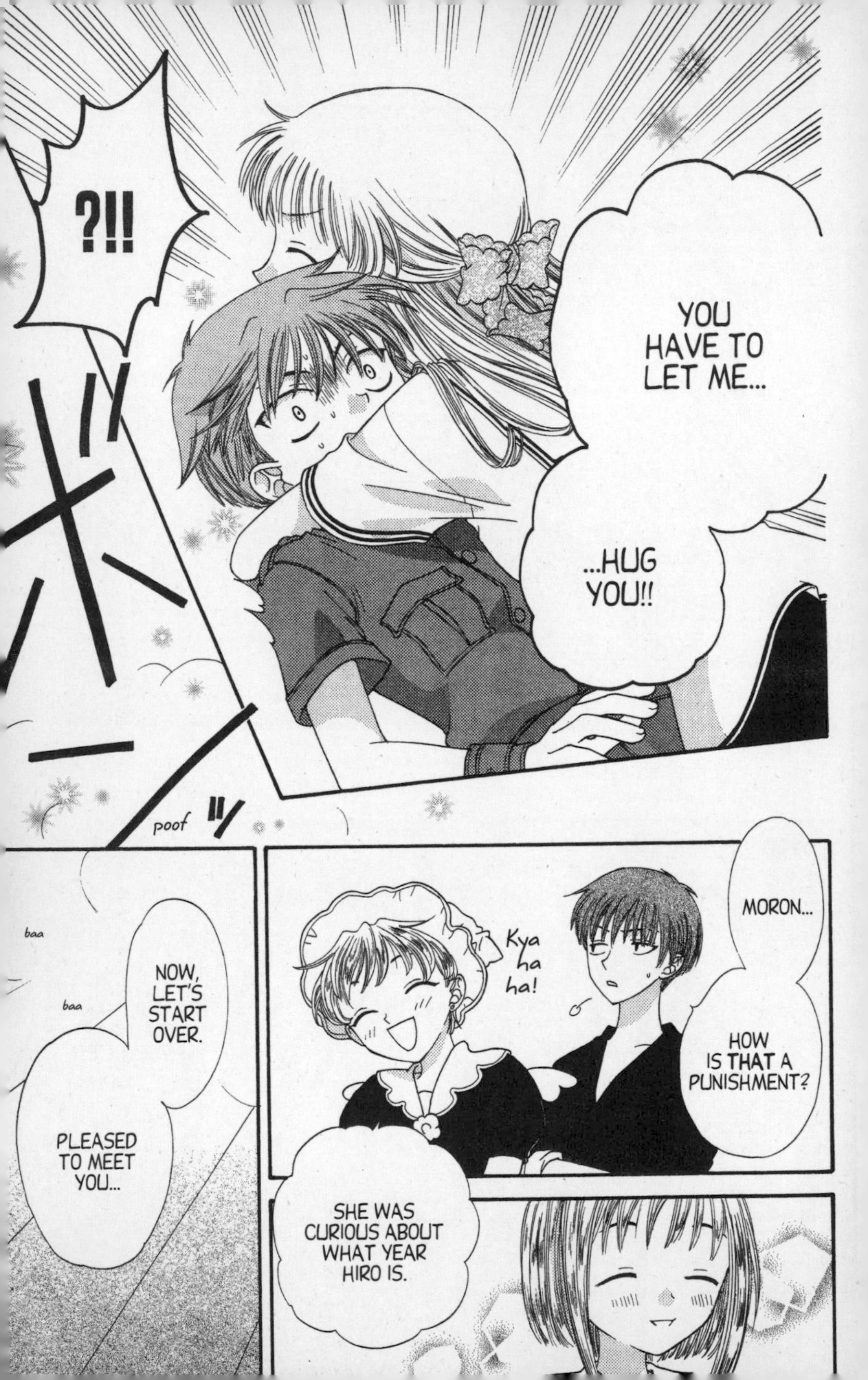
YOU HAVE TO LET ME...
...HUG YOU!!
?!!
poof
MORON...
HOW IS THAT A PUNISHMENT?
Kya ha ha!
SHE WAS CURIOUS ABOUT WHAT YEAR HIRO IS.
baa
baa
NOW, LET'S START OVER.
PLEASED TO MEET YOU...

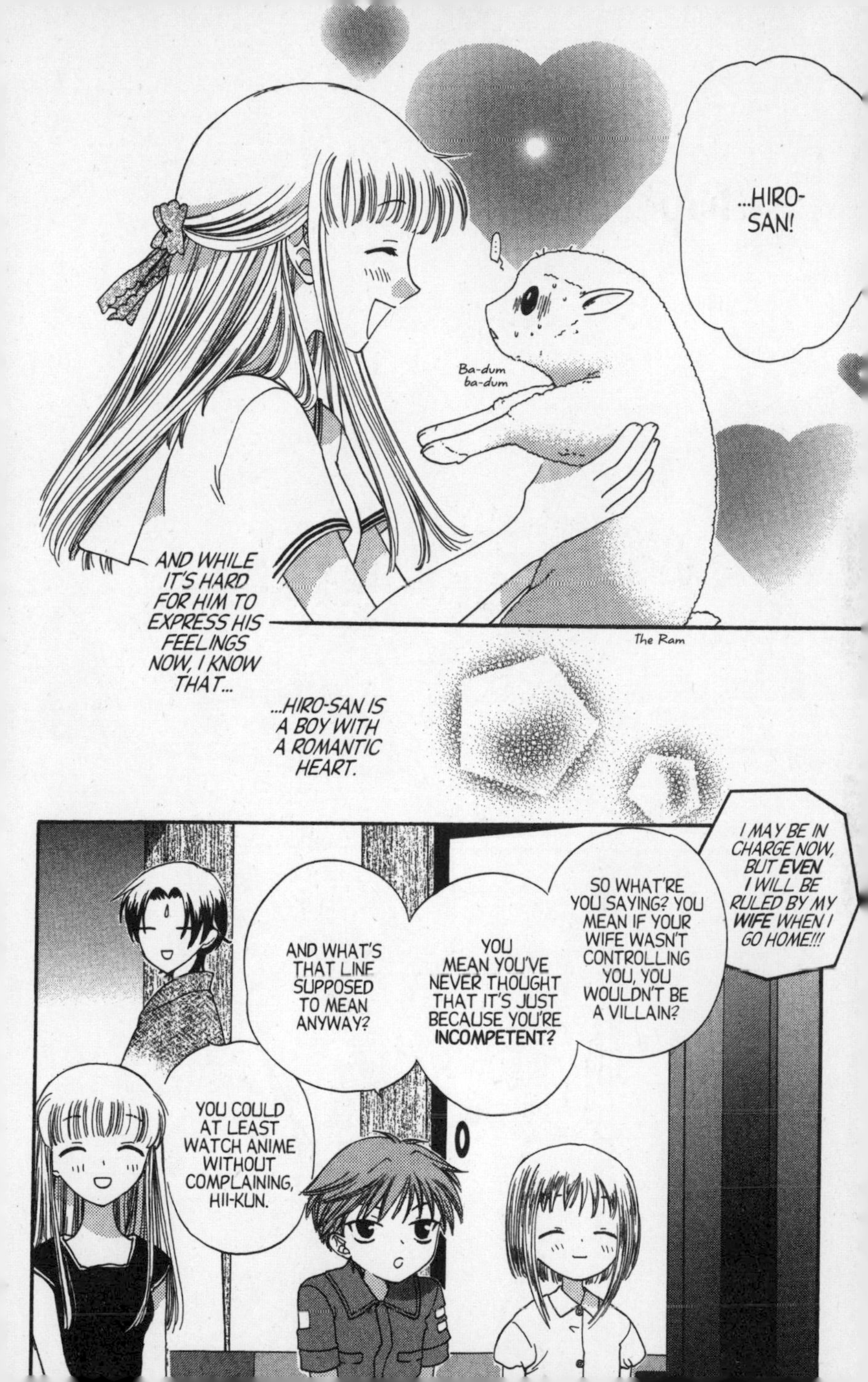
...HIRO-SAN!
Ba-dum ba-dum
The Ram
AND WHILE IT'S HARD FOR HIM TO EXPRESS HIS FEELINGS NOW, I KNOW THAT...
...HIRO-SAN IS A BOY WITH A ROMANTIC HEART.
I MAY BE IN CHARGE NOW, BUT EVEN I WILL BE RULED BY MY WIFE WHEN I GO HOME!!!
SO WHAT'RE YOU SAYING? YOU MEAN IF YOUR WIFE WASN'T CONTROLLING YOU, YOU WOULDN'T BE A VILLAIN?
YOU MEAN YOU'VE NEVER THOUGHT THAT IT'S JUST BECAUSE YOU'RE INCOMPETENT?
AND WHAT'S THAT LINE SUPPOSED TO MEAN ANYWAY?
YOU COULD AT LEAST WATCH ANIME WITHOUT COMPLAINING, HII-KUN.

Chapter 38

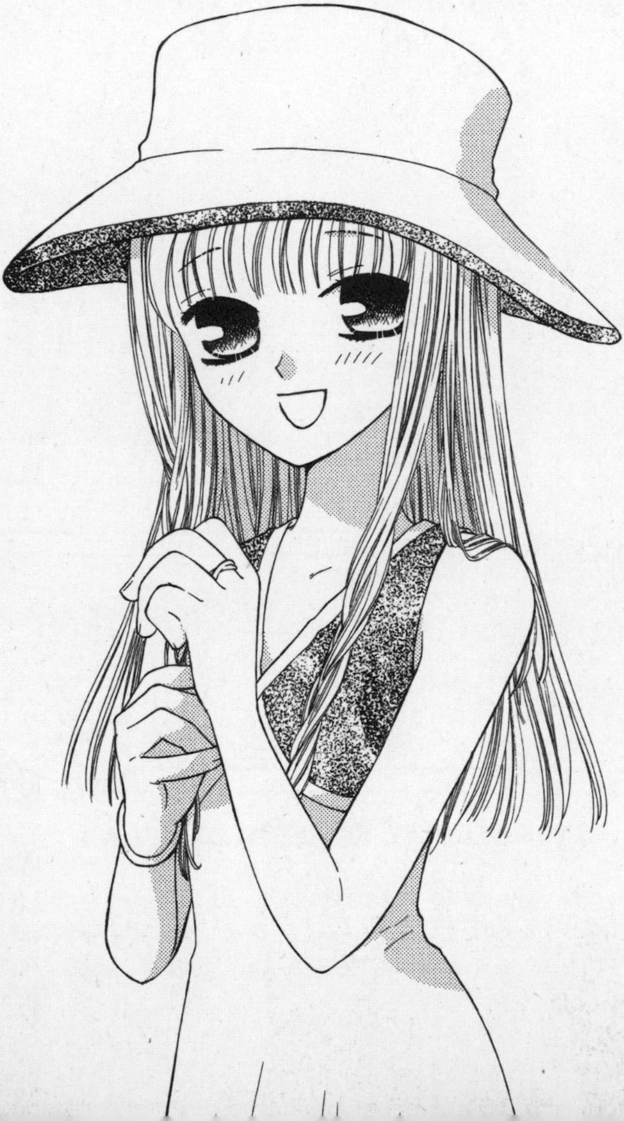

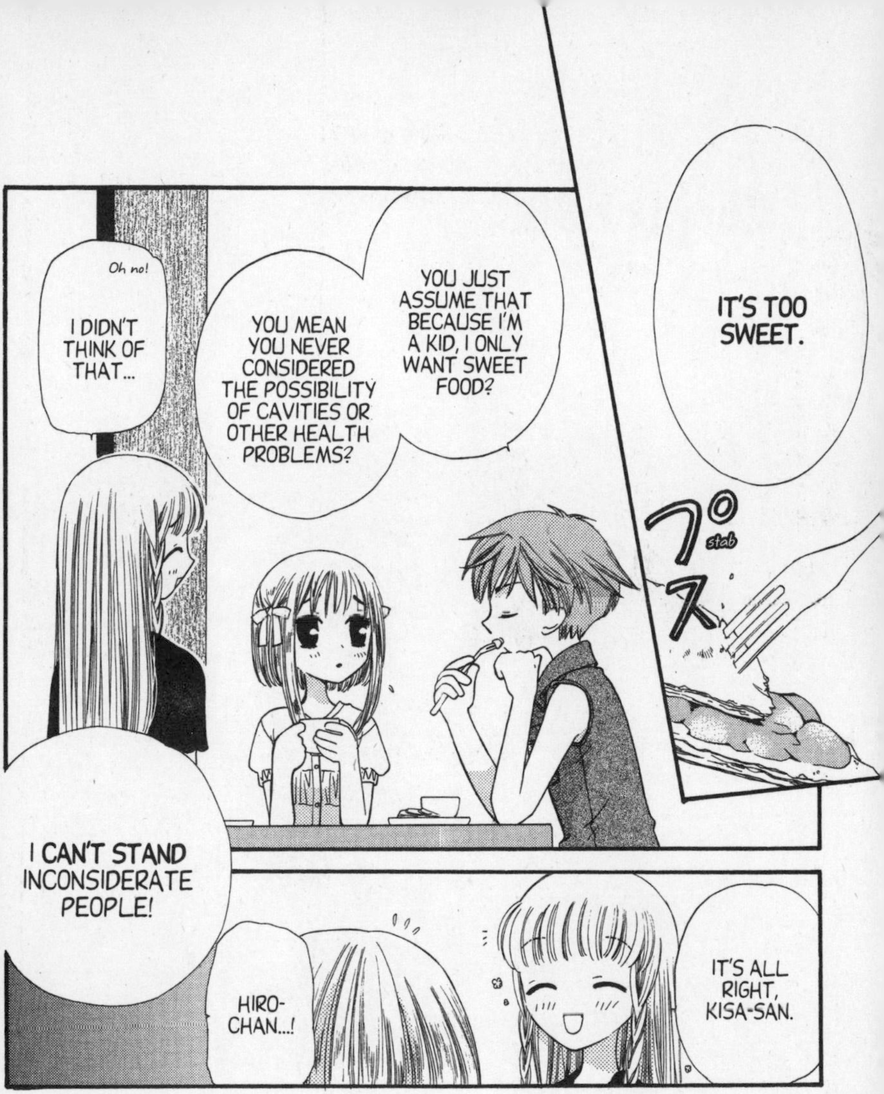
IT'S TOO SWEET.
プス
stab
YOU JUST ASSUME THAT BECAUSE I'M A KID, I ONLY WANT SWEET FOOD?
YOU MEAN YOU NEVER CONSIDERED THE POSSIBILITY OF CAVITIES OR OTHER HEALTH PROBLEMS?
Oh no!
I DIDN'T THINK OF THAT...
I CAN'T STAND INCONSIDERATE PEOPLE!
IT'S ALL RIGHT, KISA-SAN.
HIRO-CHAN...!

ULTRA-SPECIAL BLAH, BLAH, BLAH 2

By the way, I like chocolate bananas. And parfaits--I **love** chocolate parfaits. When I was in the hospital, I wanted to eat them so much. (Also steak, hamburgers, gyouza...)

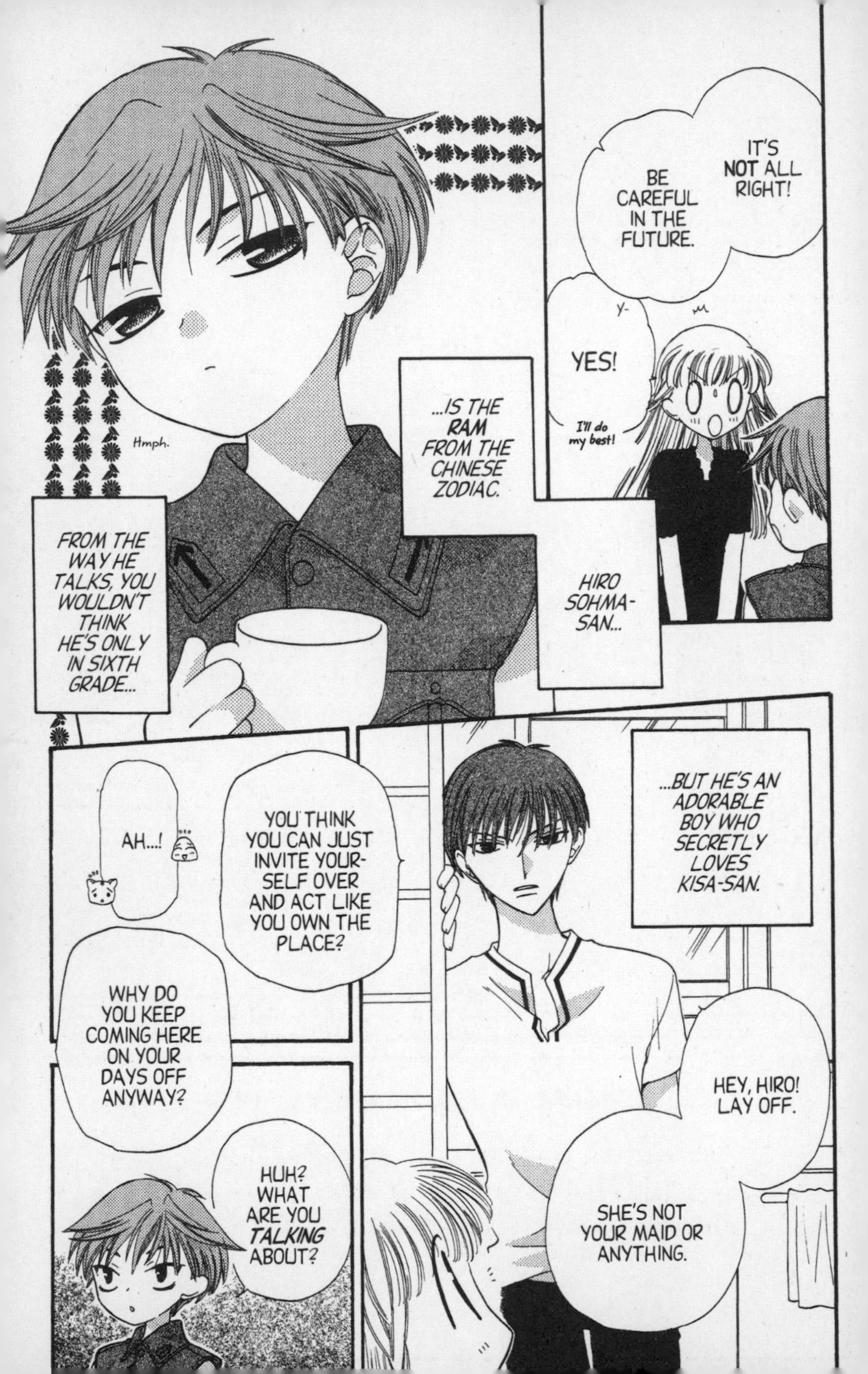
IT'S NOT ALL RIGHT! BE CAREFUL IN THE FUTURE.
Y-
YES!
I'll do my best!
HIRO SOHMA-SAN...
...IS THE RAM FROM THE CHINESE ZODIAC.
FROM THE WAY HE TALKS, YOU WOULDN'T THINK HE'S ONLY IN SIXTH GRADE...
Hmph.
...BUT HE'S AN ADORABLE BOY WHO SECRETLY LOVES KISA-SAN.
HEY, HIRO! LAY OFF.
SHE'S NOT YOUR MAID OR ANYTHING.
YOU THINK YOU CAN JUST INVITE YOUR-SELF OVER AND ACT LIKE YOU OWN THE PLACE?
AH...!
WHY DO YOU KEEP COMING HERE ON YOUR DAYS OFF ANYWAY?
HUH? WHAT ARE YOU TALKING ABOUT?

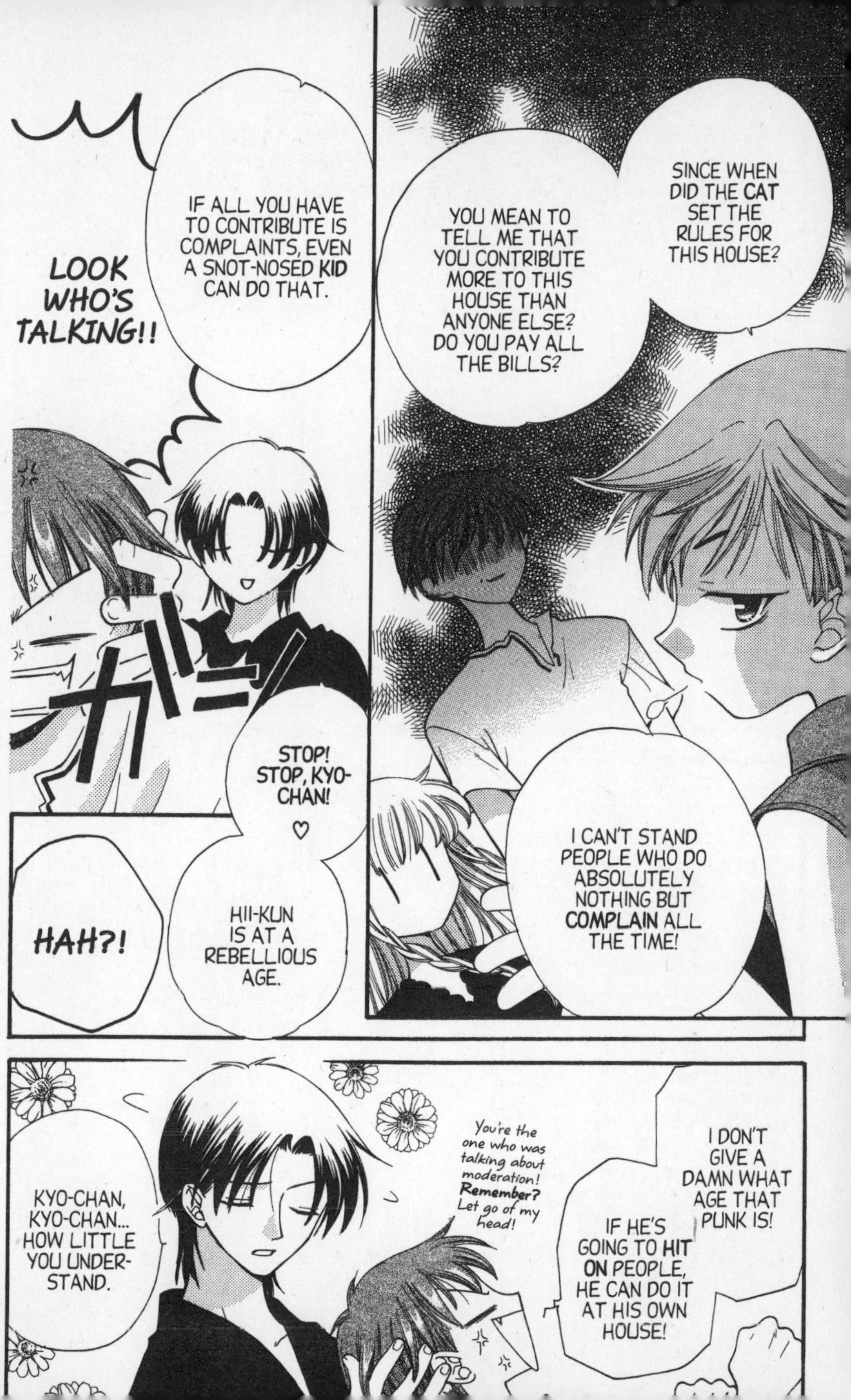
SINCE WHEN DID THE CAT SET THE RULES FOR THIS HOUSE?
YOU MEAN TO TELL ME THAT YOU CONTRIBUTE MORE TO THIS HOUSE THAN ANYONE ELSE? DO YOU PAY ALL THE BILLS?
I CAN'T STAND PEOPLE WHO DO ABSOLUTELY NOTHING BUT COMPLAIN ALL THE TIME!
IF ALL YOU HAVE TO CONTRIBUTE IS COMPLAINTS, EVEN A SNOT-NOSED KID CAN DO THAT.
LOOK WHO'S TALKING!!
STOP! STOP, KYO-CHAN! ♡
HII-KUN IS AT A REBELLIOUS AGE.
HAH?!
I DON'T GIVE A DAMN WHAT AGE THAT PUNK IS!
IF HE'S GOING TO HIT ON PEOPLE, HE CAN DO IT AT HIS OWN HOUSE!
You're the one who was talking about moderation! Remember? Let go of my head!
KYO-CHAN, KYO-CHAN... HOW LITTLE YOU UNDERSTAND.

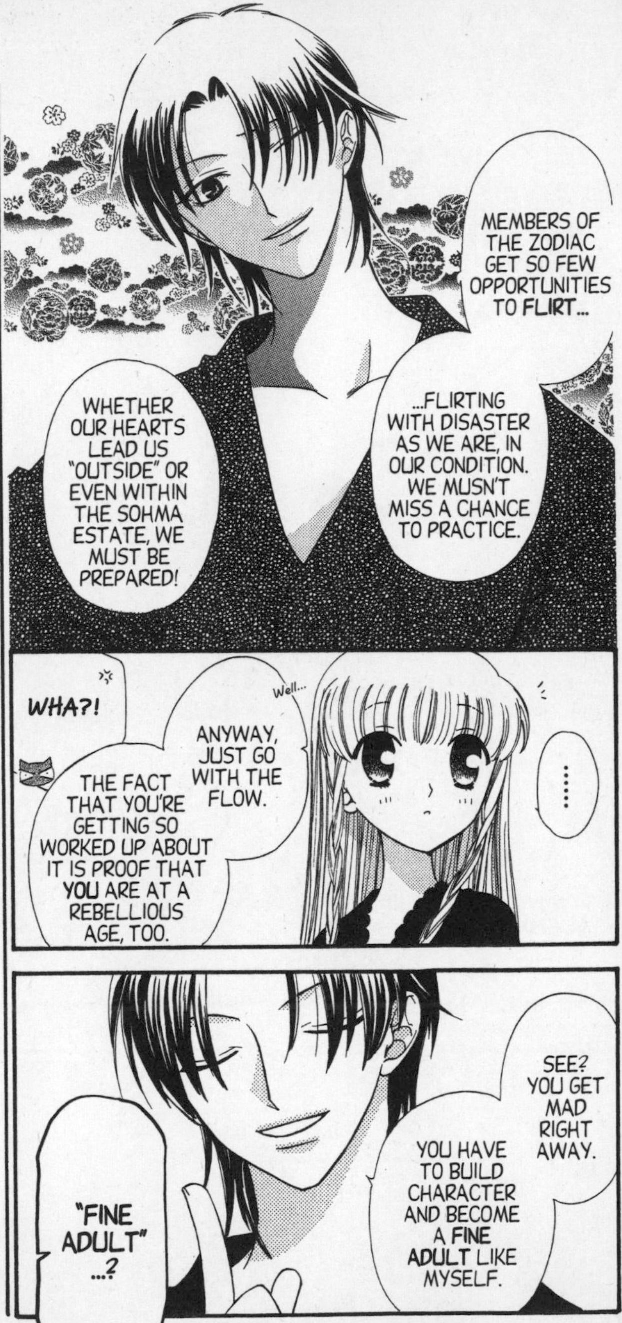
MEMBERS OF THE ZODIAC GET SO FEW OPPORTUNITIES TO FLIRT...
...FLIRTING WITH DISASTER AS WE ARE, IN OUR CONDITION. WE MUSN'T MISS A CHANCE TO PRACTICE.
WHETHER OUR HEARTS LEAD US "OUTSIDE" OR EVEN WITHIN THE SOHMA ESTATE, WE MUST BE PREPARED!
......
Well...
ANYWAY, JUST GO WITH THE FLOW.
THE FACT THAT YOU'RE GETTING SO WORKED UP ABOUT IT IS PROOF THAT YOU ARE AT A REBELLIOUS AGE, TOO.
WHA?!
SEE? YOU GET MAD RIGHT AWAY.
YOU HAVE TO BUILD CHARACTER AND BECOME A FINE ADULT LIKE MYSELF.
"FINE ADULT" ...?

Fruits Basket 7: Part 2

When I broke my left arm, I had to stay in the hospital for a while. I even had to undergo surgery, which, fortunately, was a success. And so I have returned! There may be some people who think that my handwriting's gotten sloppy since I've recovered, but my handwriting's **always** been sloppy, so please don't worry about it. And I'm sorry it's hard to read (laugh). Apparently the surgery I had came with a lot of risks, but surgery itself is like that, and I was pretty desperate, so I had no second thoughts. It was much harder for me to not be working.

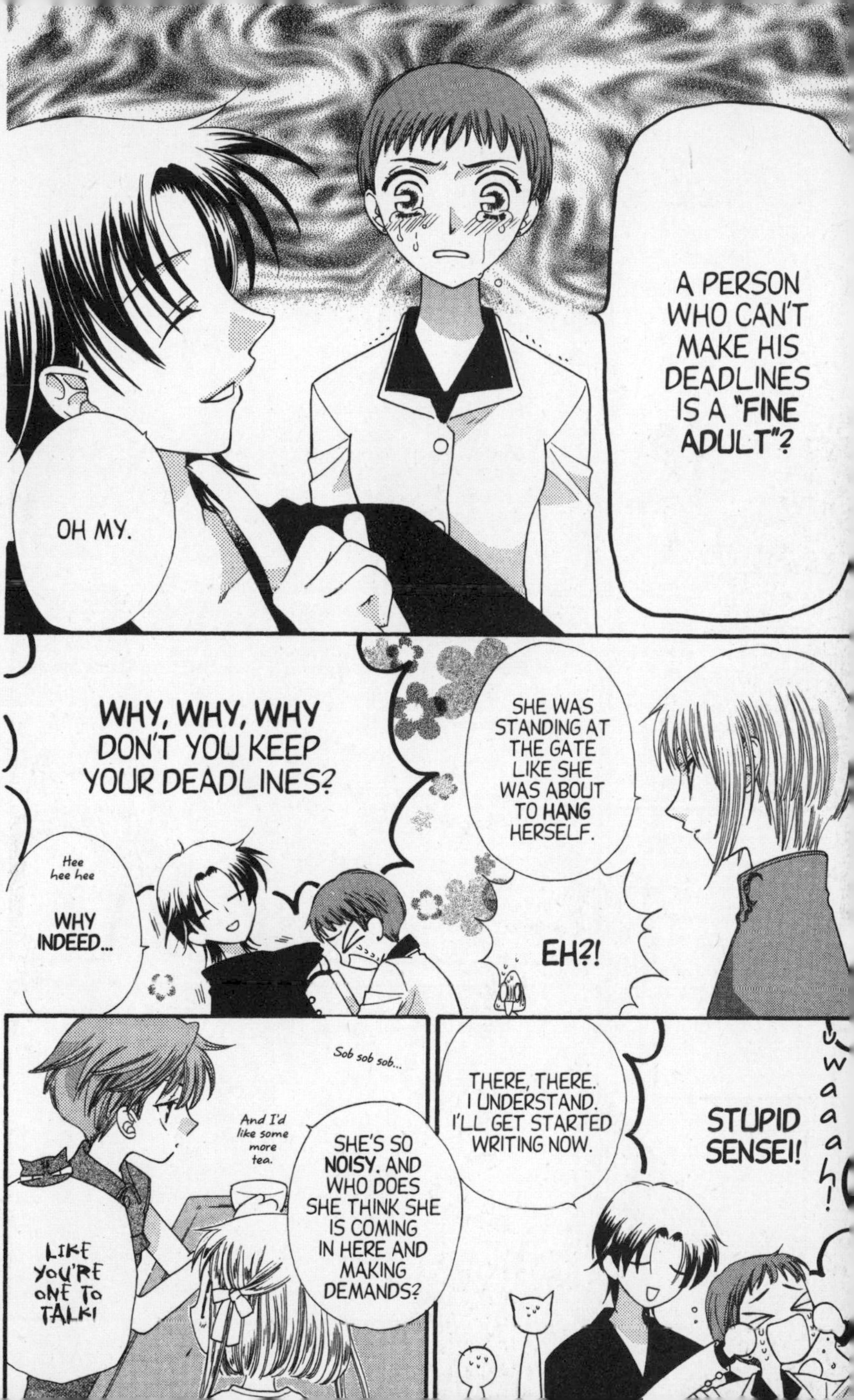
A PERSON WHO CAN'T MAKE HIS DEADLINES IS A "FINE ADULT"?
OH MY.
SHE WAS STANDING AT THE GATE LIKE SHE WAS ABOUT TO HANG HERSELF.
WHY, WHY, WHY DON'T YOU KEEP YOUR DEADLINES?
EH?!
Hee hee hee
WHY INDEED...
Uwaaaah!
STUPID SENSEI!
THERE, THERE. I UNDERSTAND. I'LL GET STARTED WRITING NOW.
Sob sob sob...
SHE'S SO NOISY. AND WHO DOES SHE THINK SHE IS COMING IN HERE AND MAKING DEMANDS?
And I'd like some more tea.
LIKE YOU'RE ONE TO TALK!

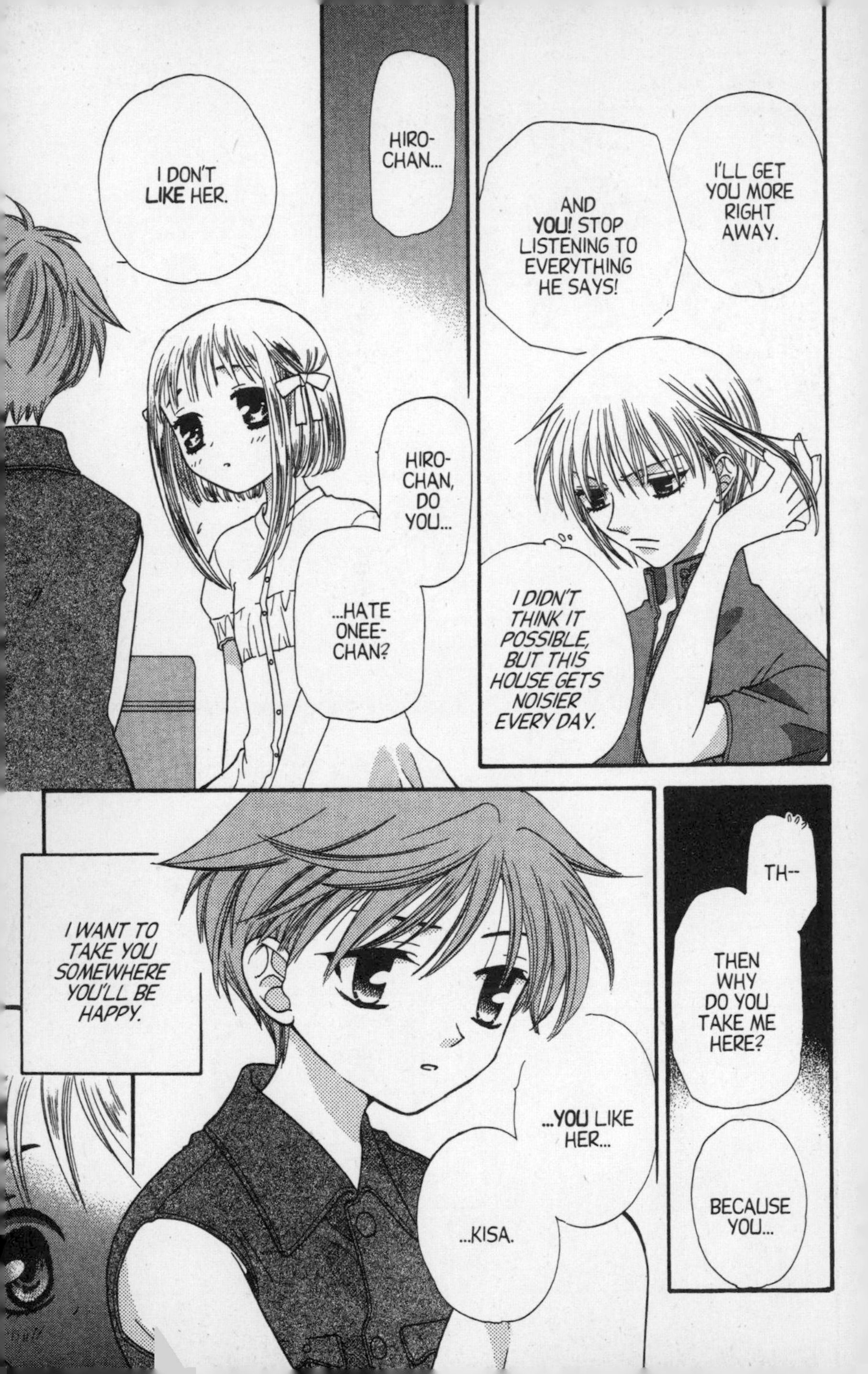

I'LL GET YOU MORE RIGHT AWAY.
AND YOU! STOP LISTENING TO EVERYTHING HE SAYS!
I DIDN'T THINK IT POSSIBLE, BUT THIS HOUSE GETS NOISIER EVERY DAY.
HIRO-CHAN...
I DON'T LIKE HER.
HIRO-CHAN, DO YOU...
...HATE ONEE-CHAN?
TH--
THEN WHY DO YOU TAKE ME HERE?
BECAUSE YOU...
...YOU LIKE HER...
...KISA.
I WANT TO TAKE YOU SOMEWHERE YOU'LL BE HAPPY.

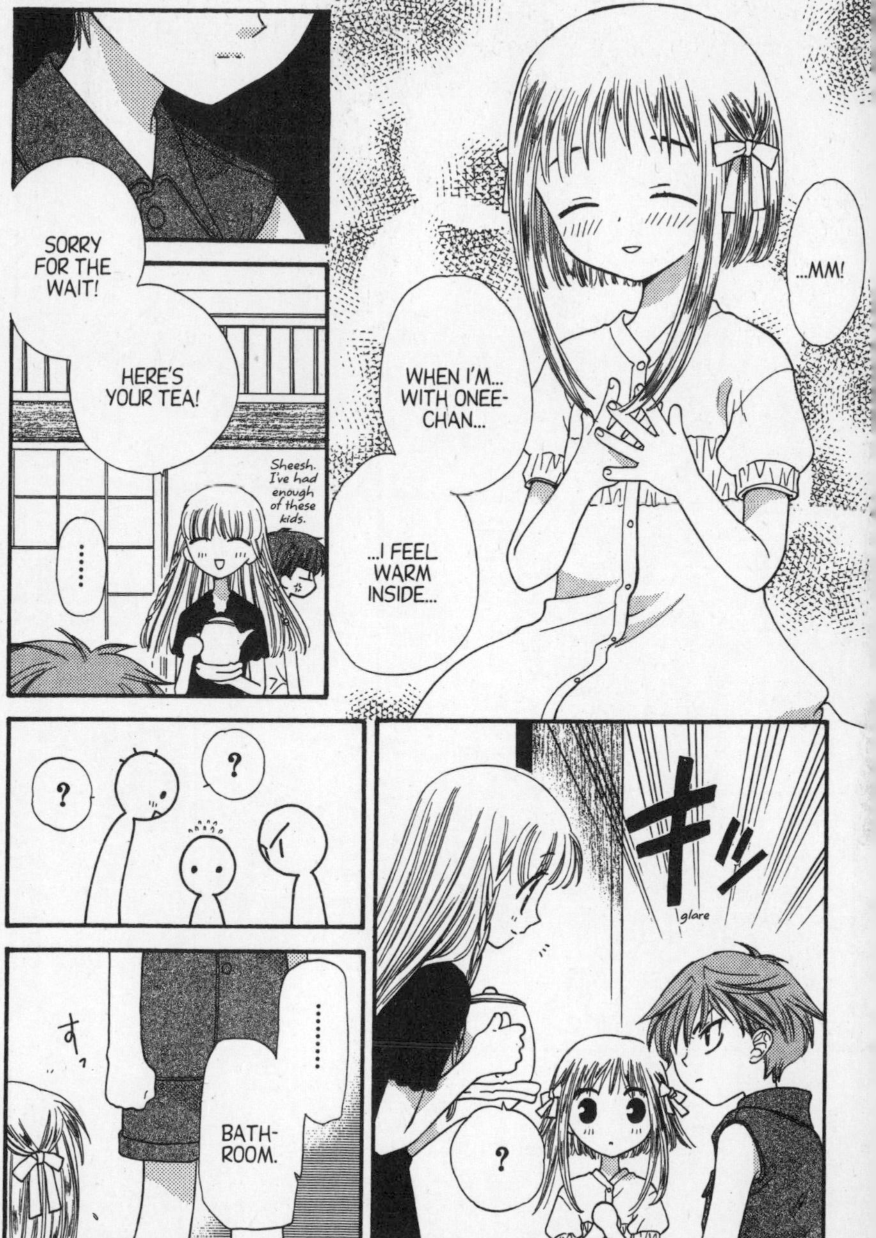

...MM!
WHEN I'M... WITH ONEE-CHAN...
...I FEEL WARM INSIDE...
SORRY FOR THE WAIT!
HERE'S YOUR TEA!
Sheesh. I've had enough of these kids.
......
キッ
glare
?
?
?
....
BATH-ROOM.
すっ

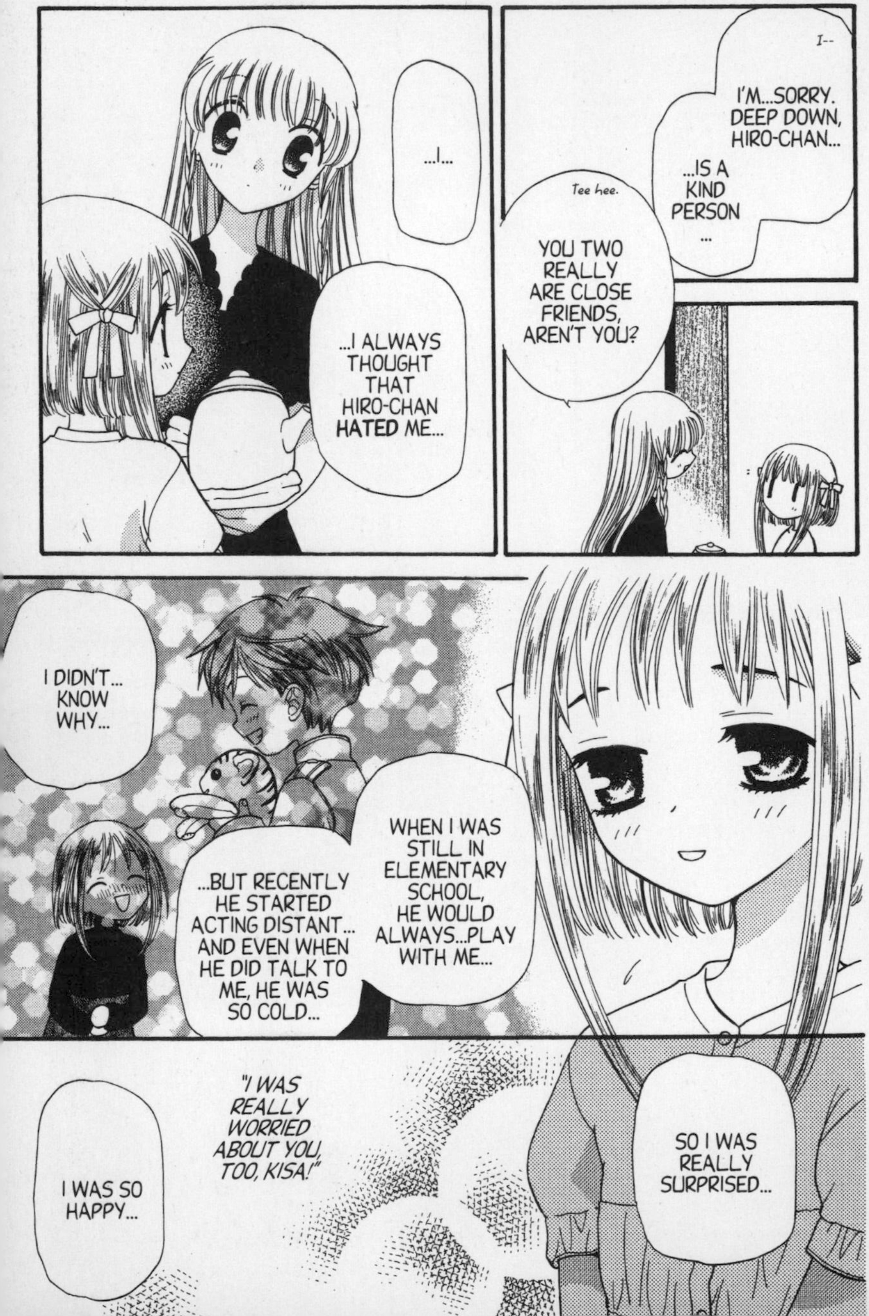
I--
I'M...SORRY. DEEP DOWN, HIRO-CHAN...
...IS A KIND PERSON ...
Tee hee.
YOU TWO REALLY ARE CLOSE FRIENDS, AREN'T YOU?
...I...
...I ALWAYS THOUGHT THAT HIRO-CHAN HATED ME...
WHEN I WAS STILL IN ELEMENTARY SCHOOL, HE WOULD ALWAYS...PLAY WITH ME...
...BUT RECENTLY HE STARTED ACTING DISTANT... AND EVEN WHEN HE DID TALK TO ME, HE WAS SO COLD...
I DIDN'T... KNOW WHY...
SO I WAS REALLY SURPRISED...
"I WAS REALLY WORRIED ABOUT YOU, TOO, KISA!"
I WAS SO HAPPY...

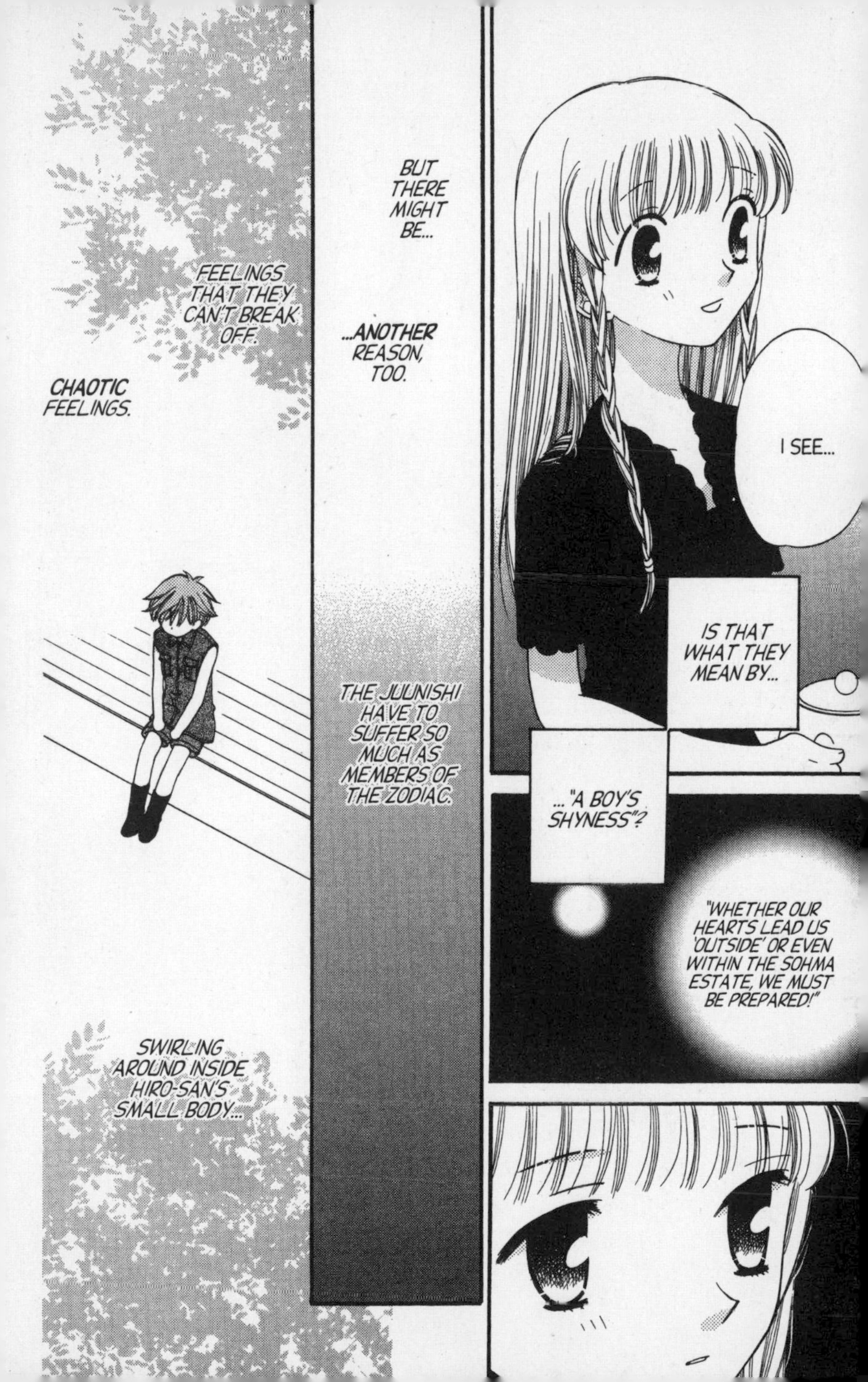
I SEE...
IS THAT WHAT THEY MEAN BY...
..."A BOY'S SHYNESS"?
"WHETHER OUR HEARTS LEAD US 'OUTSIDE' OR EVEN WITHIN THE SOHMA ESTATE, WE MUST BE PREPARED!"
BUT THERE MIGHT BE...
...ANOTHER REASON, TOO.
THE JUUNISHI HAVE TO SUFFER SO MUCH AS MEMBERS OF THE ZODIAC.
FEELINGS THAT THEY CAN'T BREAK OFF.
CHAOTIC FEELINGS.
SWIRLING AROUND INSIDE HIRO-SAN'S SMALL BODY...

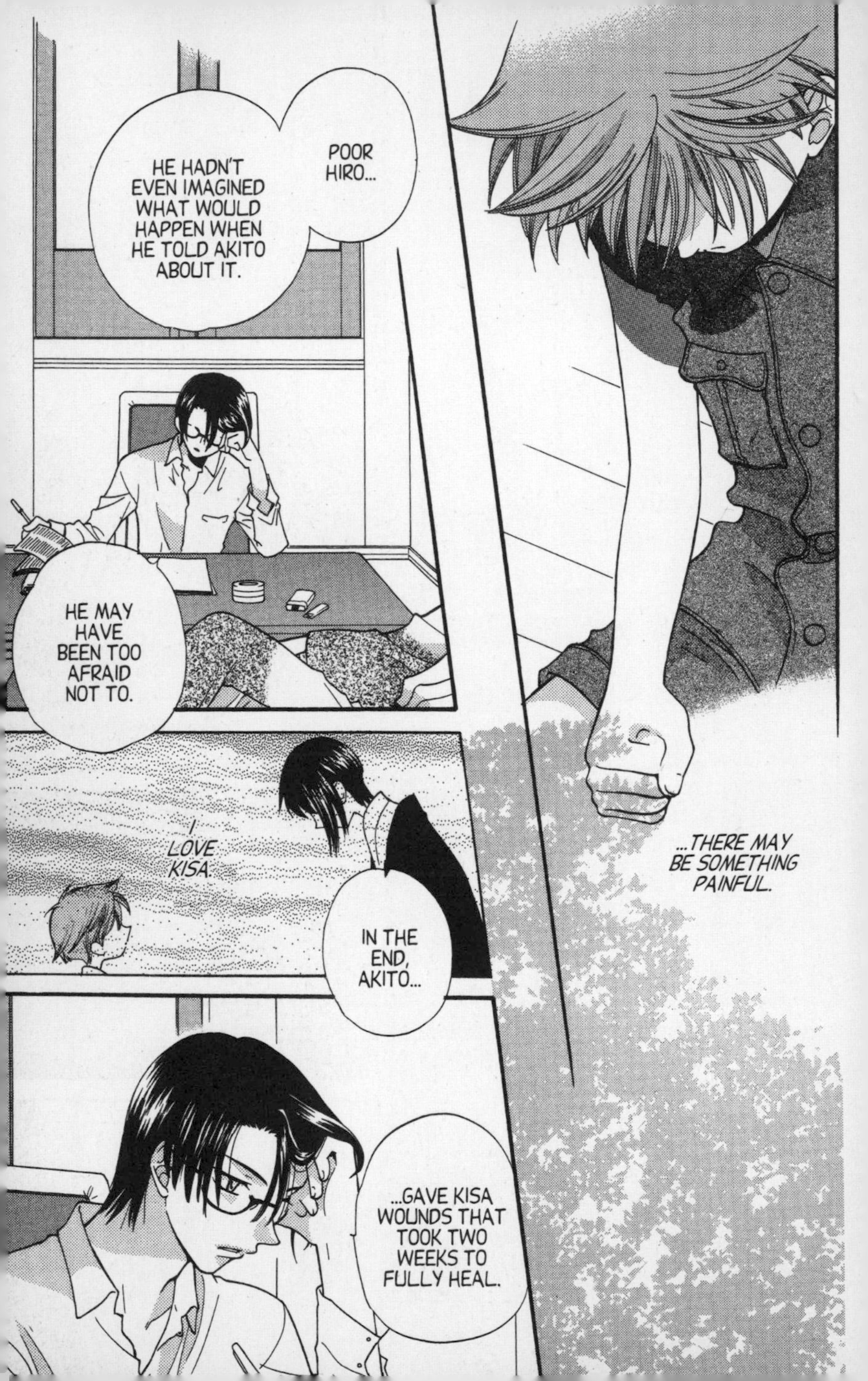
...THERE MAY BE SOMETHING PAINFUL.
POOR HIRO...
HE HADN'T EVEN IMAGINED WHAT WOULD HAPPEN WHEN HE TOLD AKITO ABOUT IT.
HE MAY HAVE BEEN TOO AFRAID NOT TO.
I LOVE KISA.
IN THE END, AKITO...
...GAVE KISA WOUNDS THAT TOOK TWO WEEKS TO FULLY HEAL.

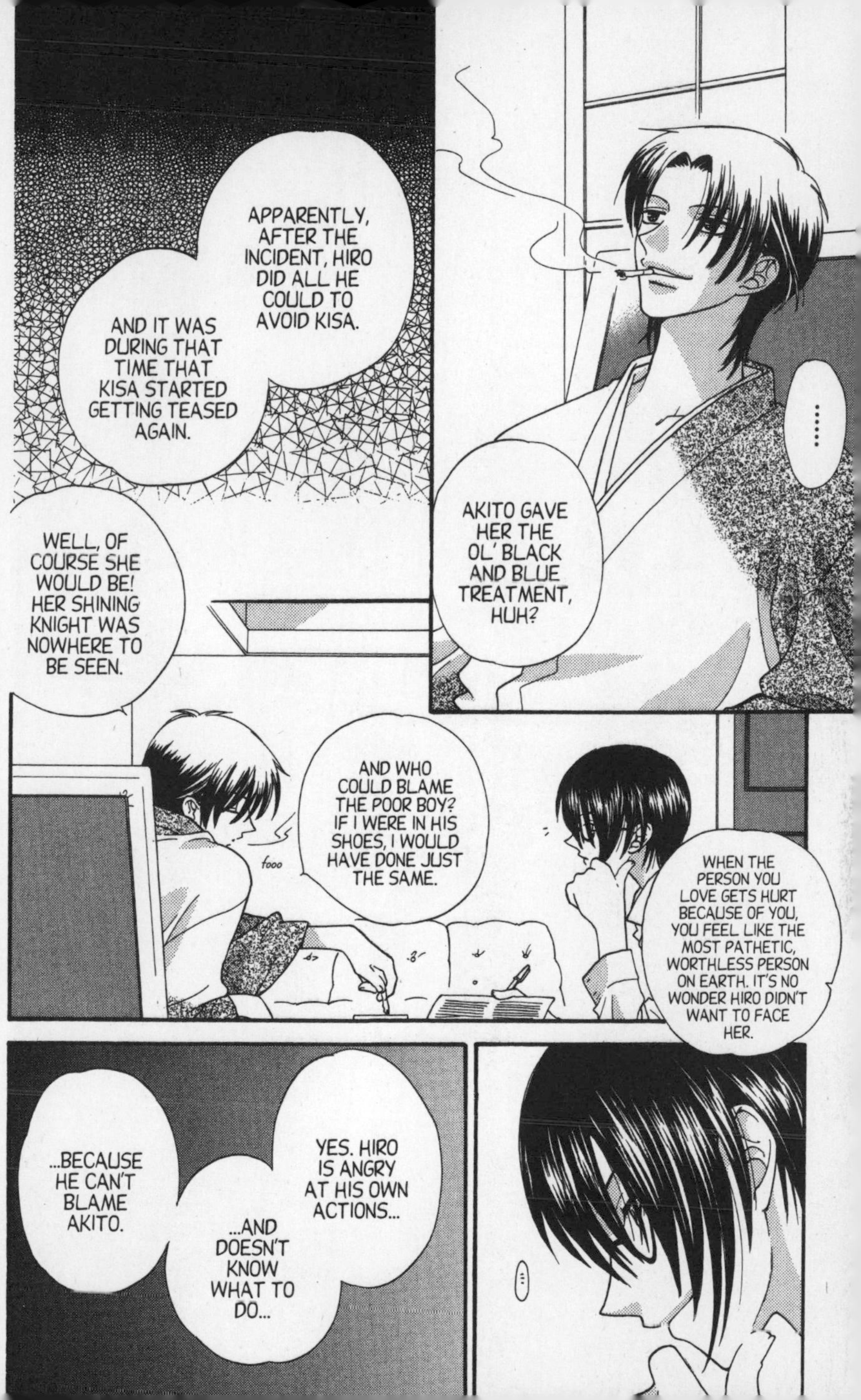
......
AKITO GAVE HER THE OL' BLACK AND BLUE TREATMENT, HUH?
APPARENTLY, AFTER THE INCIDENT, HIRO DID ALL HE COULD TO AVOID KISA.
AND IT WAS DURING THAT TIME THAT KISA STARTED GETTING TEASED AGAIN.
WELL, OF COURSE SHE WOULD BE! HER SHINING KNIGHT WAS NOWHERE TO BE SEEN.
AND WHO COULD BLAME THE POOR BOY? IF I WERE IN HIS SHOES, I WOULD HAVE DONE JUST THE SAME.
fooo
WHEN THE PERSON YOU LOVE GETS HURT BECAUSE OF YOU, YOU FEEL LIKE THE MOST PATHETIC, WORTHLESS PERSON ON EARTH. IT'S NO WONDER HIRO DIDN'T WANT TO FACE HER.
...
YES. HIRO IS ANGRY AT HIS OWN ACTIONS...
...AND DOESN'T KNOW WHAT TO DO...
...BECAUSE HE CAN'T BLAME AKITO.

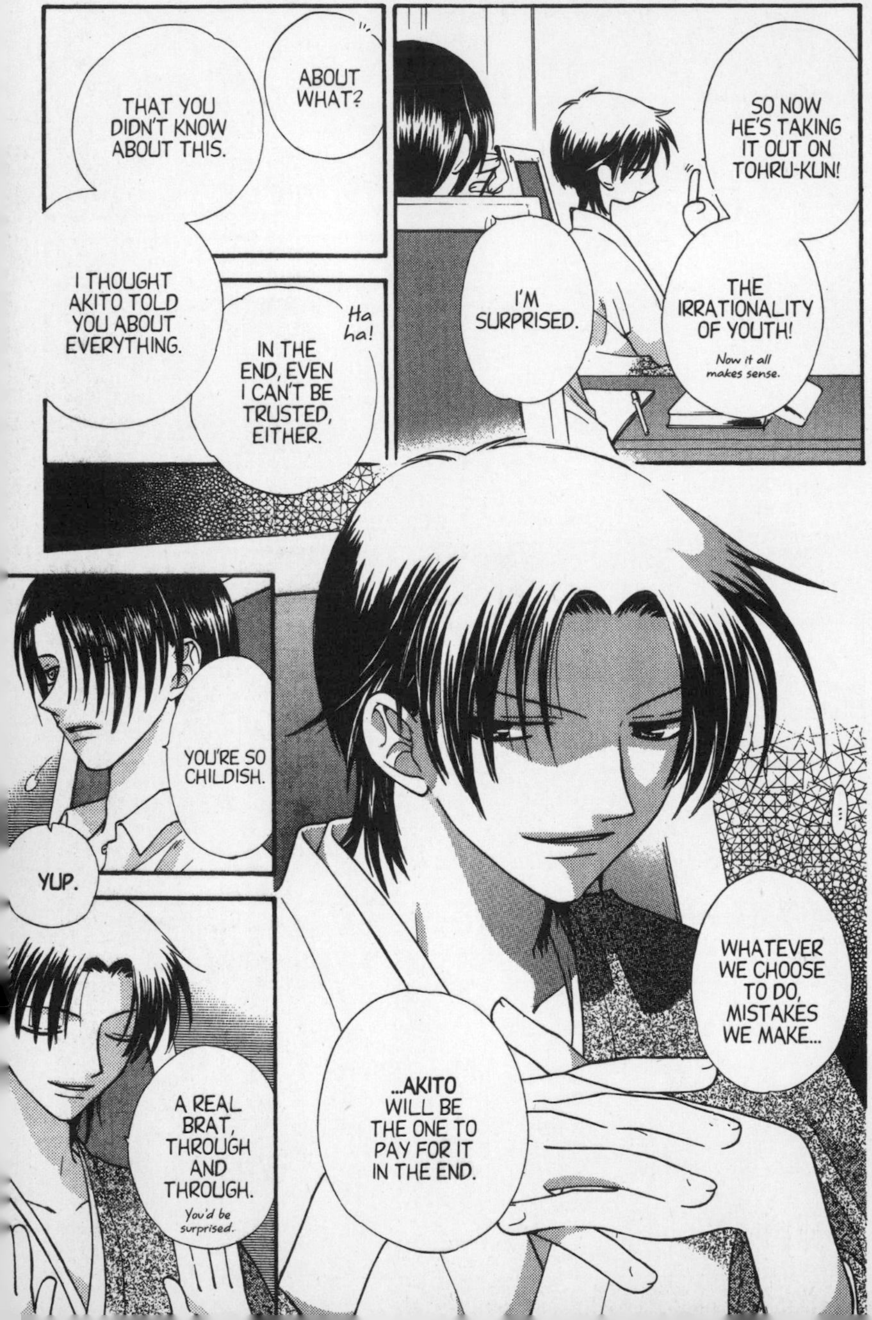
SO NOW HE'S TAKING IT OUT ON TOHRU-KUN!
THE IRRATIONALITY OF YOUTH!
Now it all makes sense.
I'M SURPRISED.
ABOUT WHAT?
THAT YOU DIDN'T KNOW ABOUT THIS.
Ha ha!
IN THE END, EVEN I CAN'T BE TRUSTED, EITHER.
I THOUGHT AKITO TOLD YOU ABOUT EVERYTHING.
...
WHATEVER WE CHOOSE TO DO, MISTAKES WE MAKE...
...AKITO WILL BE THE ONE TO PAY FOR IT IN THE END.
YOU'RE SO CHILDISH.
YUP.
A REAL BRAT, THROUGH AND THROUGH.
You'd be surprised.

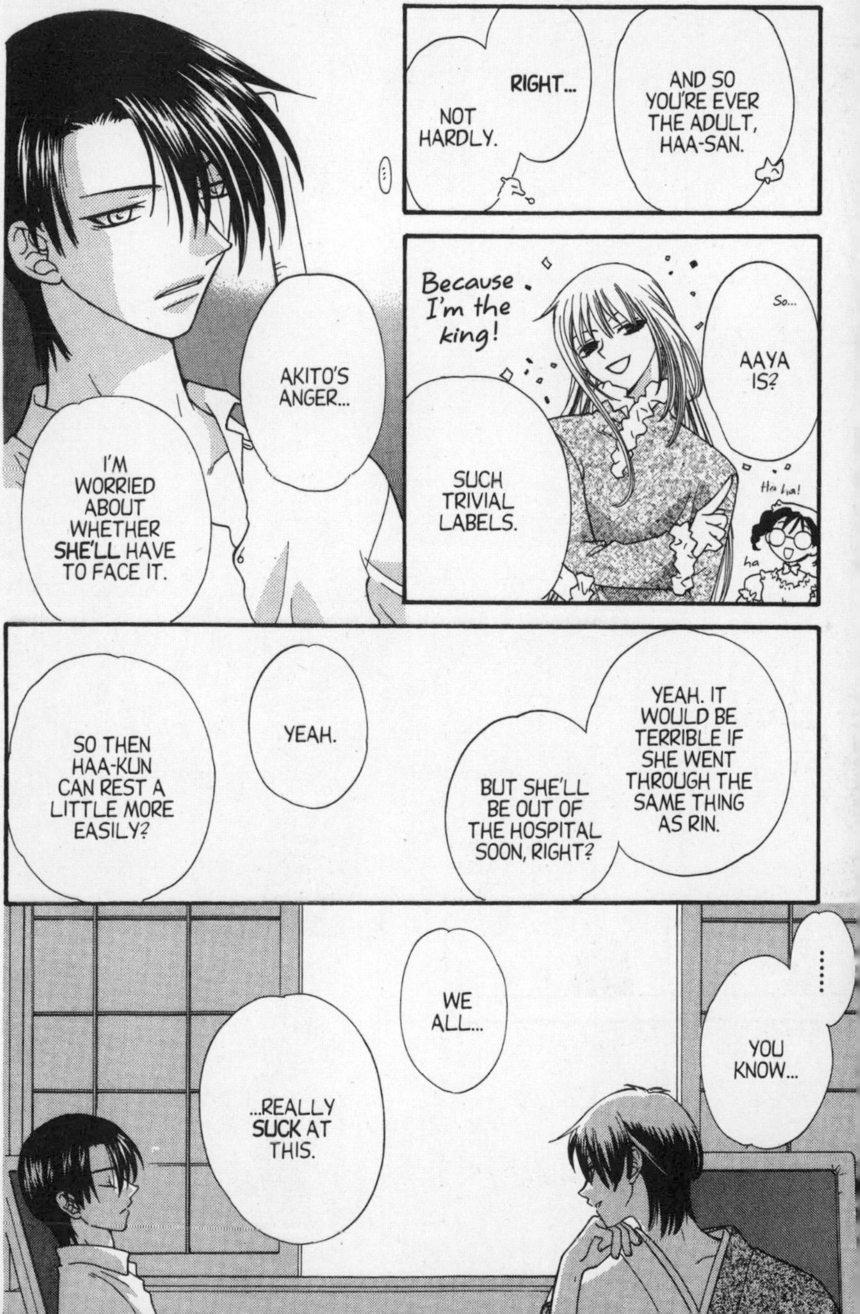
AND SO YOU'RE EVER THE ADULT, HAA-SAN.
RIGHT...
NOT HARDLY.
So...
AAYA IS?
Because I'm the king!
SUCH TRIVIAL LABELS.
Ha ha!
ha
...
AKITO'S ANGER...
I'M WORRIED ABOUT WHETHER SHE'LL HAVE TO FACE IT.
YEAH. IT WOULD BE TERRIBLE IF SHE WENT THROUGH THE SAME THING AS RIN.
BUT SHE'LL BE OUT OF THE HOSPITAL SOON, RIGHT?
YEAH.
SO THEN HAA-KUN CAN REST A LITTLE MORE EASILY?
......
YOU KNOW...
WE ALL...
...REALLY SUCK AT THIS.

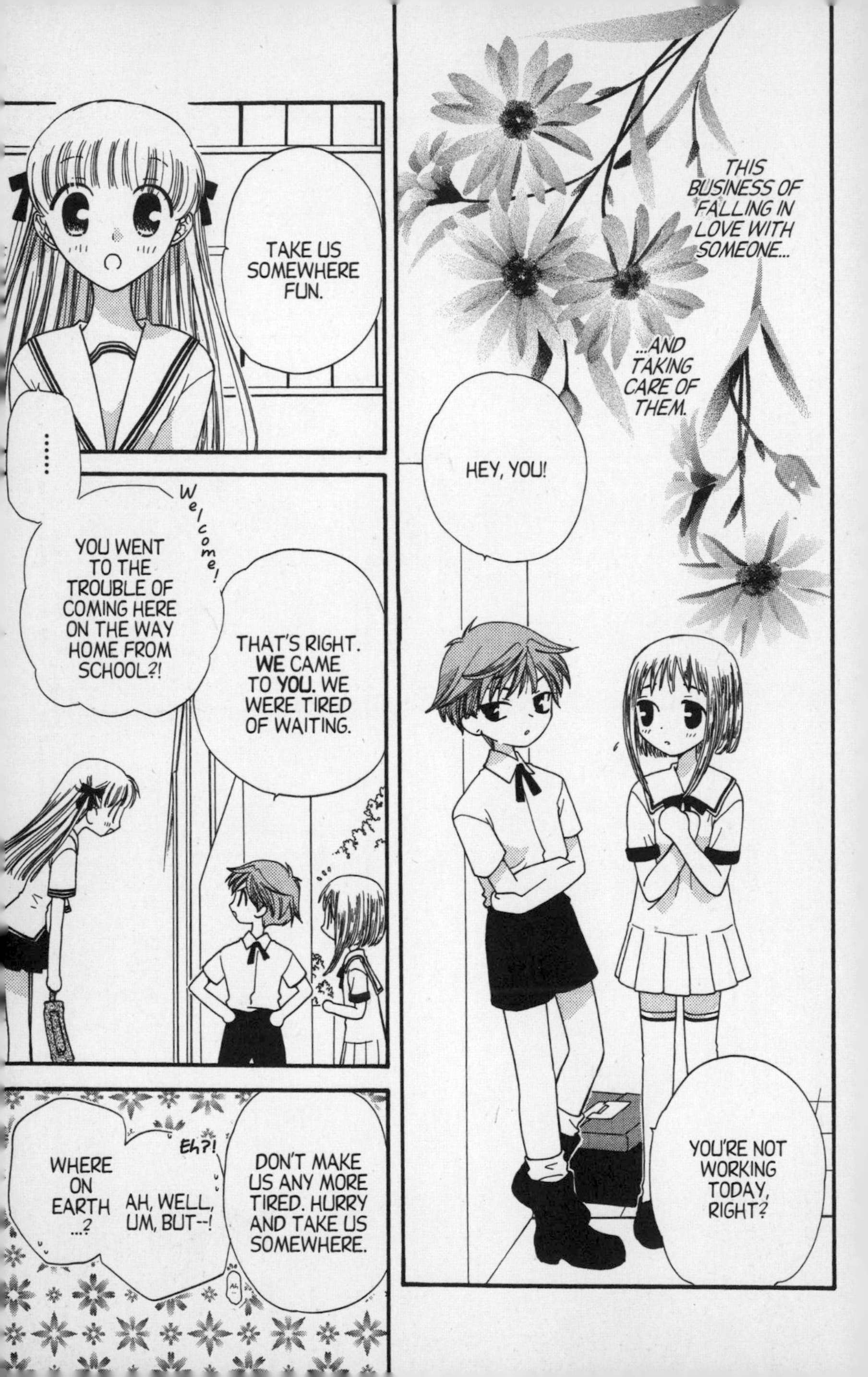
THIS BUSINESS OF FALLING IN LOVE WITH SOMEONE...
...AND TAKING CARE OF THEM.
HEY, YOU!
YOU'RE NOT WORKING TODAY, RIGHT?
TAKE US SOMEWHERE FUN.
......
Welcome!
YOU WENT TO THE TROUBLE OF COMING HERE ON THE WAY HOME FROM SCHOOL?!
THAT'S RIGHT. WE CAME TO YOU. WE WERE TIRED OF WAITING.
DON'T MAKE US ANY MORE TIRED. HURRY AND TAKE US SOMEWHERE.
Eh?!
AH, WELL, UM, BUT--!
WHERE ON EARTH ...?

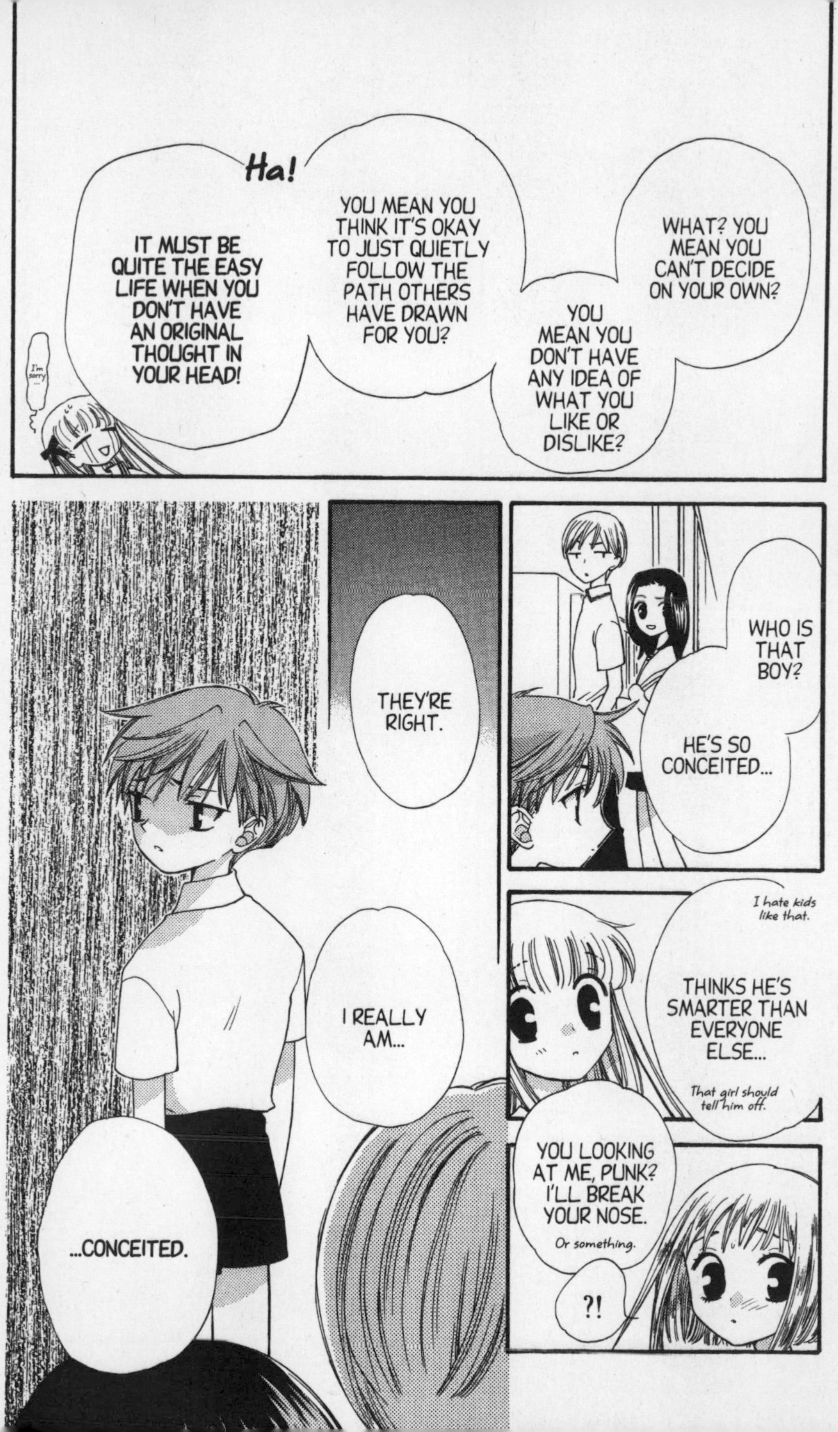
WHAT? YOU MEAN YOU CAN'T DECIDE ON YOUR OWN?
YOU MEAN YOU DON'T HAVE ANY IDEA OF WHAT YOU LIKE OR DISLIKE?
Ha!
YOU MEAN YOU THINK IT'S OKAY TO JUST QUIETLY FOLLOW THE PATH OTHERS HAVE DRAWN FOR YOU?
IT MUST BE QUITE THE EASY LIFE WHEN YOU DON'T HAVE AN ORIGINAL THOUGHT IN YOUR HEAD!
I'm sorry...
WHO IS THAT BOY?
HE'S SO CONCEITED...
I hate kids like that.
THINKS HE'S SMARTER THAN EVERYONE ELSE...
That girl should tell him off.
YOU LOOKING AT ME, PUNK? I'LL BREAK YOUR NOSE.
Or something.
?!
THEY'RE RIGHT.
I REALLY AM...
...CONCEITED.

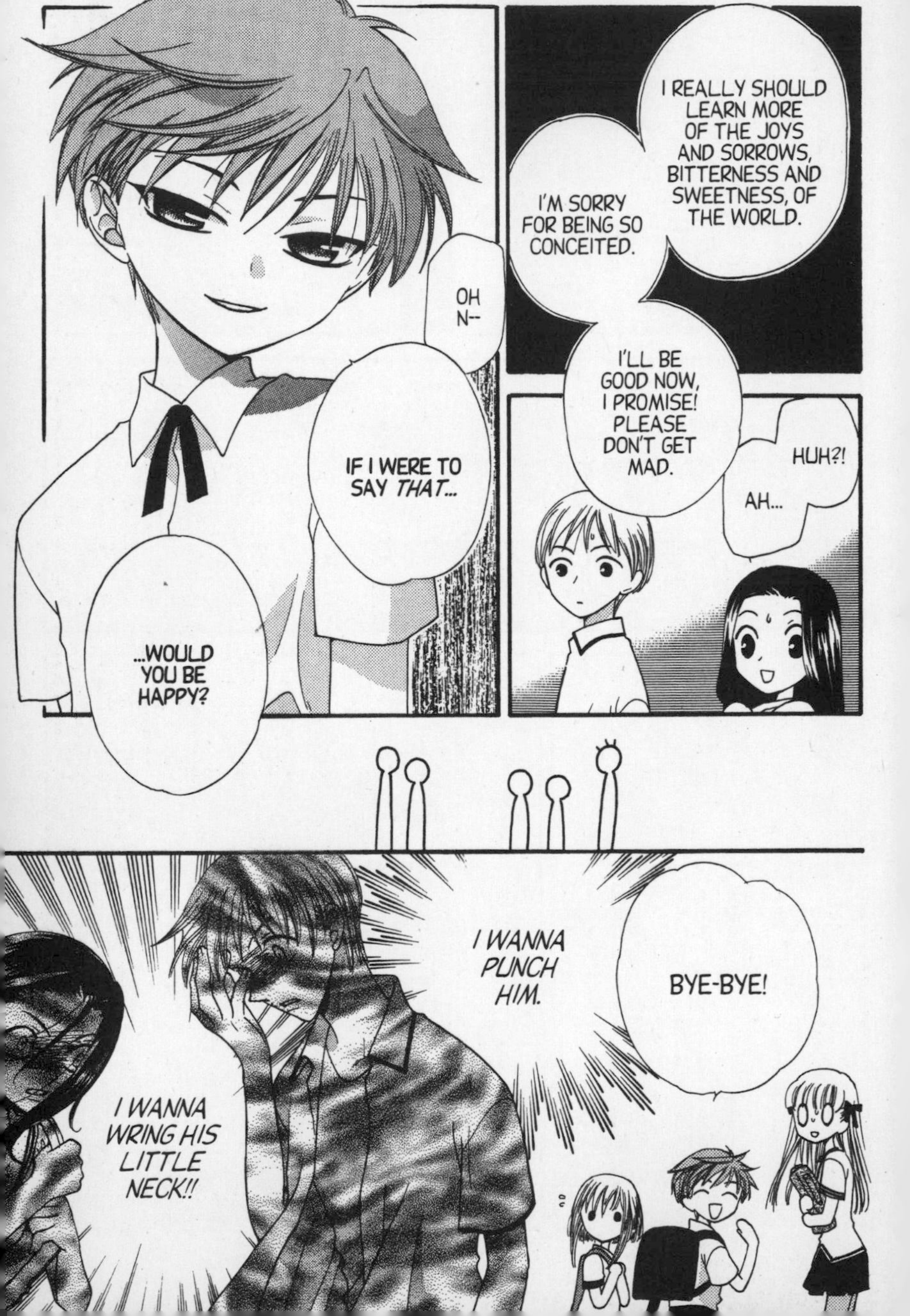
I REALLY SHOULD LEARN MORE OF THE JOYS AND SORROWS, BITTERNESS AND SWEETNESS, OF THE WORLD.
I'M SORRY FOR BEING SO CONCEITED.
I'LL BE GOOD NOW, I PROMISE! PLEASE DON'T GET MAD.
HUH?!
AH...
OH N--
IF I WERE TO SAY *THAT*...
...WOULD YOU BE HAPPY?
BYE-BYE!
I WANNA PUNCH HIM.
I WANNA WRING HIS LITTLE NECK!!

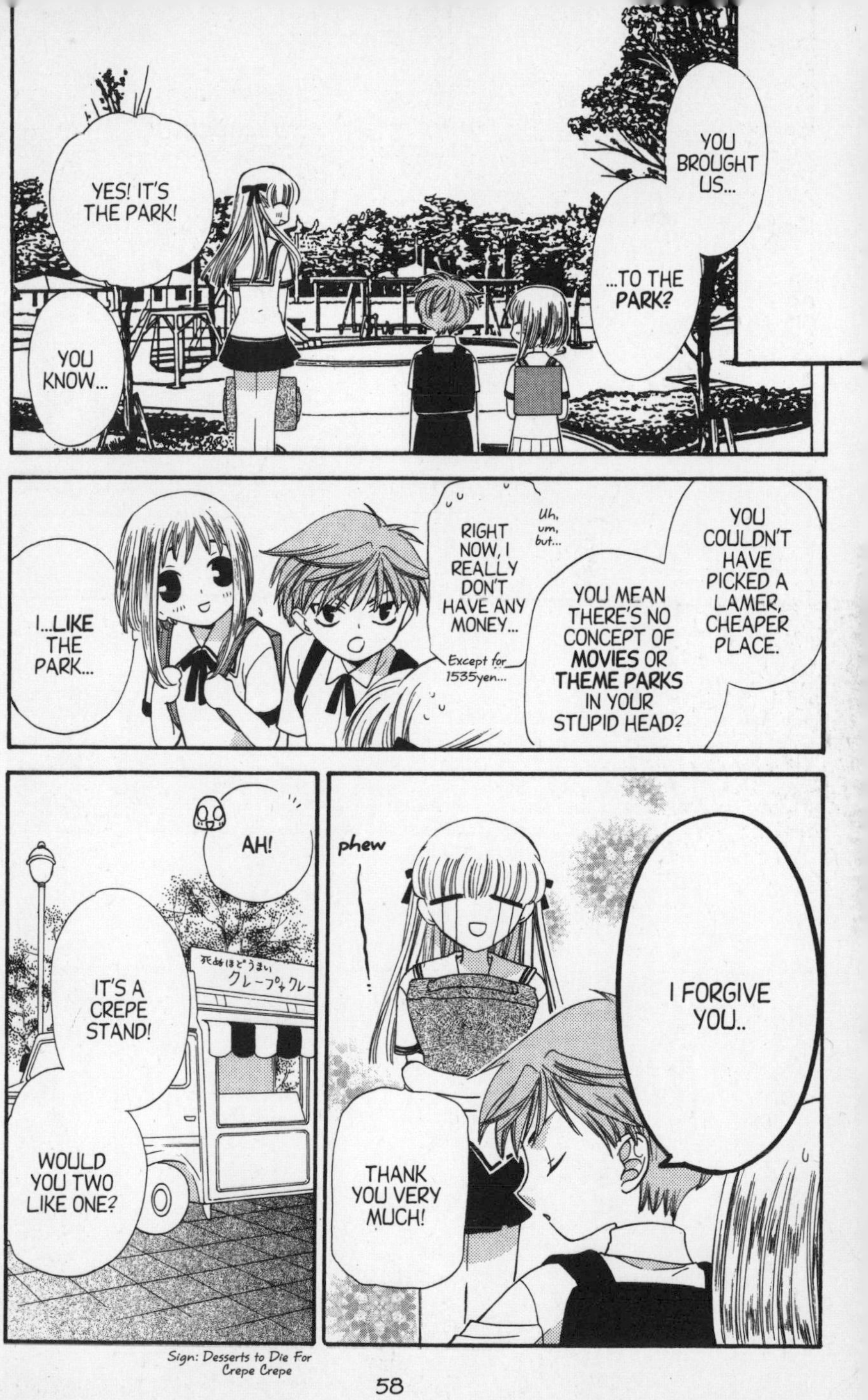
YOU BROUGHT US...
...TO THE PARK?
YES! IT'S THE PARK!
YOU KNOW...
YOU COULDN'T HAVE PICKED A LAMER, CHEAPER PLACE.
YOU MEAN THERE'S NO CONCEPT OF MOVIES OR THEME PARKS IN YOUR STUPID HEAD?
Uh, um, but...
RIGHT NOW, I REALLY DON'T HAVE ANY MONEY...
Except for 1535yen...
I...LIKE THE PARK...
I FORGIVE YOU..
phew
THANK YOU VERY MUCH!
AH!
死ぬほどうまい
IT'S A CREPE STAND!
WOULD YOU TWO LIKE ONE?

Sign: Desserts to Die For
Crepe Crepe

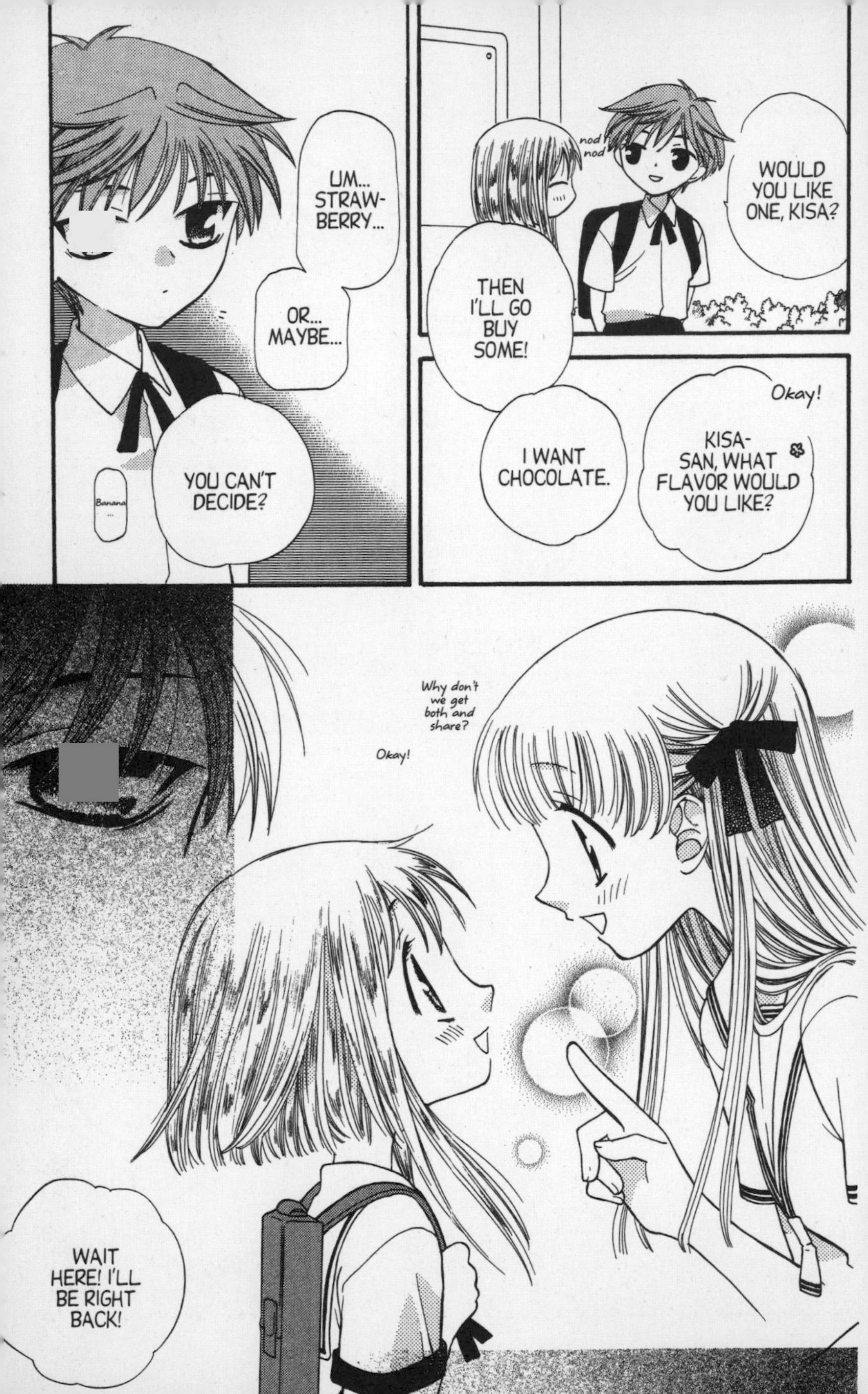
WOULD YOU LIKE ONE, KISA?
nod nod
THEN I'LL GO BUY SOME!
Okay!
KISA-SAN, WHAT FLAVOR WOULD YOU LIKE?
I WANT CHOCOLATE.
UM... STRAWBERRY...
OR... MAYBE...
YOU CAN'T DECIDE?
Banana ...
Why don't we get both and share?
Okay!
WAIT HERE! I'LL BE RIGHT BACK!

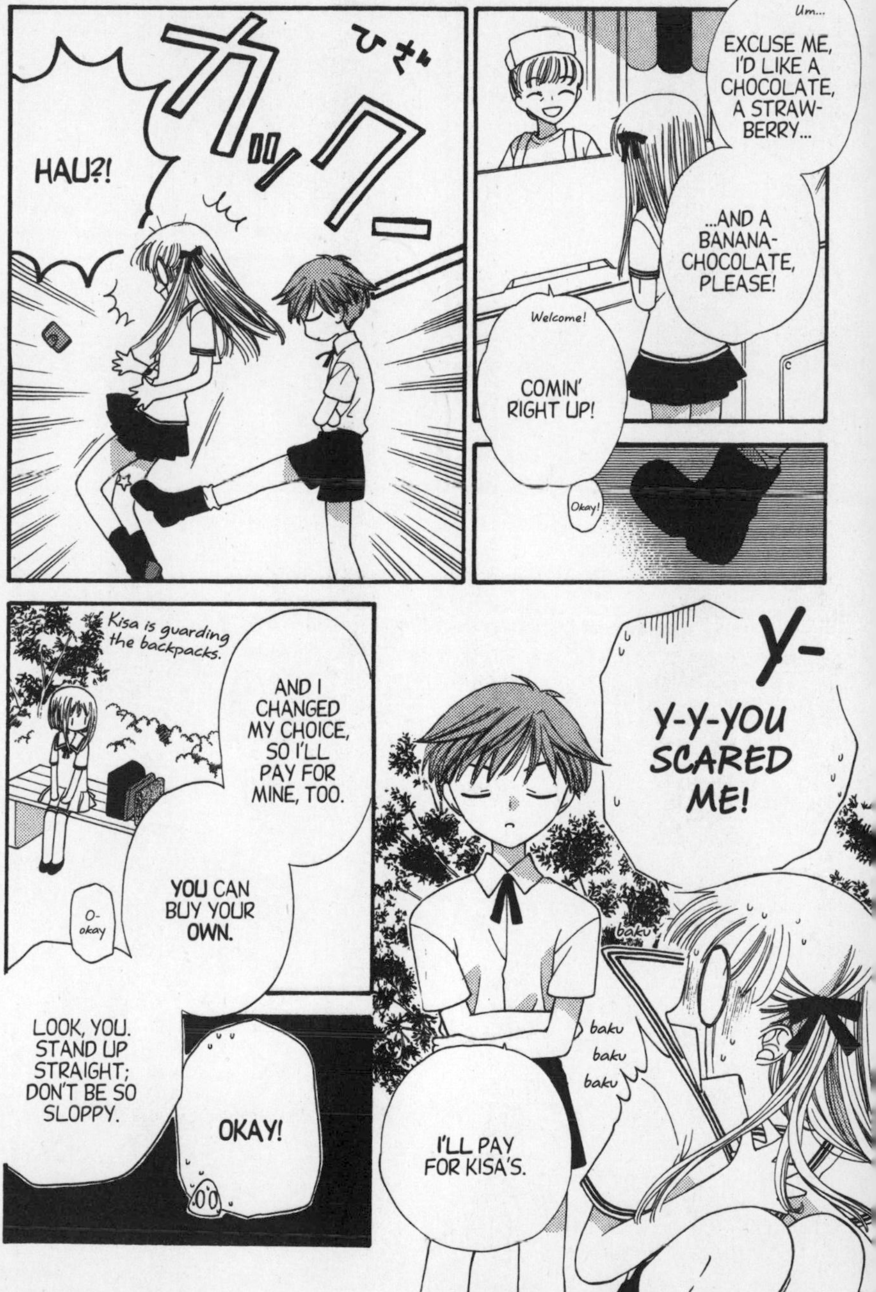
Um...
EXCUSE ME, I'D LIKE A CHOCOLATE, A STRAWBERRY...
...AND A BANANA-CHOCOLATE, PLEASE!
Welcome!
COMIN' RIGHT UP!
Okay!
ひざ
カックー
HAU?!
Y-
Y-Y-YOU SCARED ME!
baku
baku
baku
baku
I'LL PAY FOR KISA'S.
Kisa is guarding the backpacks.
AND I CHANGED MY CHOICE, SO I'LL PAY FOR MINE, TOO.
YOU CAN BUY YOUR OWN.
O-okay
LOOK, YOU. STAND UP STRAIGHT; DON'T BE SO SLOPPY.
OKAY!

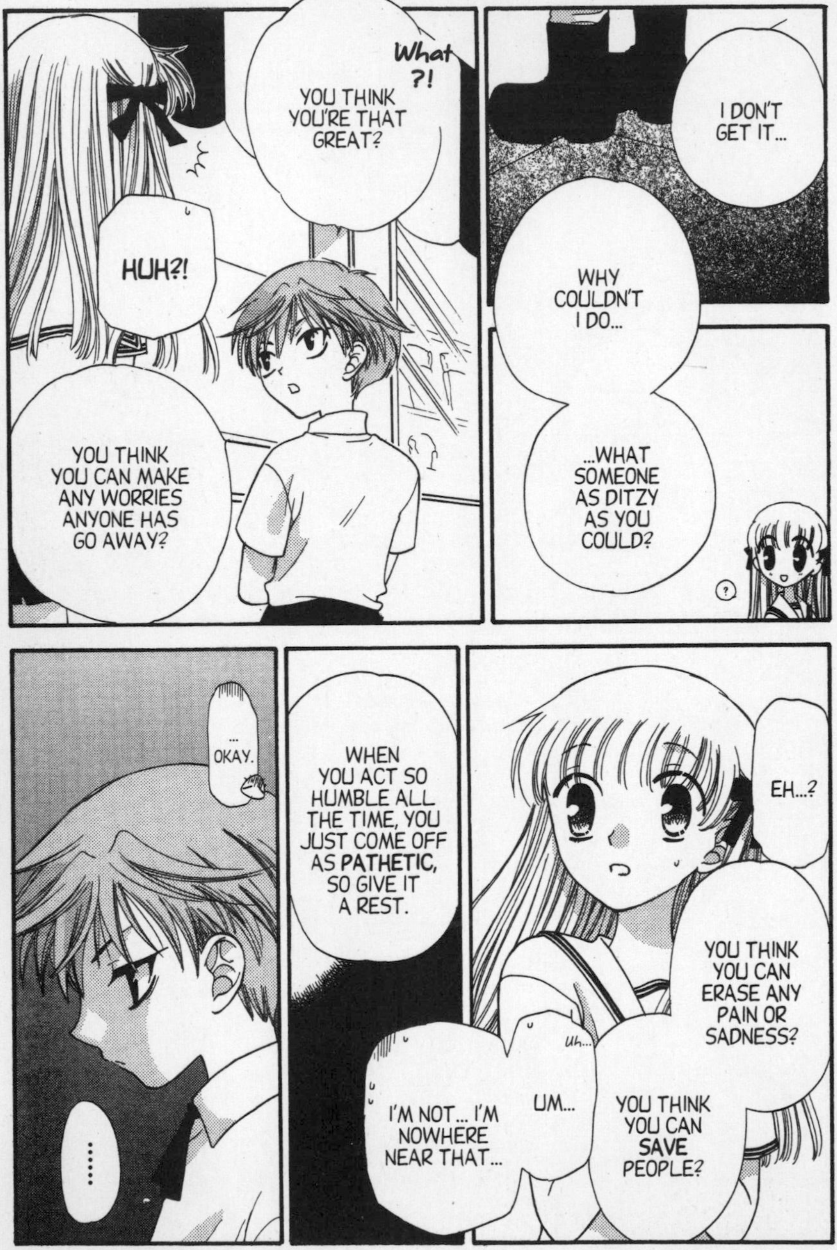
I DON'T GET IT...
WHY COULDN'T I DO...
...WHAT SOMEONE AS DITZY AS YOU COULD?
?
What ?!
YOU THINK YOU'RE THAT GREAT?
HUH?!
YOU THINK YOU CAN MAKE ANY WORRIES ANYONE HAS GO AWAY?
EH...?
YOU THINK YOU CAN ERASE ANY PAIN OR SADNESS?
YOU THINK YOU CAN SAVE PEOPLE?
Uh...
UM...
I'M NOT... I'M NOWHERE NEAR THAT...
WHEN YOU ACT SO HUMBLE ALL THE TIME, YOU JUST COME OFF AS **PATHETIC**, SO GIVE IT A REST.
... OKAY.
......

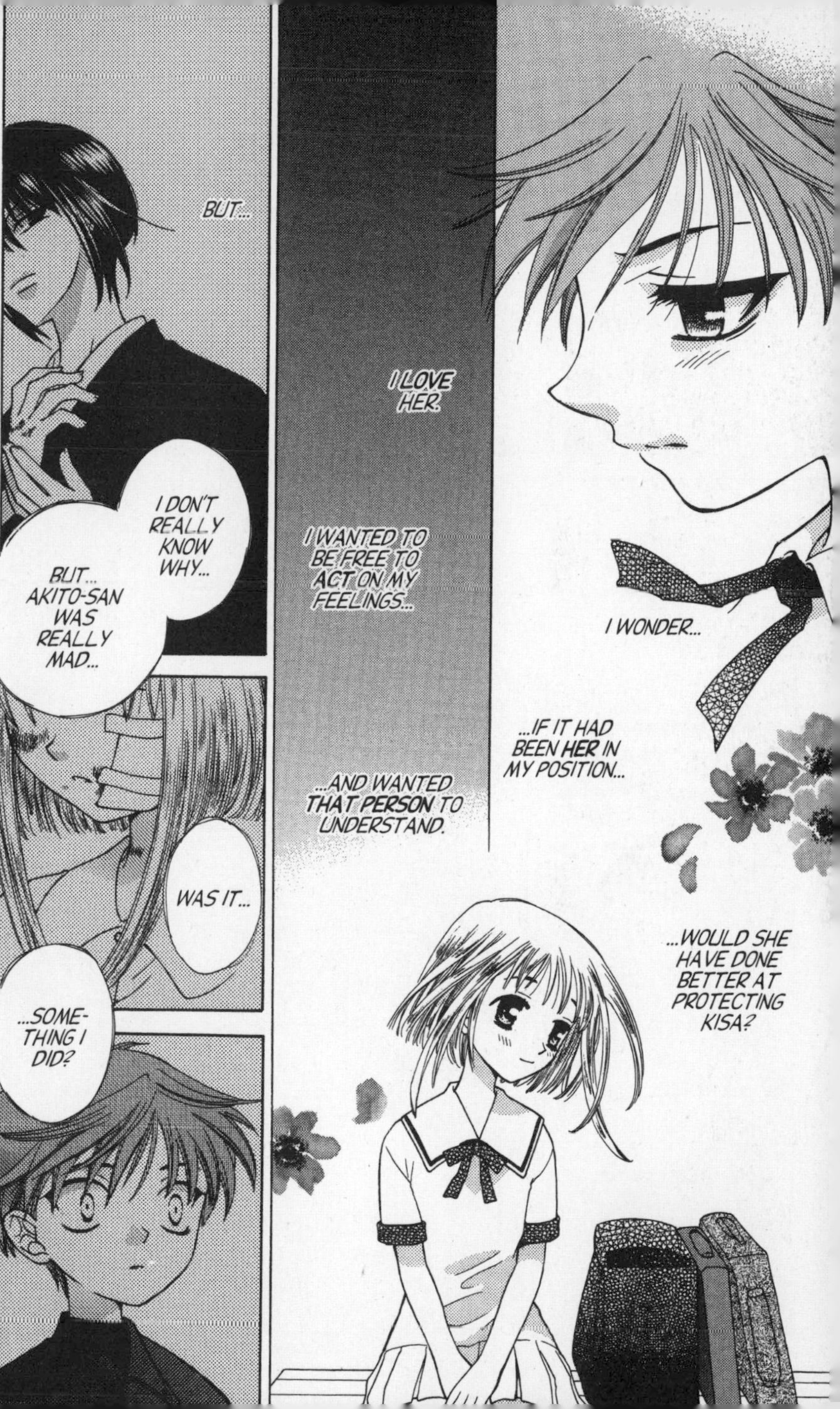
I WONDER...
...IF IT HAD BEEN HER IN MY POSITION...
...WOULD SHE HAVE DONE BETTER AT PROTECTING KISA?
I LOVE HER.
I WANTED TO BE FREE TO ACT ON MY FEELINGS...
...AND WANTED THAT PERSON TO UNDERSTAND.
BUT...
I DON'T REALLY KNOW WHY...
BUT... AKITO-SAN WAS REALLY MAD...
WAS IT...
...SOME-THING I DID?

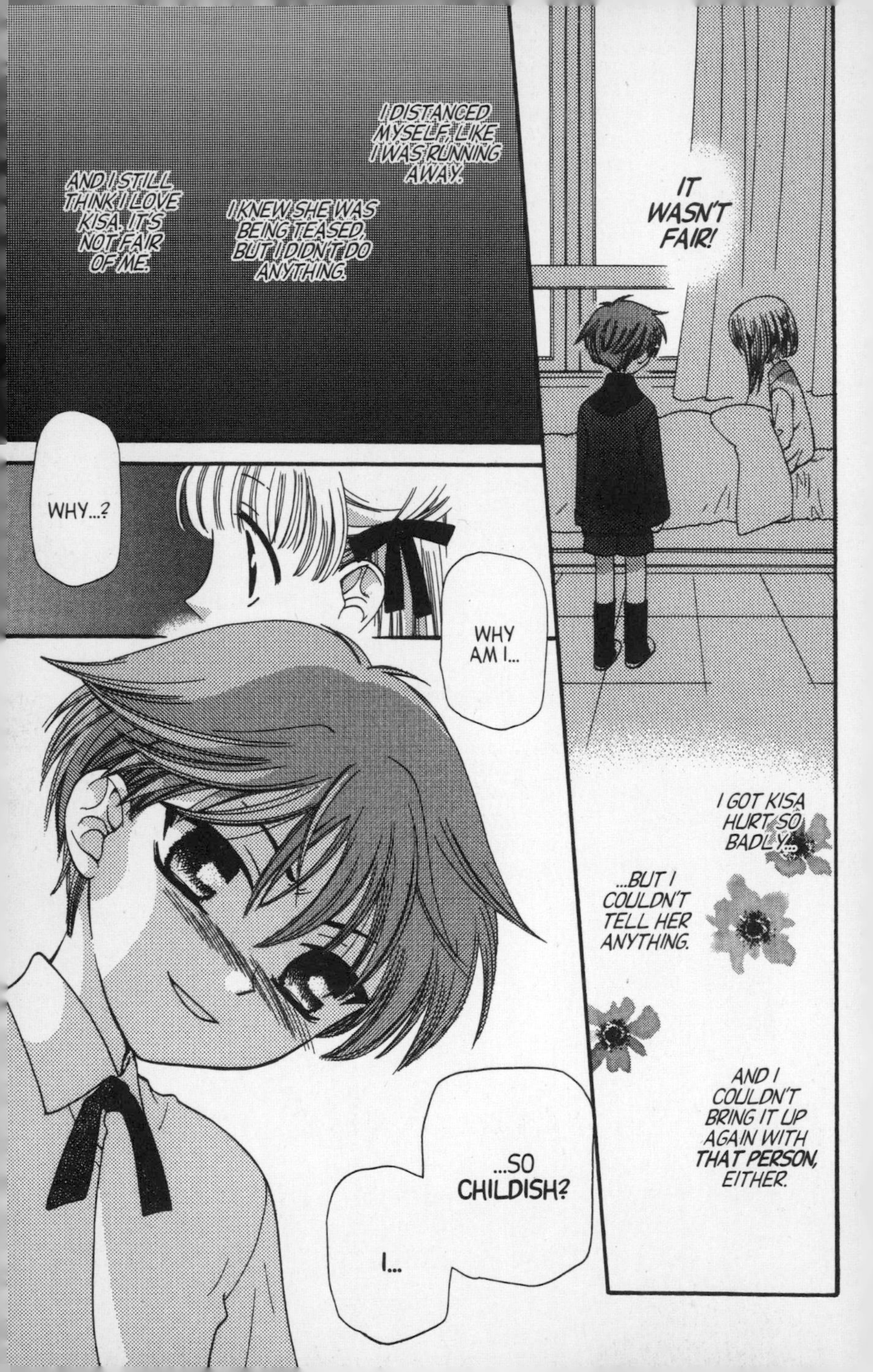
IT WASN'T FAIR!
I GOT KISA HURT SO BADLY...
...BUT I COULDN'T TELL HER ANYTHING.
AND I COULDN'T BRING IT UP AGAIN WITH THAT PERSON, EITHER.
I DISTANCED MYSELF, LIKE I WAS RUNNING AWAY.
I KNEW SHE WAS BEING TEASED, BUT I DIDN'T DO ANYTHING.
AND I STILL THINK I LOVE KISA. IT'S NOT FAIR OF ME.
WHY...?
WHY AM I...
...SO CHILDISH?
I...

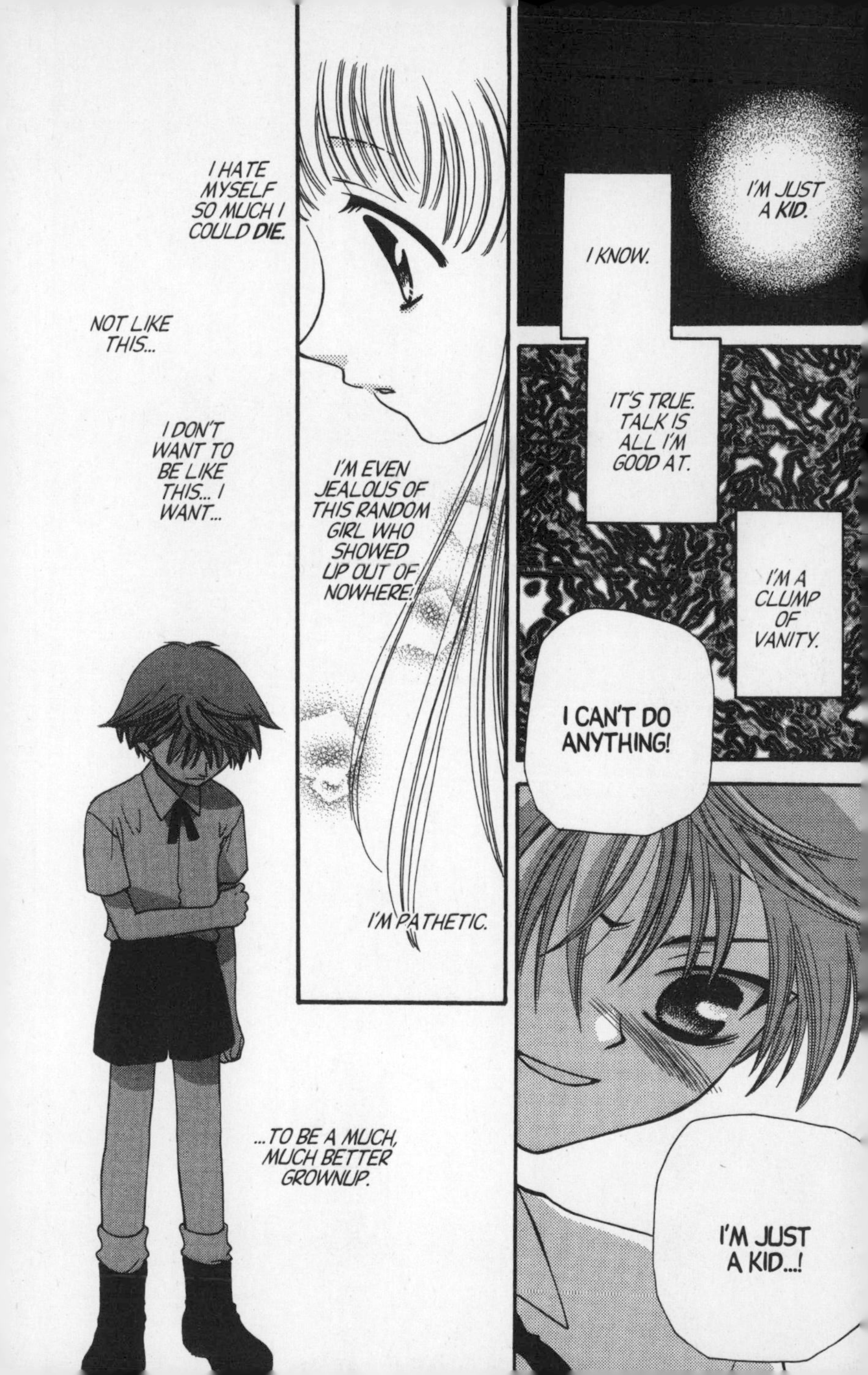
I'M JUST A KID.
I KNOW.
IT'S TRUE. TALK IS ALL I'M GOOD AT.
I'M A CLUMP OF VANITY.
I CAN'T DO ANYTHING!
I'M JUST A KID...!
I HATE MYSELF SO MUCH I COULD DIE.
I'M EVEN JEALOUS OF THIS RANDOM GIRL WHO SHOWED UP OUT OF NOWHERE!
I'M PATHETIC.
NOT LIKE THIS...
I DON'T WANT TO BE LIKE THIS... I WANT...
...TO BE A MUCH, MUCH BETTER GROWNUP.

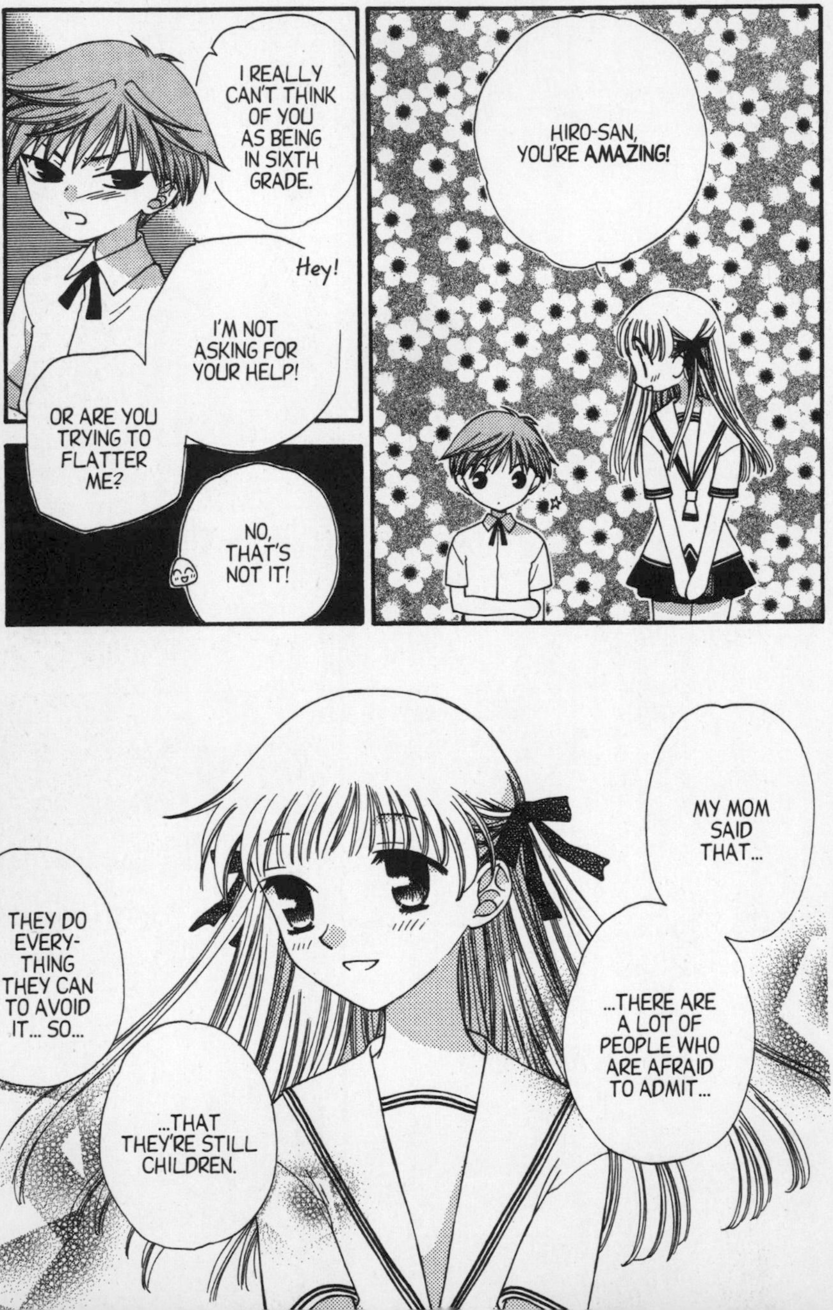
HIRO-SAN, YOU'RE **AMAZING**!
I REALLY CAN'T THINK OF YOU AS BEING IN SIXTH GRADE.
Hey!
I'M NOT ASKING FOR YOUR HELP!
OR ARE YOU TRYING TO FLATTER ME?
NO, THAT'S NOT IT!
MY MOM SAID THAT...
...THERE ARE A LOT OF PEOPLE WHO ARE AFRAID TO ADMIT...
...THAT THEY'RE STILL CHILDREN.
THEY DO EVERY-THING THEY CAN TO AVOID IT... SO...

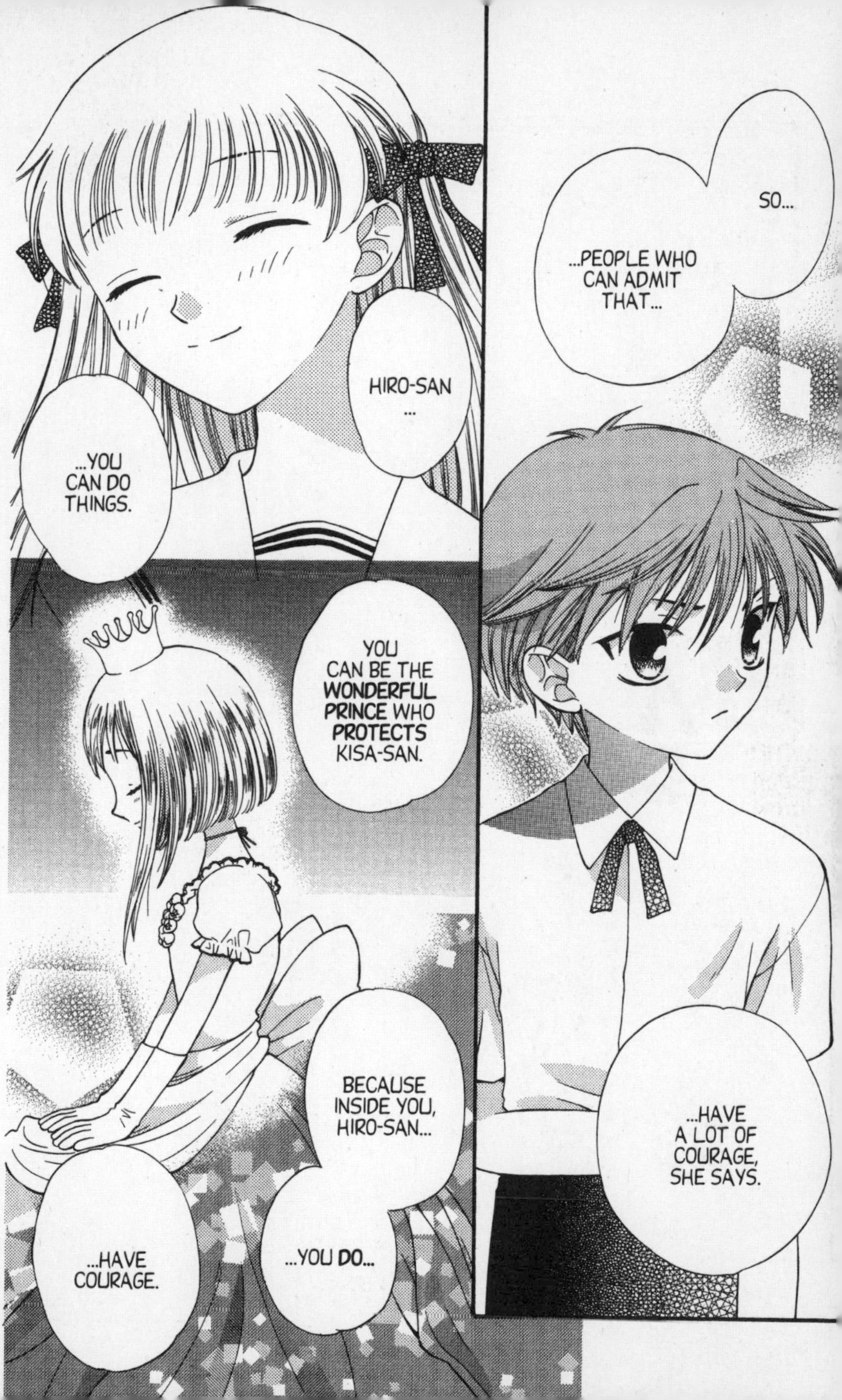
SO...
...PEOPLE WHO CAN ADMIT THAT...
...HAVE A LOT OF COURAGE, SHE SAYS.
HIRO-SAN ...
...YOU CAN DO THINGS.
YOU CAN BE THE **WONDERFUL PRINCE** WHO **PROTECTS** KISA-SAN.
BECAUSE INSIDE YOU, HIRO-SAN...
...YOU **DO**...
...HAVE COURAGE.

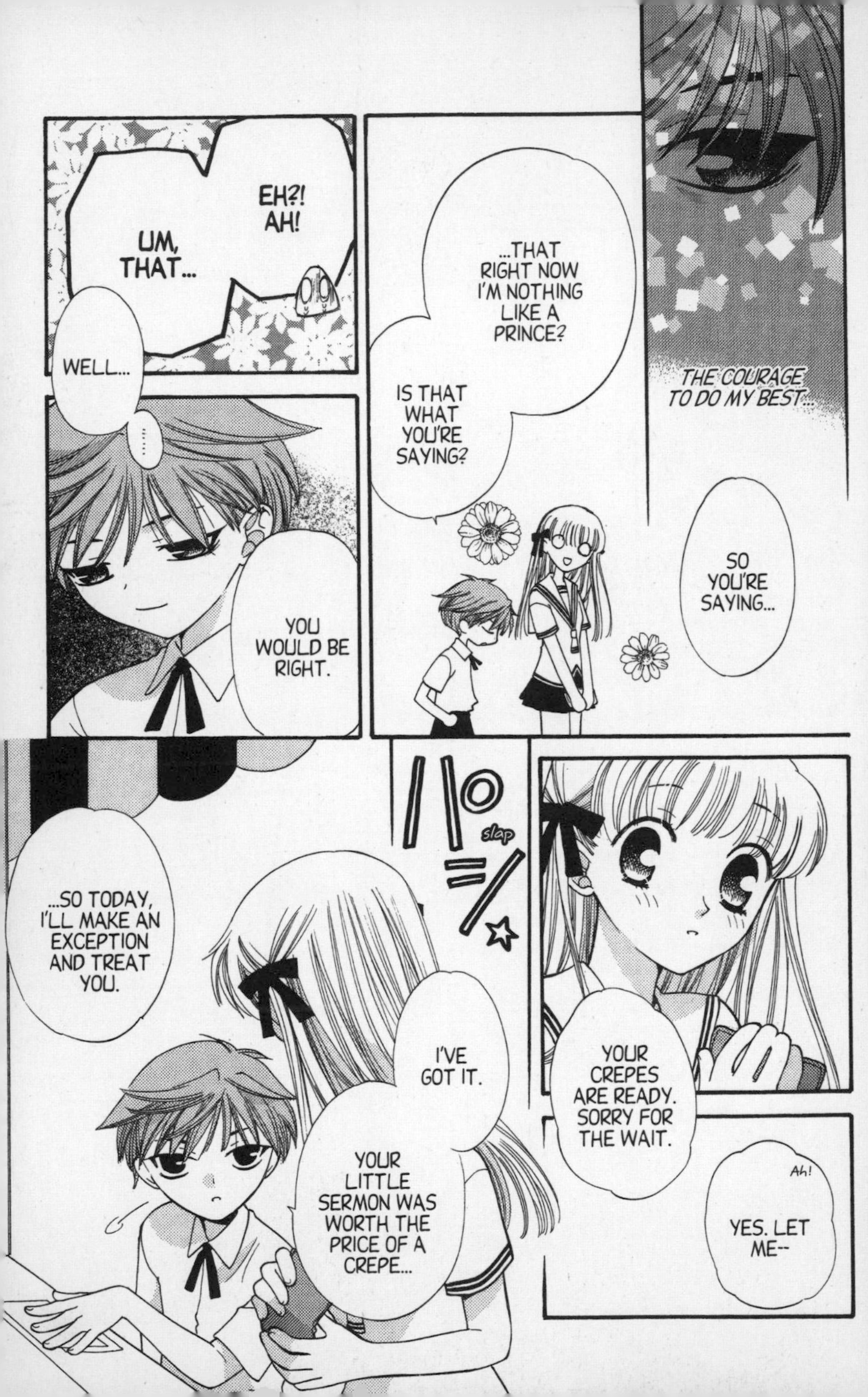
THE COURAGE TO DO MY BEST...
SO YOU'RE SAYING...
...THAT RIGHT NOW I'M NOTHING LIKE A PRINCE?
IS THAT WHAT YOU'RE SAYING?
EH?! AH!
UM, THAT...
WELL...
......
YOU WOULD BE RIGHT.
YOUR CREPES ARE READY. SORRY FOR THE WAIT.
Ah!
YES. LET ME--
slap
I'VE GOT IT.
YOUR LITTLE SERMON WAS WORTH THE PRICE OF A CREPE...
...SO TODAY, I'LL MAKE AN EXCEPTION AND TREAT YOU.

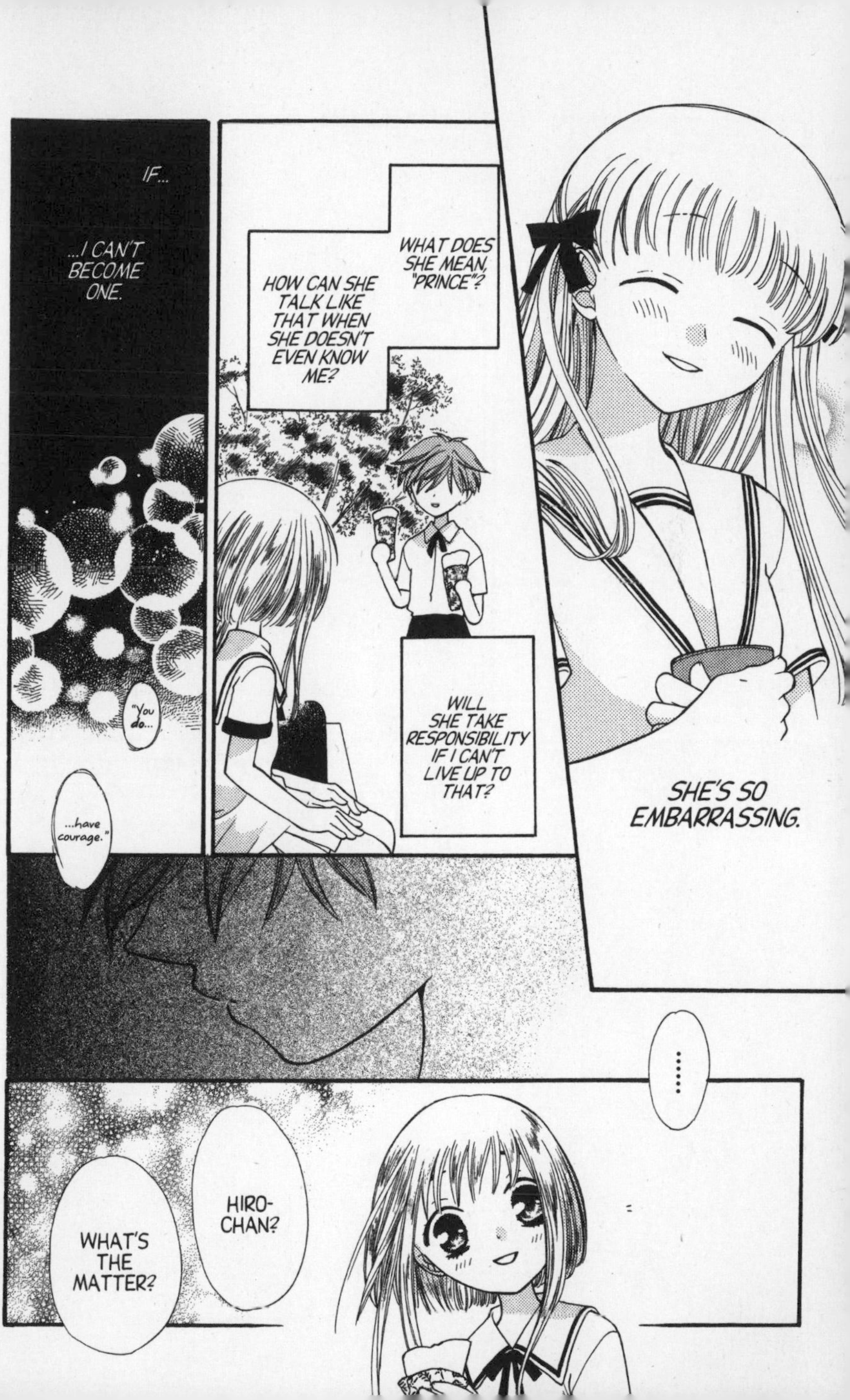
SHE'S SO EMBARRASSING.
WHAT DOES SHE MEAN, "PRINCE"?
HOW CAN SHE TALK LIKE THAT WHEN SHE DOESN'T EVEN KNOW ME?
WILL SHE TAKE RESPONSIBILITY IF I CAN'T LIVE UP TO THAT?
IF...
...I CAN'T BECOME ONE.
"You do...
...have courage."
......
HIRO-CHAN?
WHAT'S THE MATTER?

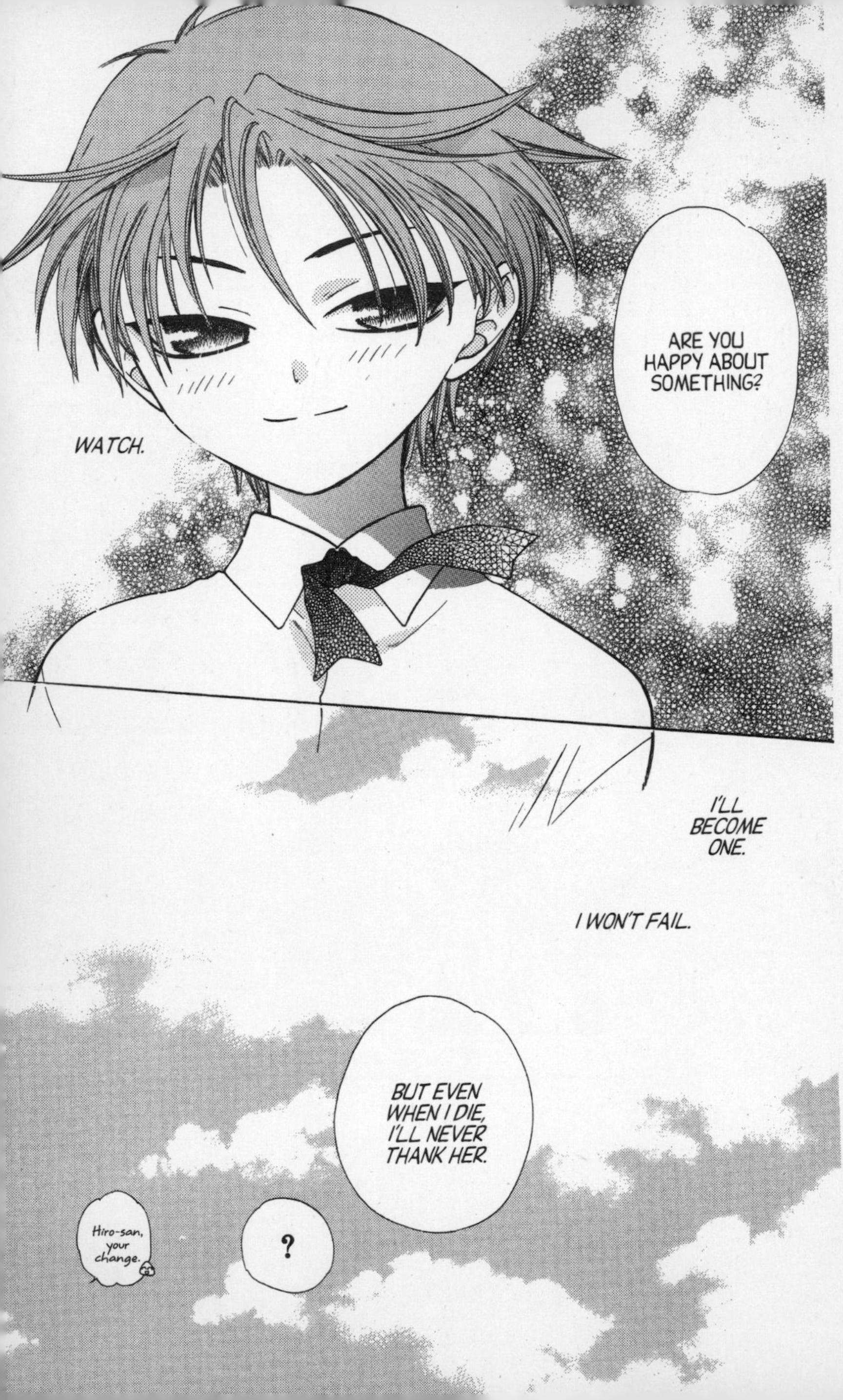
ARE YOU HAPPY ABOUT SOMETHING?
WATCH.
I'LL BECOME ONE.
I WON'T FAIL.
BUT EVEN WHEN I DIE, I'LL NEVER THANK HER.
?
Hiro-san, your change.

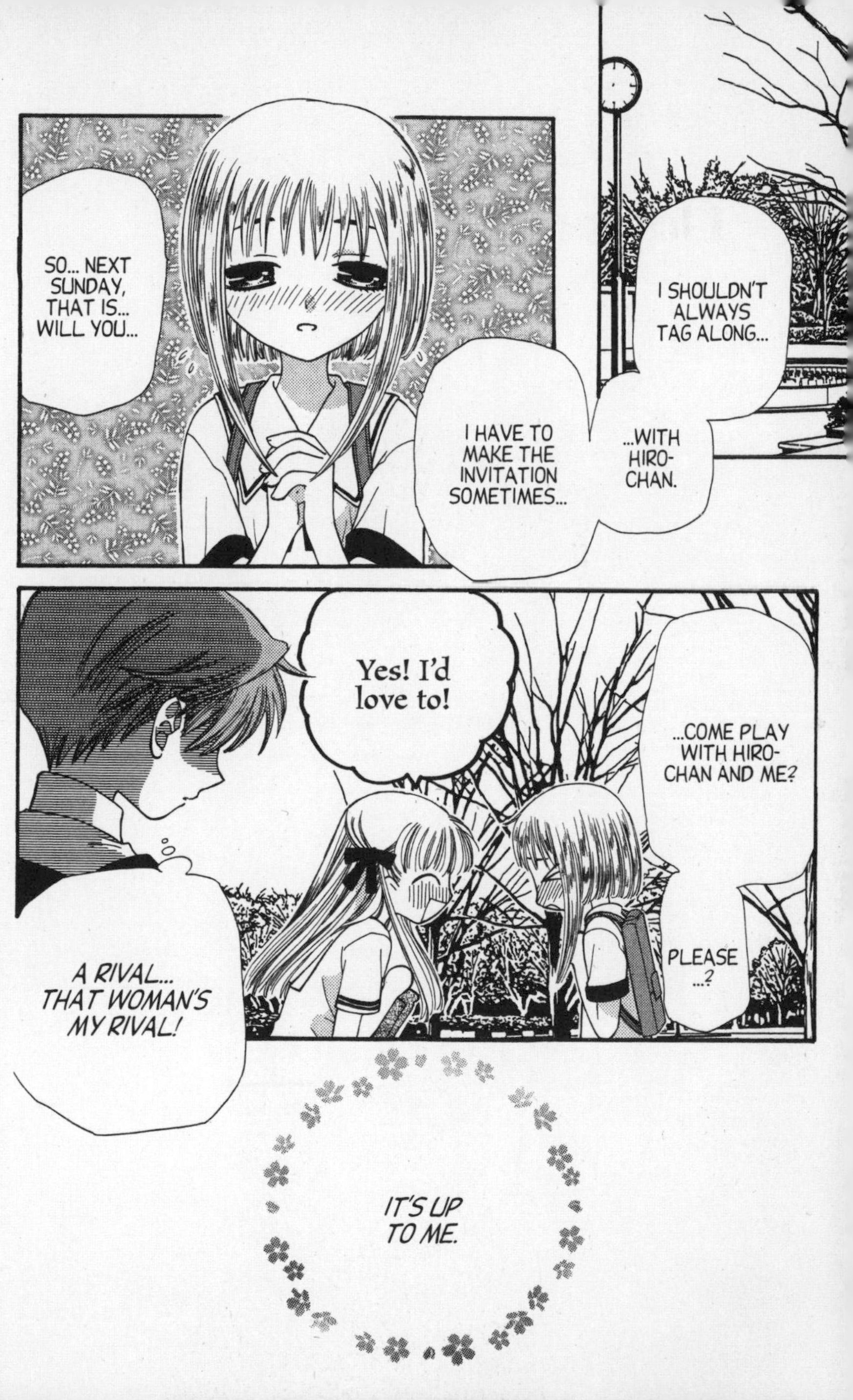
I SHOULDN'T ALWAYS TAG ALONG...
...WITH HIRO-CHAN.
I HAVE TO MAKE THE INVITATION SOMETIMES...
SO... NEXT SUNDAY, THAT IS... WILL YOU...
...COME PLAY WITH HIRO-CHAN AND ME?
PLEASE ...?
Yes! I'd love to!
A RIVAL... THAT WOMAN'S MY RIVAL!
IT'S UP TO ME.

Chapter 39

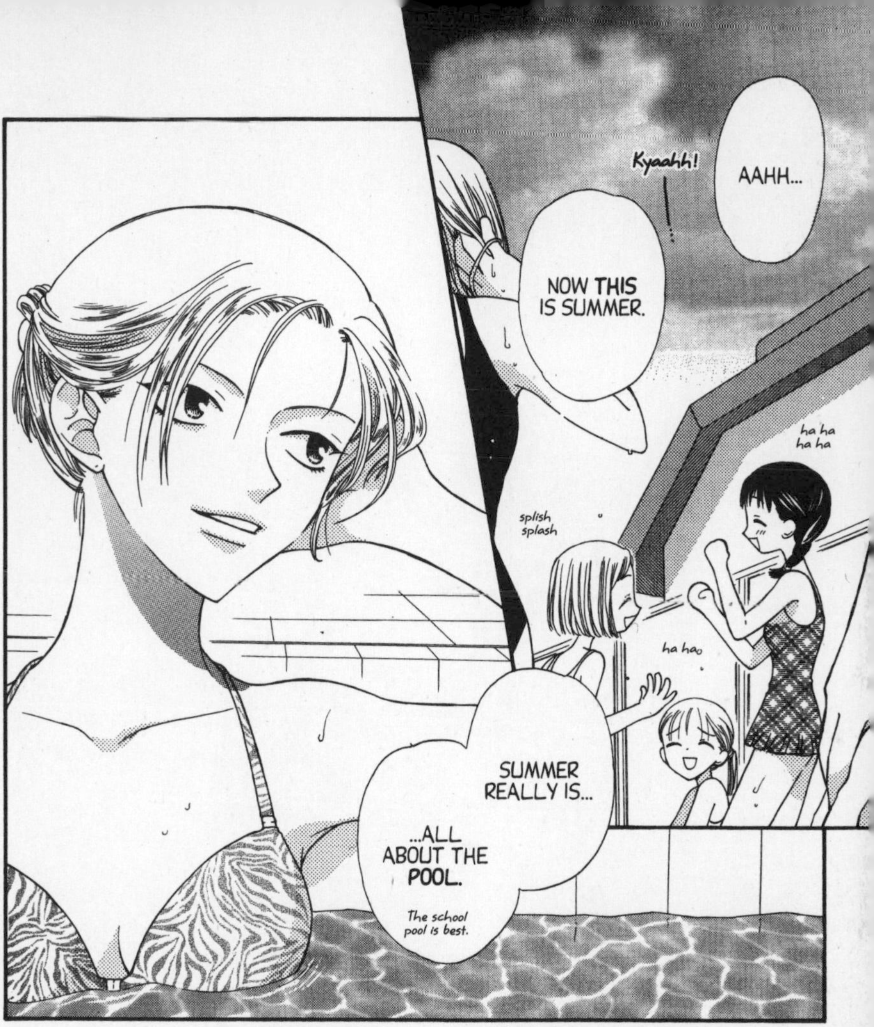
AAHH...
Kyaahh!
NOW THIS IS SUMMER.
ha ha ha ha
splish splash
ha hao
SUMMER REALLY IS...
...ALL ABOUT THE POOL.
The school pool is best.

ULTRA-SPECIAL BLAH, BLAH, BLAH. 3

There are a lot of Sohma men who hate summer, starting with the Mabudachi Trio. They prefer kotatsu (heated blankets) and oranges.

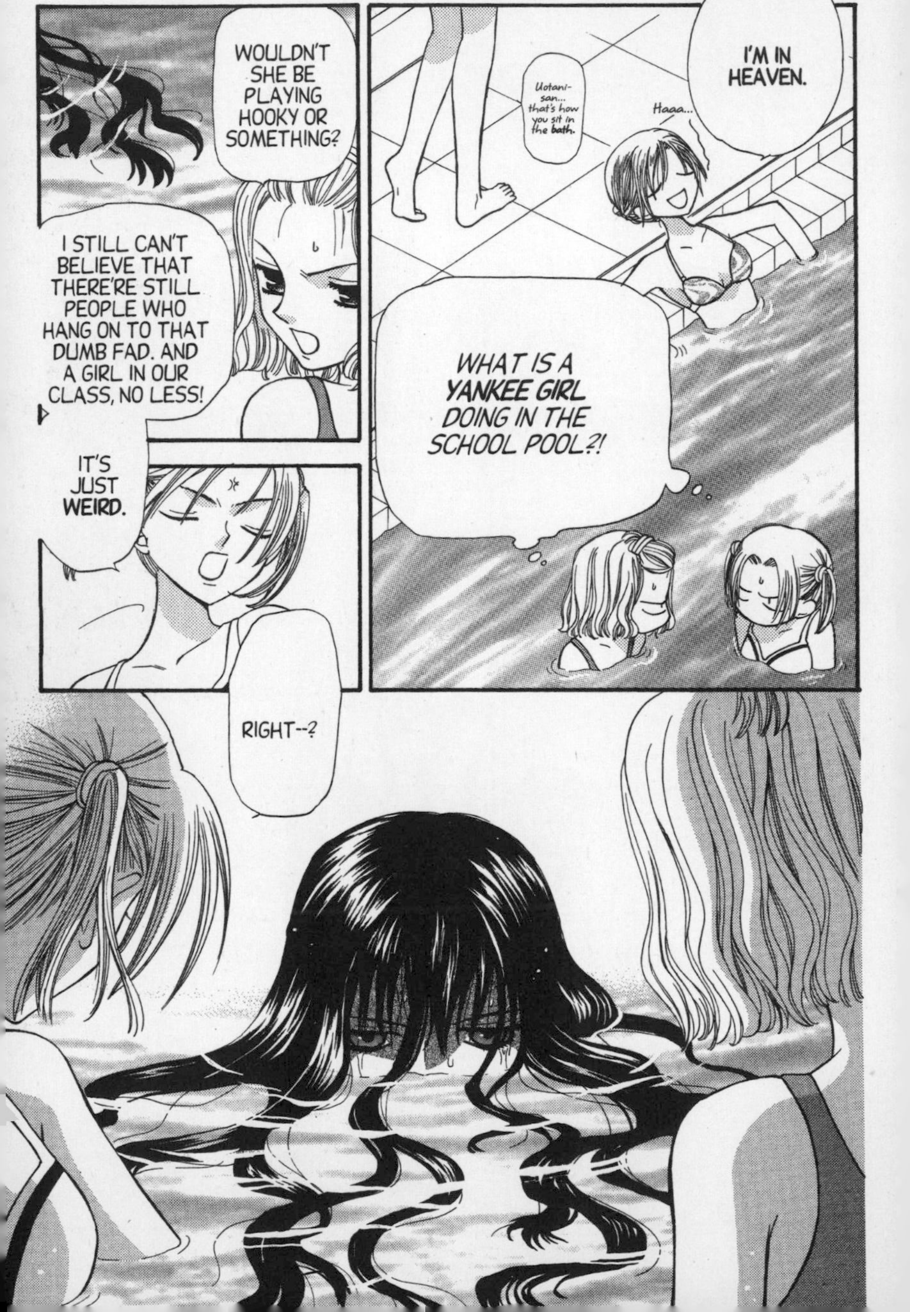
I'M IN HEAVEN.
Haaa...
Uotani-san... that's how you sit in the bath.
WHAT IS A YANKEE GIRL DOING IN THE SCHOOL POOL?!
WOULDN'T SHE BE PLAYING HOOKY OR SOMETHING?
I STILL CAN'T BELIEVE THAT THERE'RE STILL PEOPLE WHO HANG ON TO THAT DUMB FAD. AND A GIRL IN OUR CLASS, NO LESS!
IT'S JUST WEIRD.
RIGHT--?

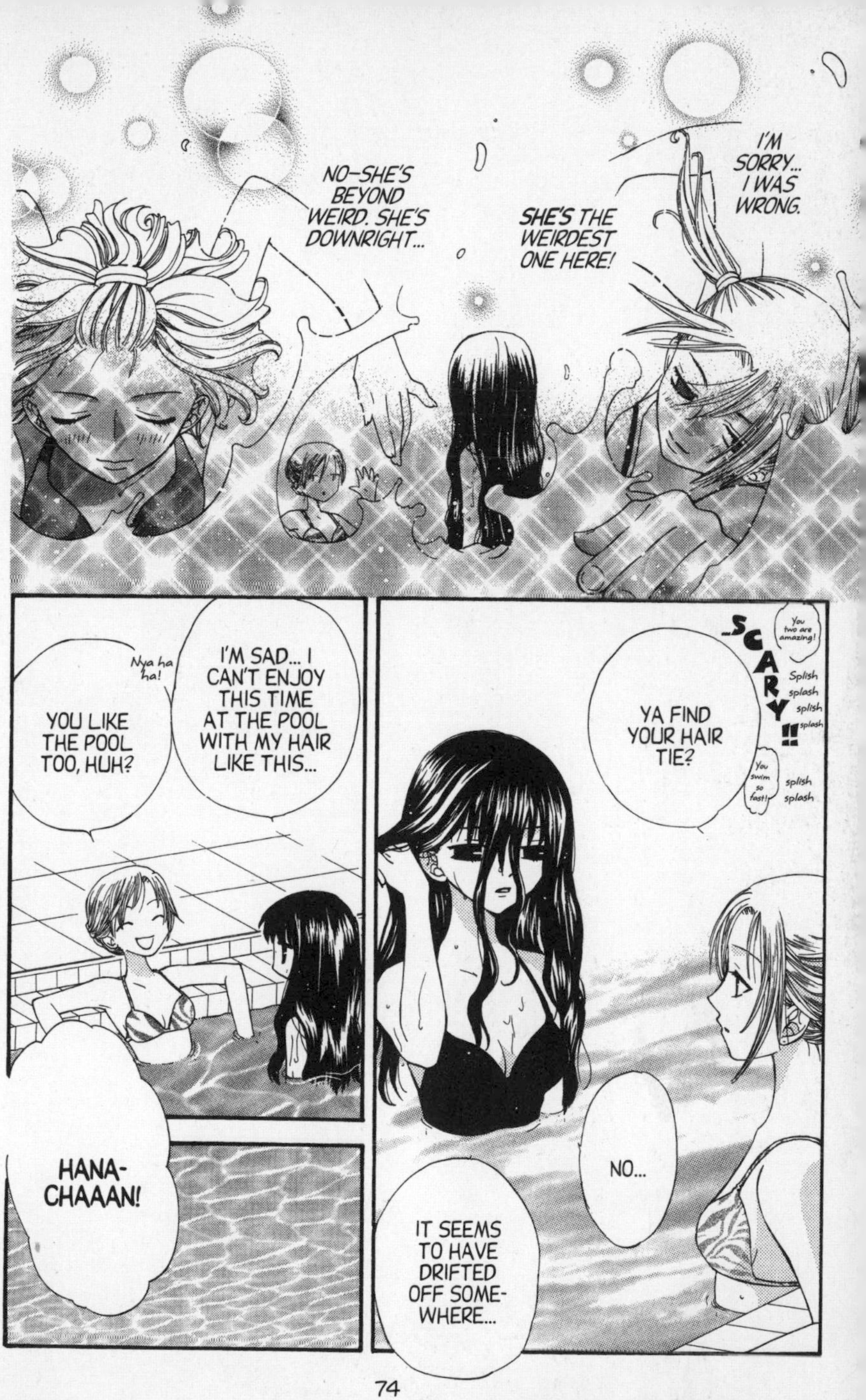
I'M SORRY... I WAS WRONG.
SHE'S THE WEIRDEST ONE HERE!
NO—SHE'S BEYOND WEIRD. SHE'S DOWNRIGHT...
...SCARY!!
You two are amazing!
Splish splash splish splash
YA FIND YOUR HAIR TIE?
You swim so fast!
splish splash
NO...
IT SEEMS TO HAVE DRIFTED OFF SOME-WHERE...
I'M SAD... I CAN'T ENJOY THIS TIME AT THE POOL WITH MY HAIR LIKE THIS...
Nya ha ha!
YOU LIKE THE POOL TOO, HUH?
HANA-CHAAAN!

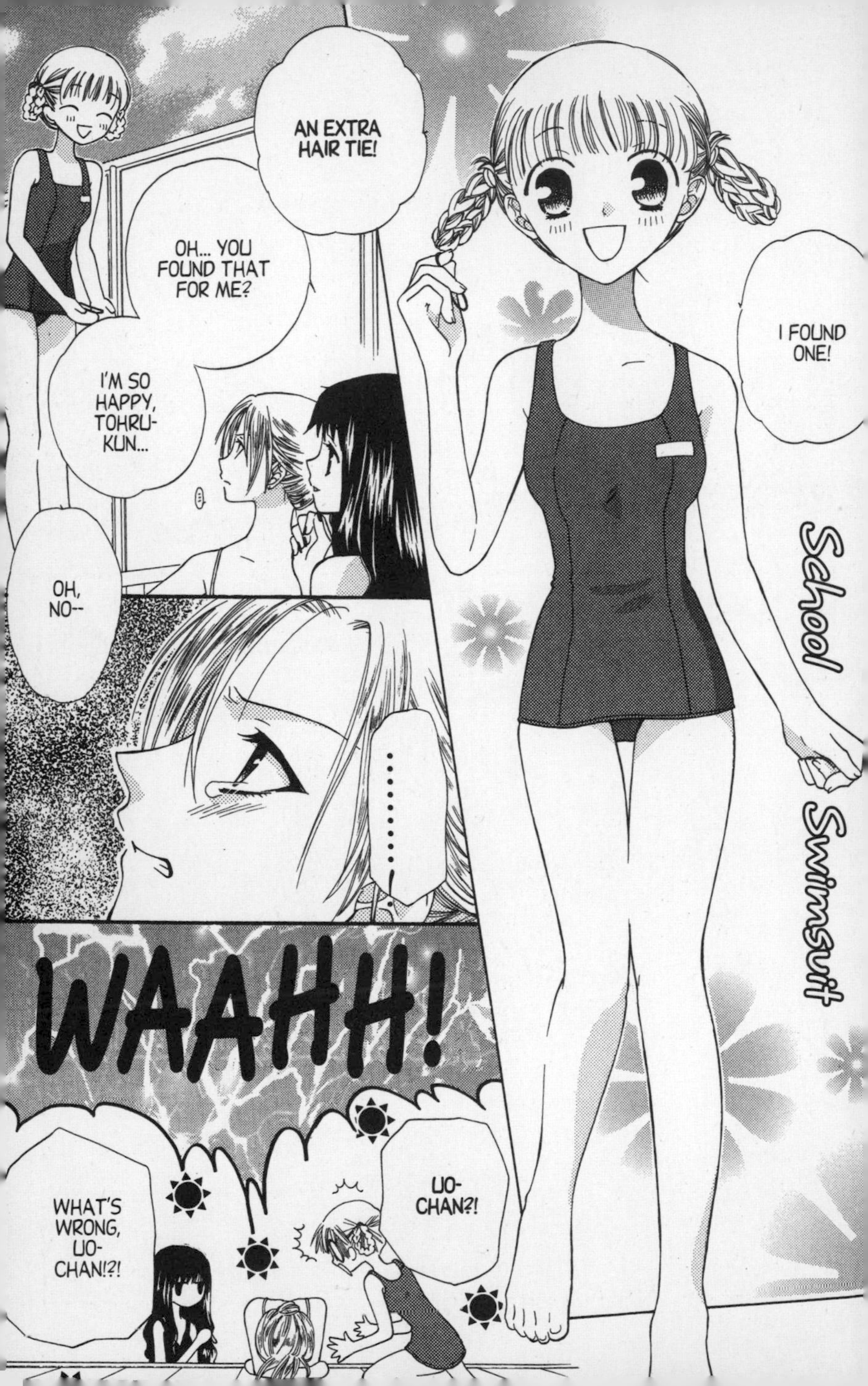
I FOUND ONE!
School Swimsuit
AN EXTRA HAIR TIE!
OH... YOU FOUND THAT FOR ME?
I'M SO HAPPY, TOHRU-KUN...
OH, NO--
......
WAAHH!
UO-CHAN?!
WHAT'S WRONG, UO-CHAN!?!

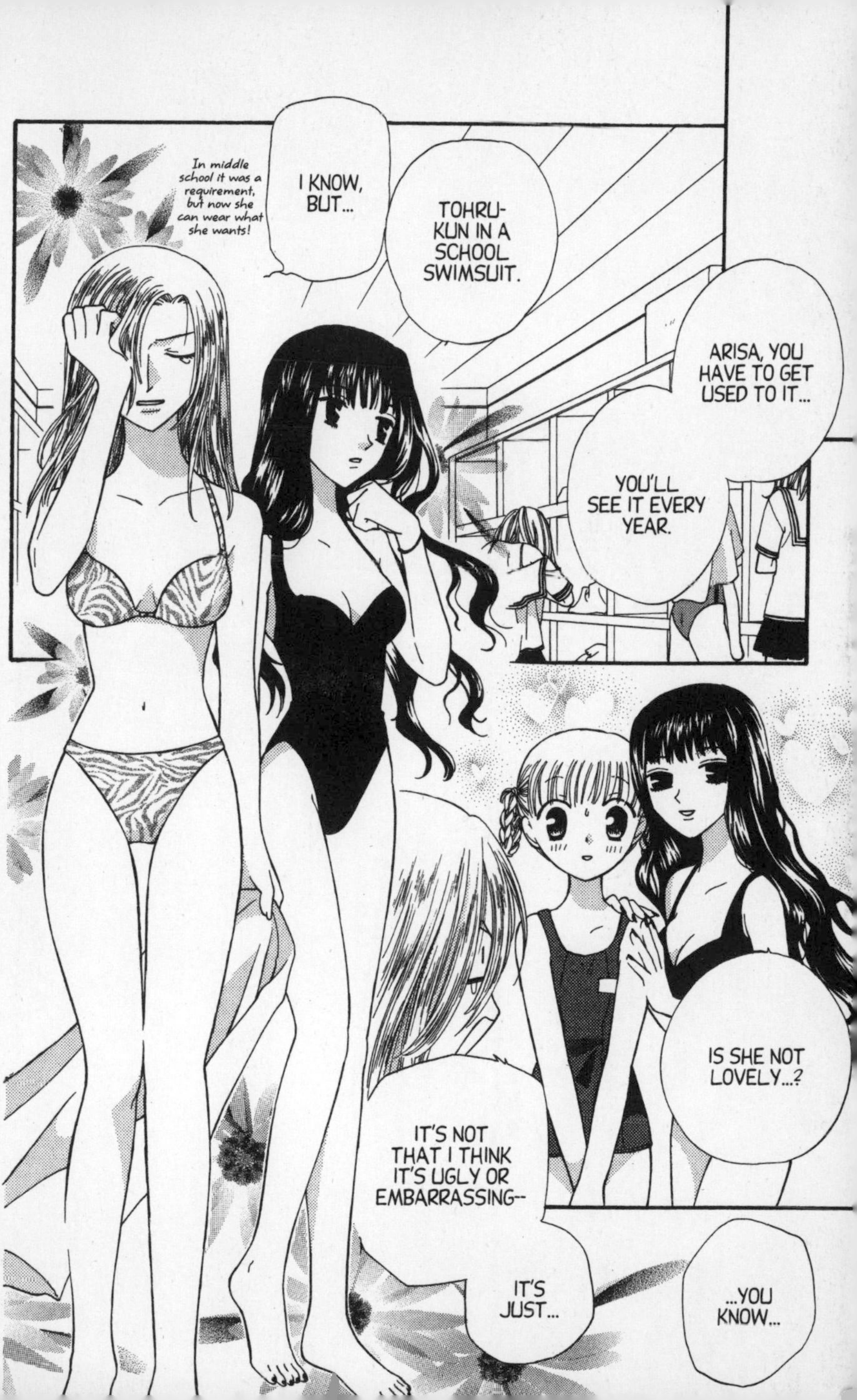
ARISA, YOU HAVE TO GET USED TO IT...
YOU'LL SEE IT EVERY YEAR.
TOHRU-KUN IN A SCHOOL SWIMSUIT.
I KNOW, BUT...
In middle school it was a requirement, but now she can wear what she wants!
IS SHE NOT LOVELY...?
IT'S NOT THAT I THINK IT'S UGLY OR EMBARRASSING--
...YOU KNOW...
IT'S JUST...

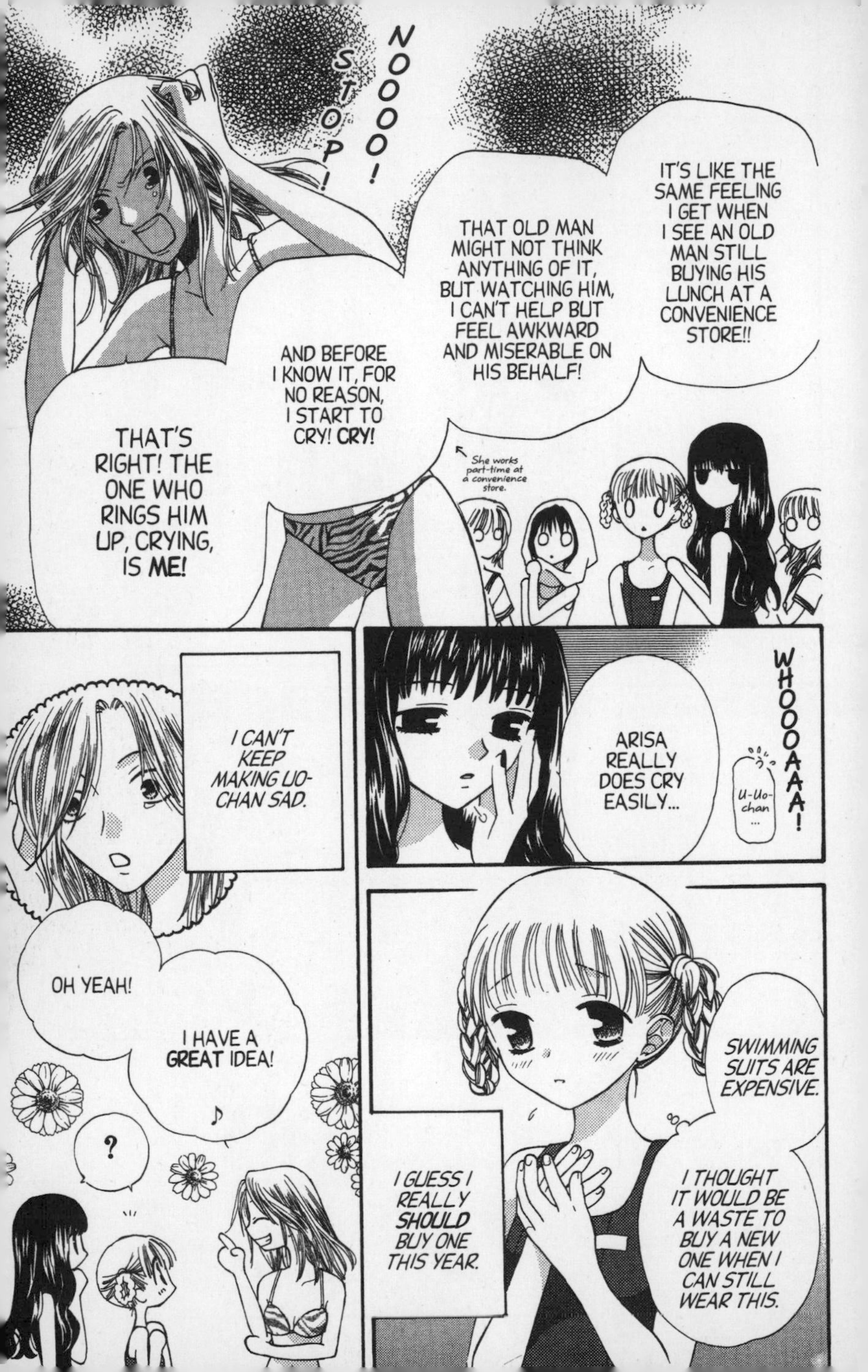
NOOOOO!
STOP!
IT'S LIKE THE SAME FEELING I GET WHEN I SEE AN OLD MAN STILL BUYING HIS LUNCH AT A CONVENIENCE STORE!!
THAT OLD MAN MIGHT NOT THINK ANYTHING OF IT, BUT WATCHING HIM, I CAN'T HELP BUT FEEL AWKWARD AND MISERABLE ON HIS BEHALF!
AND BEFORE I KNOW IT, FOR NO REASON, I START TO CRY! CRY!
She works part-time at a convenience store.
THAT'S RIGHT! THE ONE WHO RINGS HIM UP, CRYING, IS ME!
WHOOOOAAA!
U-Uo-chan ...
ARISA REALLY DOES CRY EASILY...
I CAN'T KEEP MAKING UO-CHAN SAD.
SWIMMING SUITS ARE EXPENSIVE.
I THOUGHT IT WOULD BE A WASTE TO BUY A NEW ONE WHEN I CAN STILL WEAR THIS.
I GUESS I REALLY SHOULD BUY ONE THIS YEAR.
OH YEAH!
I HAVE A GREAT IDEA! ♪
?

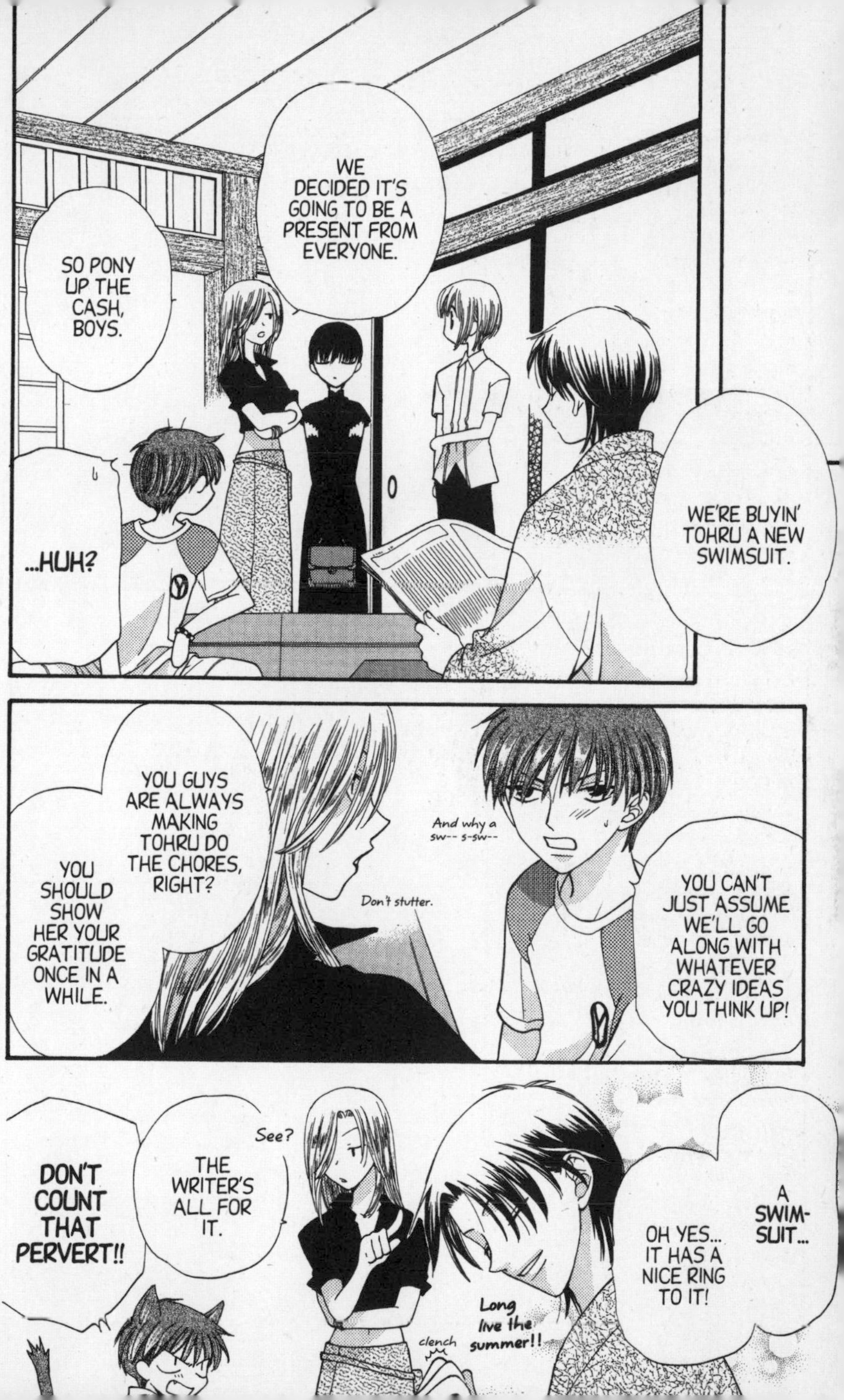
WE'RE BUYIN' TOHRU A NEW SWIMSUIT.
WE DECIDED IT'S GOING TO BE A PRESENT FROM EVERYONE.
SO PONY UP THE CASH, BOYS.
...HUH?
YOU CAN'T JUST ASSUME WE'LL GO ALONG WITH WHATEVER CRAZY IDEAS YOU THINK UP!
And why a sw-- s-sw--
Don't stutter.
YOU GUYS ARE ALWAYS MAKING TOHRU DO THE CHORES, RIGHT?
YOU SHOULD SHOW HER YOUR GRATITUDE ONCE IN A WHILE.
A SWIM-SUIT...
OH YES... IT HAS A NICE RING TO IT!
Long live the summer!!
clench
See?
THE WRITER'S ALL FOR IT.
DON'T COUNT THAT PERVERT!!

Fruits Basket 7: Part 3

When I first arrived at the hospital, I was pretty nervous, but before I knew it, I was sleeping like a baby. All night long! I would fall asleep before nine and wake up at five, and I ate three meals a day... I hadn't lived like that since middle school. Even though I was in the hospital I found myself thinking, "This is a healthy life!" (laugh). Normally I don't watch much TV, but as I had so much time on my hands I ended up watching dramas and stuff and for some reason I got hooked on baseball--it was crazy. For me. But as I had to go to sleep before nine there were a lot of times when I never found out who won... (Unless it went 'til morning, I wouldn't know the score...)

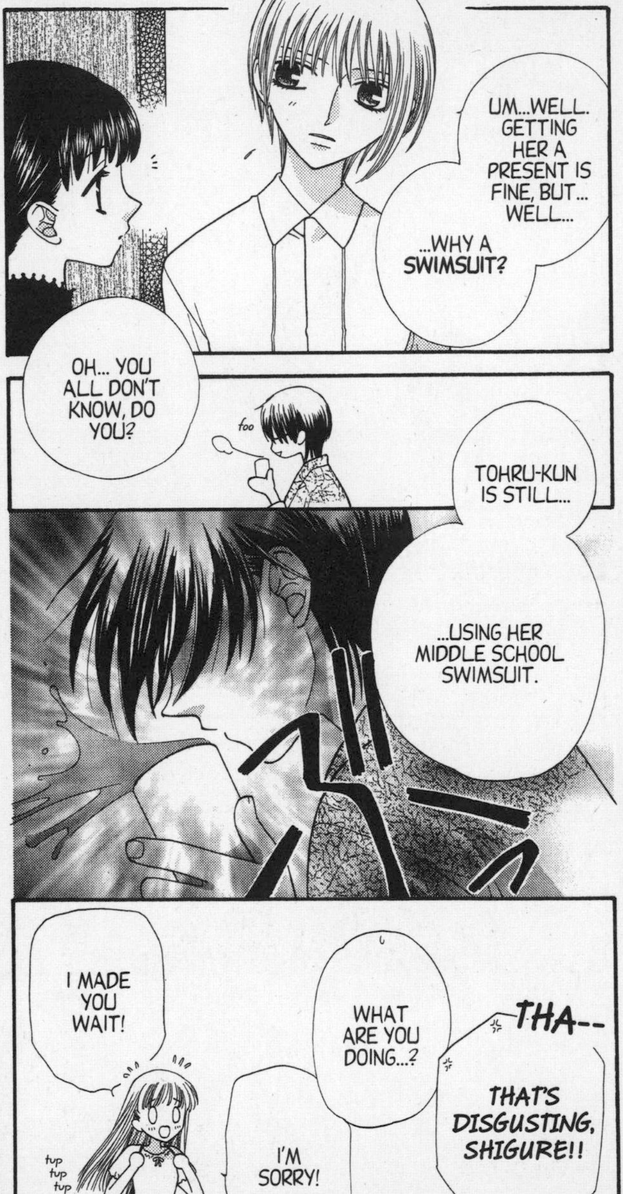
UM...WELL. GETTING HER A PRESENT IS FINE, BUT... WELL...
...WHY A SWIMSUIT?
OH... YOU ALL DON'T KNOW, DO YOU?
foo
TOHRU-KUN IS STILL...
...USING HER MIDDLE SCHOOL SWIMSUIT.
THA--
THAT'S DISGUSTING, SHIGURE!!
WHAT ARE YOU DOING...?
I MADE YOU WAIT!
I'M SORRY!
tup tup tup

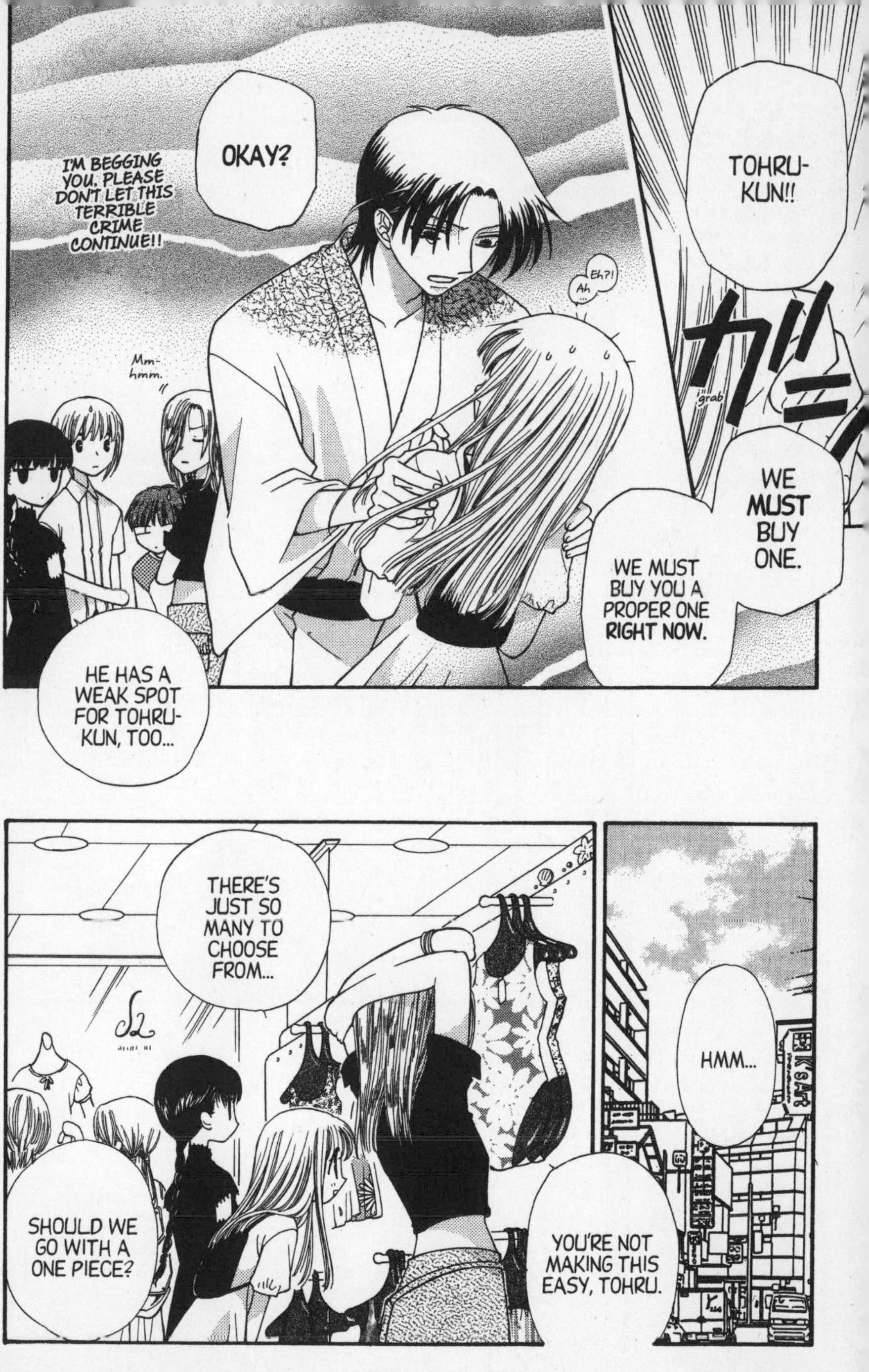
TOHRU-KUN!!
grab
WE MUST BUY ONE.
WE MUST BUY YOU A PROPER ONE RIGHT NOW.
Eh?!
Ah...
OKAY?
I'M BEGGING YOU. PLEASE DON'T LET THIS TERRIBLE CRIME CONTINUE!!
Mm-hmm.
HE HAS A WEAK SPOT FOR TOHRU-KUN, TOO...
HMM...
YOU'RE NOT MAKING THIS EASY, TOHRU.
THERE'S JUST SO MANY TO CHOOSE FROM...
SHOULD WE GO WITH A ONE PIECE?

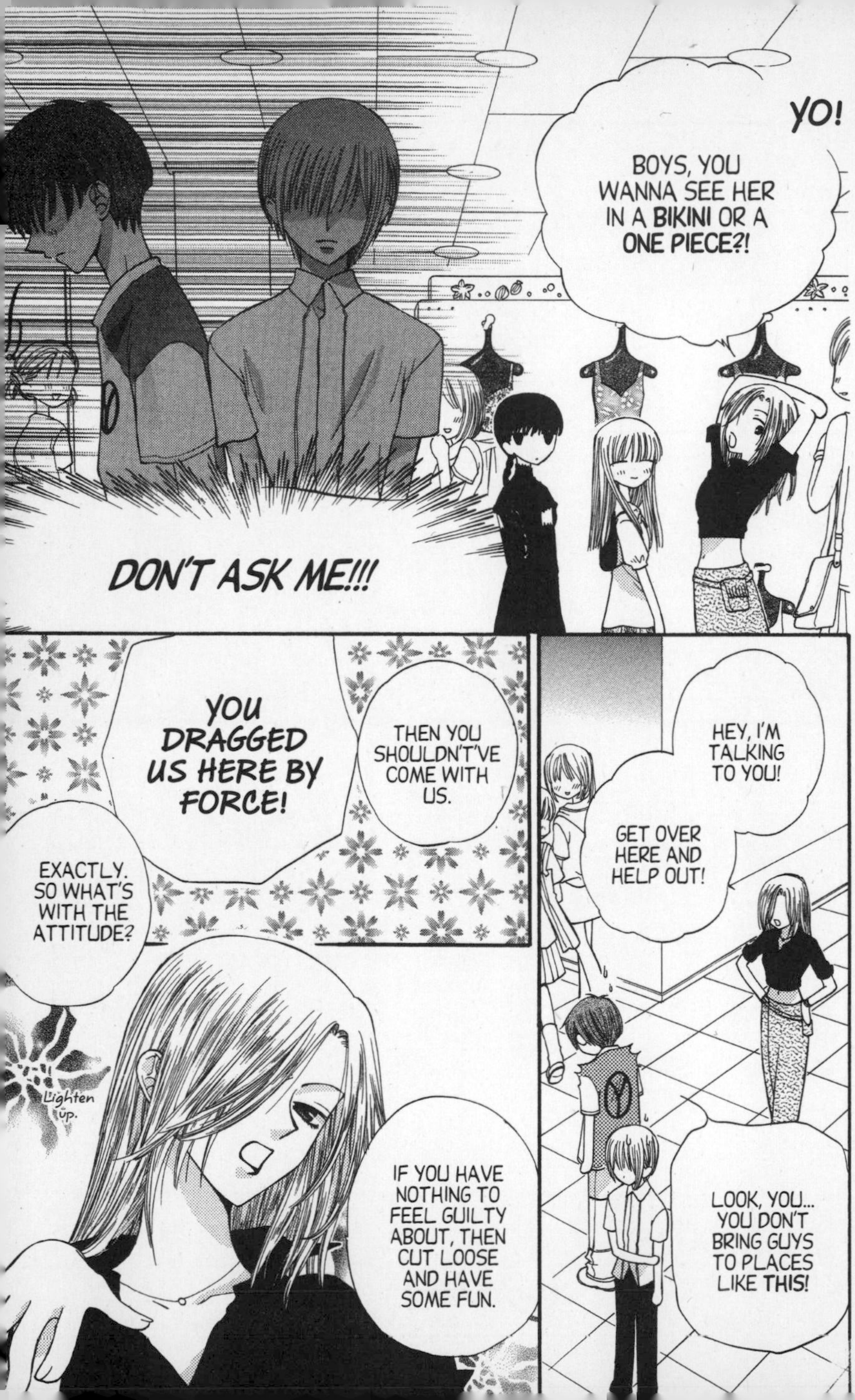
YO!
BOYS, YOU WANNA SEE HER IN A BIKINI OR A ONE PIECE?!
DON'T ASK ME!!!
HEY, I'M TALKING TO YOU!
GET OVER HERE AND HELP OUT!
LOOK, YOU... YOU DON'T BRING GUYS TO PLACES LIKE THIS!
THEN YOU SHOULDN'T'VE COME WITH US.
YOU DRAGGED US HERE BY FORCE!
EXACTLY. SO WHAT'S WITH THE ATTITUDE?
IF YOU HAVE NOTHING TO FEEL GUILTY ABOUT, THEN CUT LOOSE AND HAVE SOME FUN.
Lighten up.

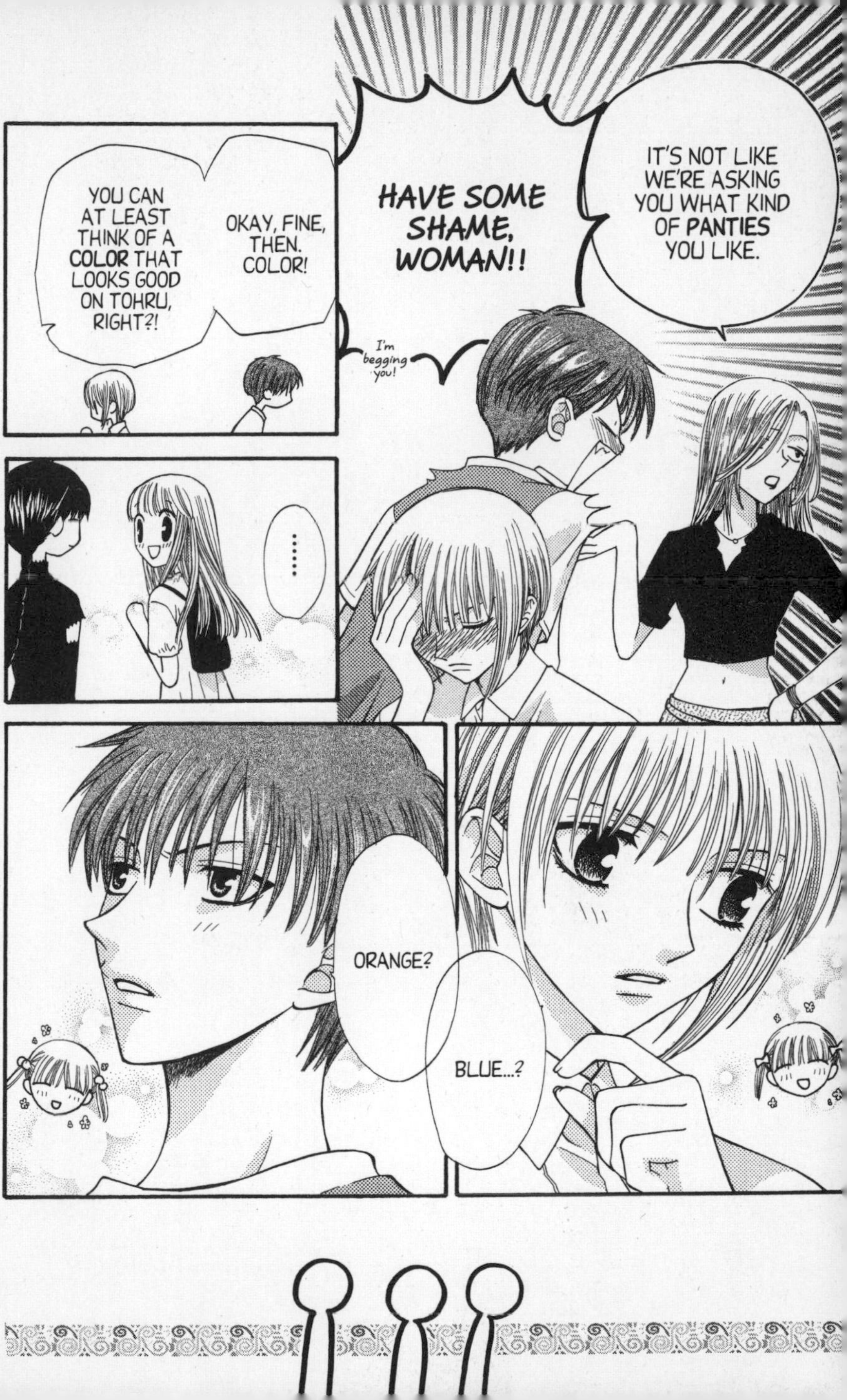
IT'S NOT LIKE WE'RE ASKING YOU WHAT KIND OF PANTIES YOU LIKE.
HAVE SOME SHAME, WOMAN!!
I'm begging you!
OKAY, FINE, THEN. COLOR!
YOU CAN AT LEAST THINK OF A COLOR THAT LOOKS GOOD ON TOHRU, RIGHT?!
......
BLUE...?
ORANGE?

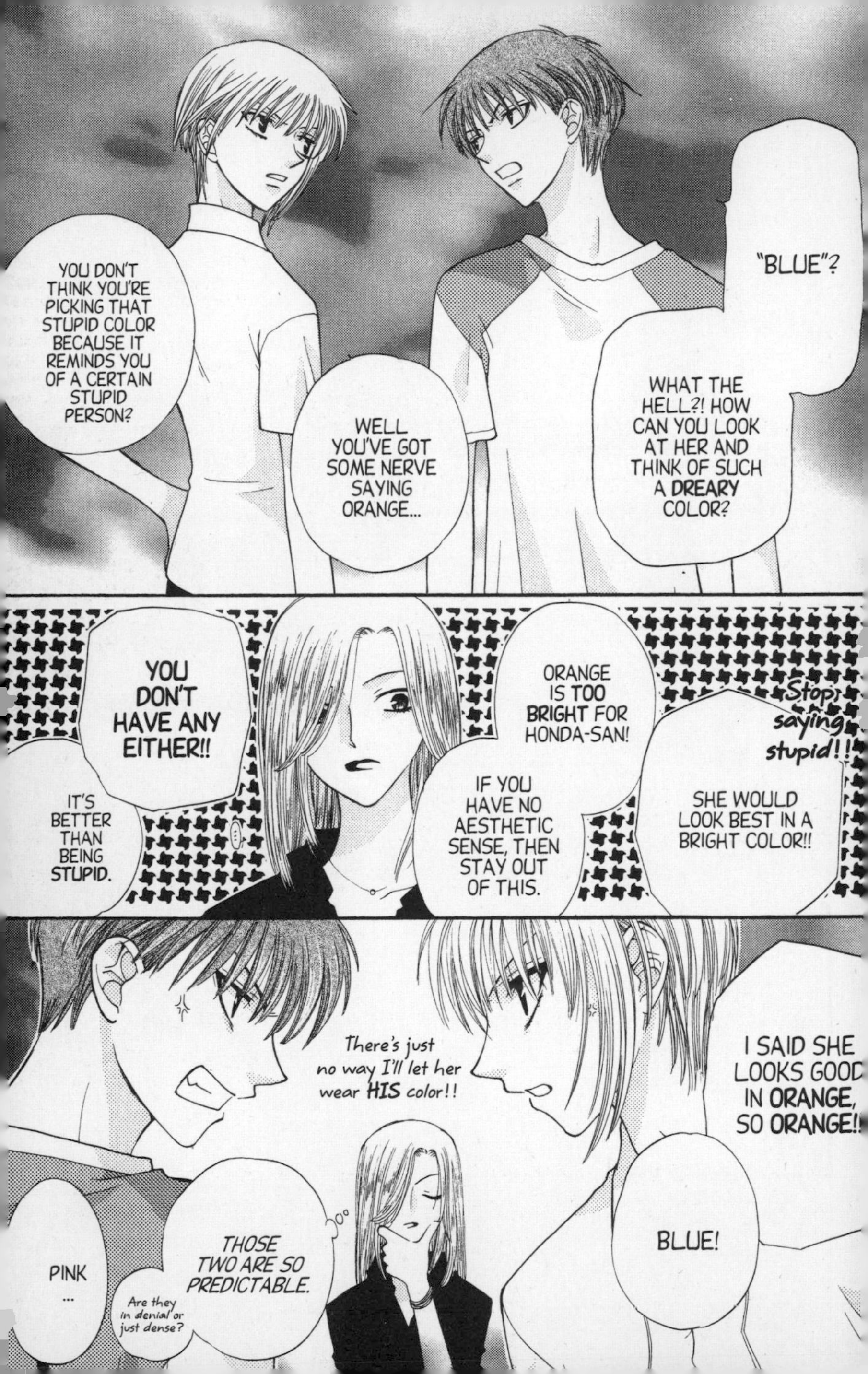
"BLUE"?
WHAT THE HELL?! HOW CAN YOU LOOK AT HER AND THINK OF SUCH A DREARY COLOR?
WELL YOU'VE GOT SOME NERVE SAYING ORANGE...
YOU DON'T THINK YOU'RE PICKING THAT STUPID COLOR BECAUSE IT REMINDS YOU OF A CERTAIN STUPID PERSON?
Stop saying stupid!!
SHE WOULD LOOK BEST IN A BRIGHT COLOR!!
ORANGE IS TOO BRIGHT FOR HONDA-SAN!
IF YOU HAVE NO AESTHETIC SENSE, THEN STAY OUT OF THIS.
YOU DON'T HAVE ANY EITHER!!
IT'S BETTER THAN BEING STUPID.
I SAID SHE LOOKS GOOD IN ORANGE, SO ORANGE!!
There's just no way I'll let her wear HIS color!!
BLUE!
THOSE TWO ARE SO PREDICTABLE.
Are they in denial or just dense?
PINK ...

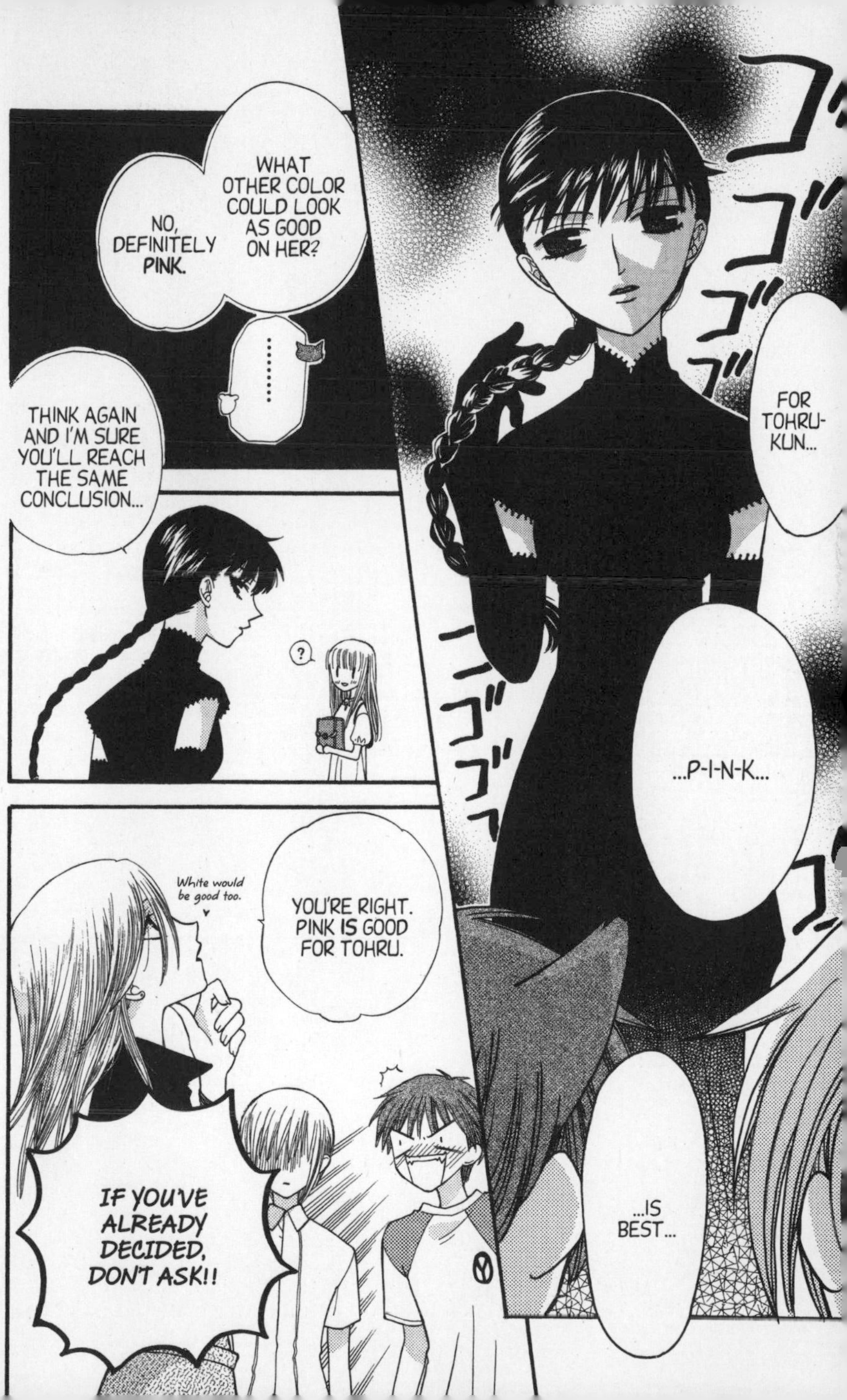
ゴゴゴ
FOR TOHRU-KUN...
ゴゴゴ
...P-I-N-K...
...IS BEST...
WHAT OTHER COLOR COULD LOOK AS GOOD ON HER?
NO, DEFINITELY PINK.
......
THINK AGAIN AND I'M SURE YOU'LL REACH THE SAME CONCLUSION...
?
YOU'RE RIGHT. PINK IS GOOD FOR TOHRU.
White would be good too.
IF YOU'VE ALREADY DECIDED, DON'T ASK!!

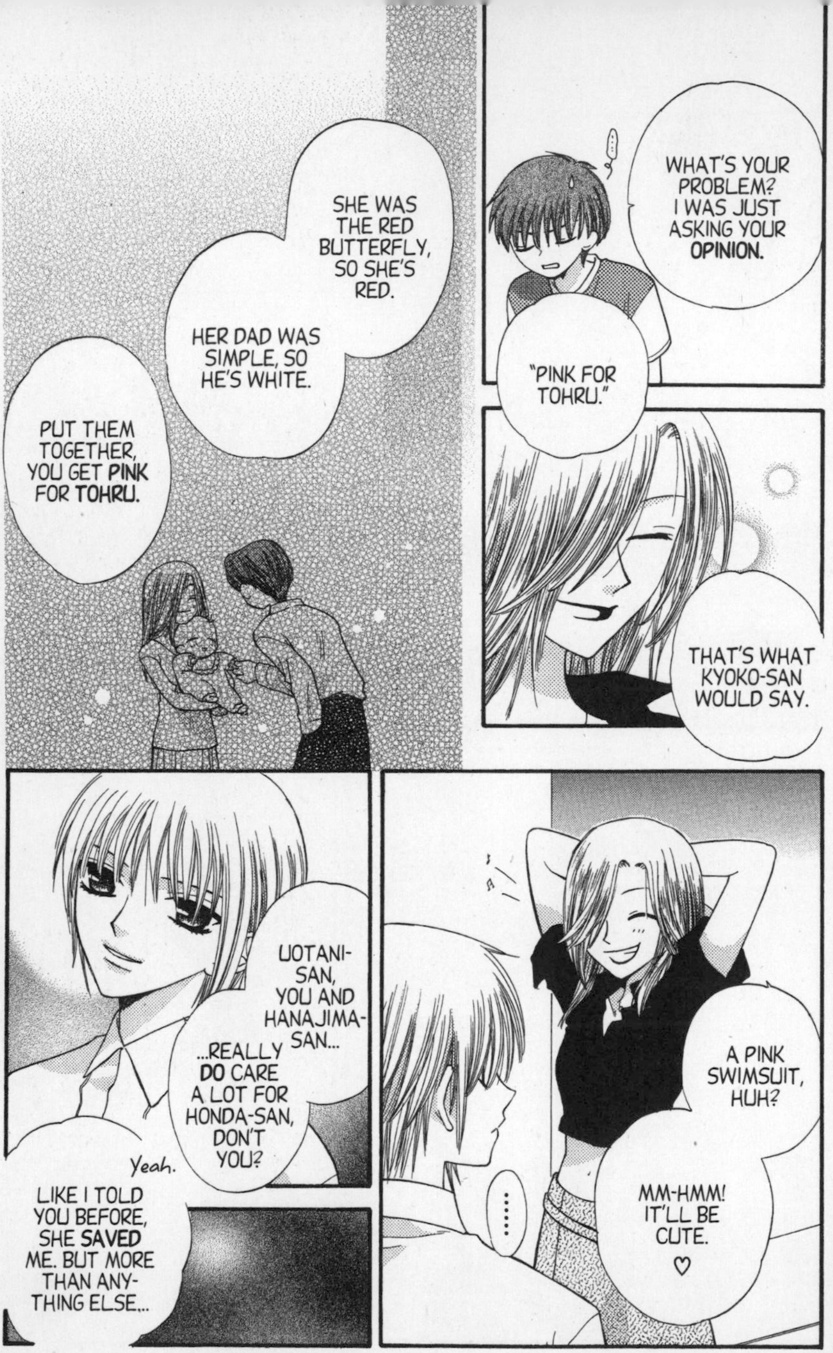
WHAT'S YOUR PROBLEM? I WAS JUST ASKING YOUR **OPINION.**
"PINK FOR TOHRU."
THAT'S WHAT KYOKO-SAN WOULD SAY.
SHE WAS THE RED BUTTERFLY, SO SHE'S RED.
HER DAD WAS SIMPLE, SO HE'S WHITE.
PUT THEM TOGETHER, YOU GET **PINK** FOR **TOHRU.**
A PINK SWIMSUIT, HUH?
MM-HMM! IT'LL BE CUTE. ♡
......
UOTANI-SAN, YOU AND HANAJIMA-SAN...
...REALLY **DO** CARE A LOT FOR HONDA-SAN, DON'T YOU?
Yeah.
LIKE I TOLD YOU BEFORE, SHE **SAVED** ME. BUT MORE THAN ANY-THING ELSE...

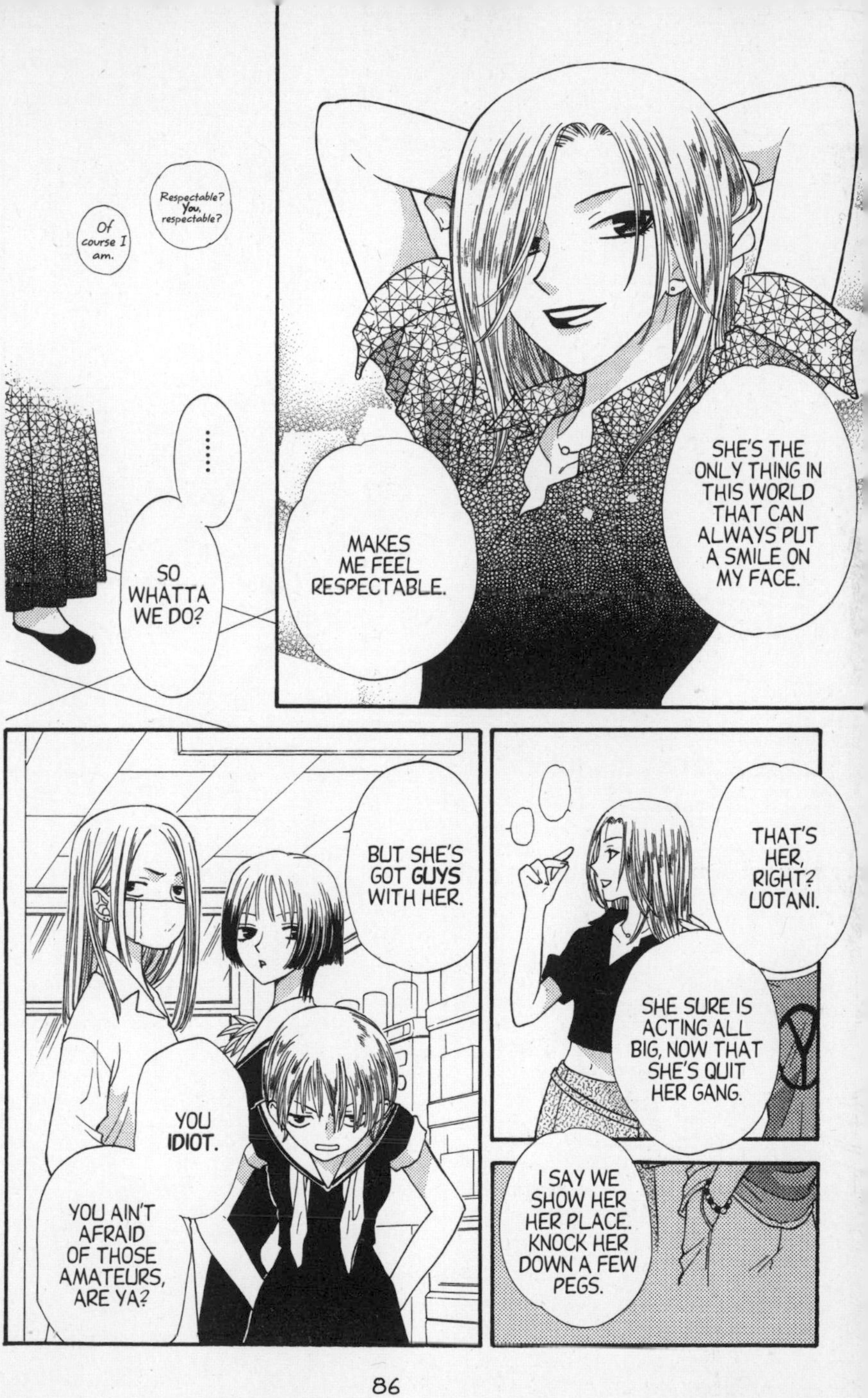
SHE'S THE ONLY THING IN THIS WORLD THAT CAN ALWAYS PUT A SMILE ON MY FACE.
MAKES ME FEEL RESPECTABLE.
Respectable? **You,** respectable?
Of course I am.
......
SO WHATTA WE DO?
THAT'S HER, RIGHT? UOTANI.
SHE SURE IS ACTING ALL BIG, NOW THAT SHE'S QUIT HER GANG.
I SAY WE SHOW HER HER PLACE. KNOCK HER DOWN A FEW PEGS.
BUT SHE'S GOT **GUYS** WITH HER.
YOU **IDIOT.**
YOU AIN'T AFRAID OF THOSE AMATEURS, ARE YA?

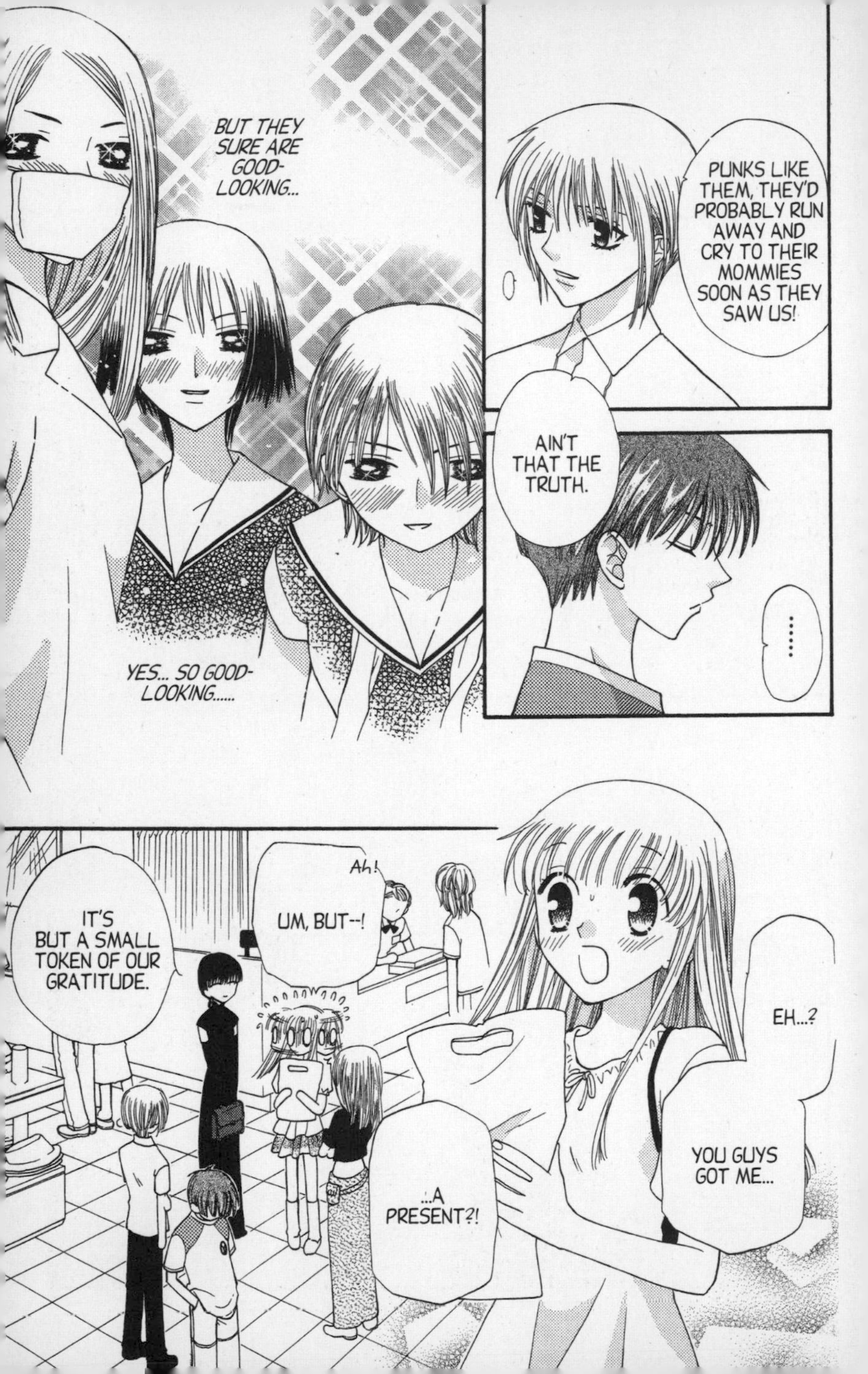
PUNKS LIKE THEM, THEY'D PROBABLY RUN AWAY AND CRY TO THEIR MOMMIES SOON AS THEY SAW US!
AIN'T THAT THE TRUTH.
......
BUT THEY SURE ARE GOOD-LOOKING...
YES... SO GOOD-LOOKING......
EH...?
YOU GUYS GOT ME...
..A PRESENT?!
Ah!
UM, BUT--!
IT'S BUT A SMALL TOKEN OF OUR GRATITUDE.

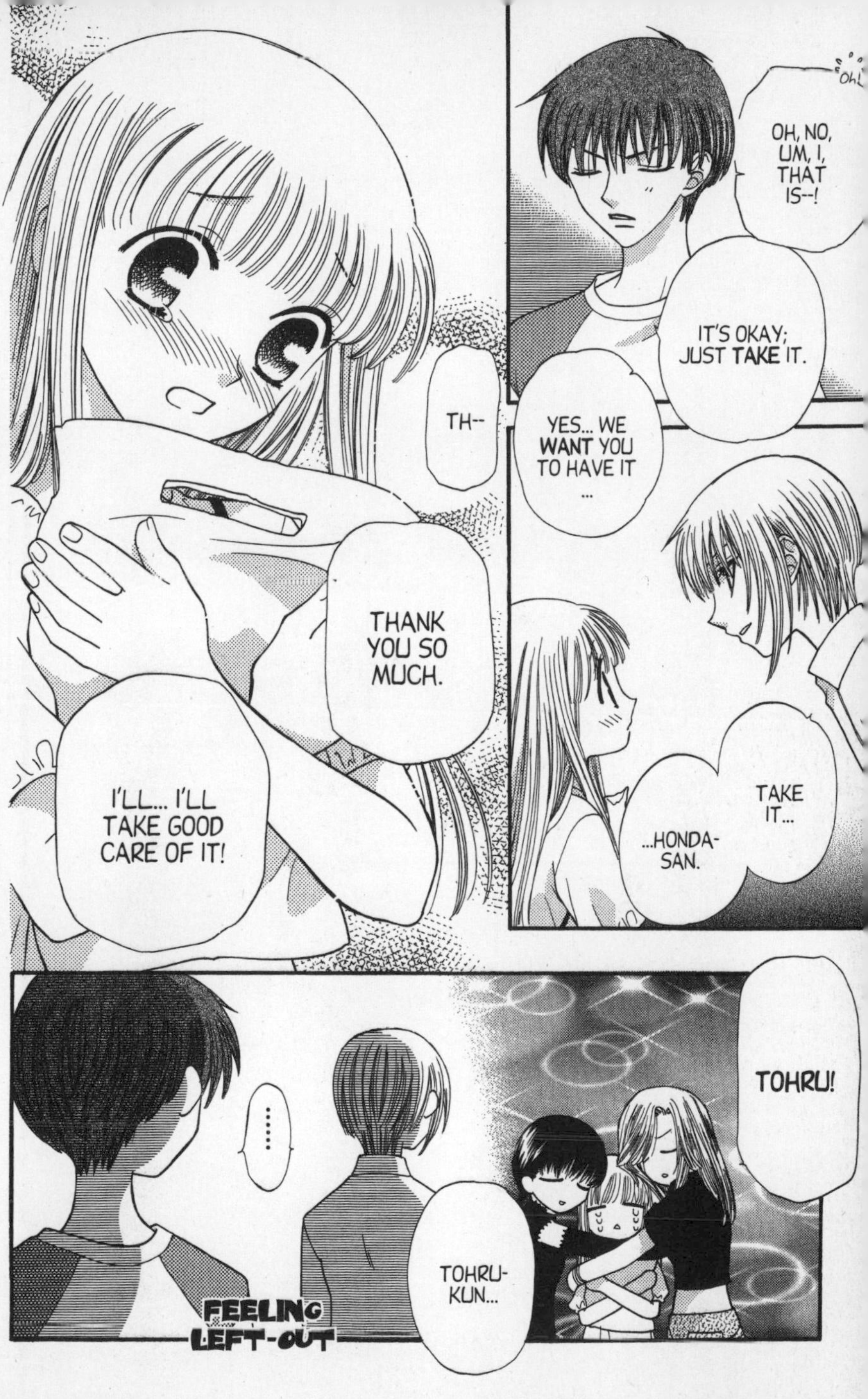
OH!
OH, NO, UM, I, THAT IS--!
IT'S OKAY; JUST TAKE IT.
YES... WE WANT YOU TO HAVE IT ...
TAKE IT...
...HONDA-SAN.
TH--
THANK YOU SO MUCH.
I'LL... I'LL TAKE GOOD CARE OF IT!
TOHRU!
TOHRU-KUN...
......
FEELING LEFT-OUT

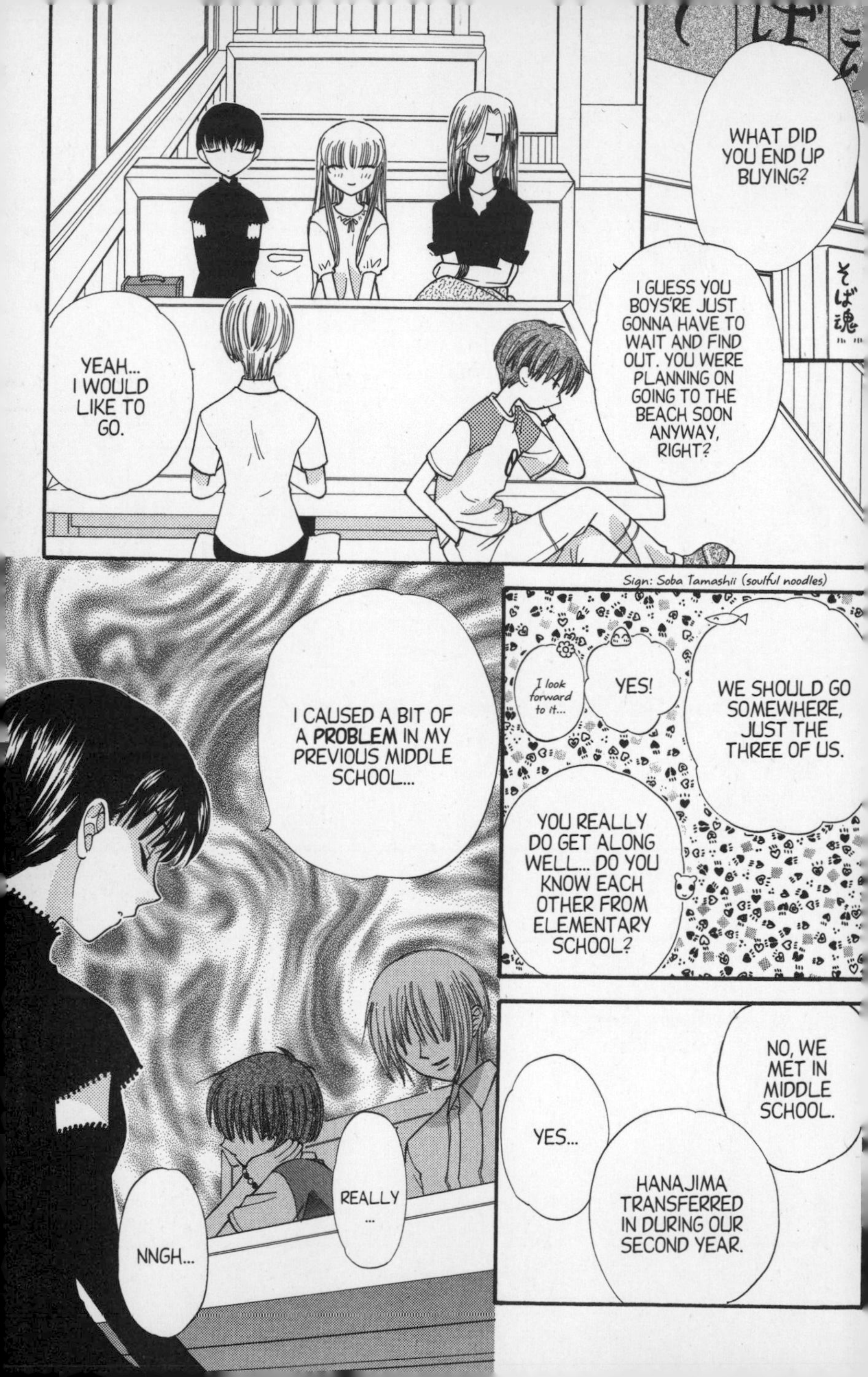
そば魂
WHAT DID YOU END UP BUYING?
I GUESS YOU BOYS'RE JUST GONNA HAVE TO WAIT AND FIND OUT. YOU WERE PLANNING ON GOING TO THE BEACH SOON ANYWAY, RIGHT?
YEAH... I WOULD LIKE TO GO.
Sign: Soba Tamashii (soulful noodles)
WE SHOULD GO SOMEWHERE, JUST THE THREE OF US.
YES!
I look forward to it...
YOU REALLY DO GET ALONG WELL... DO YOU KNOW EACH OTHER FROM ELEMENTARY SCHOOL?
NO, WE MET IN MIDDLE SCHOOL.
YES...
HANAJIMA TRANSFERRED IN DURING OUR SECOND YEAR.
I CAUSED A BIT OF A PROBLEM IN MY PREVIOUS MIDDLE SCHOOL...
REALLY...
NNGH...

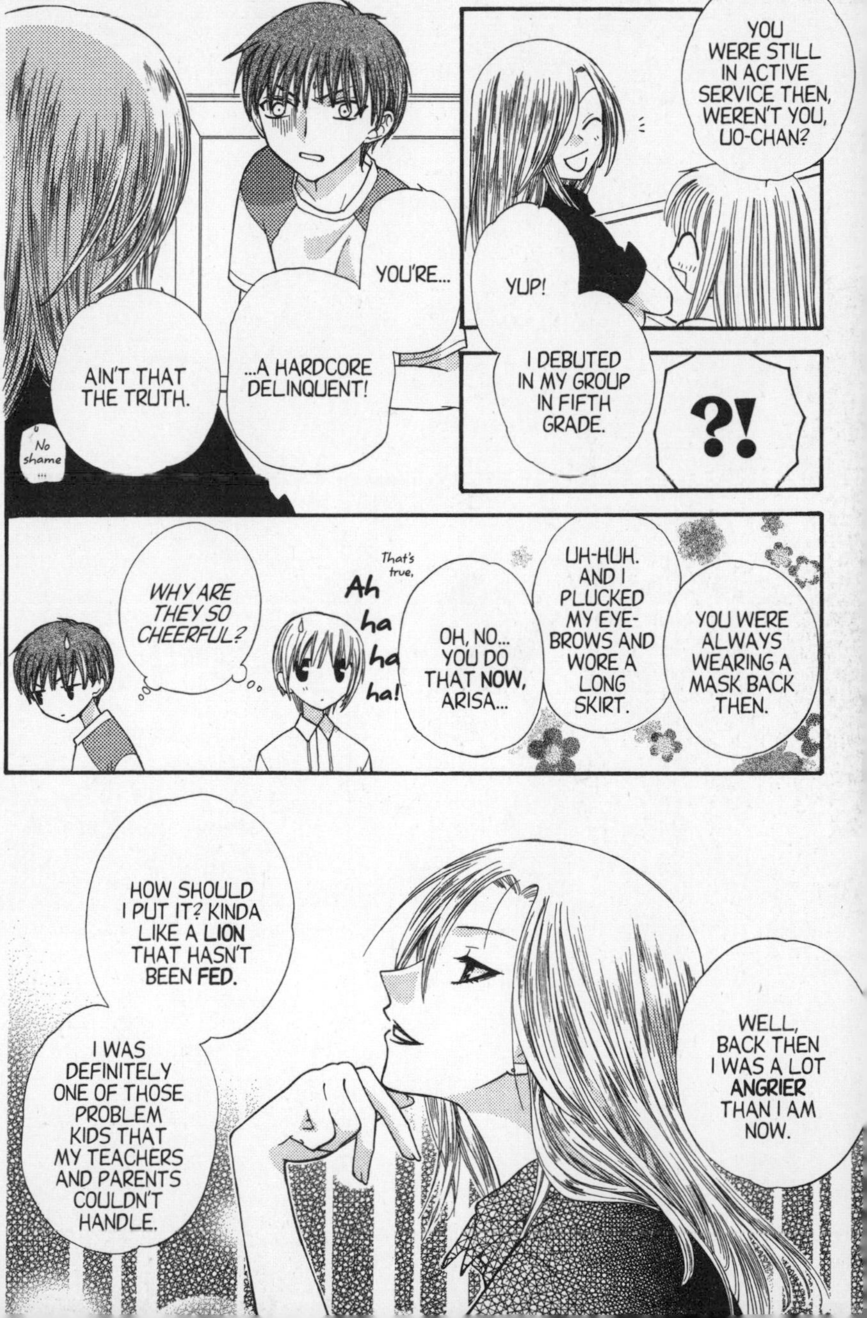
YOU WERE STILL IN ACTIVE SERVICE THEN, WEREN'T YOU, UO-CHAN?
YUP!
?!
I DEBUTED IN MY GROUP IN FIFTH GRADE.
YOU'RE...
...A HARDCORE DELINQUENT!
AIN'T THAT THE TRUTH.
No shame...
YOU WERE ALWAYS WEARING A MASK BACK THEN.
UH-HUH. AND I PLUCKED MY EYE-BROWS AND WORE A LONG SKIRT.
OH, NO... YOU DO THAT NOW, ARISA...
That's true,
Ah ha ha ha!
WHY ARE THEY SO CHEERFUL?
WELL, BACK THEN I WAS A LOT ANGRIER THAN I AM NOW.
HOW SHOULD I PUT IT? KINDA LIKE A LION THAT HASN'T BEEN FED.
I WAS DEFINITELY ONE OF THOSE PROBLEM KIDS THAT MY TEACHERS AND PARENTS COULDN'T HANDLE.

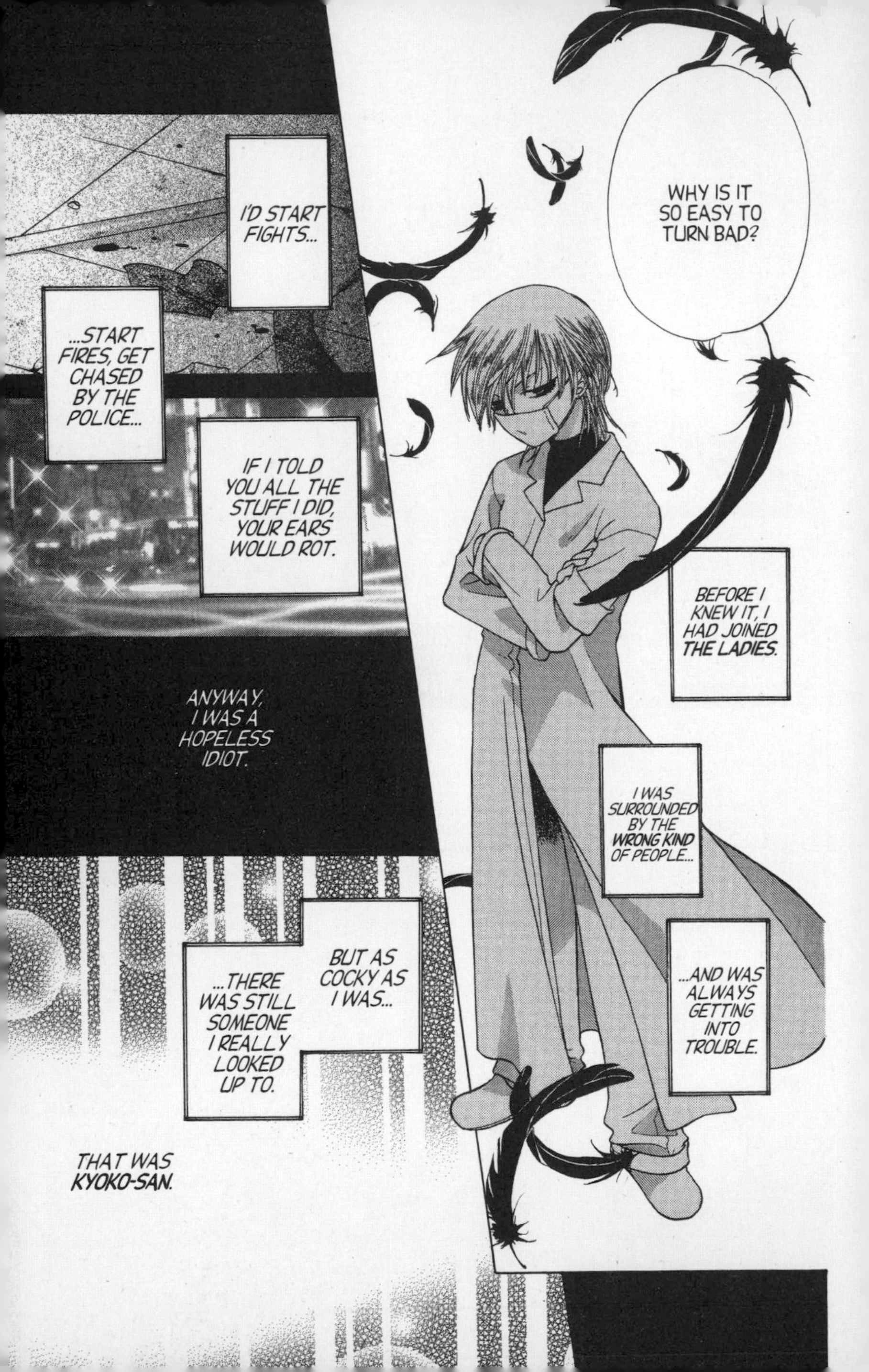
WHY IS IT SO EASY TO TURN BAD?
BEFORE I KNEW IT, I HAD JOINED THE LADIES.
I WAS SURROUNDED BY THE WRONG KIND OF PEOPLE...
...AND WAS ALWAYS GETTING INTO TROUBLE.
I'D START FIGHTS...
...START FIRES, GET CHASED BY THE POLICE...
IF I TOLD YOU ALL THE STUFF I DID, YOUR EARS WOULD ROT.
ANYWAY, I WAS A HOPELESS IDIOT.
BUT AS COCKY AS I WAS...
...THERE WAS STILL SOMEONE I REALLY LOOKED UP TO.
THAT WAS KYOKO-SAN.

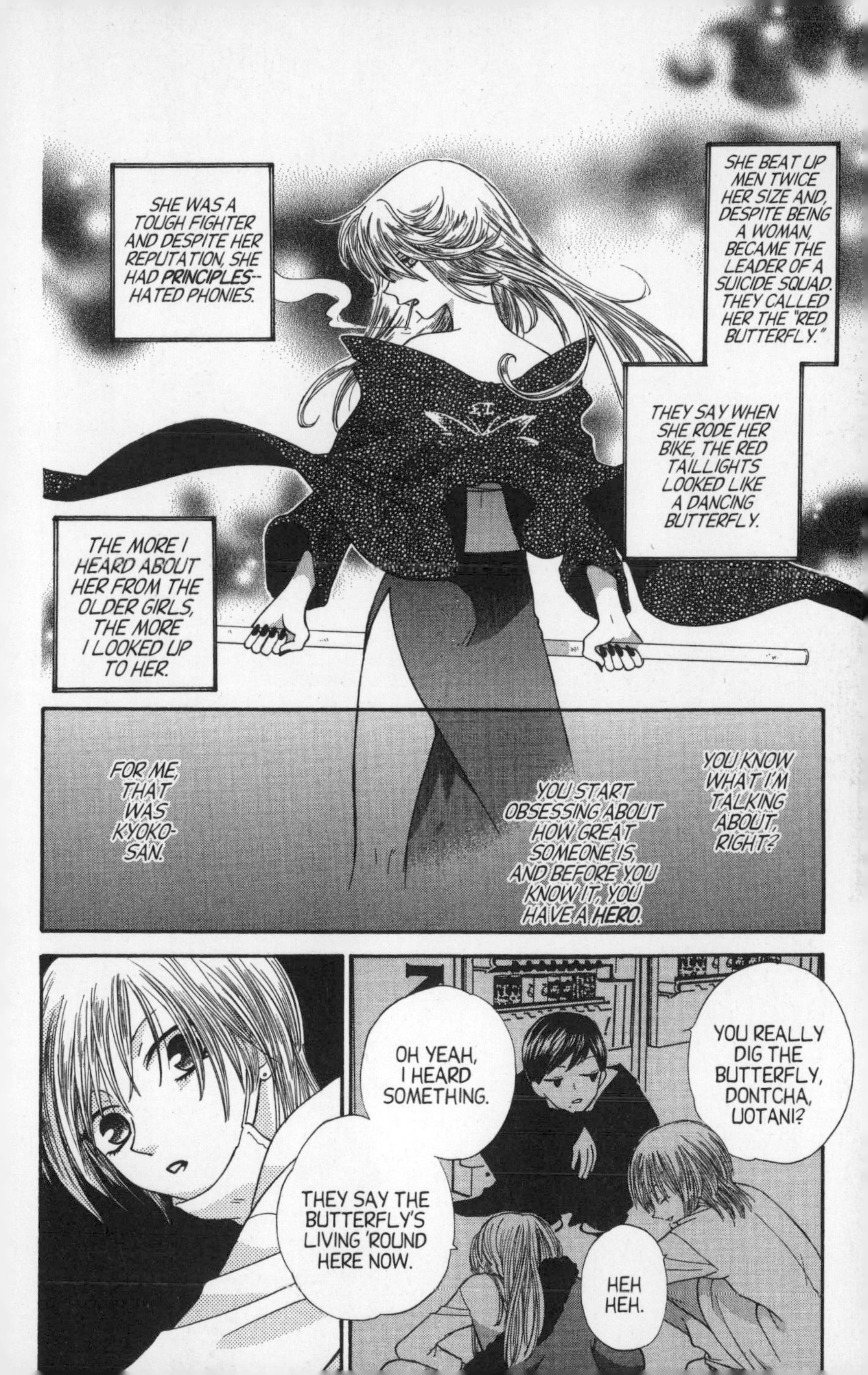

SHE BEAT UP MEN TWICE HER SIZE AND, DESPITE BEING A WOMAN, BECAME THE LEADER OF A SUICIDE SQUAD. THEY CALLED HER THE "RED BUTTERFLY."
SHE WAS A TOUGH FIGHTER AND DESPITE HER REPUTATION, SHE HAD **PRINCIPLES**--HATED PHONIES.
THEY SAY WHEN SHE RODE HER BIKE, THE RED TAILLIGHTS LOOKED LIKE A DANCING BUTTERFLY.
THE MORE I HEARD ABOUT HER FROM THE OLDER GIRLS, THE MORE I LOOKED UP TO HER.
YOU KNOW WHAT I'M TALKING ABOUT, RIGHT?
YOU START OBSESSING ABOUT HOW GREAT SOMEONE IS, AND BEFORE YOU KNOW IT, YOU HAVE A **HERO**.
FOR ME, THAT WAS KYOKO-SAN.
YOU REALLY DIG THE BUTTERFLY, DONTCHA, UOTANI?
OH YEAH, I HEARD SOMETHING.
THEY SAY THE BUTTERFLY'S LIVING 'ROUND HERE NOW.
HEH HEH.

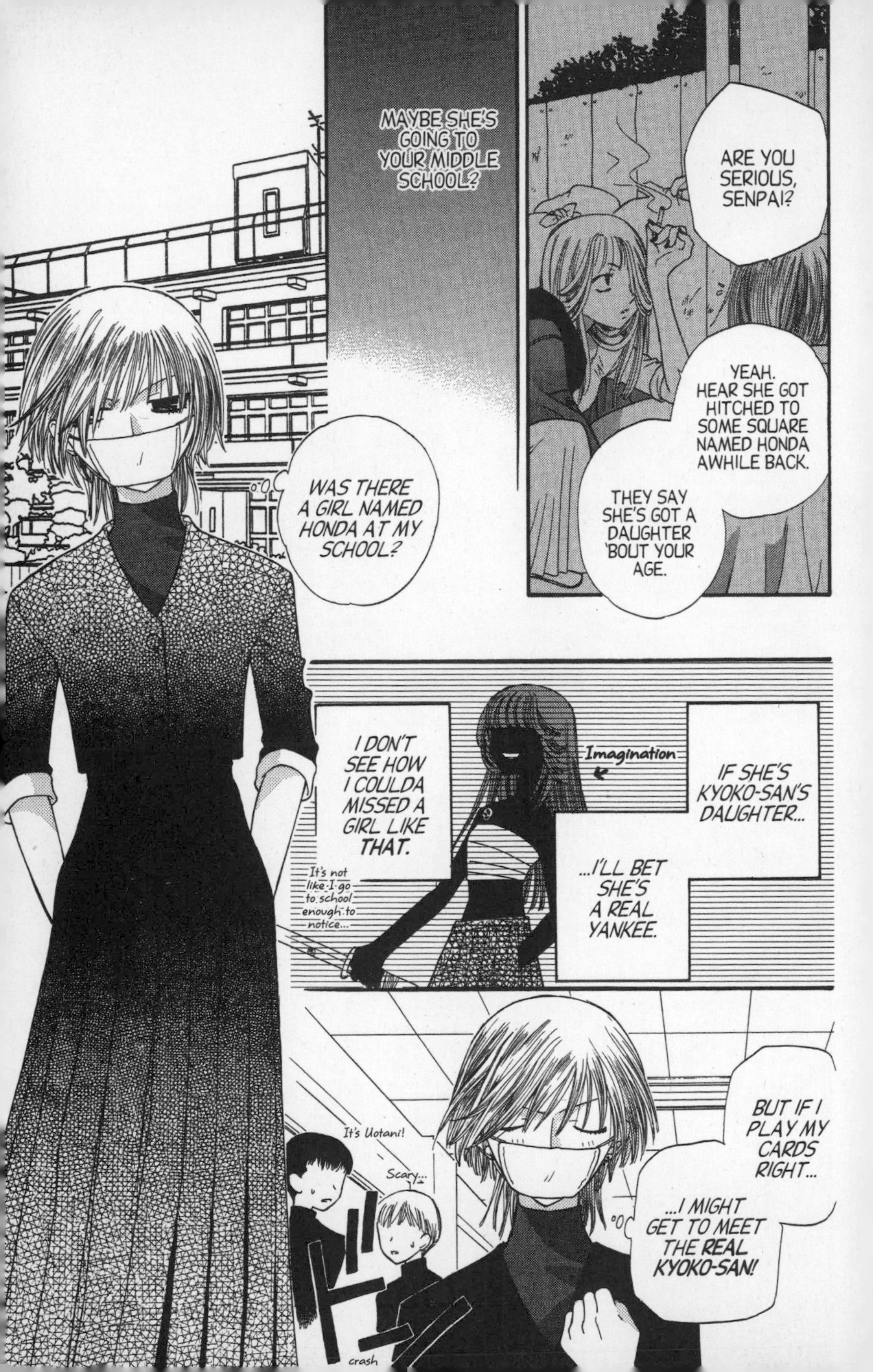
ARE YOU SERIOUS, SENPAI?
YEAH. HEAR SHE GOT HITCHED TO SOME SQUARE NAMED HONDA AWHILE BACK.
THEY SAY SHE'S GOT A DAUGHTER 'BOUT YOUR AGE.
MAYBE SHE'S GOING TO YOUR MIDDLE SCHOOL?
WAS THERE A GIRL NAMED HONDA AT MY SCHOOL?
IF SHE'S KYOKO-SAN'S DAUGHTER...
...I'LL BET SHE'S A REAL YANKEE.
Imagination
I DON'T SEE HOW I COULDA MISSED A GIRL LIKE THAT.
It's not like I go to school enough to notice...
BUT IF I PLAY MY CARDS RIGHT...
...I MIGHT GET TO MEET THE REAL KYOKO-SAN!
Scary...
It's Uotani!
crash

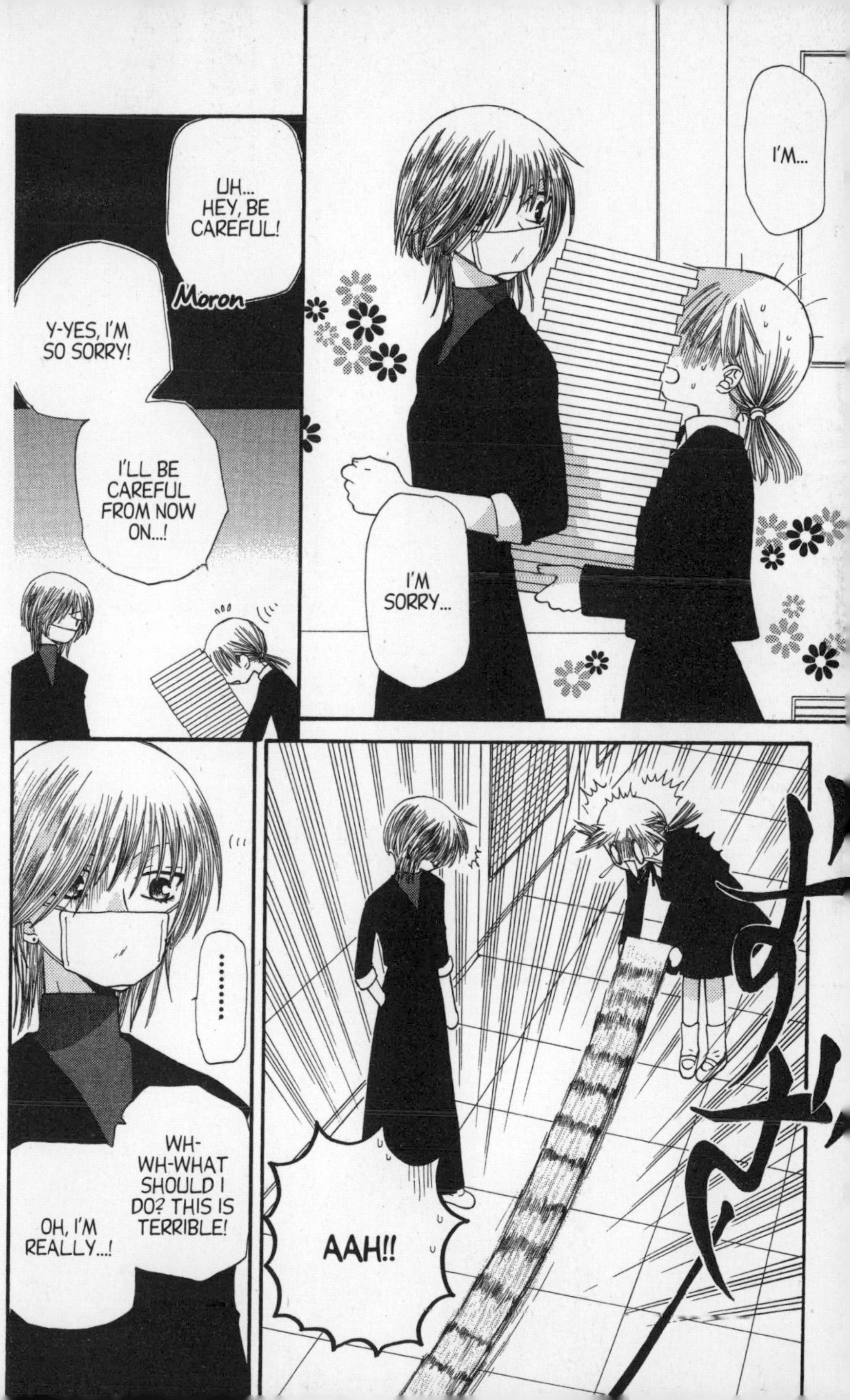
I'M...
I'M SORRY...
UH... HEY, BE CAREFUL!
Moron
Y-YES, I'M SO SORRY!
I'LL BE CAREFUL FROM NOW ON...!
AAH!!
....
WH-WH-WHAT SHOULD I DO? THIS IS TERRIBLE!
OH, I'M REALLY...!

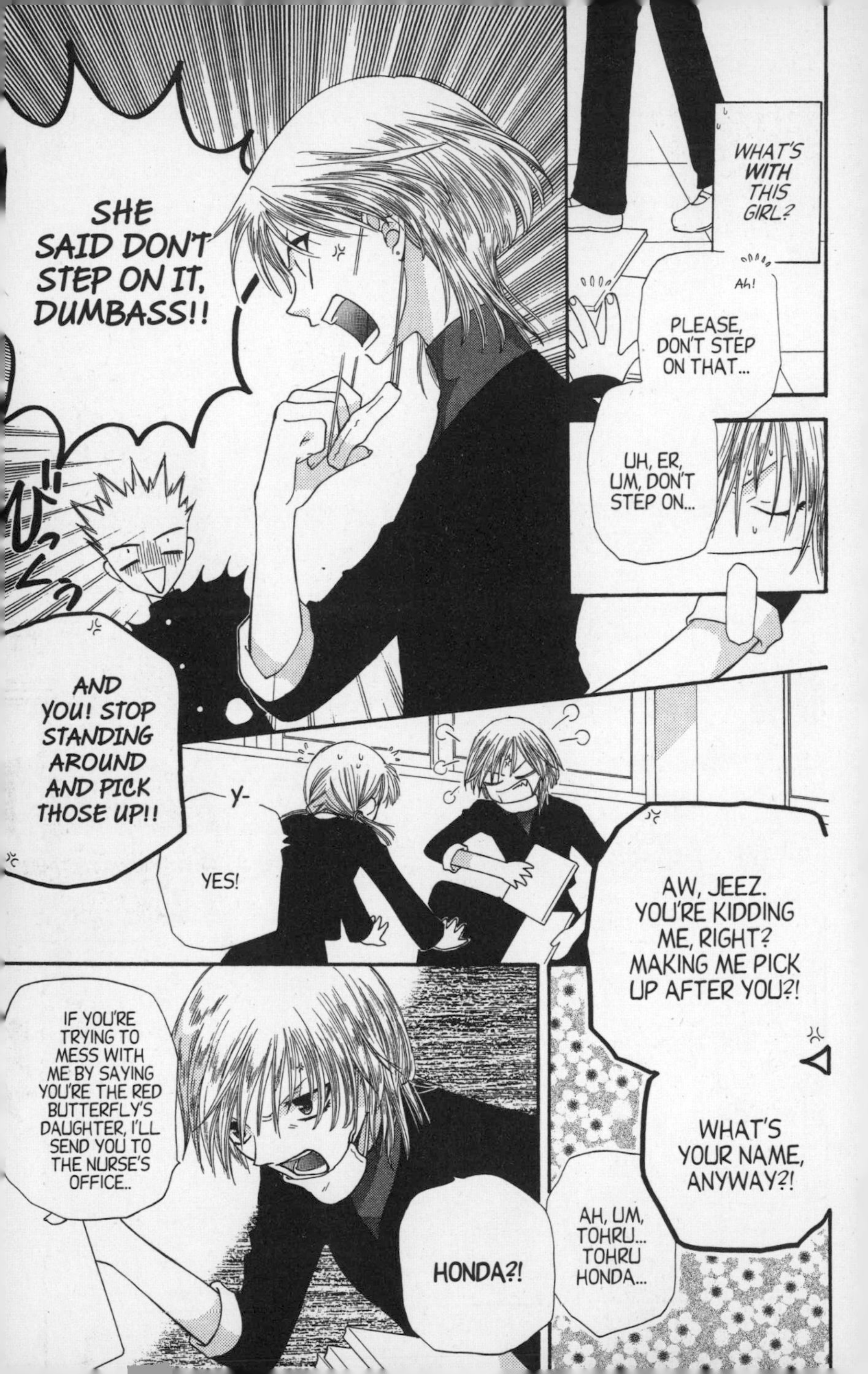
WHAT'S WITH THIS GIRL?
Ah!
PLEASE, DON'T STEP ON THAT...
UH, ER, UM, DON'T STEP ON...
SHE SAID DON'T STEP ON IT, DUMBASS!!
AND YOU! STOP STANDING AROUND AND PICK THOSE UP!!
AW, JEEZ. YOU'RE KIDDING ME, RIGHT? MAKING ME PICK UP AFTER YOU?!
Y-
YES!
WHAT'S YOUR NAME, ANYWAY?!
AH, UM, TOHRU... TOHRU HONDA...
HONDA?!
IF YOU'RE TRYING TO MESS WITH ME BY SAYING YOU'RE THE RED BUTTERFLY'S DAUGHTER, I'LL SEND YOU TO THE NURSE'S OFFICE..

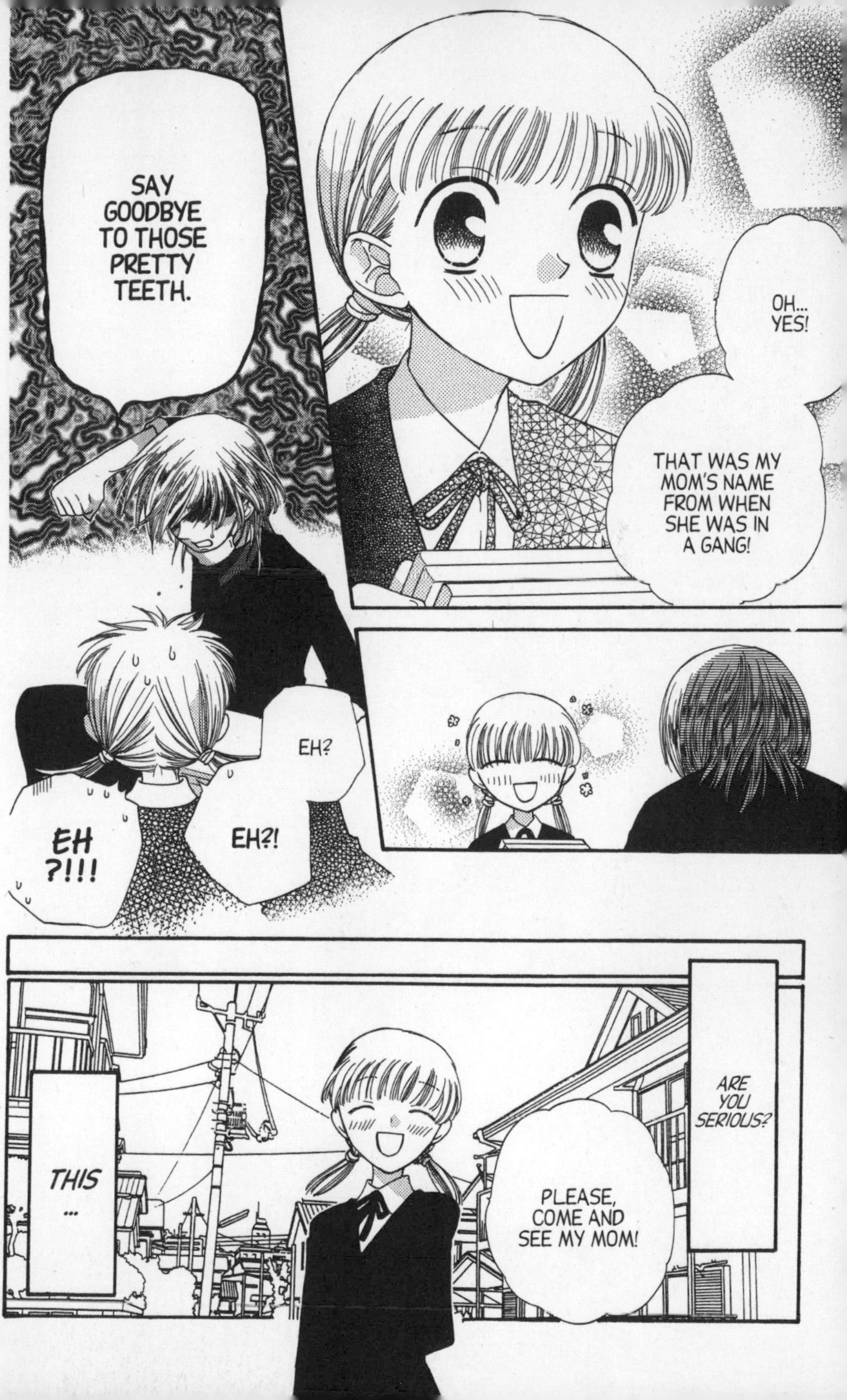
OH... YES!
THAT WAS MY MOM'S NAME FROM WHEN SHE WAS IN A GANG!
SAY GOODBYE TO THOSE PRETTY TEETH.
EH?
EH?!
EH ?!!!
ARE YOU SERIOUS?
PLEASE, COME AND SEE MY MOM!
THIS ...

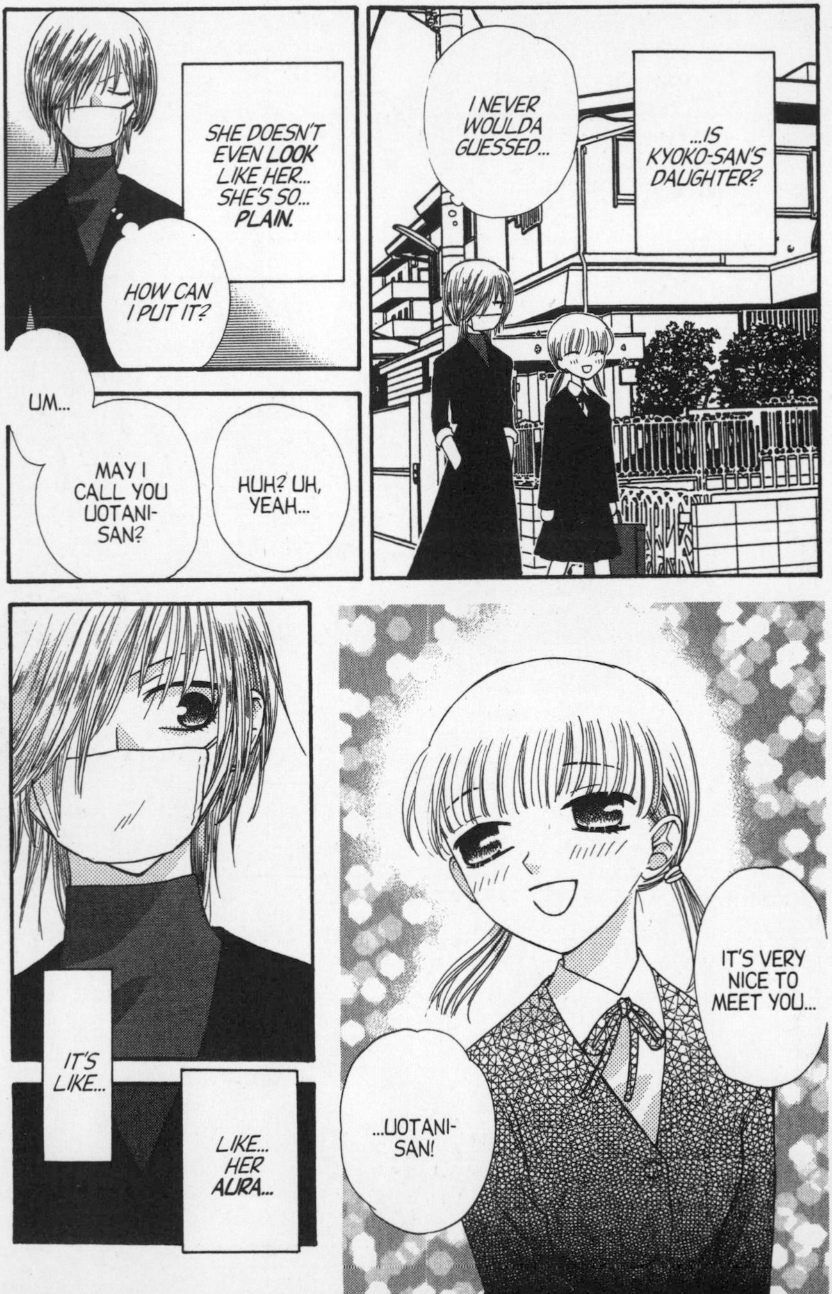
...IS KYOKO-SAN'S DAUGHTER?
I NEVER WOULDA GUESSED...
SHE DOESN'T EVEN LOOK LIKE HER... SHE'S SO... PLAIN.
HOW CAN I PUT IT?
UM...
MAY I CALL YOU UOTANI-SAN?
HUH? UH, YEAH...
IT'S VERY NICE TO MEET YOU...
...UOTANI-SAN!
IT'S LIKE...
LIKE... HER AURA...

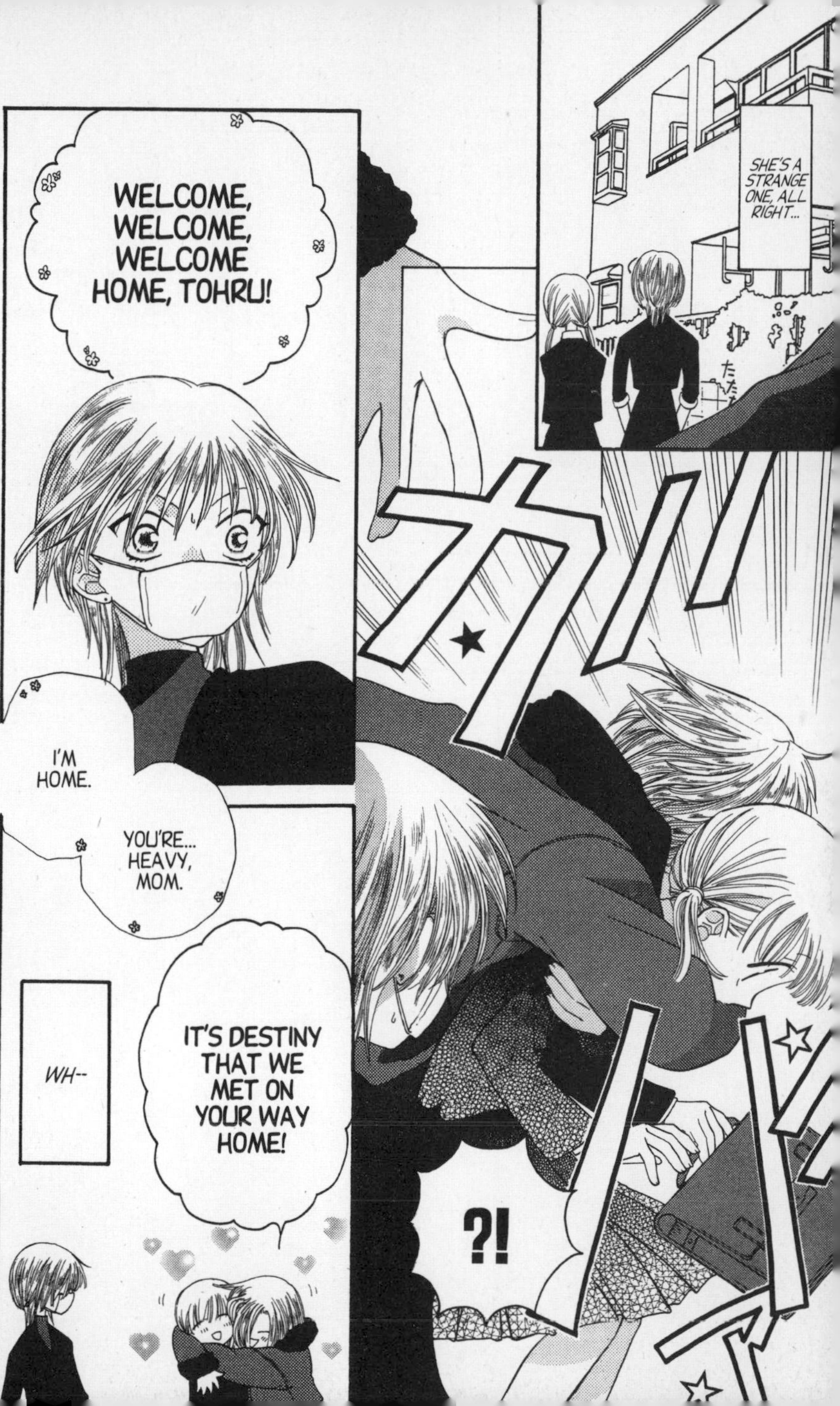
SHE'S A STRANGE ONE, ALL RIGHT...
?!
WELCOME, WELCOME, WELCOME HOME, TOHRU!
I'M HOME.
YOU'RE... HEAVY, MOM.
IT'S DESTINY THAT WE MET ON YOUR WAY HOME!
WH--

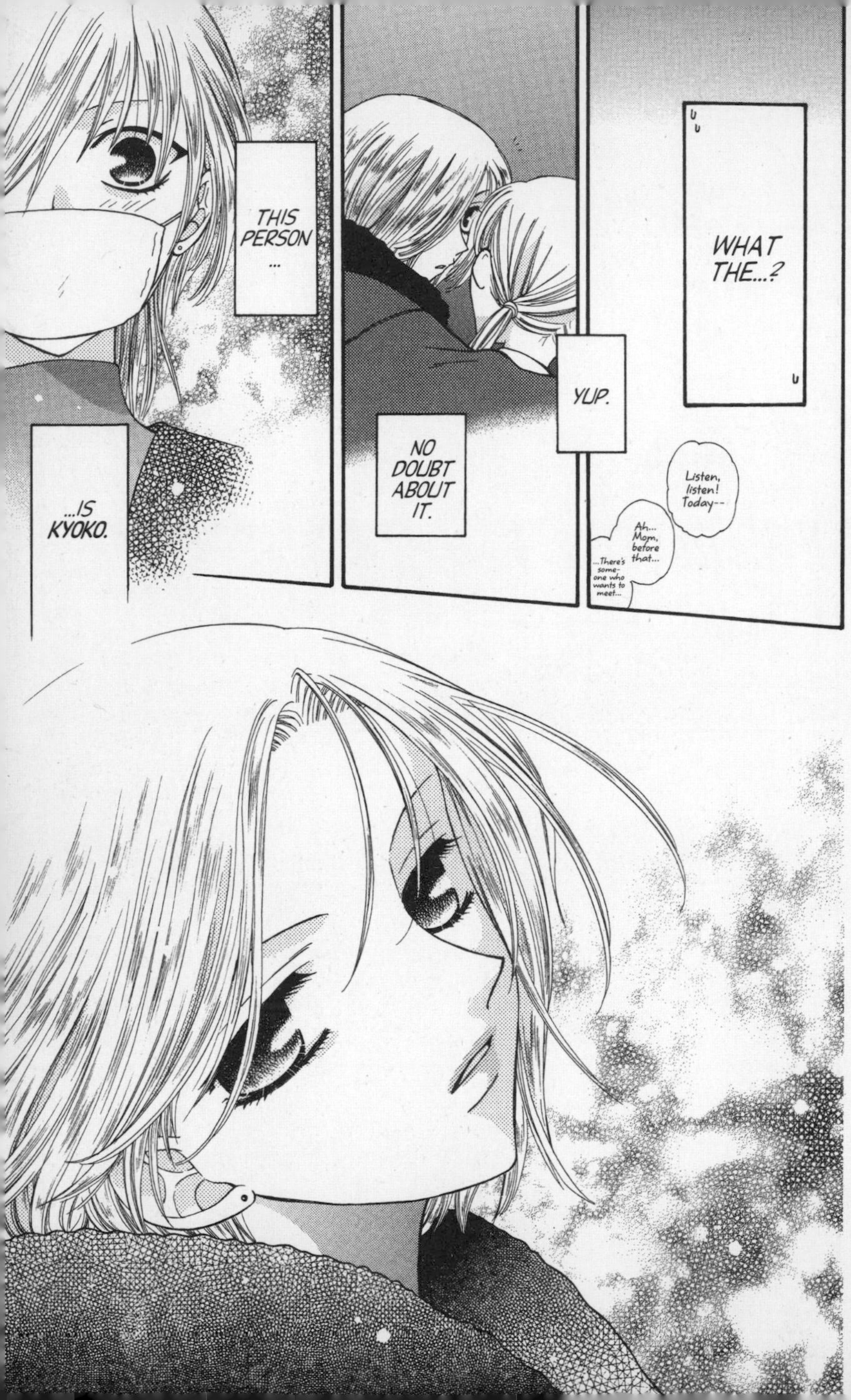
WHAT THE...?
Listen, listen! Today--
Ah... Mom, before that...
...There's someone who wants to meet...
YUP.
NO DOUBT ABOUT IT.
THIS PERSON ...
...IS KYOKO.

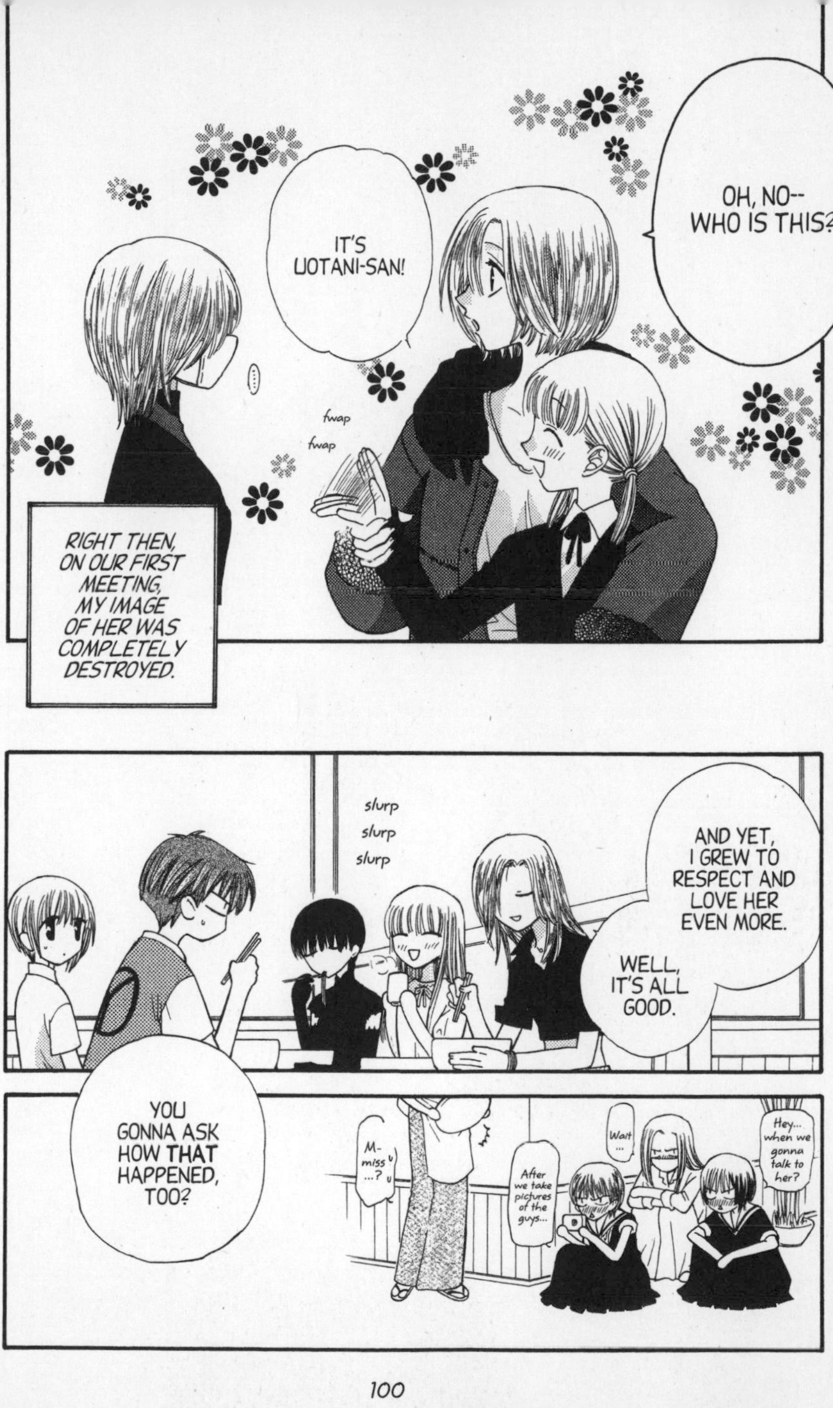
OH, NO--
WHO IS THIS?
IT'S UOTANI-SAN!
...
fwap
fwap
RIGHT THEN, ON OUR FIRST MEETING, MY IMAGE OF HER WAS COMPLETELY DESTROYED.
AND YET, I GREW TO RESPECT AND LOVE HER EVEN MORE.
WELL, IT'S ALL GOOD.
slurp
slurp
slurp
Hey... when we gonna talk to her?
Wait...
After we take pictures of the guys...
M-miss...?
YOU GONNA ASK HOW THAT HAPPENED, TOO?

Chapter 40

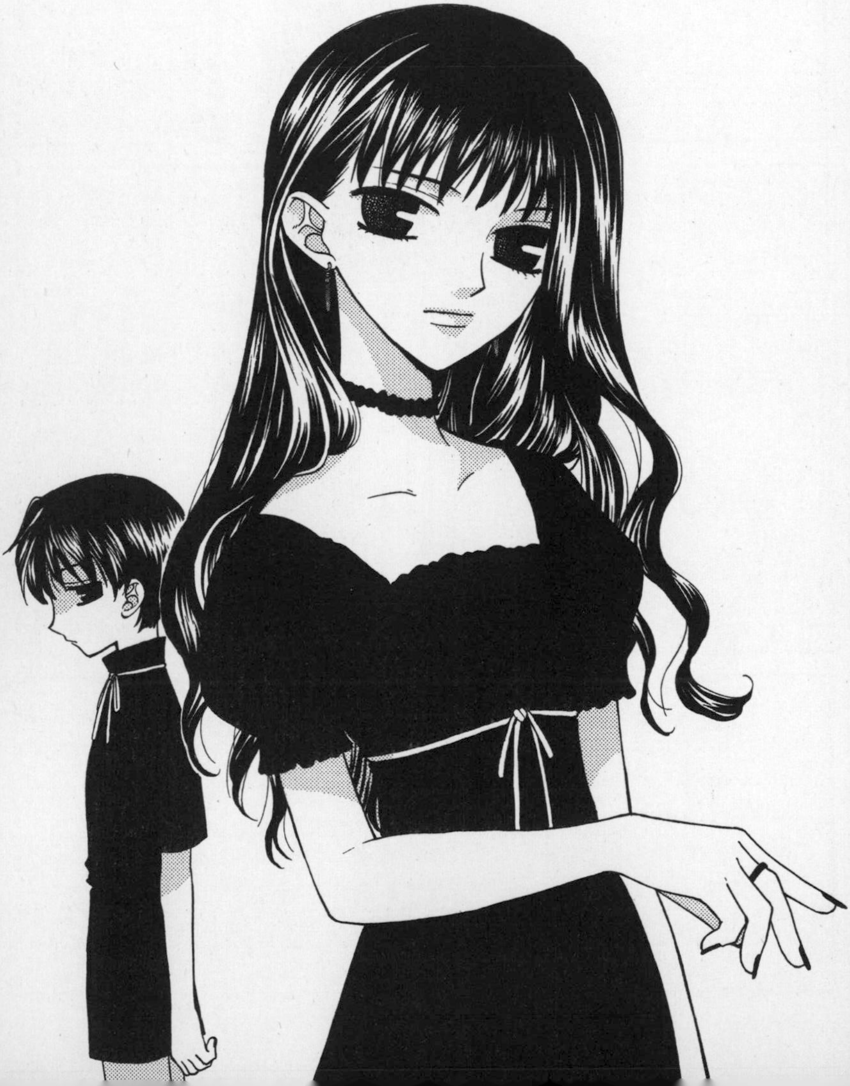

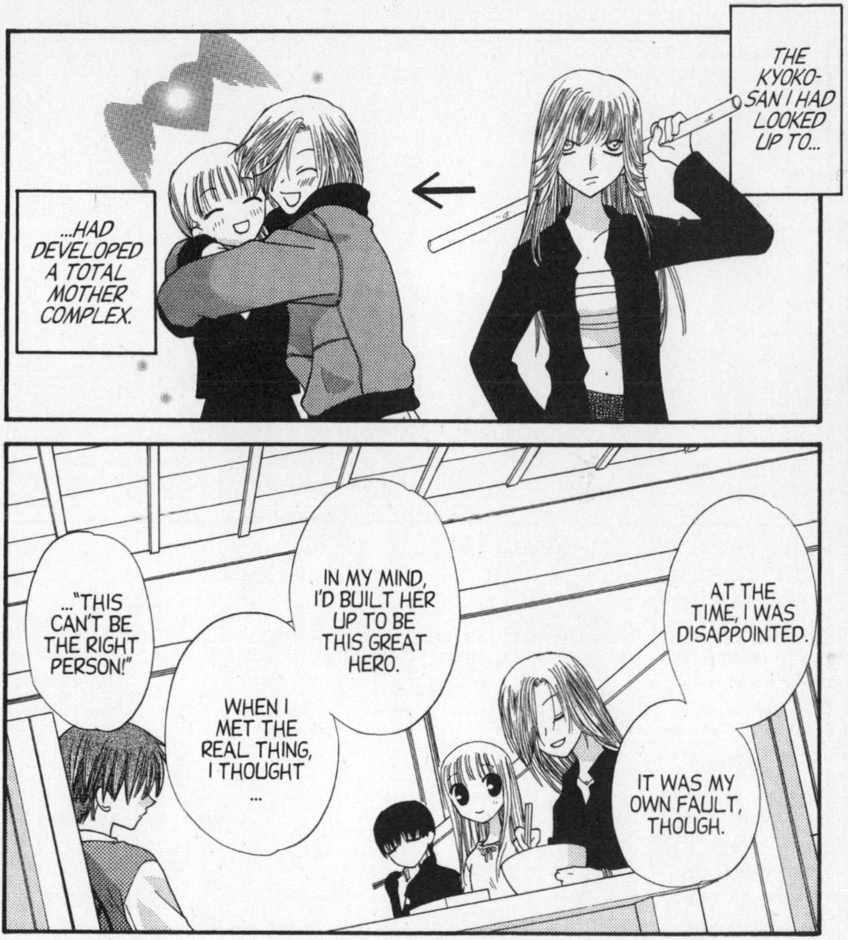
THE KYOKO-SAN I HAD LOOKED UP TO...
...HAD DEVELOPED A TOTAL MOTHER COMPLEX.
AT THE TIME, I WAS DISAPPOINTED.
IT WAS MY OWN FAULT, THOUGH.
IN MY MIND, I'D BUILT HER UP TO BE THIS GREAT HERO.
WHEN I MET THE REAL THING, I THOUGHT ...
..."THIS CAN'T BE THE RIGHT PERSON!"

ULTRA-SPECIAL BLAH, BLAH, BLAH 4

Having your heart shaken by a fictional character, or being made to cry for them, is very sad, but I think it's a good thing. I know it sounds negative, but it's really a positive experience. It is! I'm not making any sense, am I? No, I'm sorry.

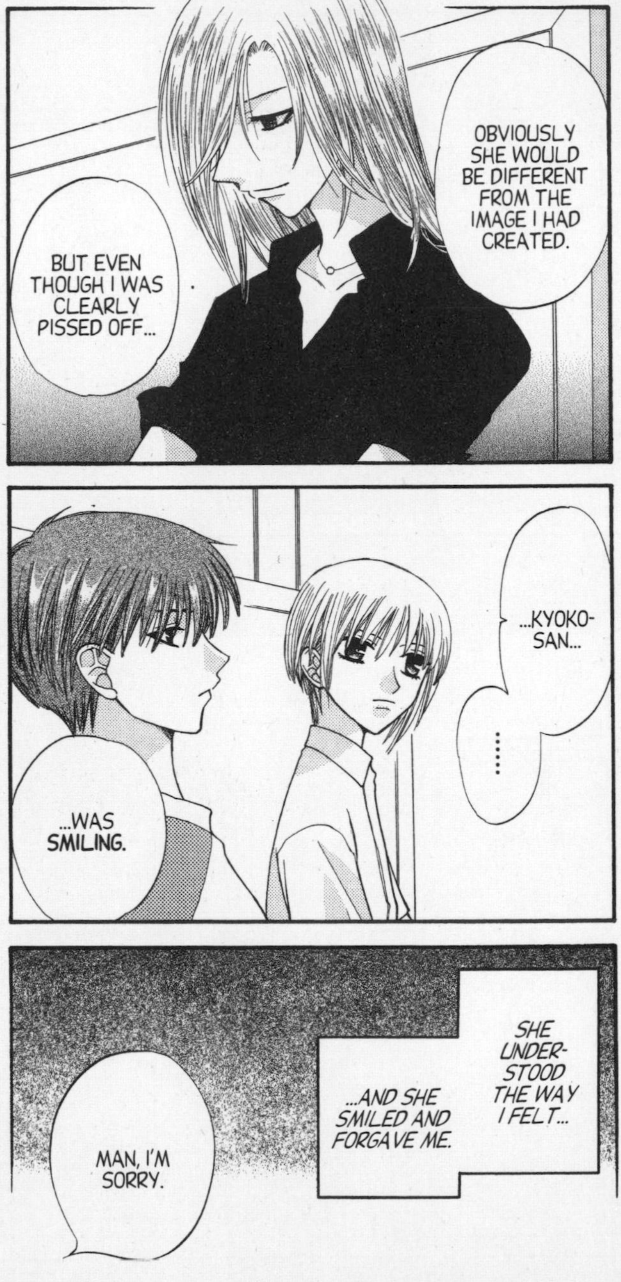
OBVIOUSLY SHE WOULD BE DIFFERENT FROM THE IMAGE I HAD CREATED.
BUT EVEN THOUGH I WAS CLEARLY PISSED OFF...
...KYOKO-SAN... ......
...WAS SMILING.
SHE UNDER-STOOD THE WAY I FELT...
...AND SHE SMILED AND FORGAVE ME.
MAN, I'M SORRY.

Fruits Basket 7: Part 4

It was strange that, as the days went on, the hospital bed became "my bed." There was more and more of my stuff nearby. I hated that I couldn't play video games (laugh). Apparently, the day before my operation, my mother and people couldn't sleep. But, as usual, Takaya slept like a log! I thought again about how those situations are harder on the loved ones than they are on the actual patient. (It's a kind of torture, especially for family.) But when it came time for the actual surgery, even I had a hard time. Yup—I finally got scared. Yeah, it's scary, really...

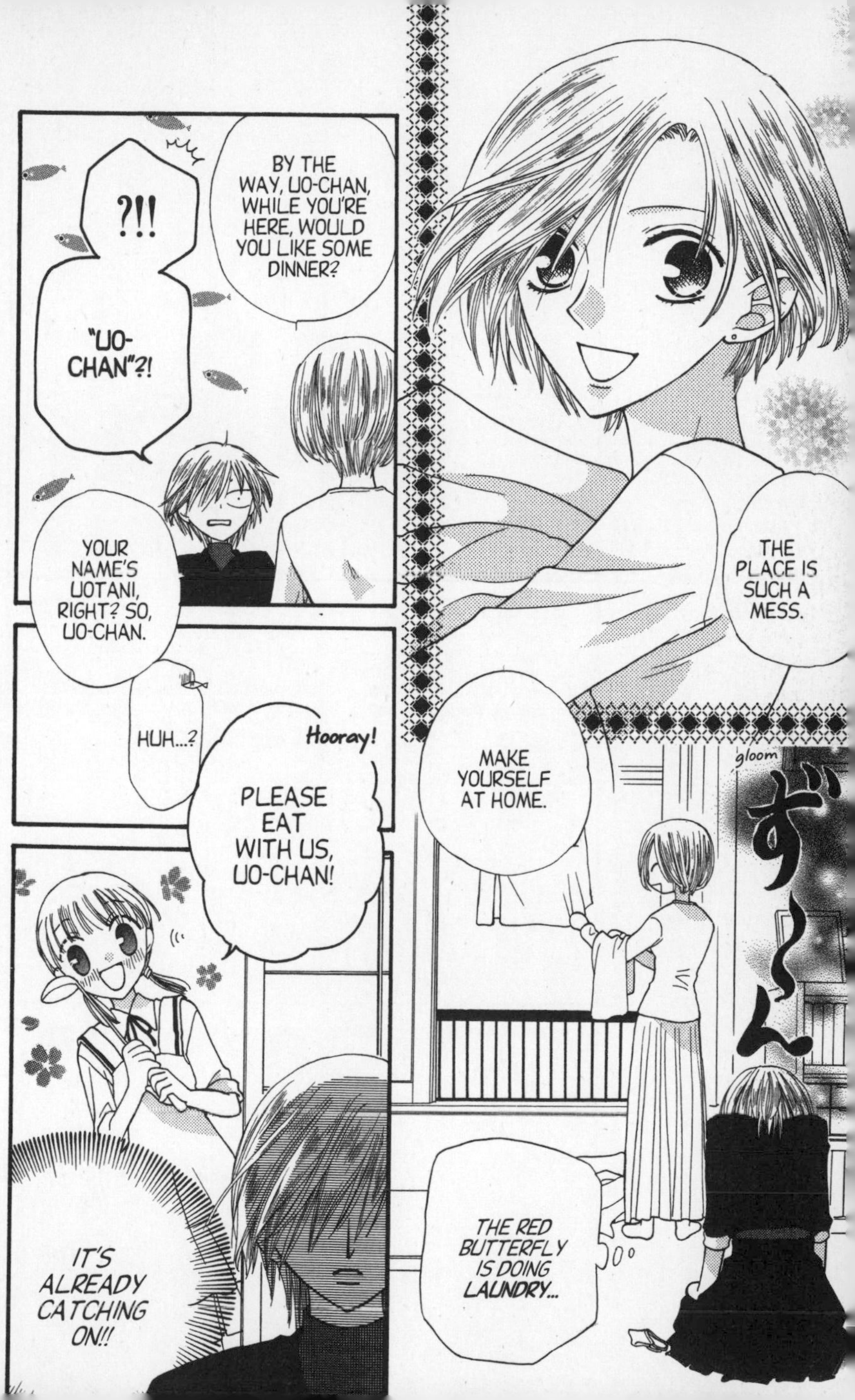
THE PLACE IS SUCH A MESS.
MAKE YOURSELF AT HOME.
gloom
ず〜ん
THE RED BUTTERFLY IS DOING LAUNDRY...
BY THE WAY, UO-CHAN, WHILE YOU'RE HERE, WOULD YOU LIKE SOME DINNER?
?!!
"UO-CHAN"?!
YOUR NAME'S UOTANI, RIGHT? SO, UO-CHAN.
HUH...?
Hooray!
PLEASE EAT WITH US, UO-CHAN!
IT'S ALREADY CATCHING ON!!

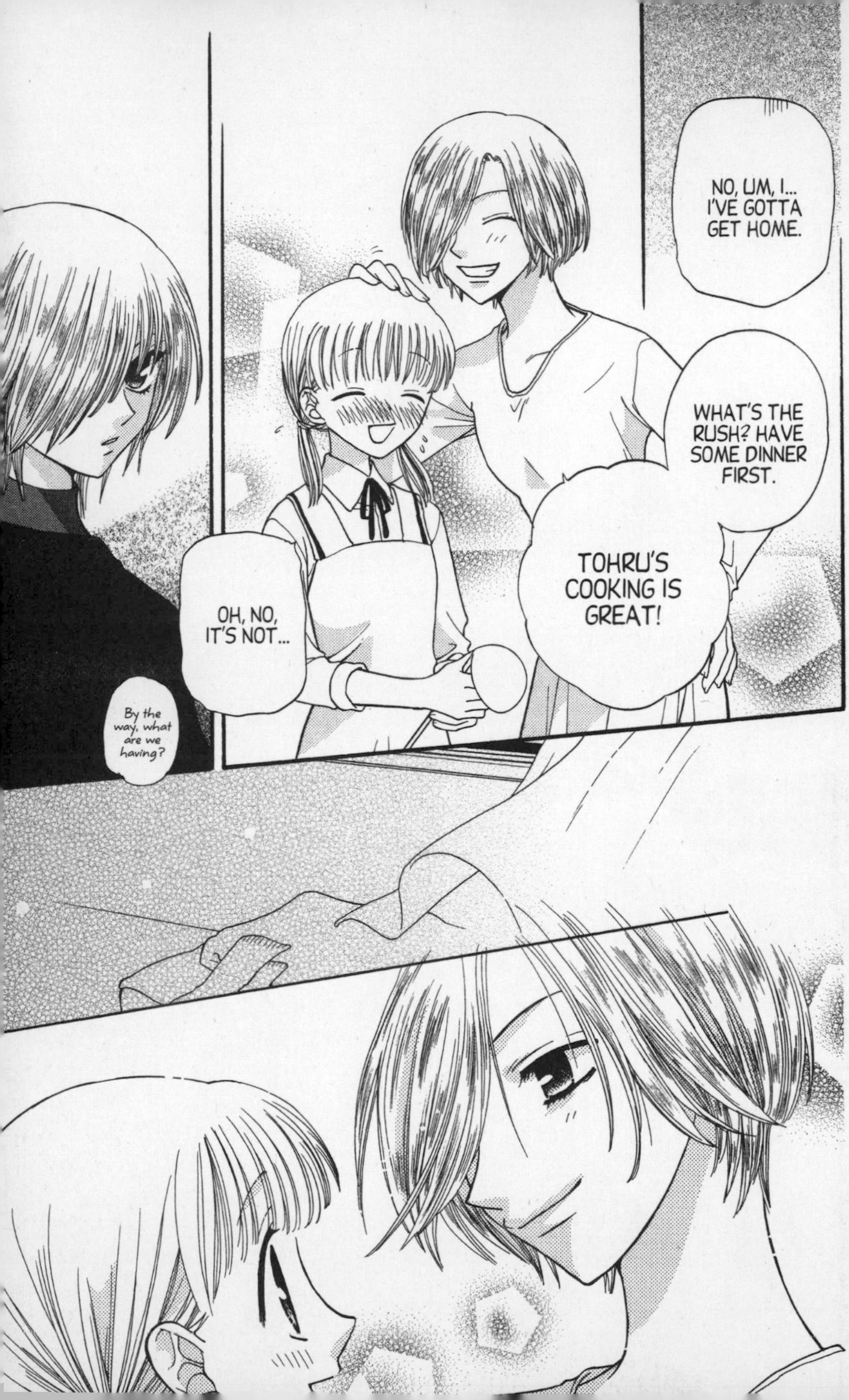
NO, UM, I... I'VE GOTTA GET HOME.
WHAT'S THE RUSH? HAVE SOME DINNER FIRST.
TOHRU'S COOKING IS GREAT!
OH, NO, IT'S NOT...
By the way, what are we having?

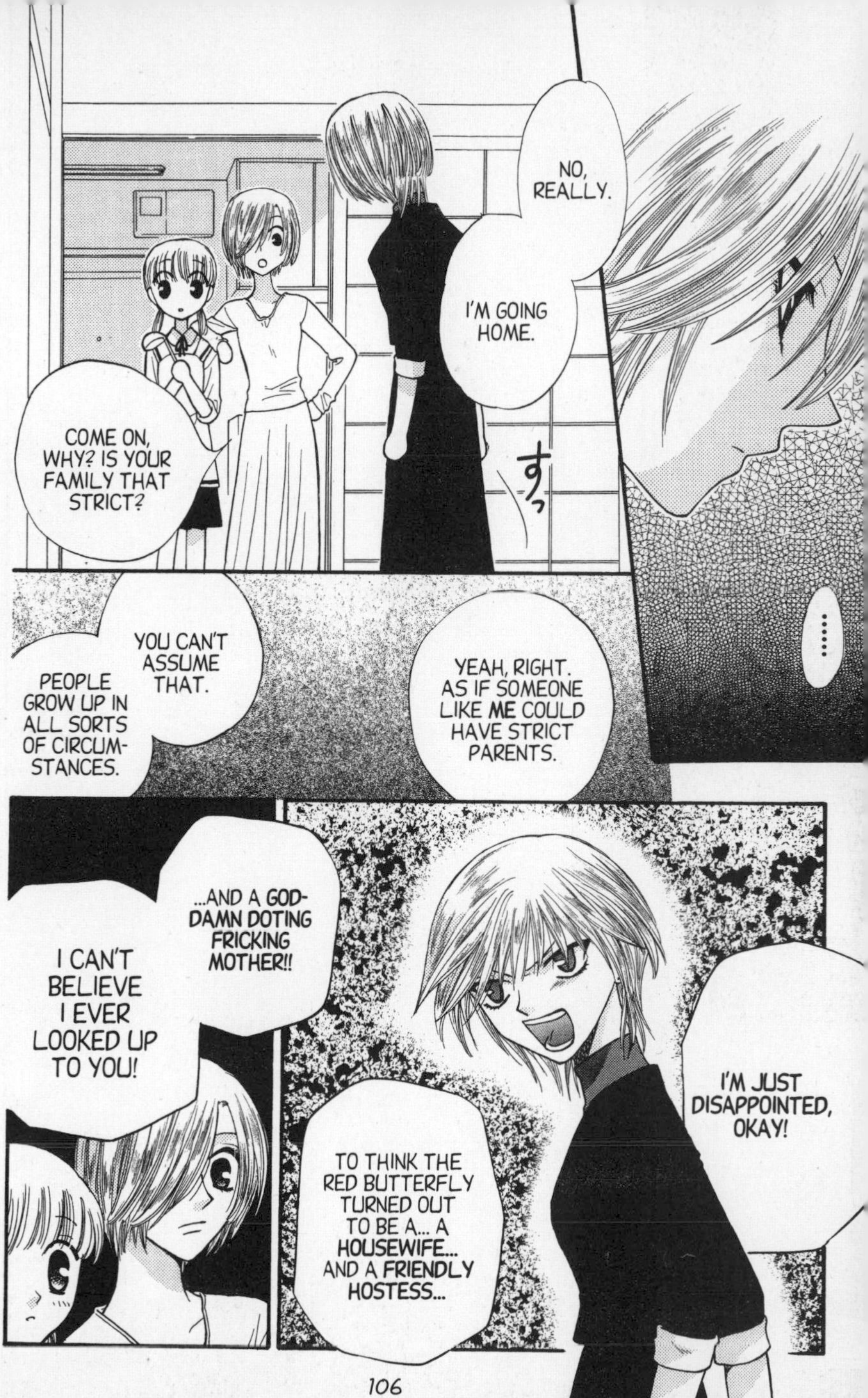
......
NO, REALLY.
I'M GOING HOME.
すっ
COME ON, WHY? IS YOUR FAMILY THAT STRICT?
YEAH, RIGHT. AS IF SOMEONE LIKE ME COULD HAVE STRICT PARENTS.
YOU CAN'T ASSUME THAT.
PEOPLE GROW UP IN ALL SORTS OF CIRCUM-STANCES.
I'M JUST DISAPPOINTED, OKAY!
TO THINK THE RED BUTTERFLY TURNED OUT TO BE A... A HOUSEWIFE... AND A FRIENDLY HOSTESS...
...AND A GOD-DAMN DOTING FRICKING MOTHER!!
I CAN'T BELIEVE I EVER LOOKED UP TO YOU!

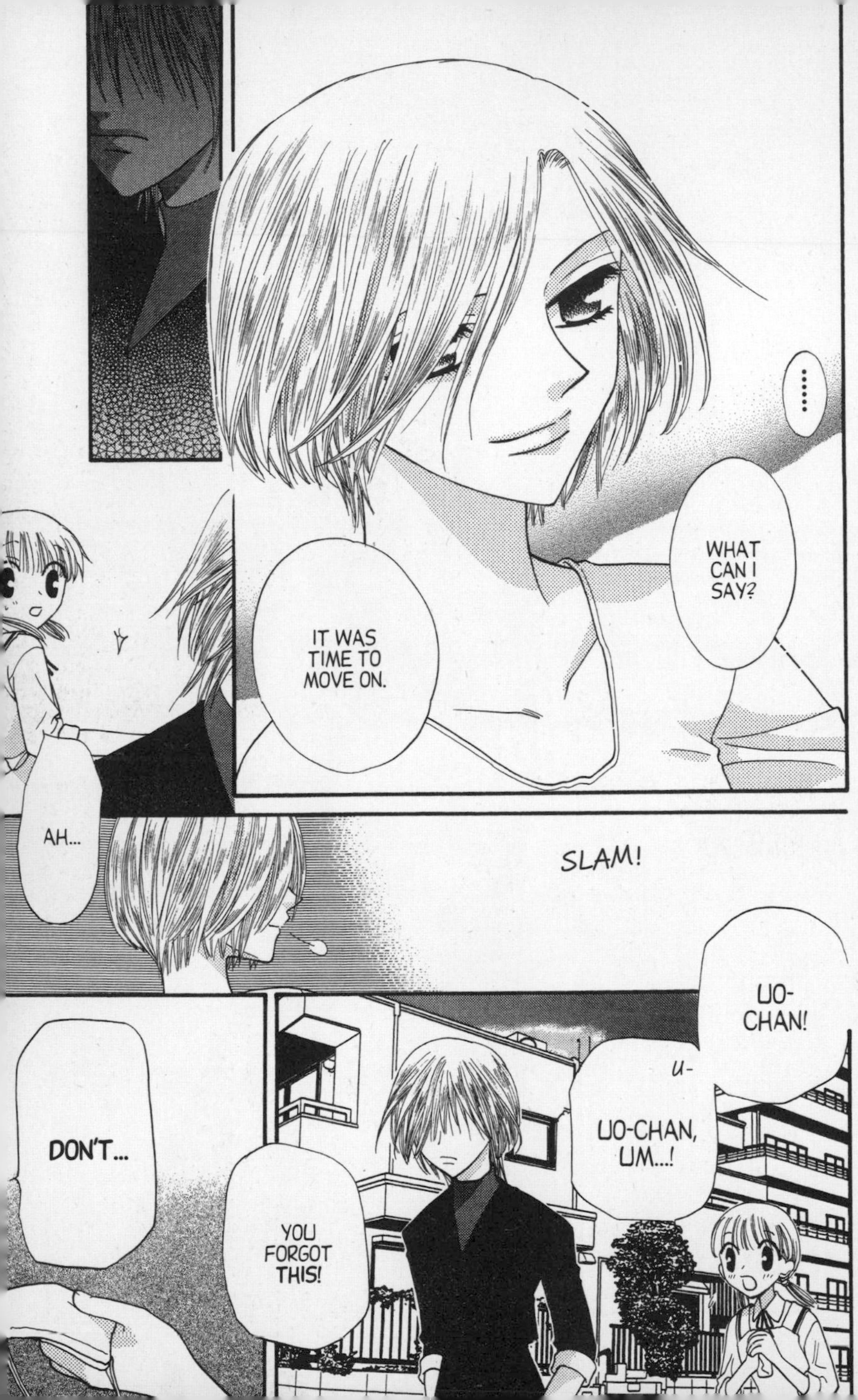
......
WHAT CAN I SAY?
IT WAS TIME TO MOVE ON.
AH...
SLAM!
UO-CHAN!
U-
UO-CHAN, UM...!
YOU FORGOT THIS!
DON'T...

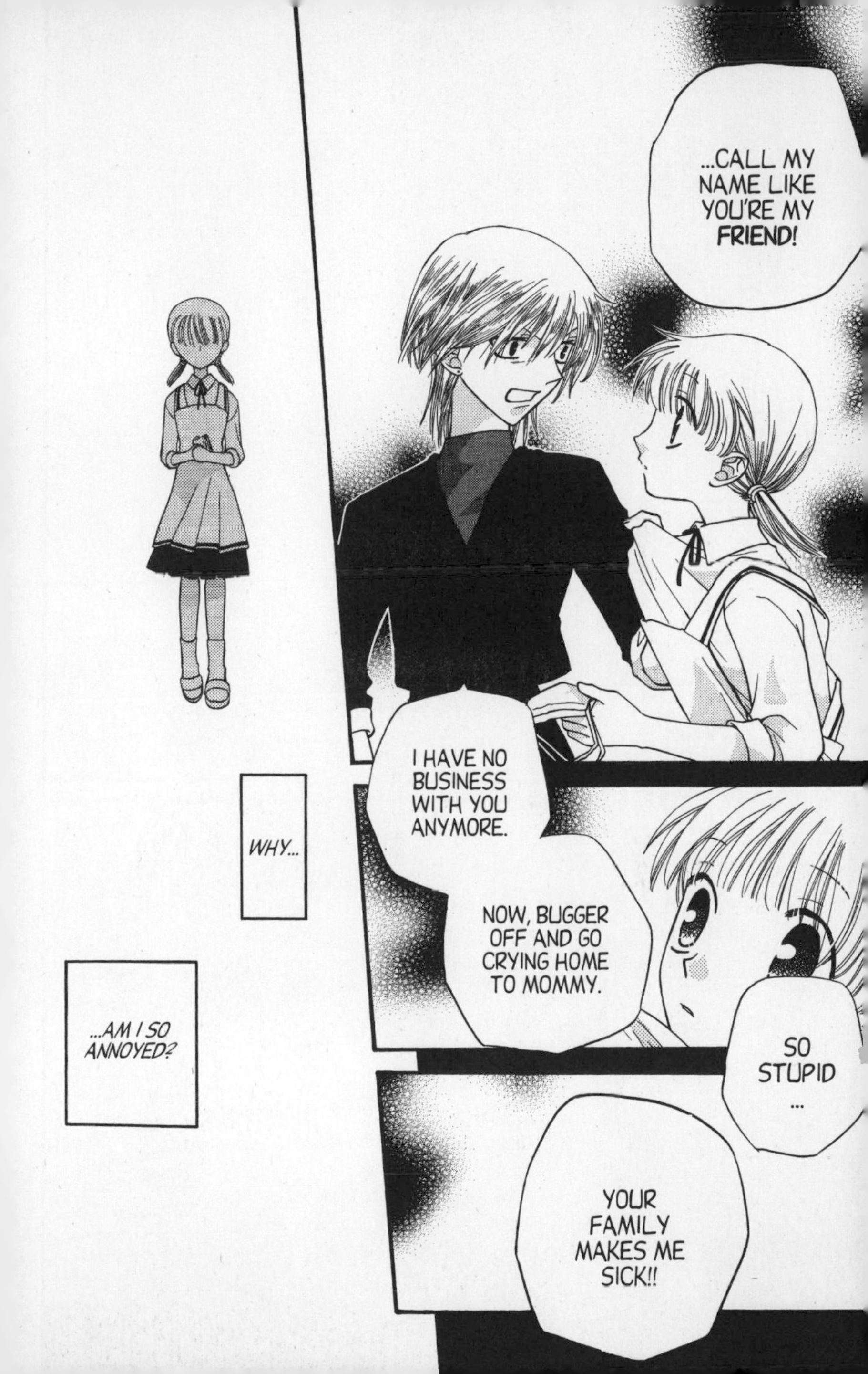
...CALL MY NAME LIKE YOU'RE MY FRIEND!
I HAVE NO BUSINESS WITH YOU ANYMORE.
NOW, BUGGER OFF AND GO CRYING HOME TO MOMMY.
SO STUPID ...
YOUR FAMILY MAKES ME SICK!!
WHY...
...AM I SO ANNOYED?

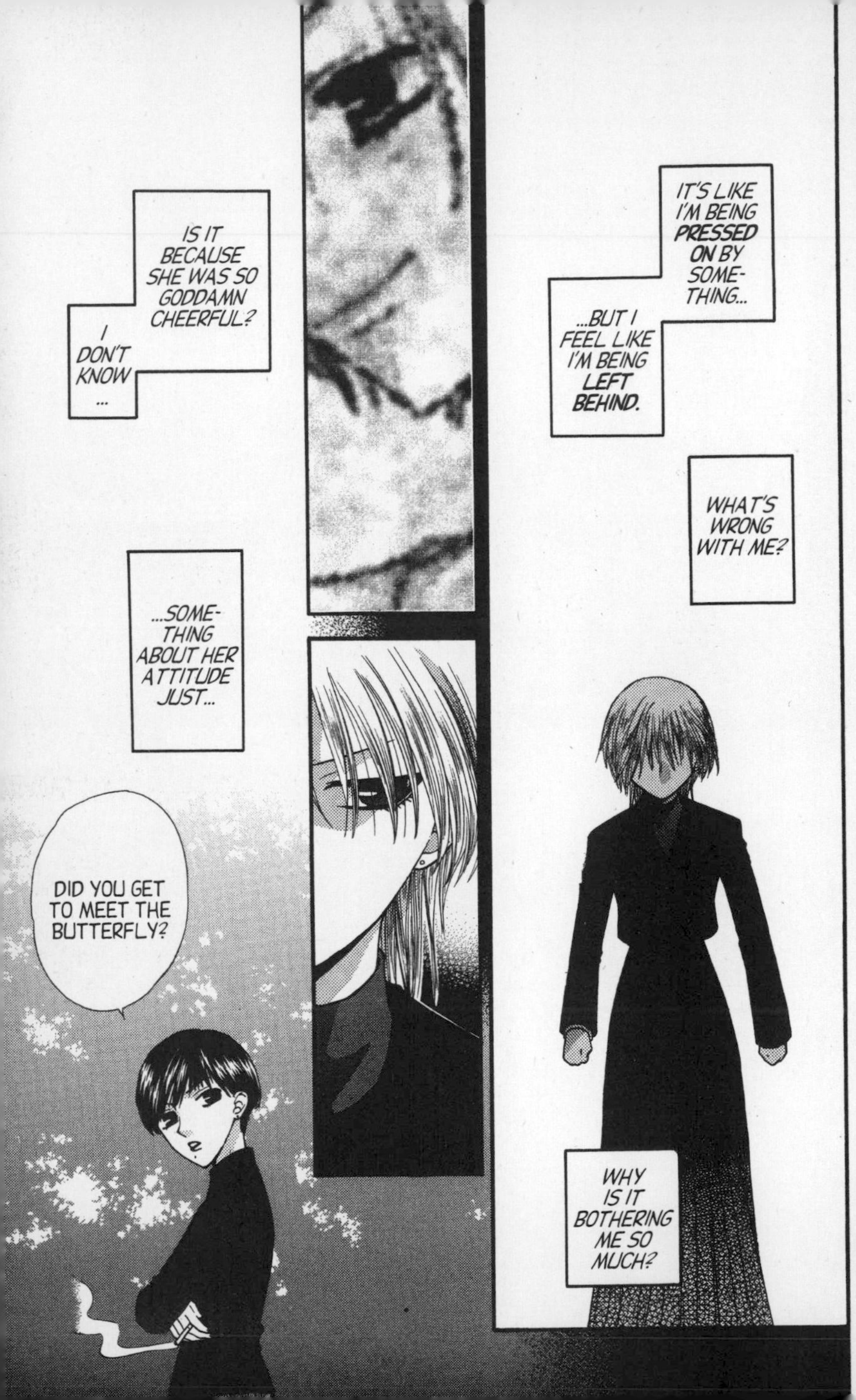
IT'S LIKE I'M BEING PRESSED ON BY SOME-THING...
...BUT I FEEL LIKE I'M BEING LEFT BEHIND.
WHAT'S WRONG WITH ME?
WHY IS IT BOTHERING ME SO MUCH?
IS IT BECAUSE SHE WAS SO GODDAMN CHEERFUL?
I DON'T KNOW ...
...SOME-THING ABOUT HER ATTITUDE JUST...
DID YOU GET TO MEET THE BUTTERFLY?

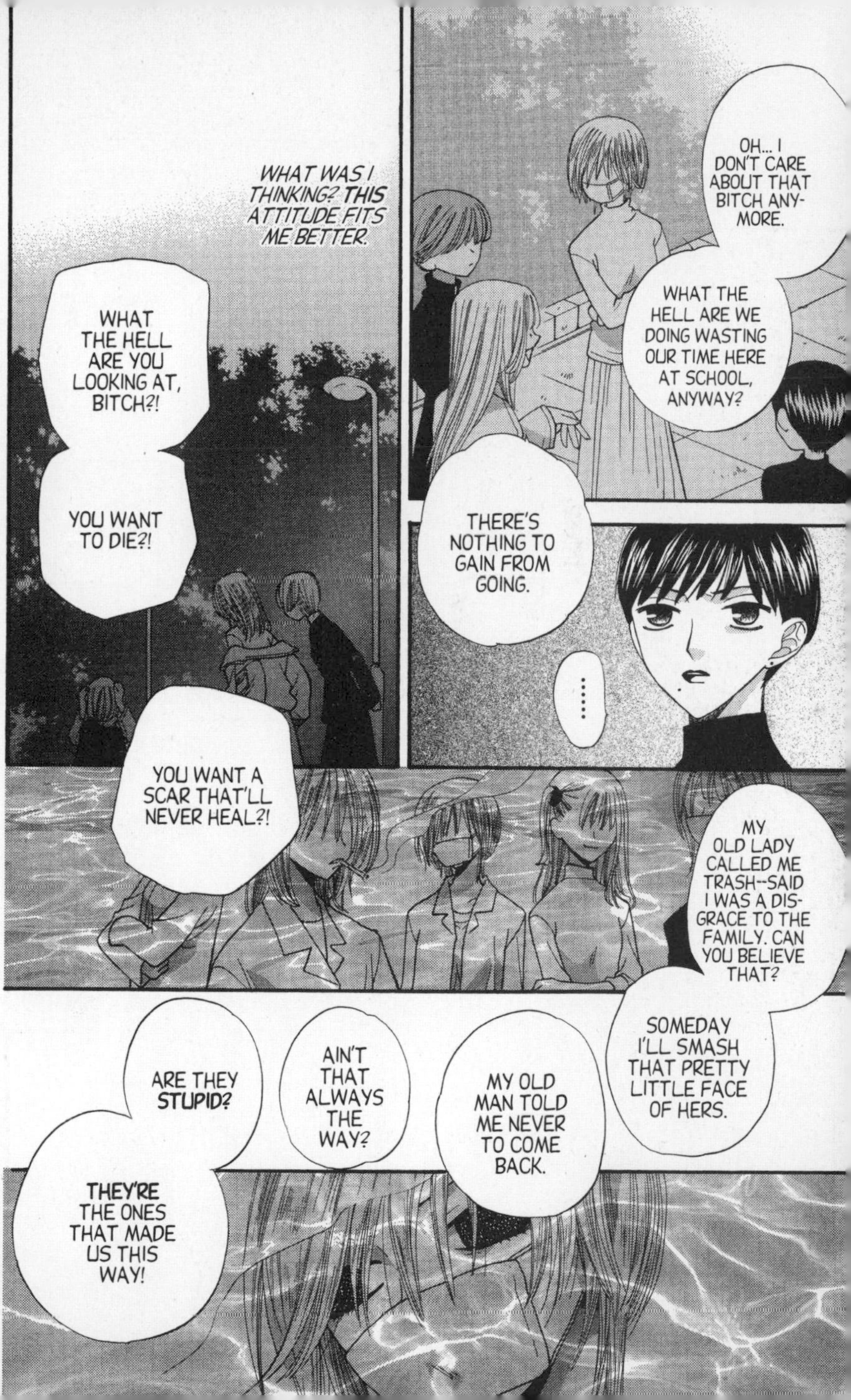
OH... I DON'T CARE ABOUT THAT BITCH ANY-MORE.
WHAT THE HELL ARE WE DOING WASTING OUR TIME HERE AT SCHOOL, ANYWAY?
THERE'S NOTHING TO GAIN FROM GOING.
......
WHAT WAS I THINKING? THIS ATTITUDE FITS ME BETTER.
WHAT THE HELL ARE YOU LOOKING AT, BITCH?!
YOU WANT TO DIE?!
YOU WANT A SCAR THAT'LL NEVER HEAL?!
MY OLD LADY CALLED ME TRASH--SAID I WAS A DIS-GRACE TO THE FAMILY. CAN YOU BELIEVE THAT?
SOMEDAY I'LL SMASH THAT PRETTY LITTLE FACE OF HERS.
MY OLD MAN TOLD ME NEVER TO COME BACK.
AIN'T THAT ALWAYS THE WAY?
ARE THEY STUPID?
THEY'RE THE ONES THAT MADE US THIS WAY!

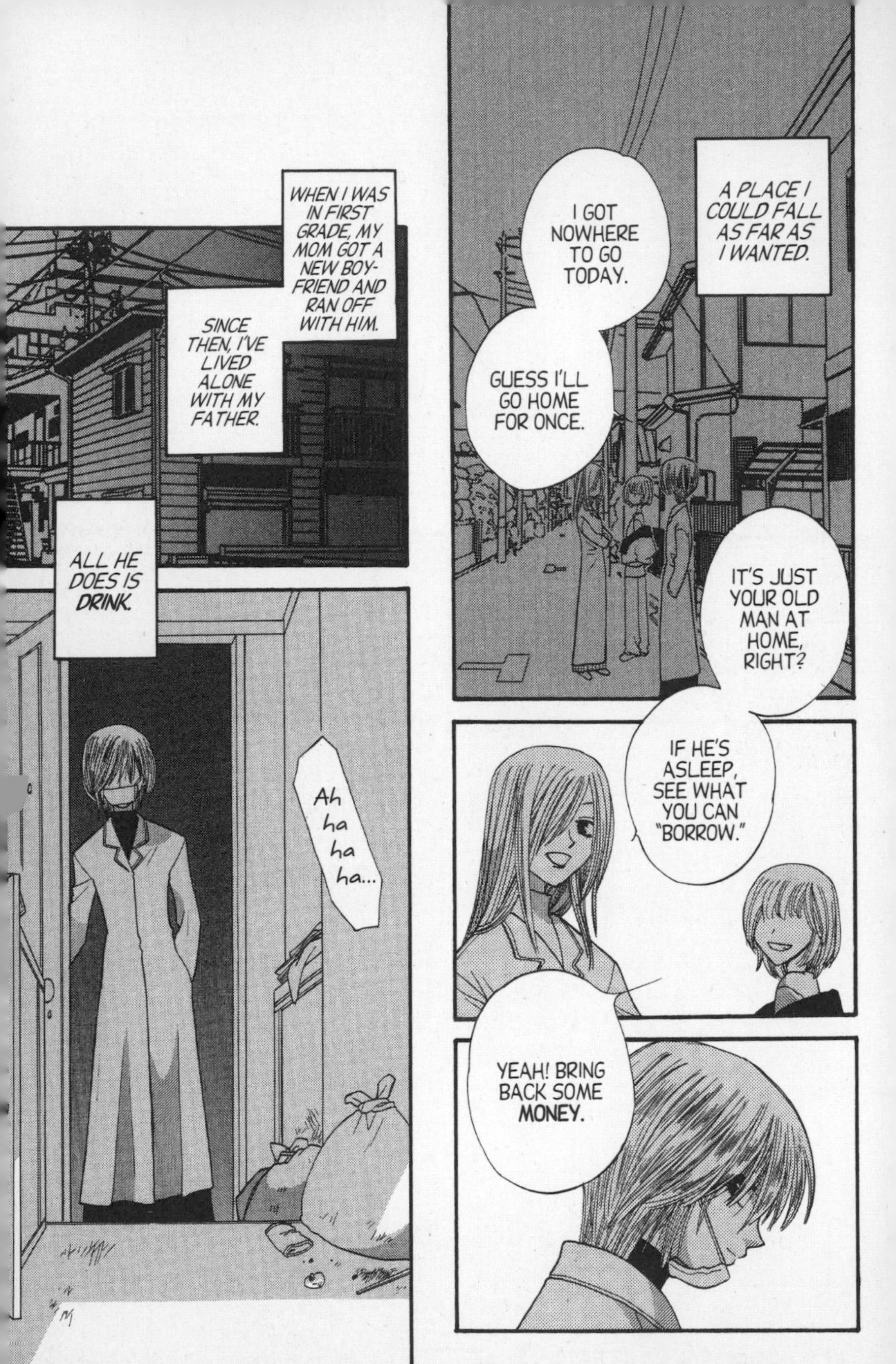
A PLACE I COULD FALL AS FAR AS I WANTED.
I GOT NOWHERE TO GO TODAY.
GUESS I'LL GO HOME FOR ONCE.
IT'S JUST YOUR OLD MAN AT HOME, RIGHT?
IF HE'S ASLEEP, SEE WHAT YOU CAN "BORROW."
YEAH! BRING BACK SOME MONEY.
WHEN I WAS IN FIRST GRADE, MY MOM GOT A NEW BOY-FRIEND AND RAN OFF WITH HIM.
SINCE THEN, I'VE LIVED ALONE WITH MY FATHER.
ALL HE DOES IS DRINK.
Ah ha ha ha...

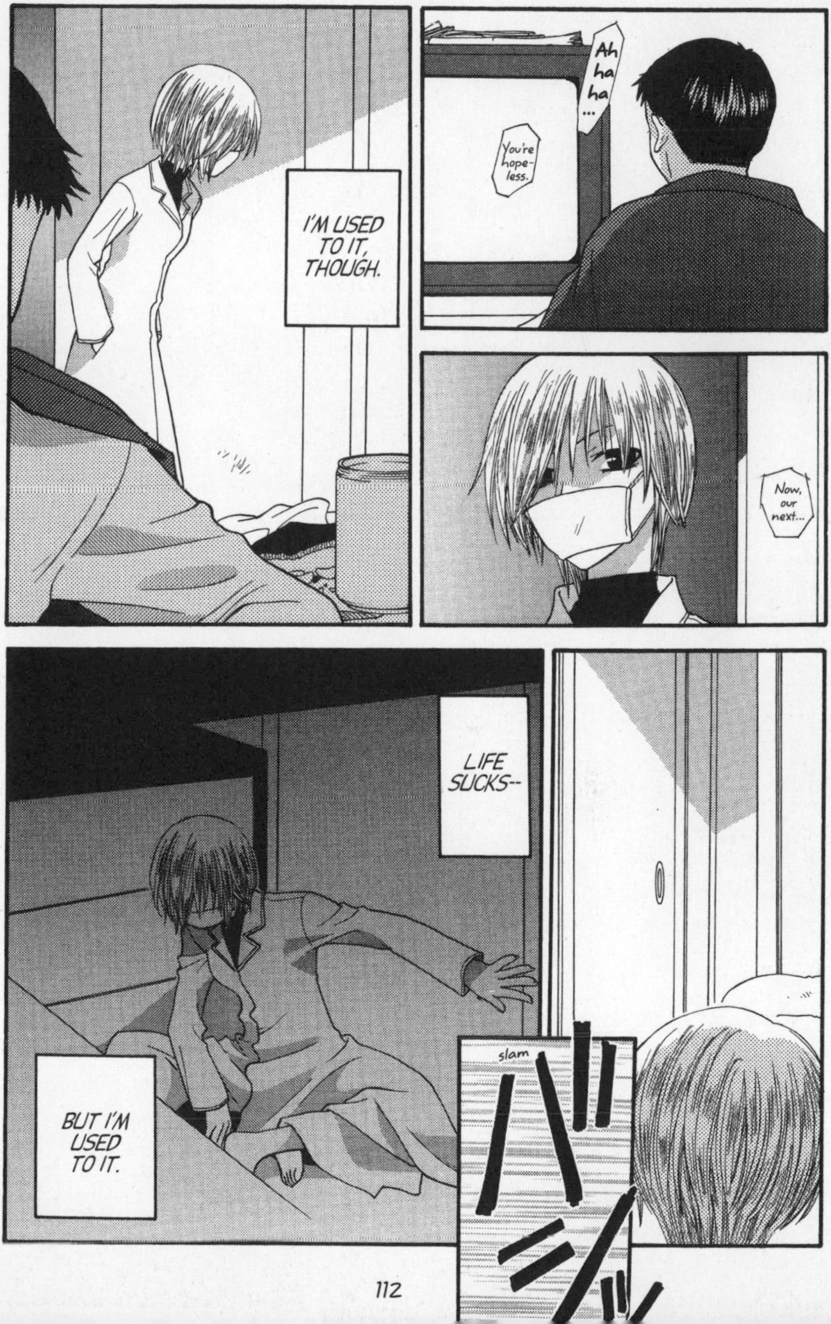

Ah ha ha ...
You're hope-less.
Now, our next...
I'M USED TO IT, THOUGH.
slam
LIFE SUCKS--
BUT I'M USED TO IT.

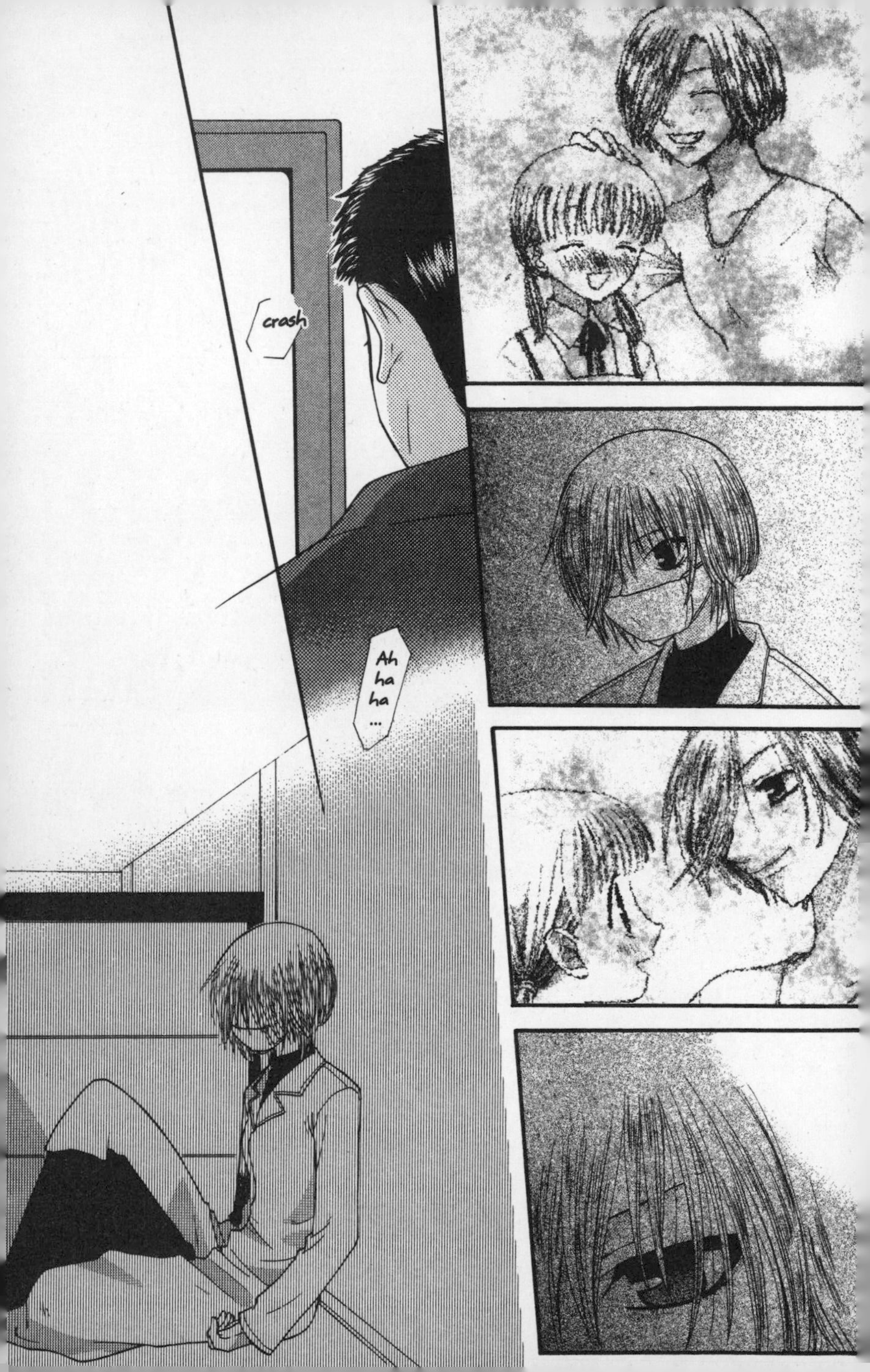
crash
Ah ha ha ...

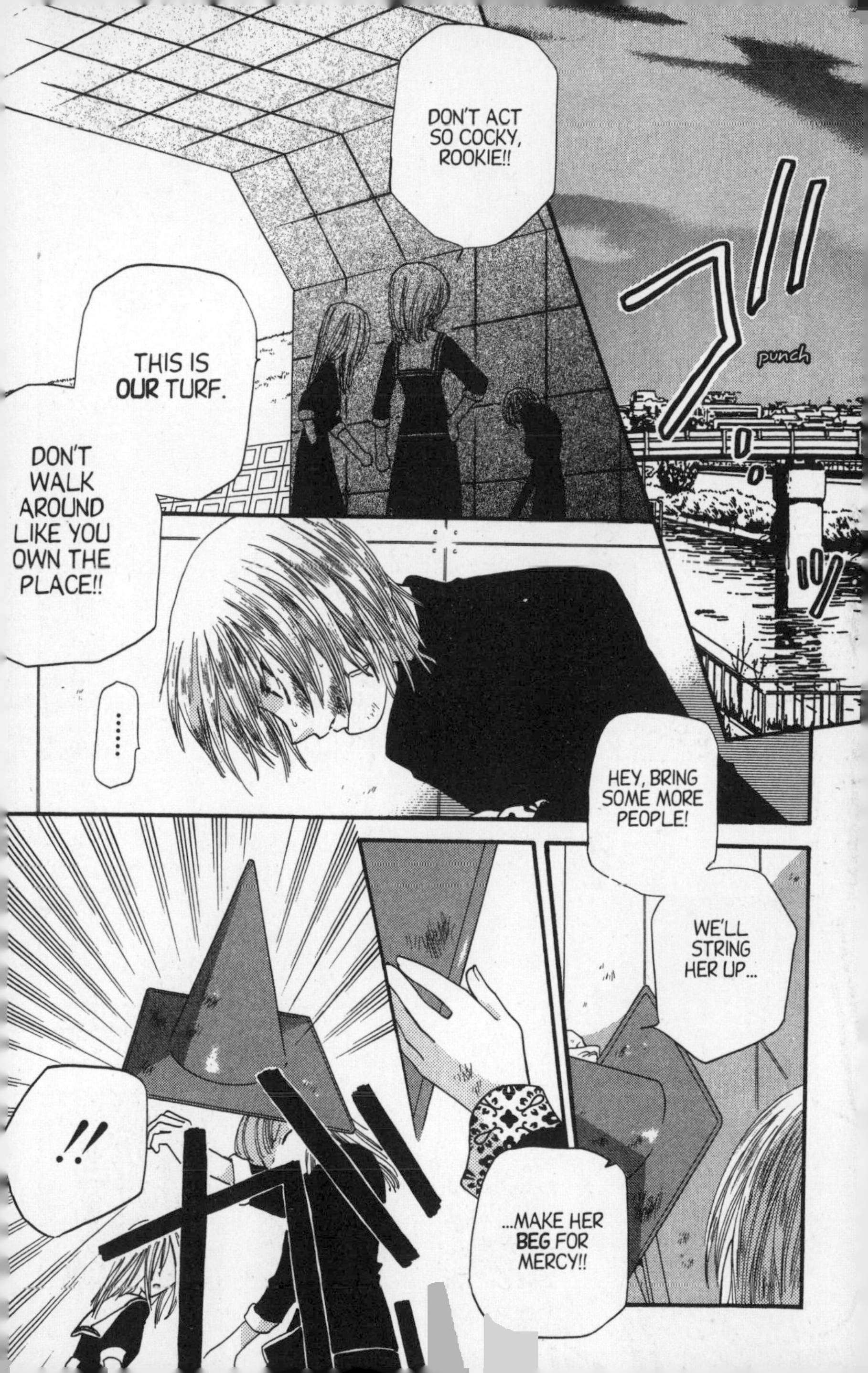
punch
DON'T ACT SO COCKY, ROOKIE!!
THIS IS OUR TURF.
DON'T WALK AROUND LIKE YOU OWN THE PLACE!!
......
HEY, BRING SOME MORE PEOPLE!
WE'LL STRING HER UP...
...MAKE HER BEG FOR MERCY!!
!!

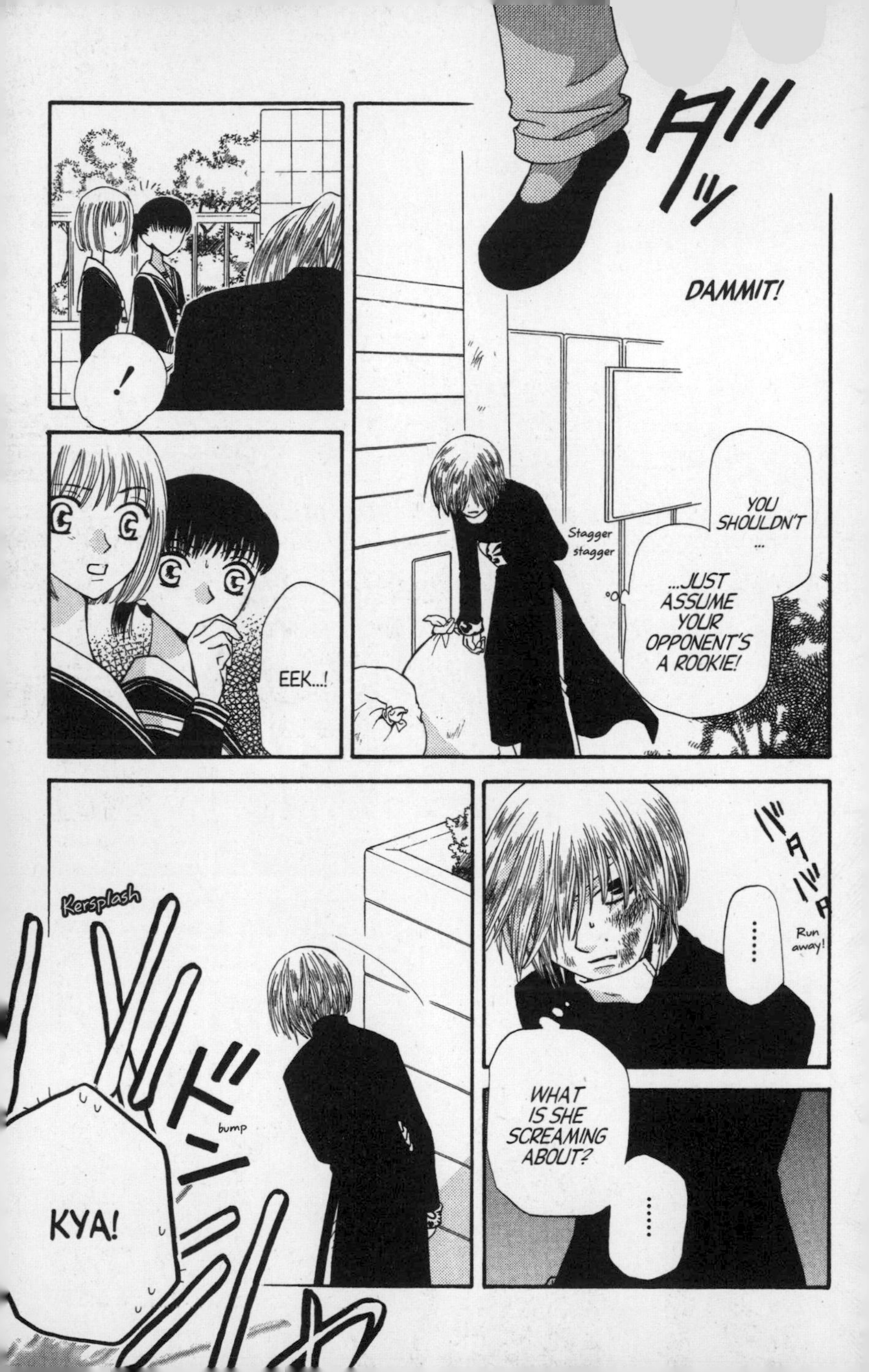
ダッ
DAMMIT!
Stagger stagger
YOU SHOULDN'T ...
...JUST ASSUME YOUR OPPONENT'S A ROOKIE!
!
EEK...!
......
Run away!
WHAT IS SHE SCREAMING ABOUT?
......
Kersplash
bump
KYA!

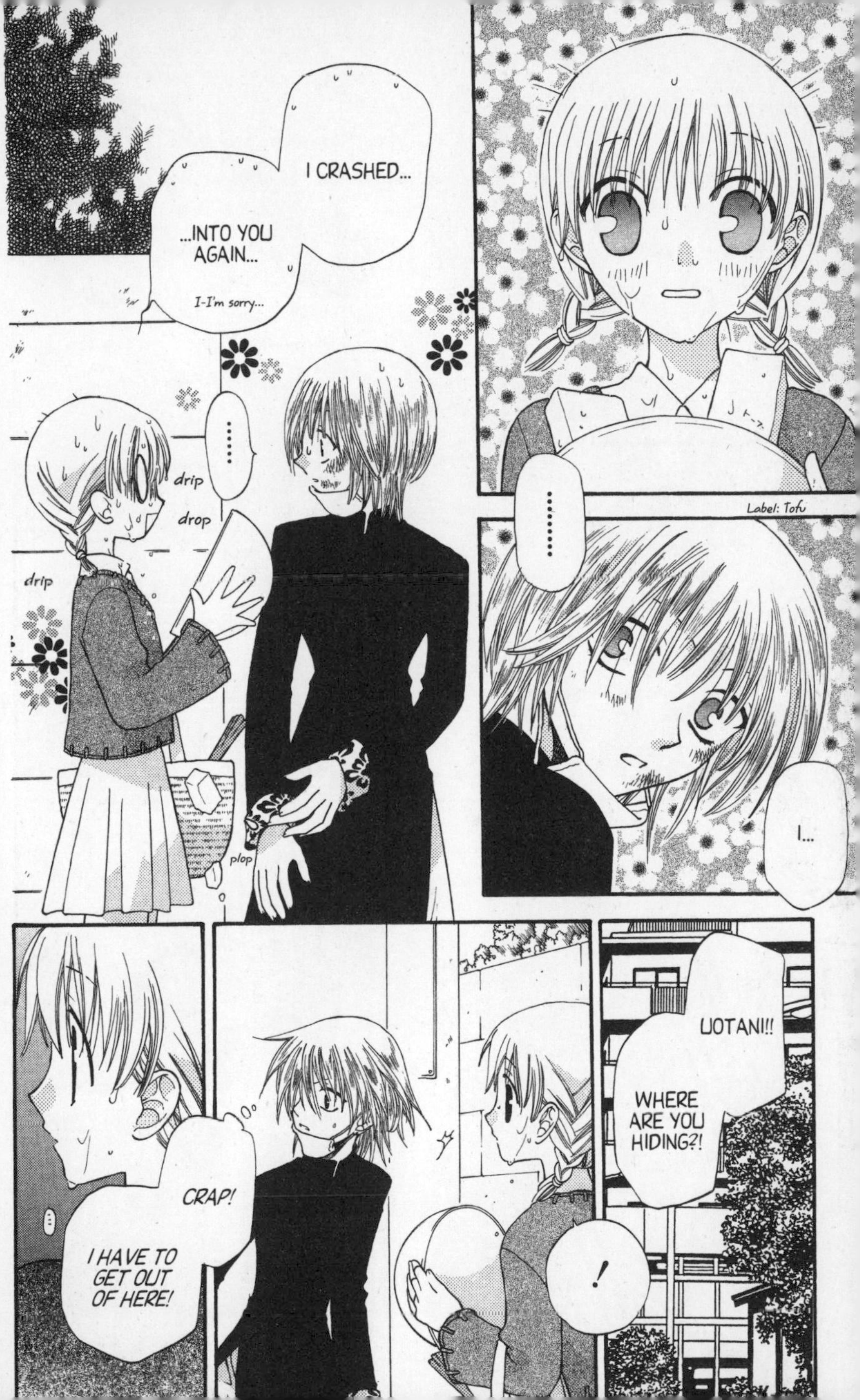
Label: Tofu
....
I...
I CRASHED...
...INTO YOU AGAIN...
I-I'm sorry...
......
drip
drop
drip
plop
UOTANI!!
WHERE ARE YOU HIDING?!
!
CRAP!
I HAVE TO GET OUT OF HERE!
...

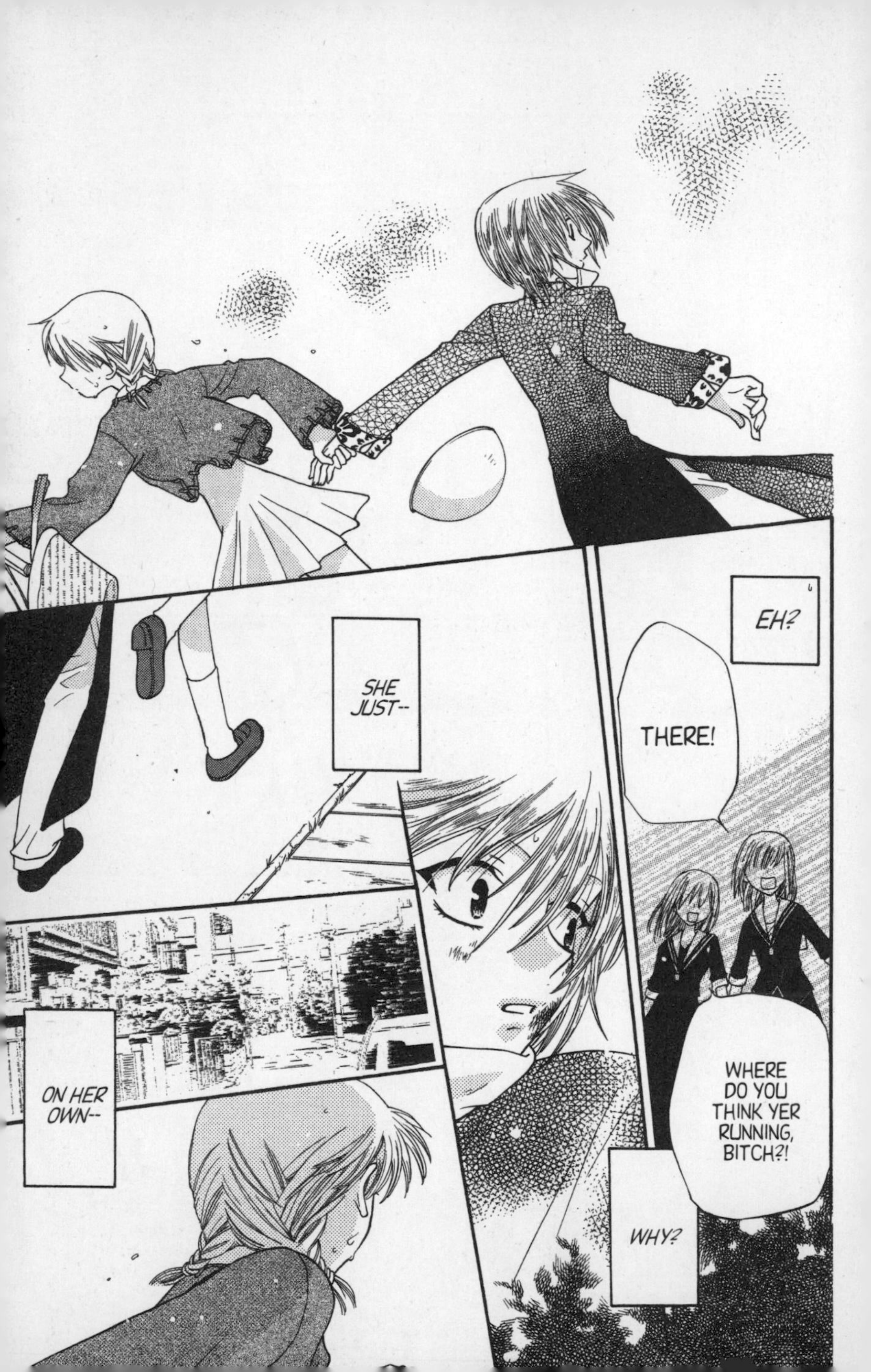

EH?
THERE!
WHERE DO YOU THINK YER RUNNING, BITCH?!
WHY?
SHE JUST--
ON HER OWN--

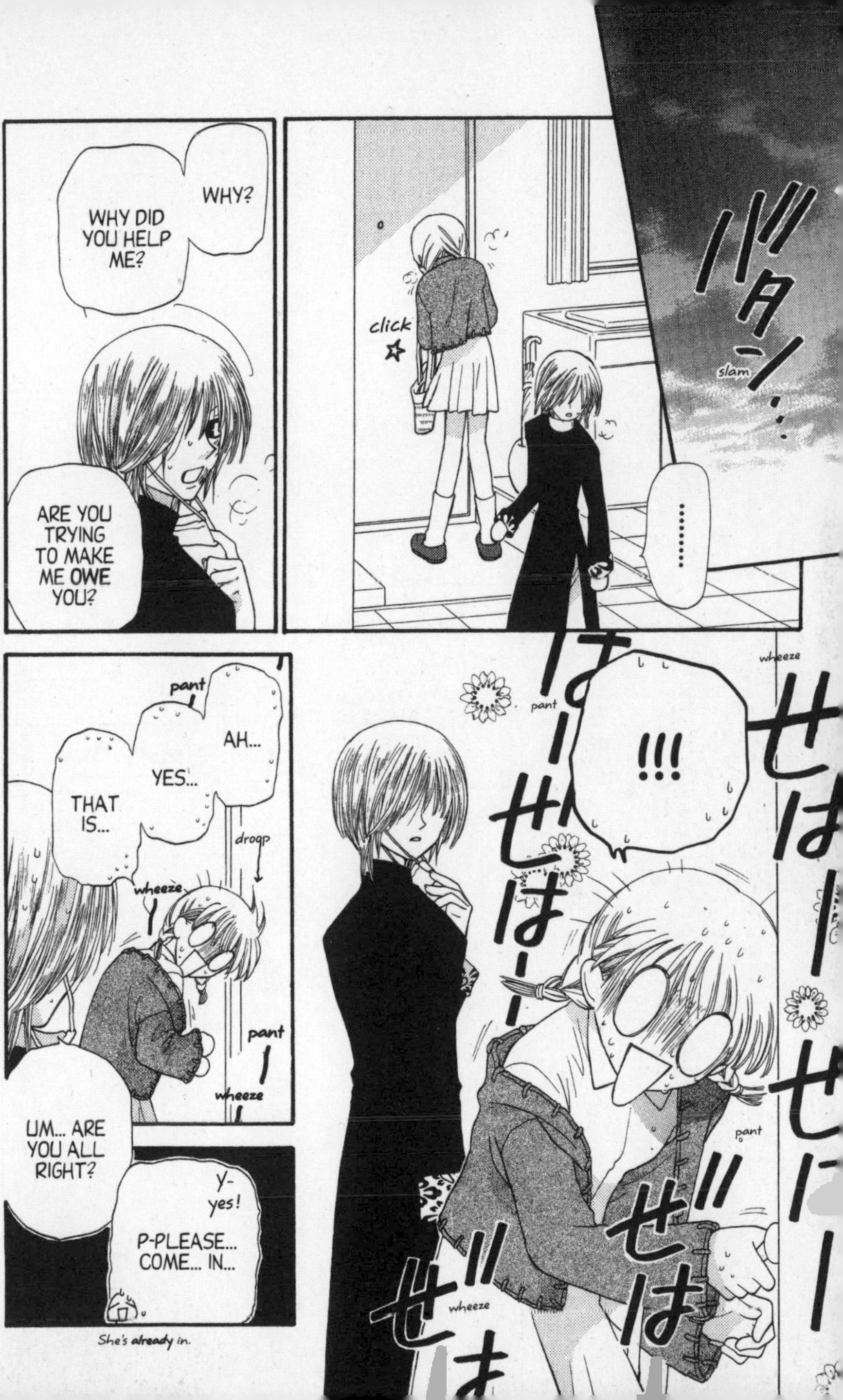
バタン…
slam
click
......
WHY?
WHY DID YOU HELP ME?
ARE YOU TRYING TO MAKE ME OWE YOU?
wheeze
pant
!!!
pant
wheeze
pant
AH...
YES...
THAT IS...
droop
wheeze
pant
wheeze
UM... ARE YOU ALL RIGHT?
Y-yes!
P-PLEASE... COME... IN...
She's already in.

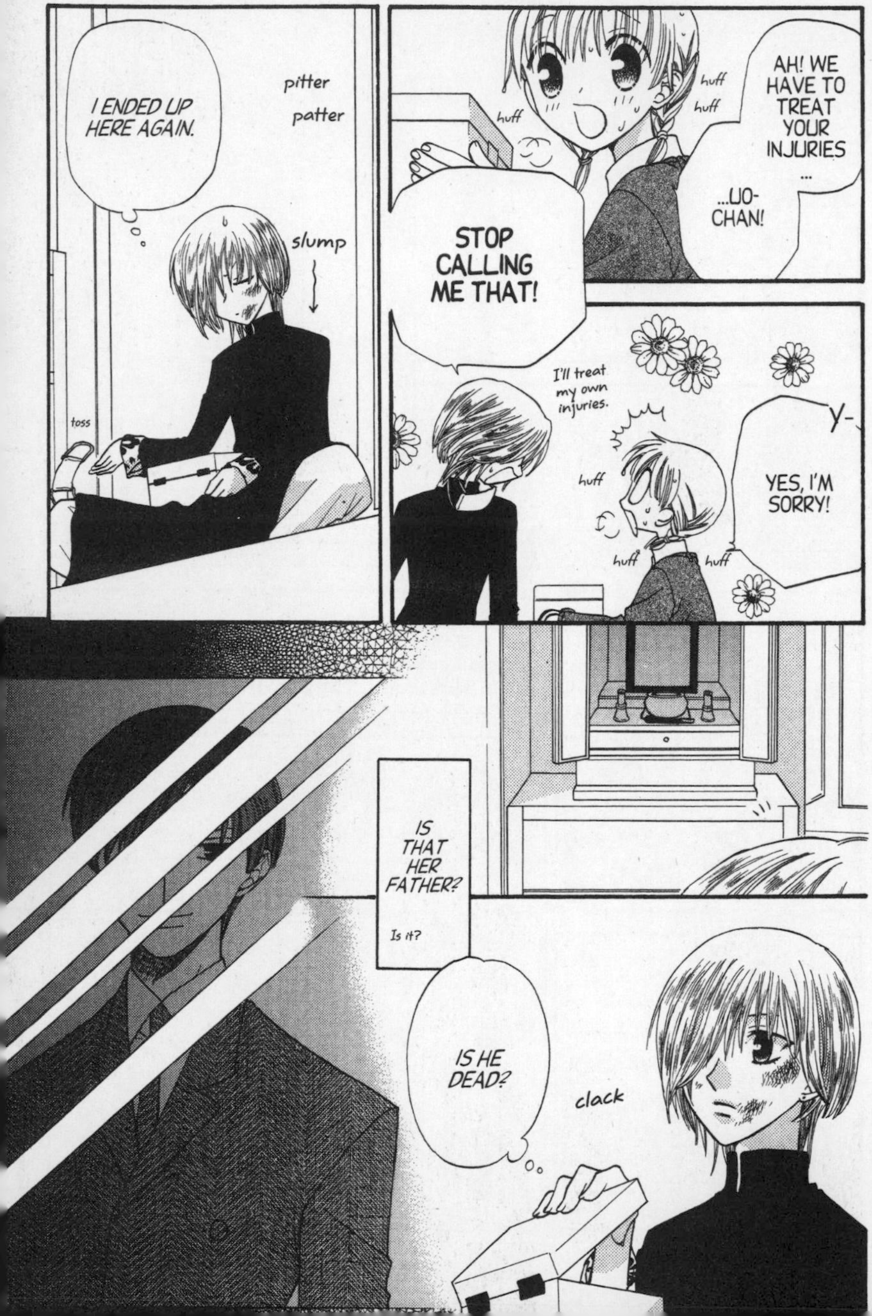
huff
huff
huff
AH! WE HAVE TO TREAT YOUR INJURIES ...
...UO-CHAN!
STOP CALLING ME THAT!
I'll treat my own injuries.
Y-
YES, I'M SORRY!
huff
huff
huff
I ENDED UP HERE AGAIN.
pitter
patter
slump
toss
IS THAT HER FATHER?
Is it?
IS HE DEAD?
clack

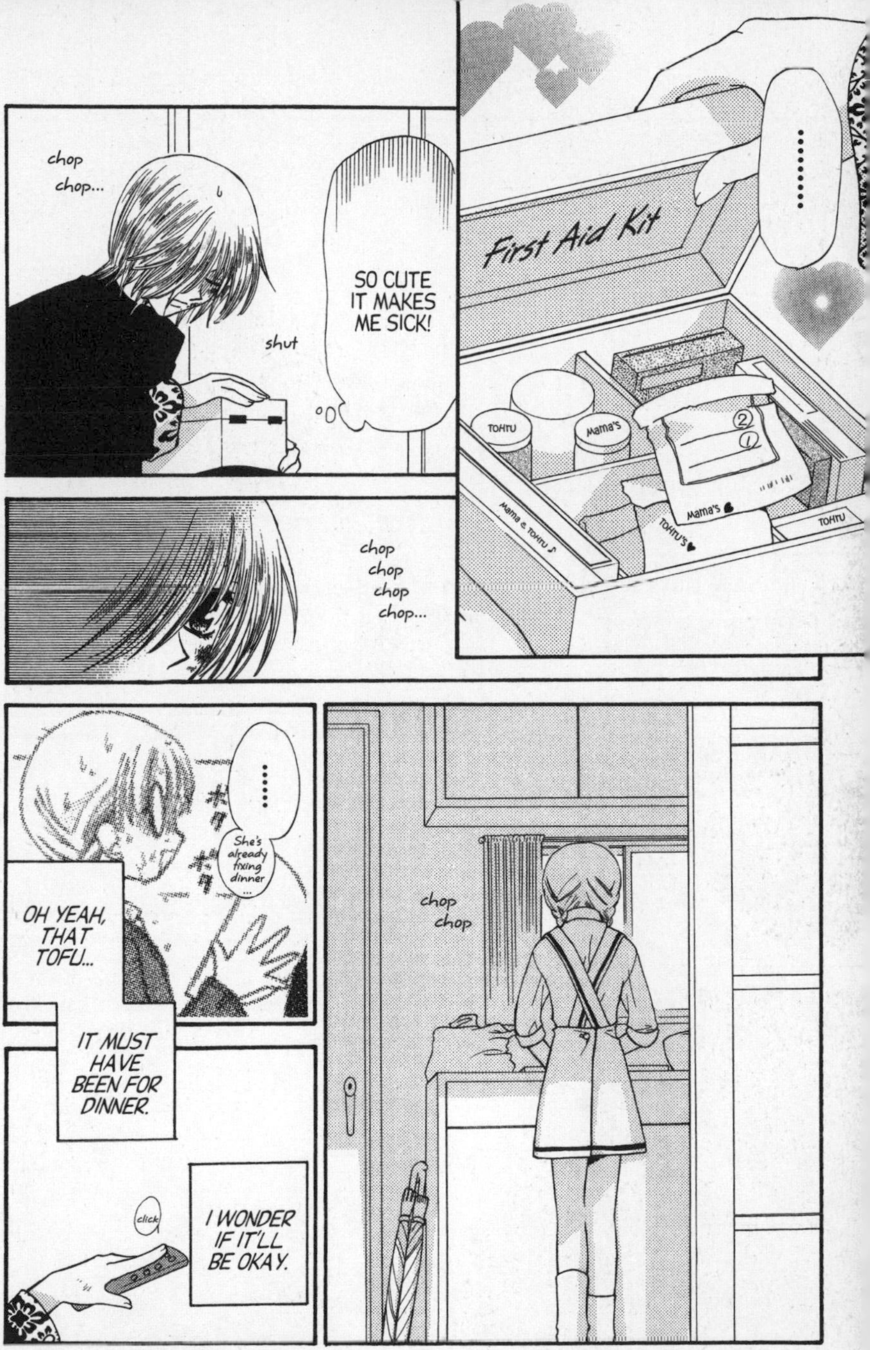
......
First Aid Kit
TOHTU
Mama's
Mama's
TOHTU'S
TOHTU
Mama & TOHTU
SO CUTE IT MAKES ME SICK!
shut
chop chop...
chop chop chop chop...
chop chop
......
She's already fixing dinner ...
OH YEAH, THAT TOFU...
IT MUST HAVE BEEN FOR DINNER.
I WONDER IF IT'LL BE OKAY.
click

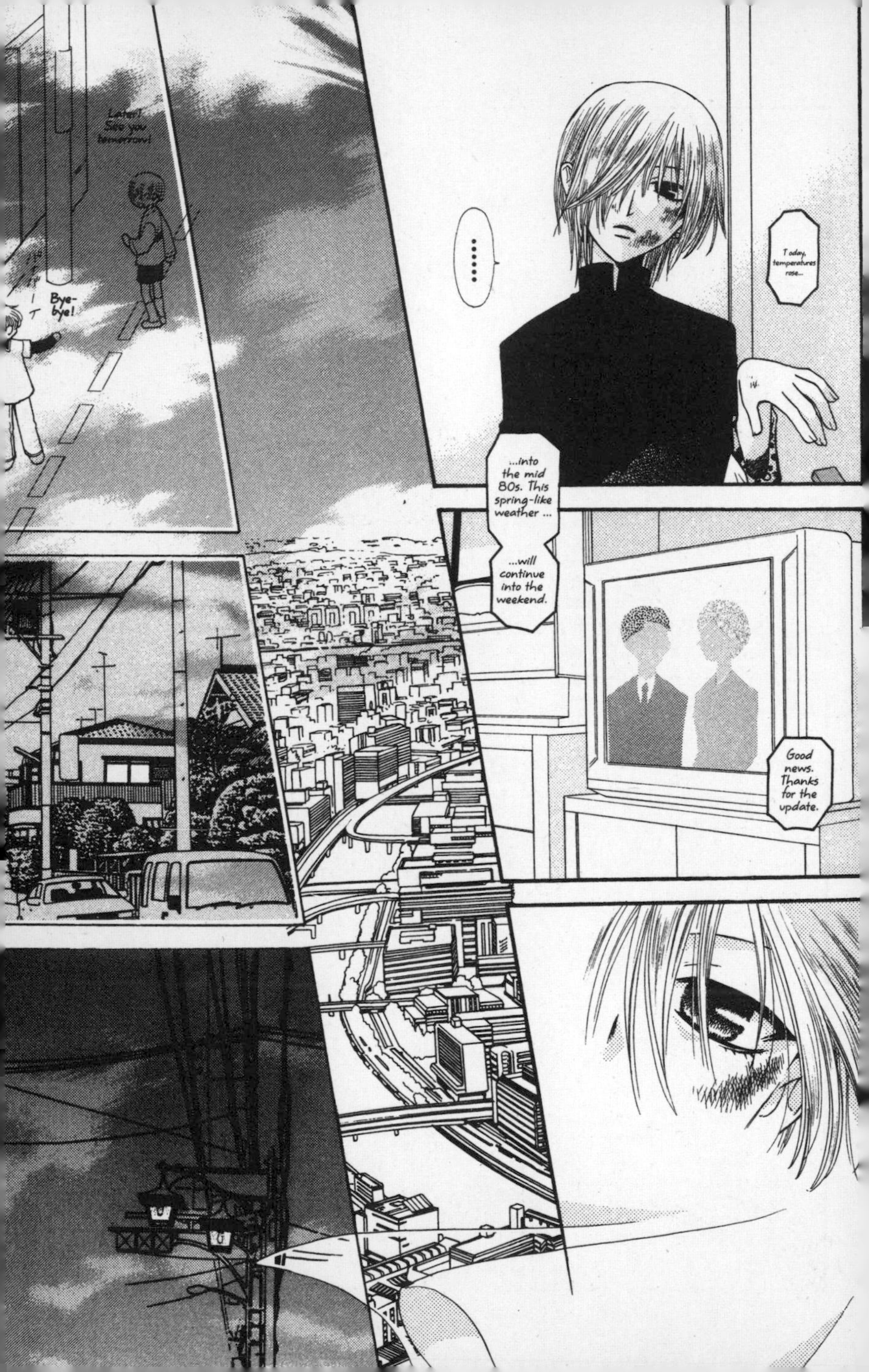
Today, temperatures rose...
......
...into the mid 80s. This spring-like weather ...
...will continue into the weekend.
Later! See you tomorrow!
Bye-bye!
Good news. Thanks for the update.

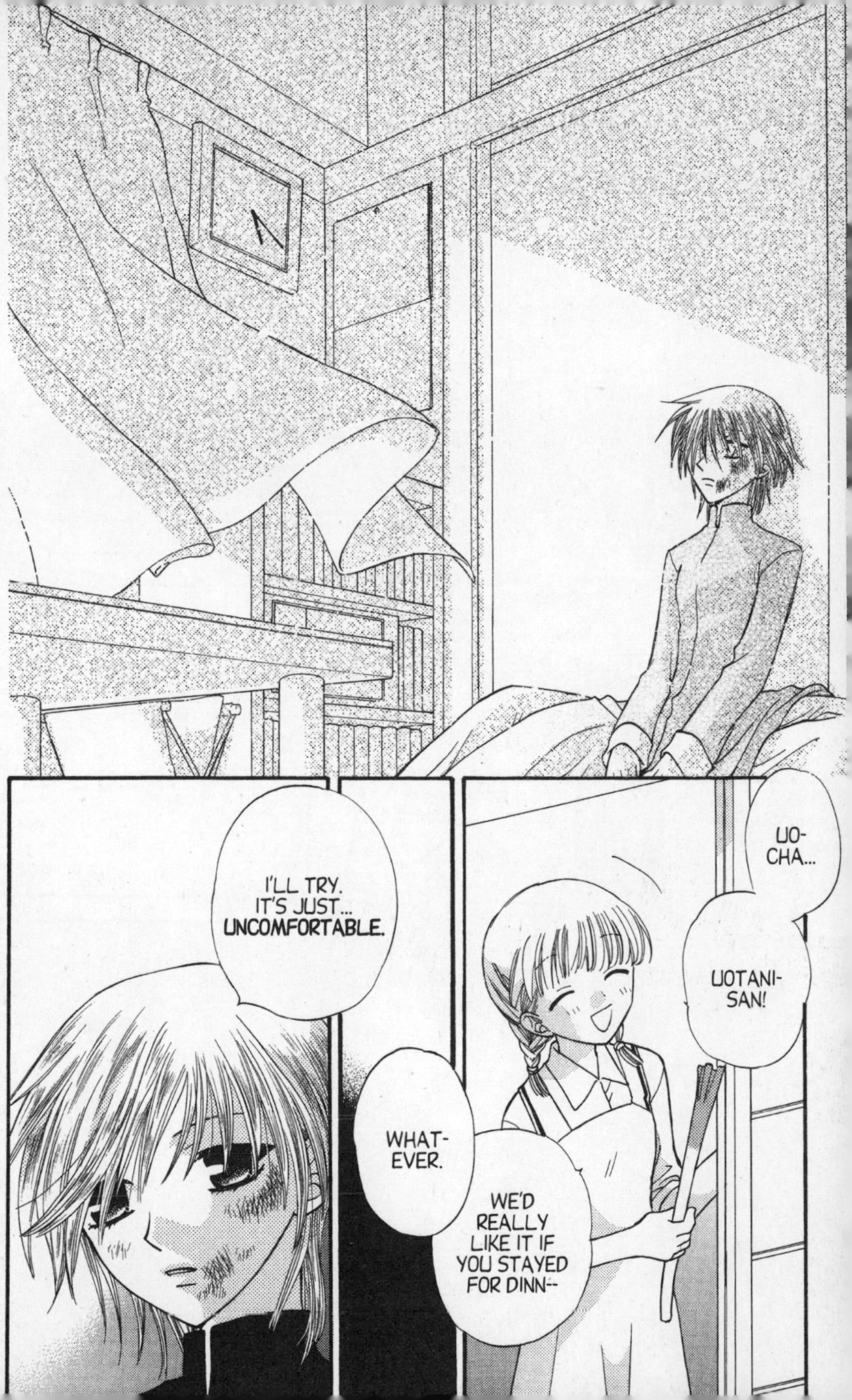
UO-CHA...
UOTANI-SAN!
WE'D REALLY LIKE IT IF YOU STAYED FOR DINN--
WHAT-EVER.
I'LL TRY. IT'S JUST... UNCOMFORTABLE.

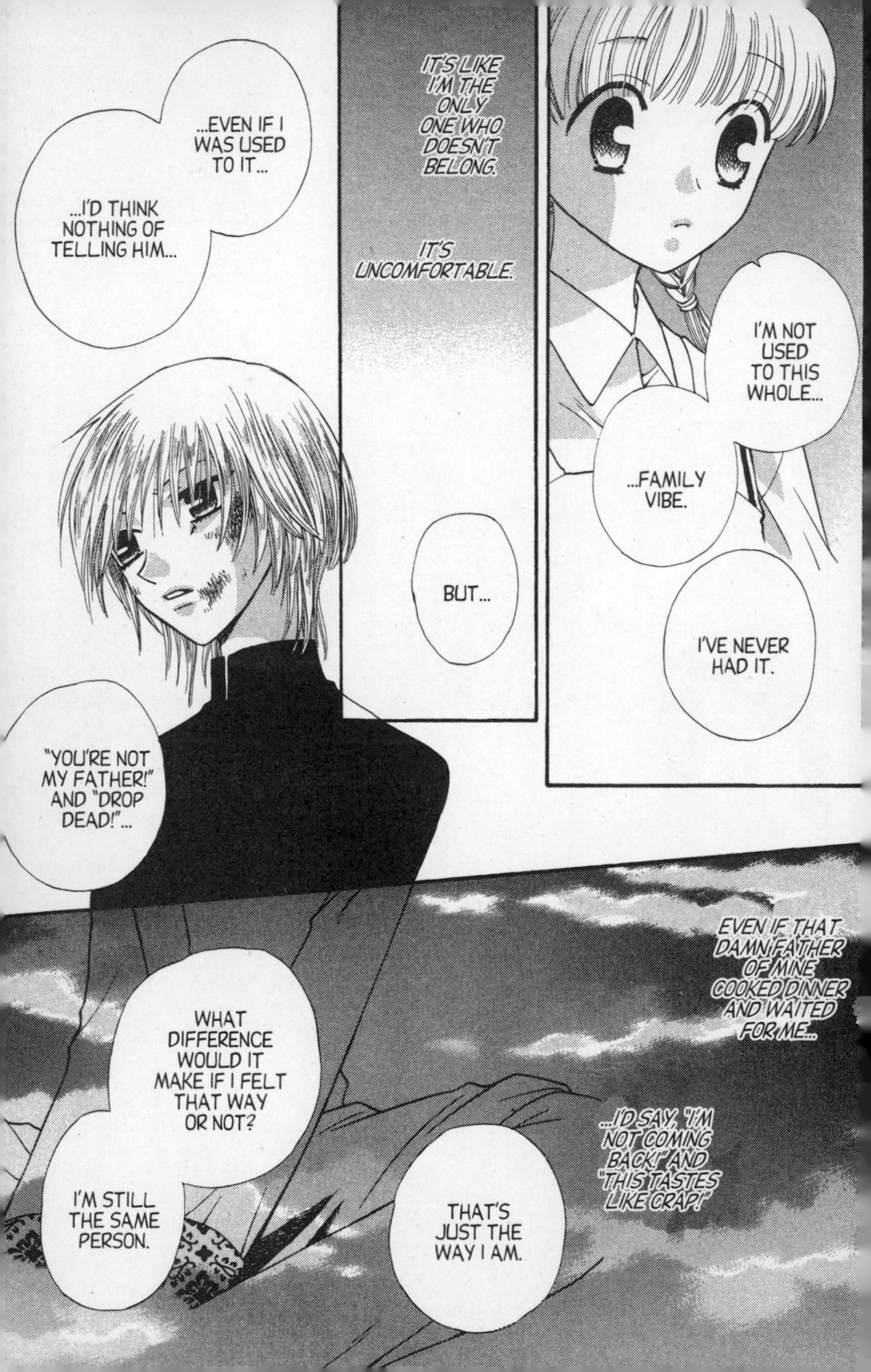
I'M NOT USED TO THIS WHOLE...
...FAMILY VIBE.
I'VE NEVER HAD IT.
IT'S LIKE I'M THE ONLY ONE WHO DOESN'T BELONG.
IT'S UNCOMFORTABLE.
BUT...
...EVEN IF I WAS USED TO IT...
...I'D THINK NOTHING OF TELLING HIM...
"YOU'RE NOT MY FATHER!" AND "DROP DEAD!"...
EVEN IF THAT DAMN FATHER OF MINE COOKED DINNER AND WAITED FOR ME...
...I'D SAY, "I'M NOT COMING BACK!" AND "THIS TASTES LIKE CRAP!"
THAT'S JUST THE WAY I AM.
WHAT DIFFERENCE WOULD IT MAKE IF I FELT THAT WAY OR NOT?
I'M STILL THE SAME PERSON.

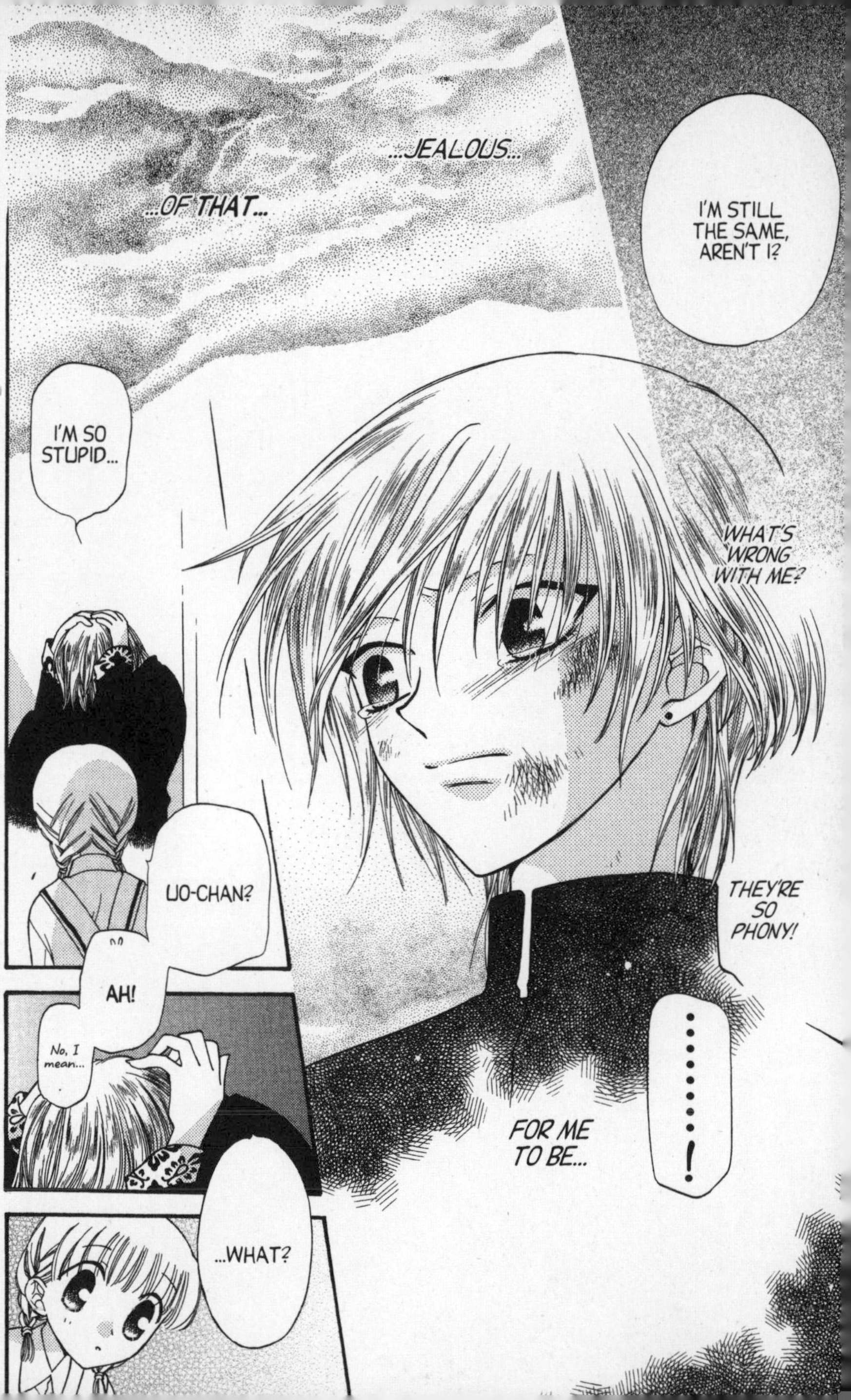
I'M STILL THE SAME, AREN'T I?
...JEALOUS...
...OF THAT...
WHAT'S WRONG WITH ME?
THEY'RE SO PHONY!
......!
FOR ME TO BE...
I'M SO STUPID...
UO-CHAN?
AH!
No, I mean...
...WHAT?

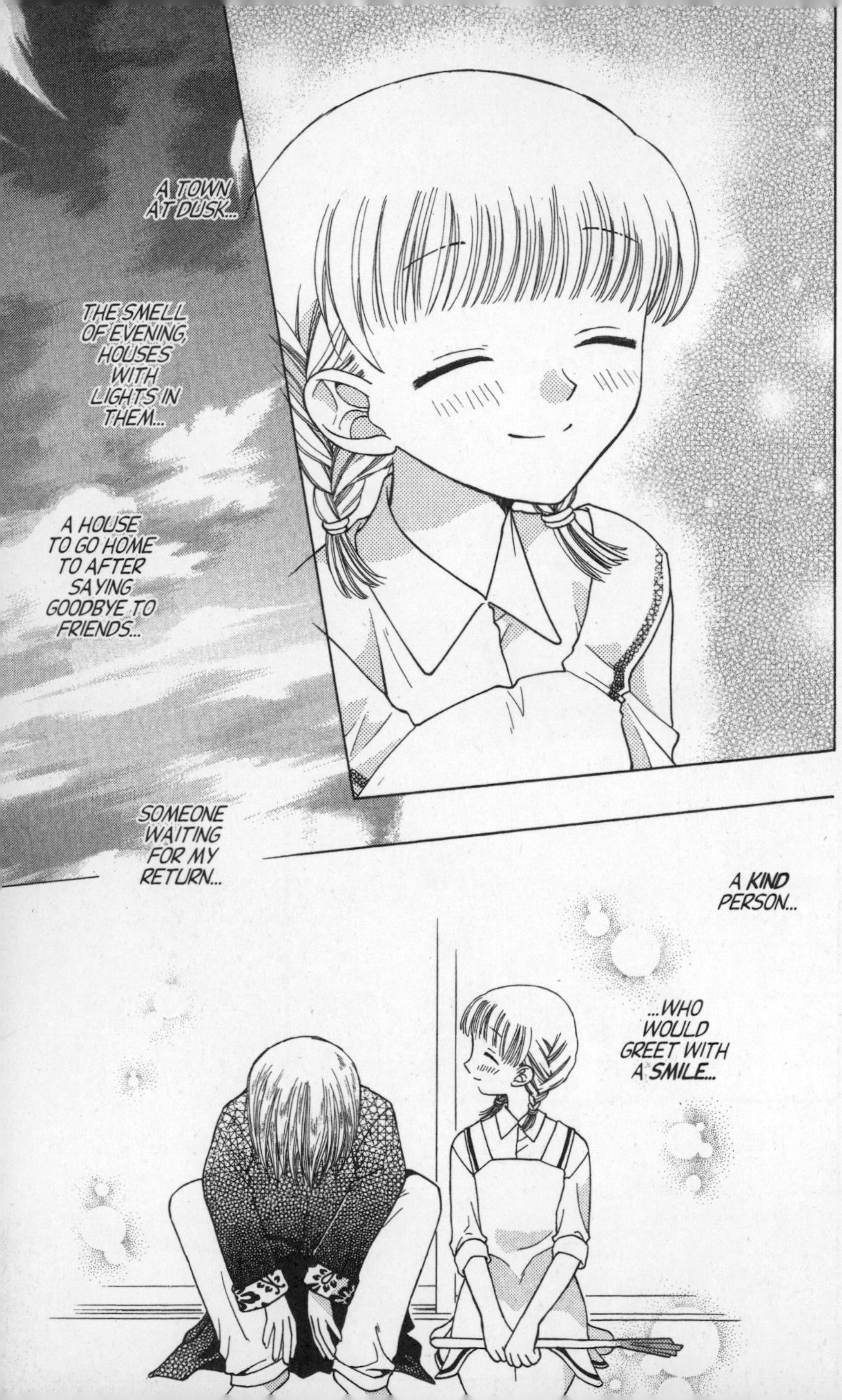
A TOWN AT DUSK...
THE SMELL OF EVENING, HOUSES WITH LIGHTS IN THEM...
A HOUSE TO GO HOME TO AFTER SAYING GOODBYE TO FRIENDS...
SOMEONE WAITING FOR MY RETURN...
A KIND PERSON...
...WHO WOULD GREET WITH A SMILE...

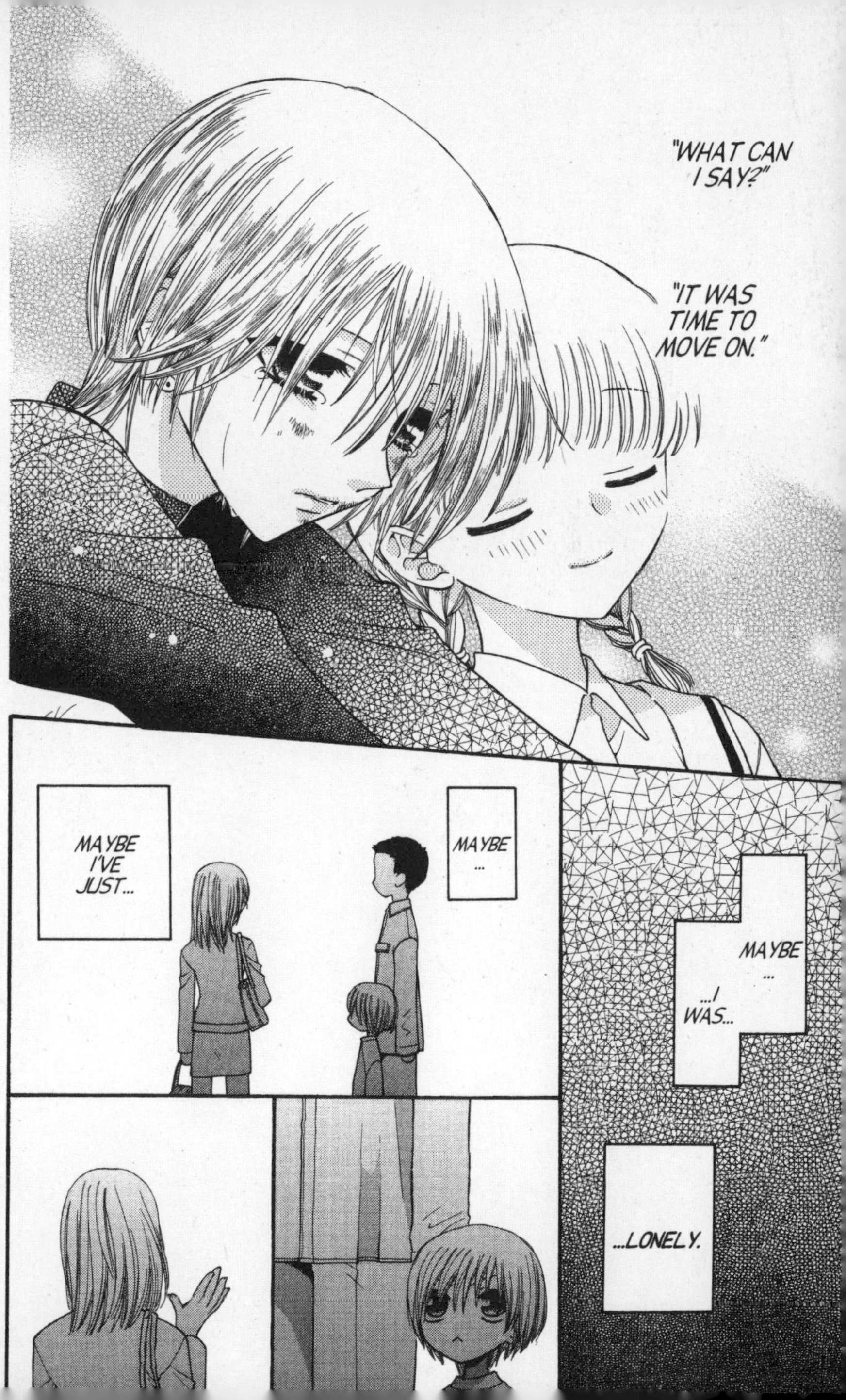
"WHAT CAN I SAY?"
"IT WAS TIME TO MOVE ON."
MAYBE ...
...I WAS...
...LONELY.
MAYBE ...
MAYBE I'VE JUST...

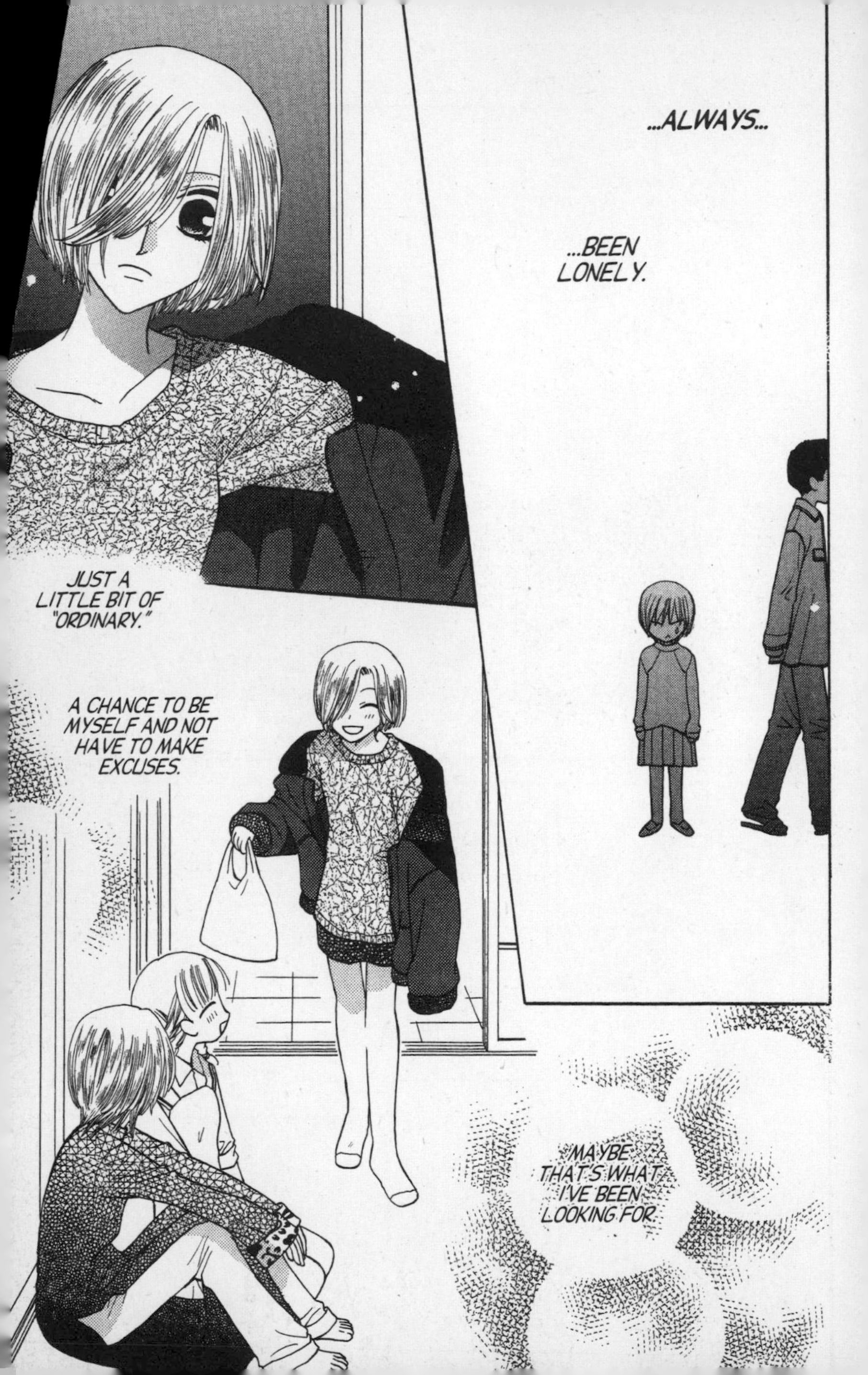
...ALWAYS...
...BEEN LONELY.
JUST A LITTLE BIT OF "ORDINARY."
A CHANCE TO BE MYSELF AND NOT HAVE TO MAKE EXCUSES.
MAYBE THAT'S WHAT I'VE BEEN LOOKING FOR.

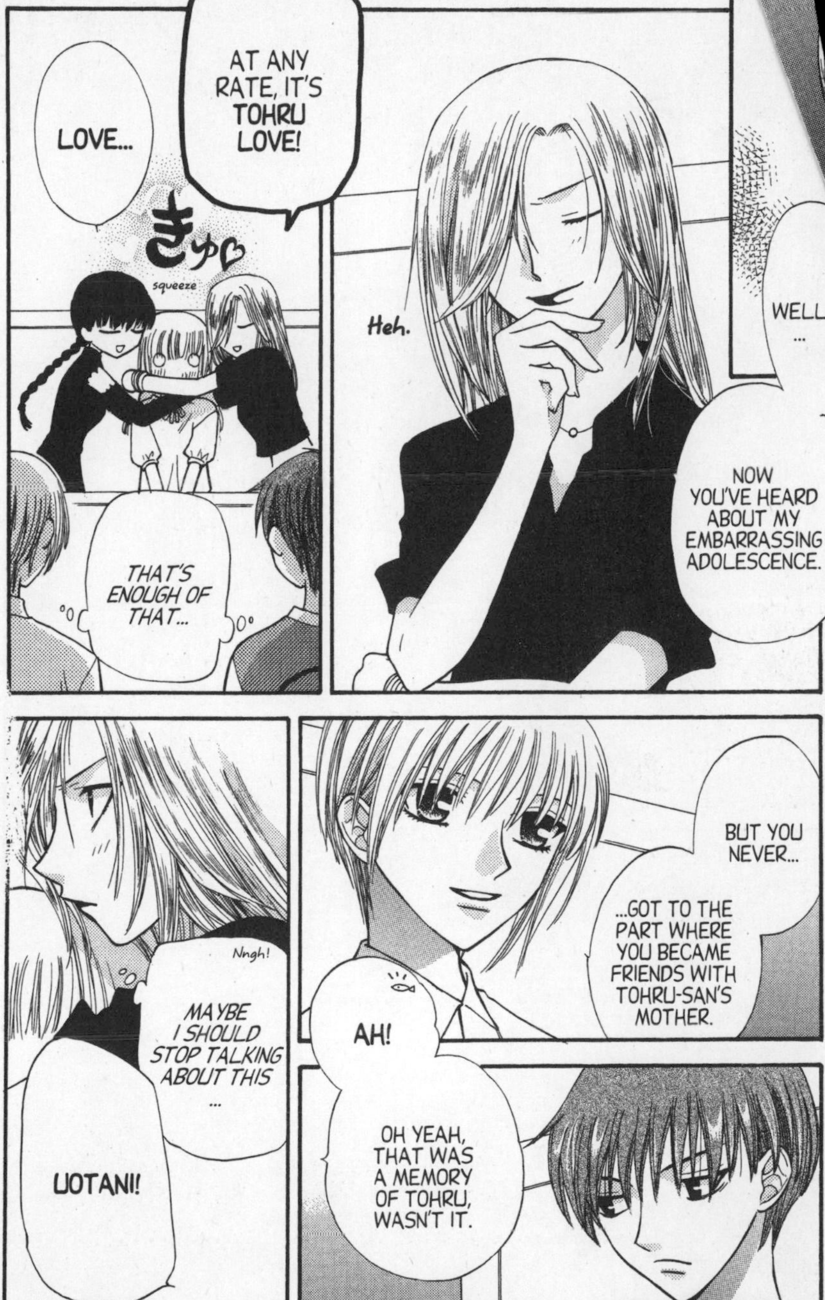
WELL ...
Heh.
NOW YOU'VE HEARD ABOUT MY EMBARRASSING ADOLESCENCE.
AT ANY RATE, IT'S TOHRU LOVE!
LOVE...
きゅ♡
squeeze
THAT'S ENOUGH OF THAT...
BUT YOU NEVER...
...GOT TO THE PART WHERE YOU BECAME FRIENDS WITH TOHRU-SAN'S MOTHER.
AH!
OH YEAH, THAT WAS A MEMORY OF TOHRU, WASN'T IT.
Nngh!
MAYBE I SHOULD STOP TALKING ABOUT THIS ...
UOTANI!

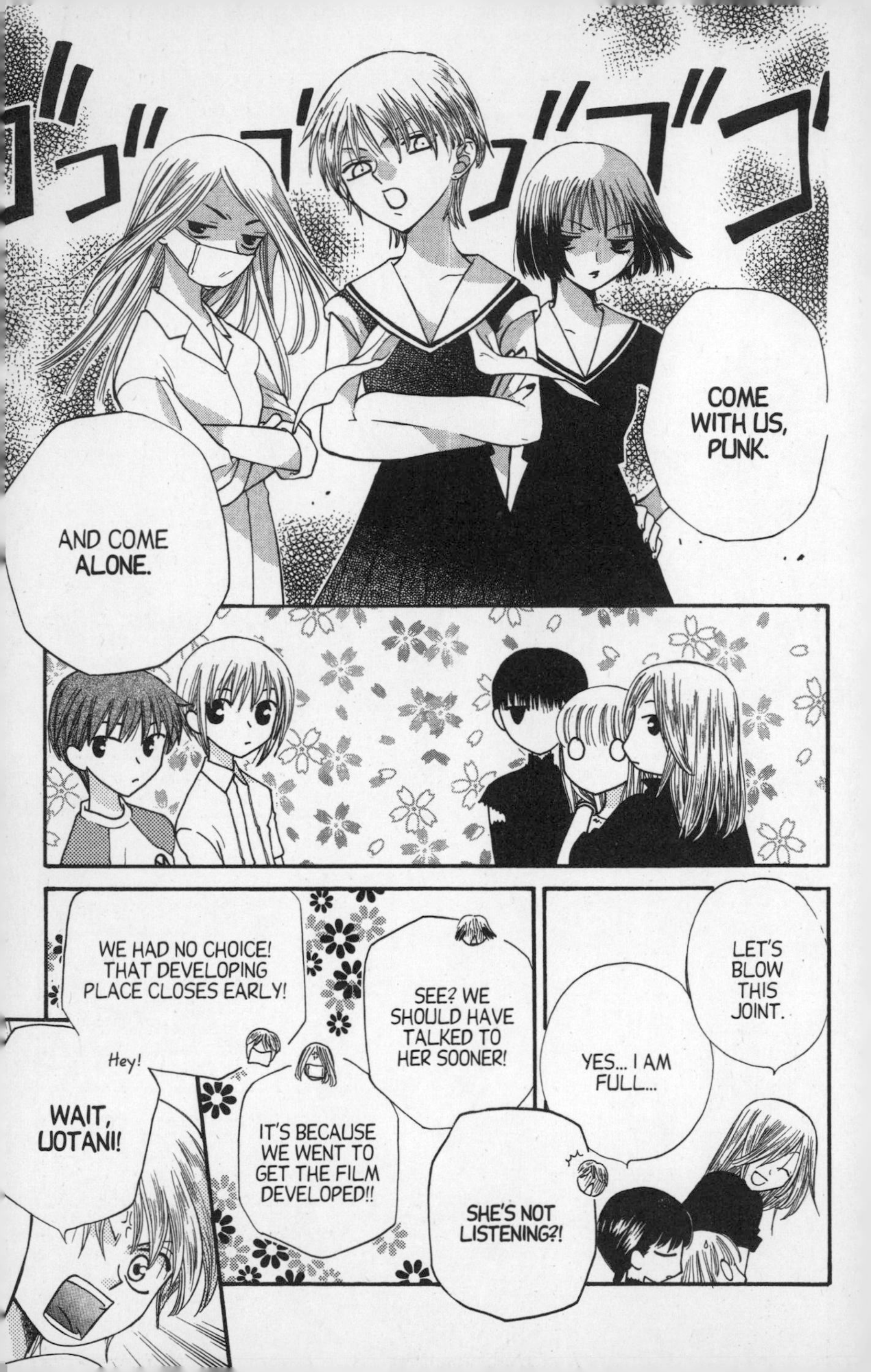
COME WITH US, PUNK.
AND COME ALONE.
LET'S BLOW THIS JOINT.
YES... I AM FULL...
SHE'S NOT LISTENING?!
SEE? WE SHOULD HAVE TALKED TO HER SOONER!
WE HAD NO CHOICE! THAT DEVELOPING PLACE CLOSES EARLY!
IT'S BECAUSE WE WENT TO GET THE FILM DEVELOPED!!
Hey!
WAIT, UOTANI!

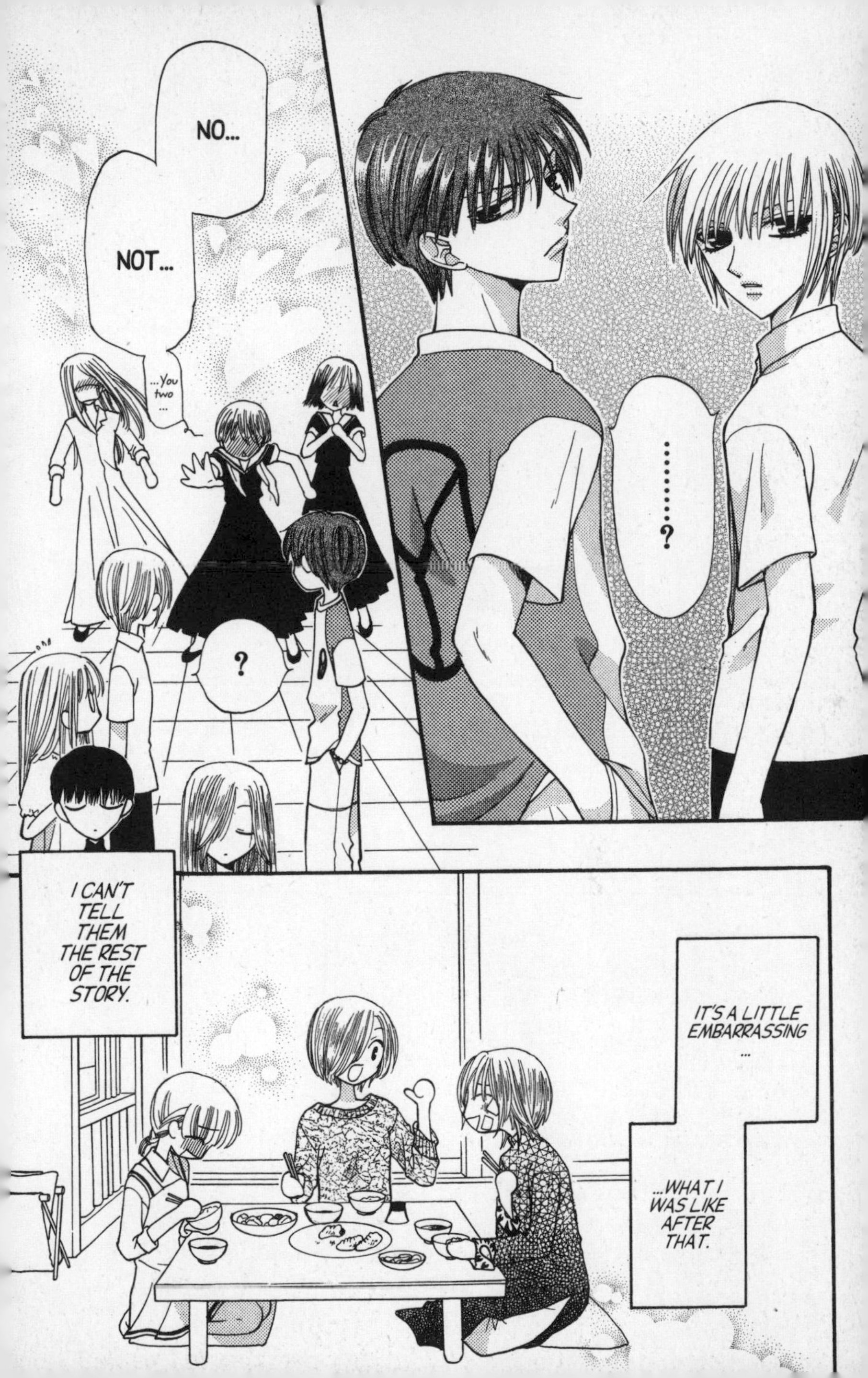

......?
NO...
NOT...
...You two ...
?
IT'S A LITTLE EMBARRASSING ...
...WHAT I WAS LIKE AFTER THAT.
I CAN'T TELL THEM THE REST OF THE STORY.

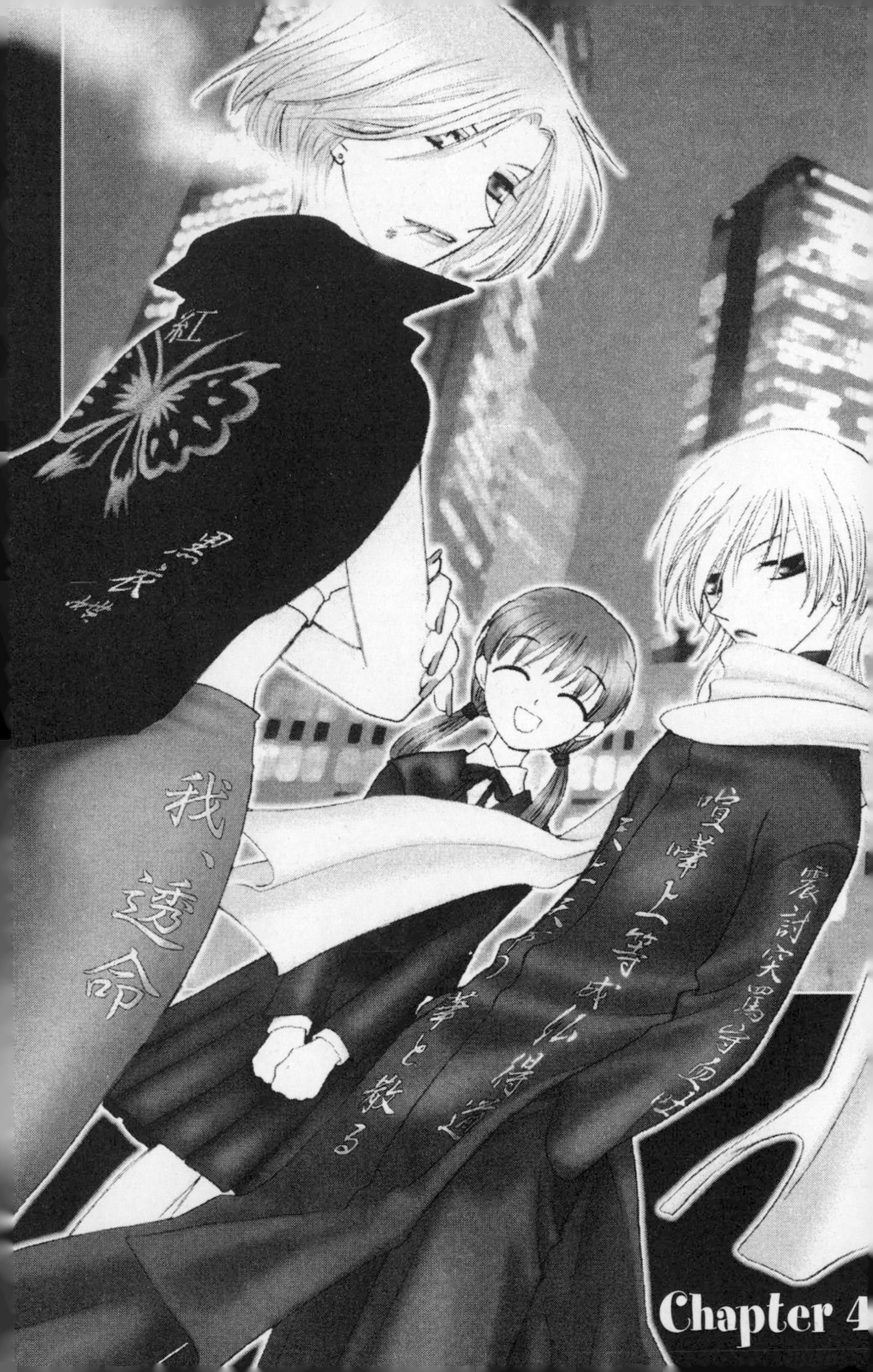
紅
喧嘩上等
Chapter 4

I feel so grateful!

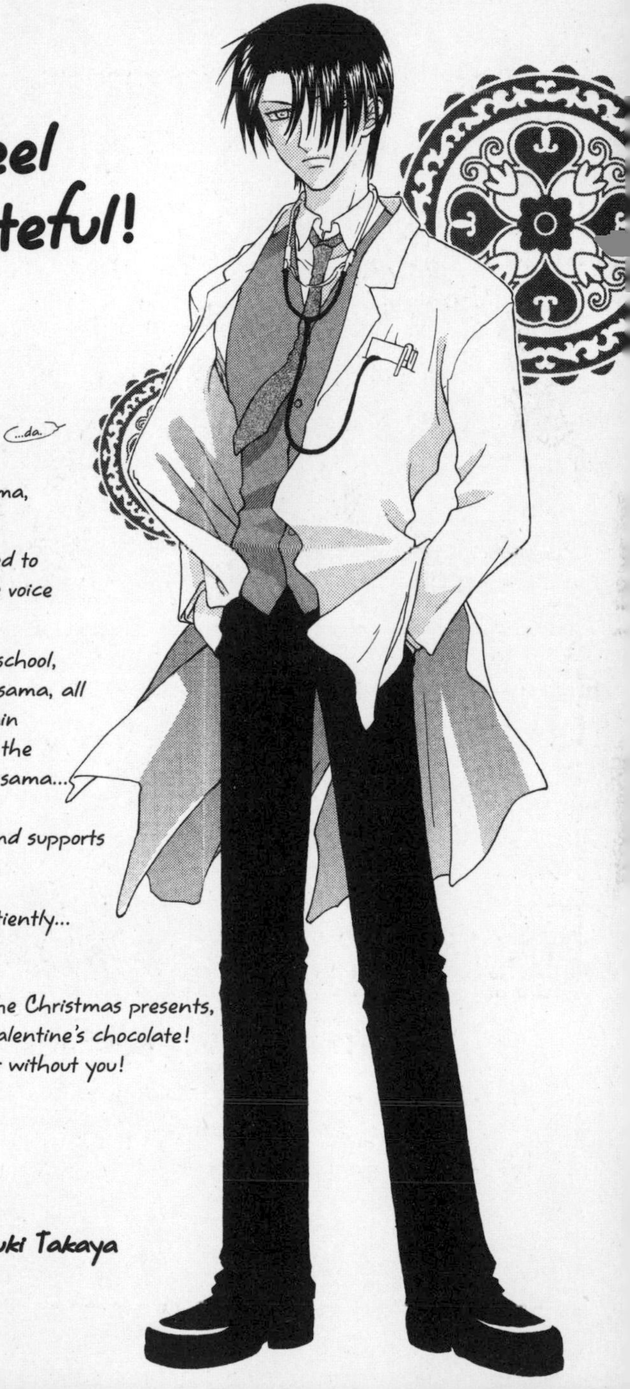
...da.

Harada-sama, Araki-sama, Mom, Dad...

All the people who worked to create the anime, all the voice actors...

From a certain medical school, T-sensei-sama, I-sensei-sama, all the nurses...From a certain hospital, K-sensei-sama, the accupuncturist, K-sensei-sama...

To everyone who reads and supports this manga...

Everyone who waited patiently...

And...

Thank you so much for the Christmas presents, birthday presents and Valentine's chocolate! I couldn't have got better without you!

Next is Haru.

—Natsuki Takaya

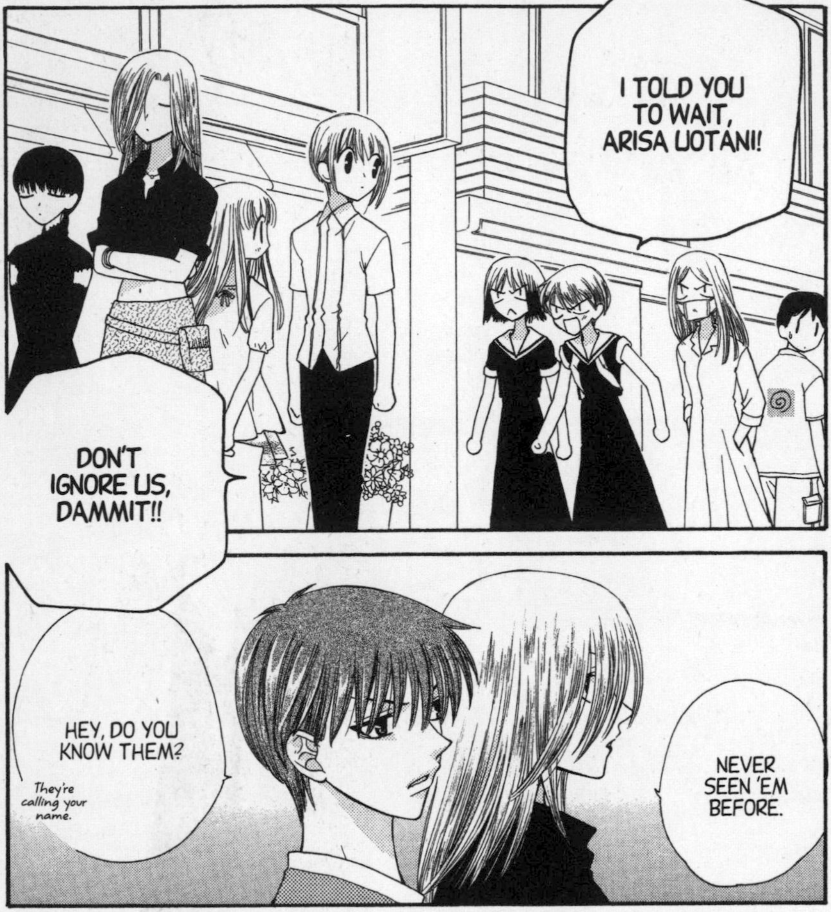
I TOLD YOU TO WAIT, ARISA UOTANI!
DON'T IGNORE US, DAMMIT!!
HEY, DO YOU KNOW THEM?
They're calling your name.
NEVER SEEN 'EM BEFORE.

ULTRA-SPECIAL BLAH, BLAH, BLAH 5

Has anyone noticed what's written on Uo-chan's sleeve on the title page to this chapter? It says "Fruits Basket" in phonetic kanji. I was playing around. I'm sorry (laugh).

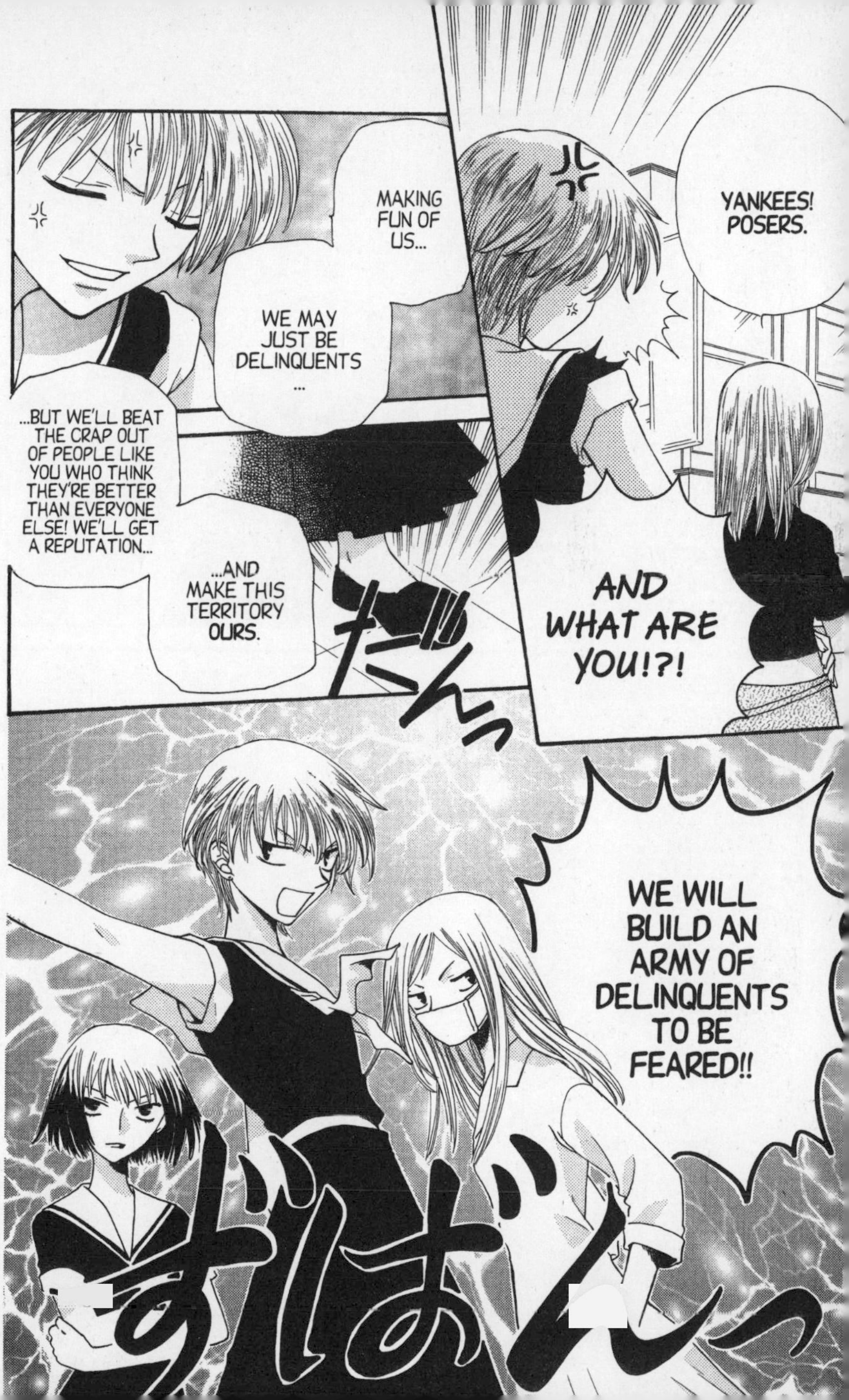
YANKEES! POSERS.
AND WHAT ARE YOU!?!
MAKING FUN OF US...
WE MAY JUST BE DELINQUENTS ...
...BUT WE'LL BEAT THE CRAP OUT OF PEOPLE LIKE YOU WHO THINK THEY'RE BETTER THAN EVERYONE ELSE! WE'LL GET A REPUTATION...
...AND MAKE THIS TERRITORY OURS.
だんっ
WE WILL BUILD AN ARMY OF DELINQUENTS TO BE FEARED!!

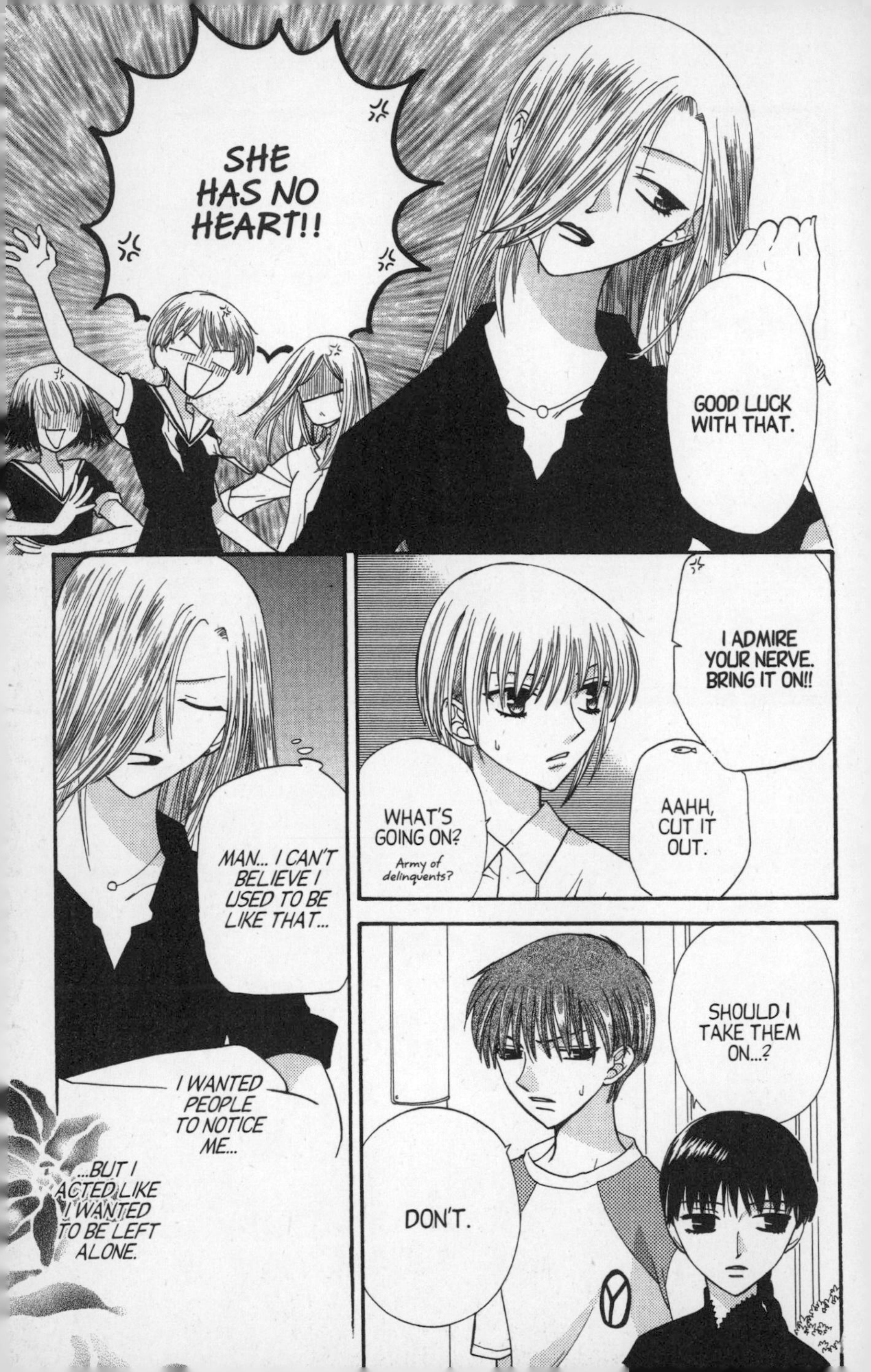
GOOD LUCK WITH THAT.
SHE HAS NO HEART!!
I ADMIRE YOUR NERVE. BRING IT ON!!
AAHH, CUT IT OUT.
WHAT'S GOING ON?
Army of delinquents?
SHOULD I TAKE THEM ON...?
DON'T.
MAN... I CAN'T BELIEVE I USED TO BE LIKE THAT...
I WANTED PEOPLE TO NOTICE ME...
...BUT I ACTED LIKE I WANTED TO BE LEFT ALONE.

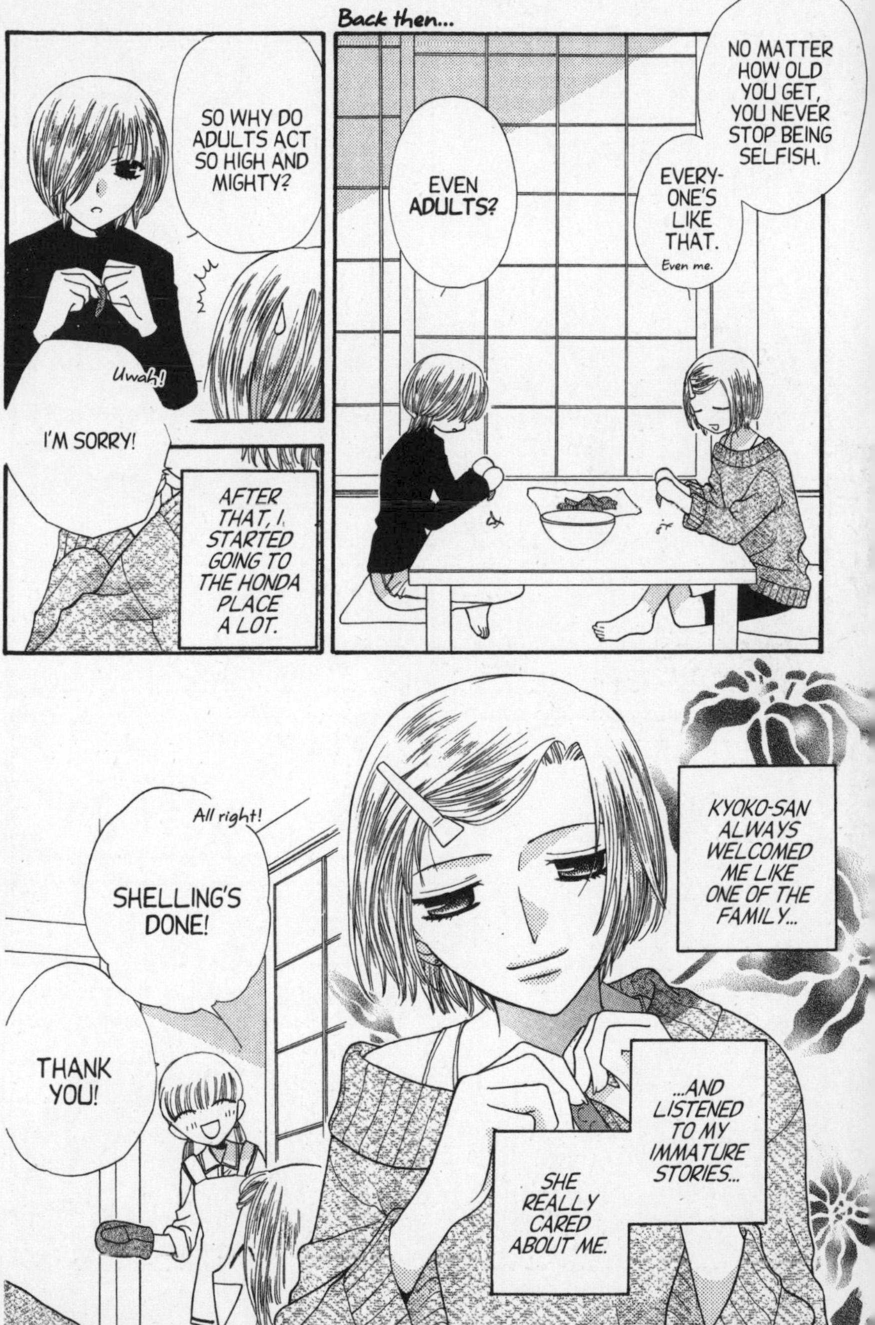
Back then...
NO MATTER HOW OLD YOU GET, YOU NEVER STOP BEING SELFISH.
EVEN ADULTS?
EVERY-ONE'S LIKE THAT.
Even me.
SO WHY DO ADULTS ACT SO HIGH AND MIGHTY?
Uwah!
I'M SORRY!
AFTER THAT, I STARTED GOING TO THE HONDA PLACE A LOT.
KYOKO-SAN ALWAYS WELCOMED ME LIKE ONE OF THE FAMILY...
...AND LISTENED TO MY IMMATURE STORIES...
SHE REALLY CARED ABOUT ME.
All right!
SHELLING'S DONE!
THANK YOU!

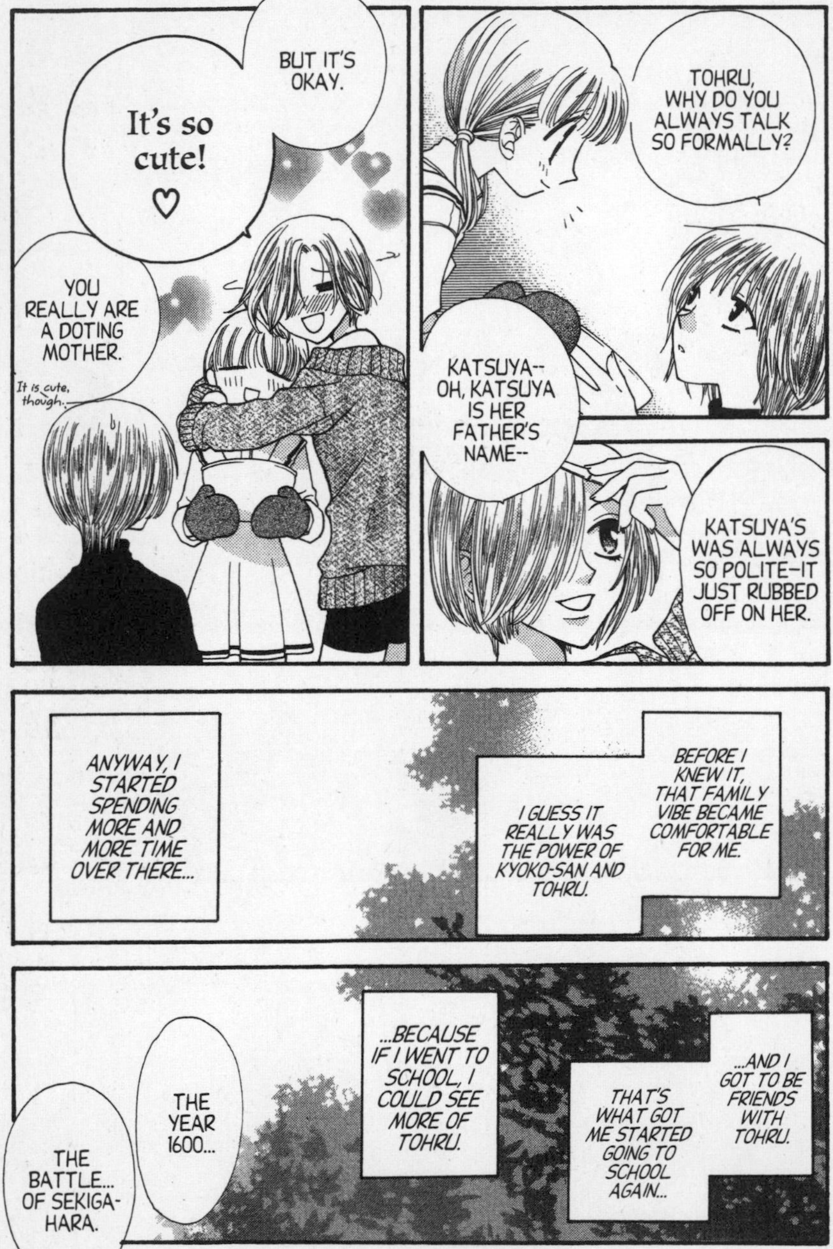
TOHRU, WHY DO YOU ALWAYS TALK SO FORMALLY?
KATSUYA-- OH, KATSUYA IS HER FATHER'S NAME--
KATSUYA'S WAS ALWAYS SO POLITE—IT JUST RUBBED OFF ON HER.
BUT IT'S OKAY.
It's so cute! ♡
YOU REALLY ARE A DOTING MOTHER.
It is cute, though.
BEFORE I KNEW IT, THAT FAMILY VIBE BECAME COMFORTABLE FOR ME.
I GUESS IT REALLY WAS THE POWER OF KYOKO-SAN AND TOHRU.
ANYWAY, I STARTED SPENDING MORE AND MORE TIME OVER THERE...
...AND I GOT TO BE FRIENDS WITH TOHRU.
THAT'S WHAT GOT ME STARTED GOING TO SCHOOL AGAIN...
...BECAUSE IF I WENT TO SCHOOL, I COULD SEE MORE OF TOHRU.
THE YEAR 1600...
THE BATTLE... OF SEKIGA-HARA.

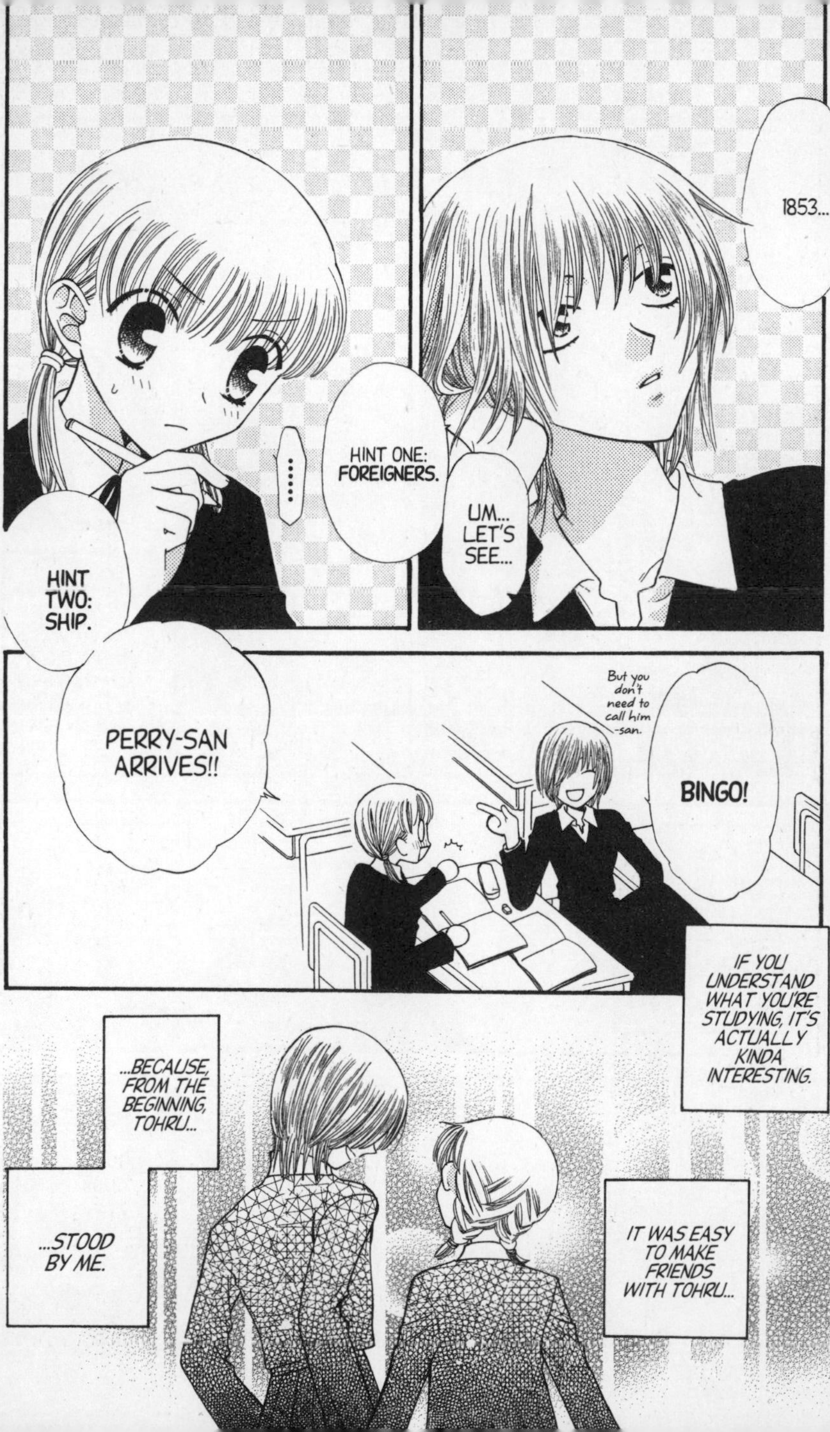
1853...
UM... LET'S SEE...
HINT ONE: FOREIGNERS.
......
HINT TWO: SHIP.
PERRY-SAN ARRIVES!!
BINGO!
But you don't need to call him -san.
IF YOU UNDERSTAND WHAT YOU'RE STUDYING, IT'S ACTUALLY KINDA INTERESTING.
IT WAS EASY TO MAKE FRIENDS WITH TOHRU...
...BECAUSE, FROM THE BEGINNING, TOHRU...
...STOOD BY ME.

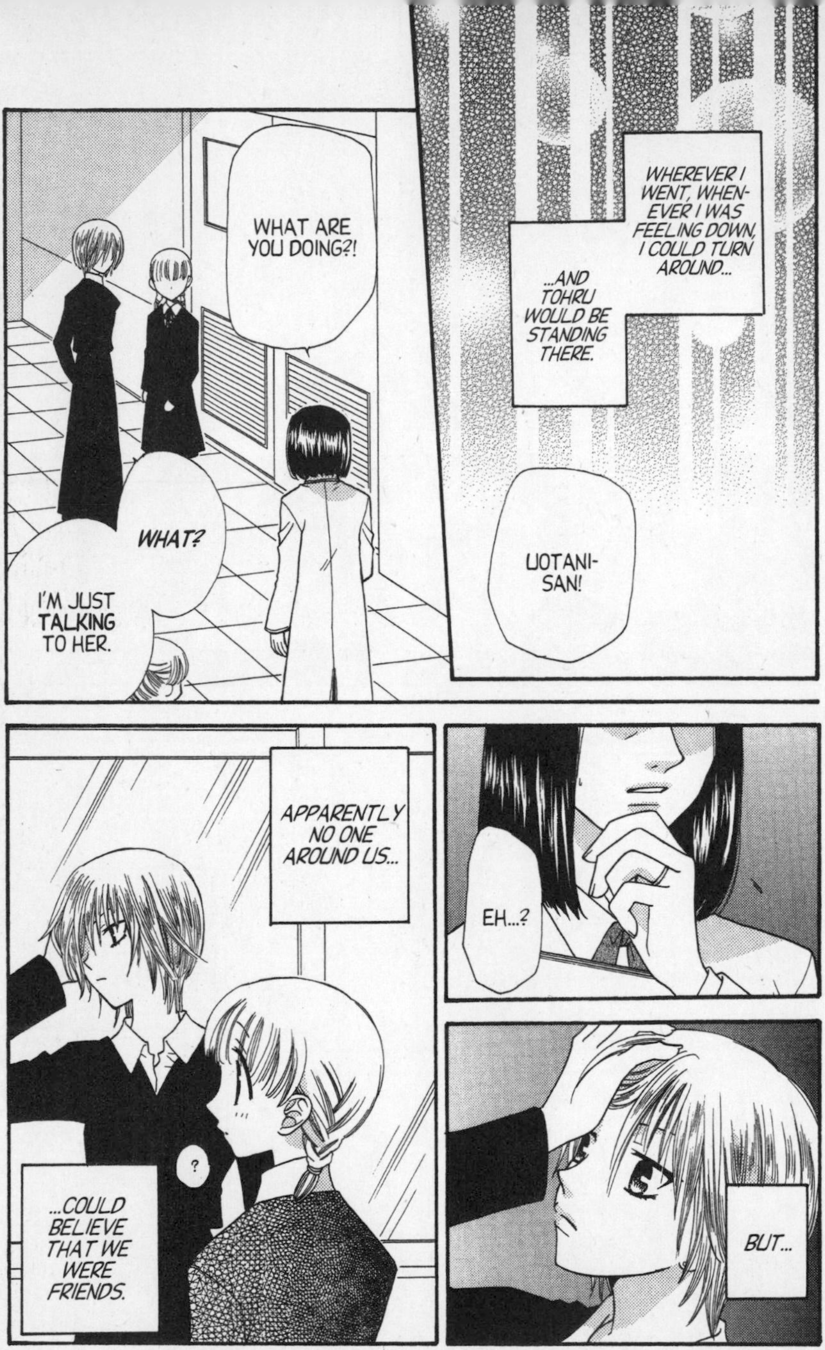
WHEREVER I WENT, WHEN-EVER I WAS FEELING DOWN, I COULD TURN AROUND...
...AND TOHRU WOULD BE STANDING THERE.
UOTANI-SAN!
WHAT ARE YOU DOING?!
WHAT?
I'M JUST TALKING TO HER.
EH...?
BUT...
APPARENTLY NO ONE AROUND US...
?
...COULD BELIEVE THAT WE WERE FRIENDS.

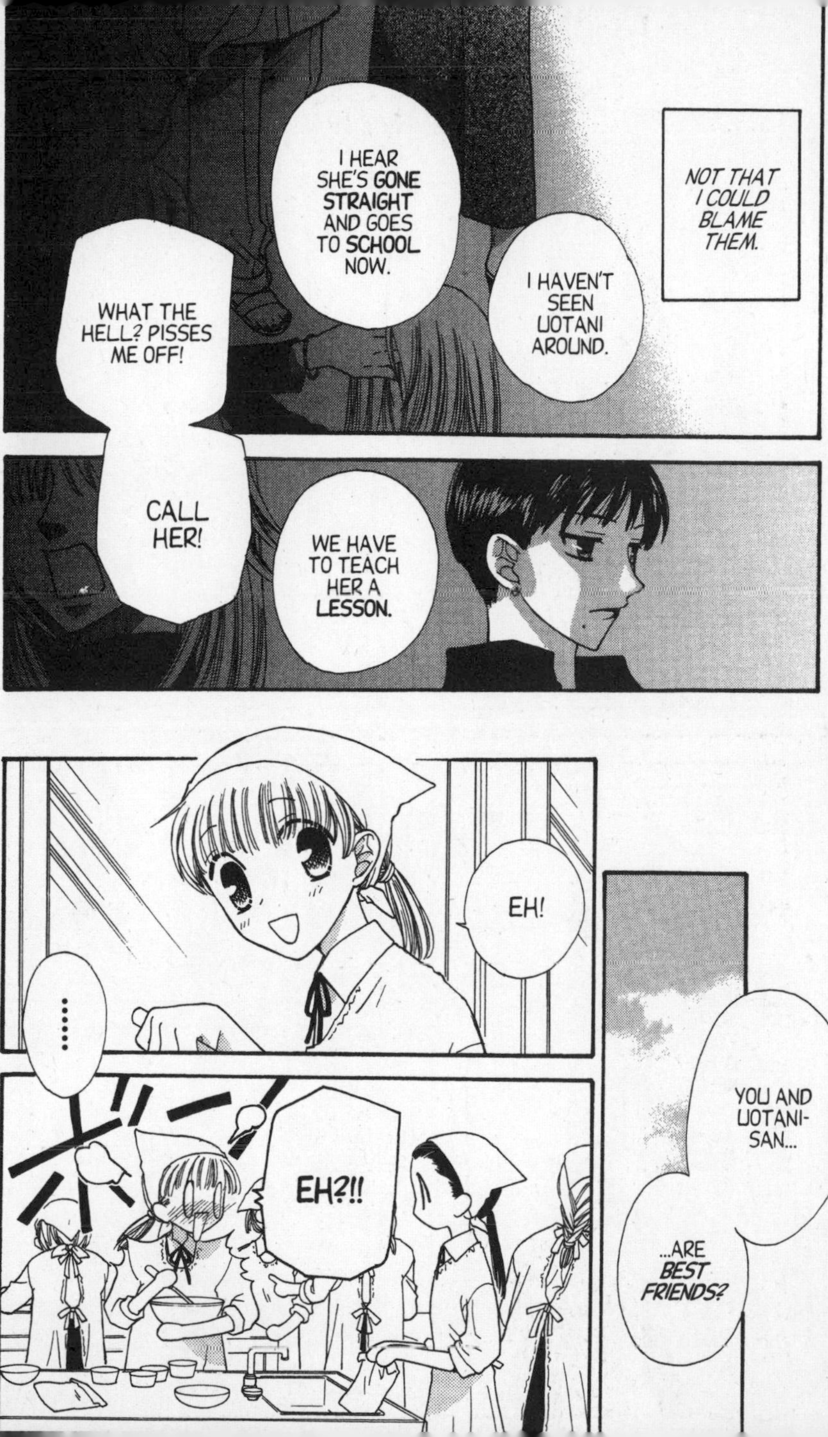
NOT THAT I COULD BLAME THEM.
I HAVEN'T SEEN UOTANI AROUND.
I HEAR SHE'S GONE STRAIGHT AND GOES TO SCHOOL NOW.
WHAT THE HELL? PISSES ME OFF!
WE HAVE TO TEACH HER A LESSON.
CALL HER!
YOU AND UOTANI-SAN...
...ARE BEST FRIENDS?
EH!
......
EH?!!

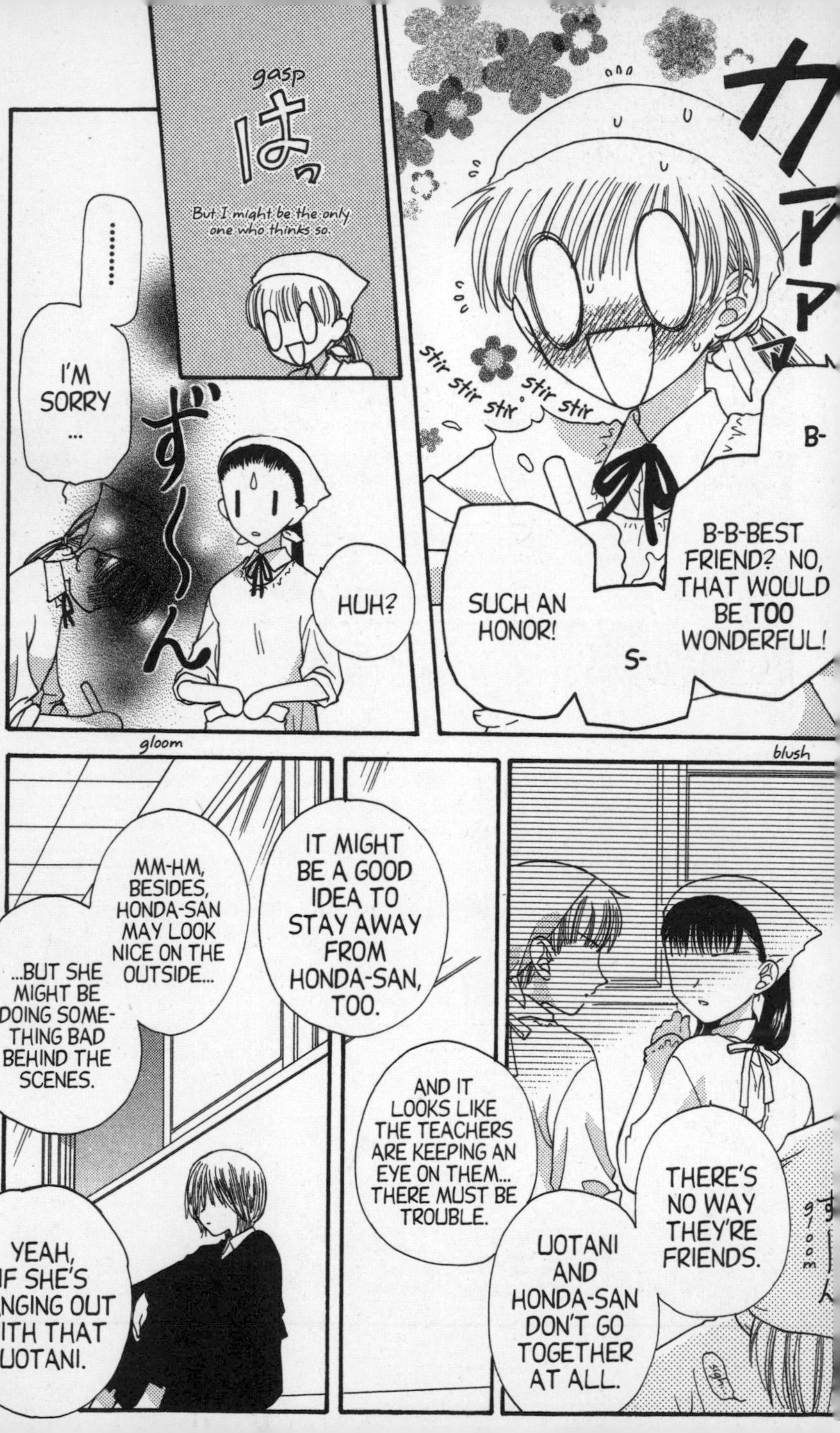
カァァ
B-
B-B-BEST FRIEND? NO, THAT WOULD BE TOO WONDERFUL!
S-
SUCH AN HONOR!
stir stir stir stir stir
blush
gasp
はっ
But I might be the only one who thinks so.
......
I'M SORRY ...
ずーん
HUH?
gloom
THERE'S NO WAY THEY'RE FRIENDS.
UOTANI AND HONDA-SAN DON'T GO TOGETHER AT ALL.
AND IT LOOKS LIKE THE TEACHERS ARE KEEPING AN EYE ON THEM... THERE MUST BE TROUBLE.
gloom
すーん
sigh
IT MIGHT BE A GOOD IDEA TO STAY AWAY FROM HONDA-SAN, TOO.
MM-HM, BESIDES, HONDA-SAN MAY LOOK NICE ON THE OUTSIDE...
...BUT SHE MIGHT BE DOING SOMETHING BAD BEHIND THE SCENES.
YEAH, IF SHE'S HANGING OUT WITH THAT UOTANI.

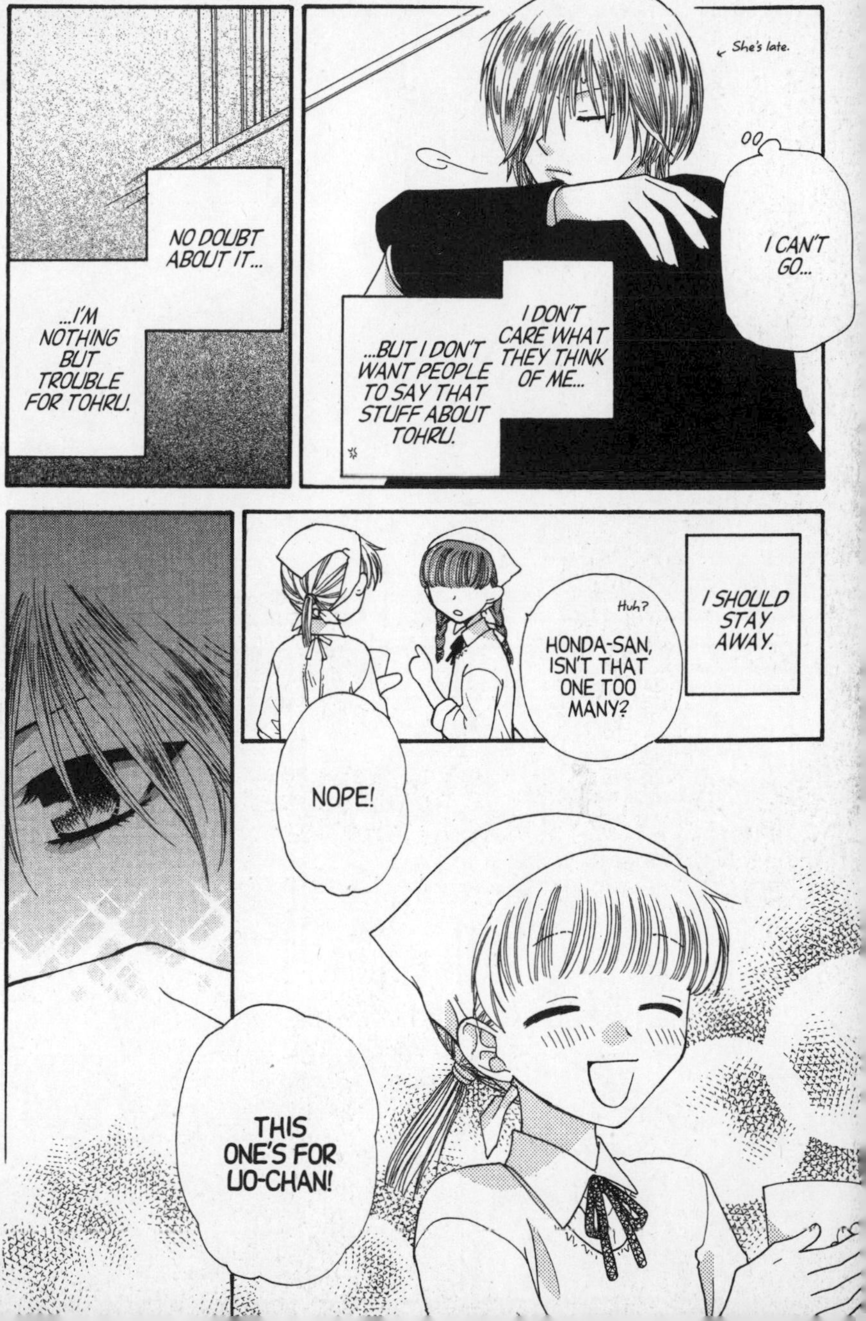
She's late.
I CAN'T GO...
I DON'T CARE WHAT THEY THINK OF ME...
...BUT I DON'T WANT PEOPLE TO SAY THAT STUFF ABOUT TOHRU.
NO DOUBT ABOUT IT...
...I'M NOTHING BUT TROUBLE FOR TOHRU.
I SHOULD STAY AWAY.
Huh?
HONDA-SAN, ISN'T THAT ONE TOO MANY?
NOPE!
THIS ONE'S FOR UO-CHAN!

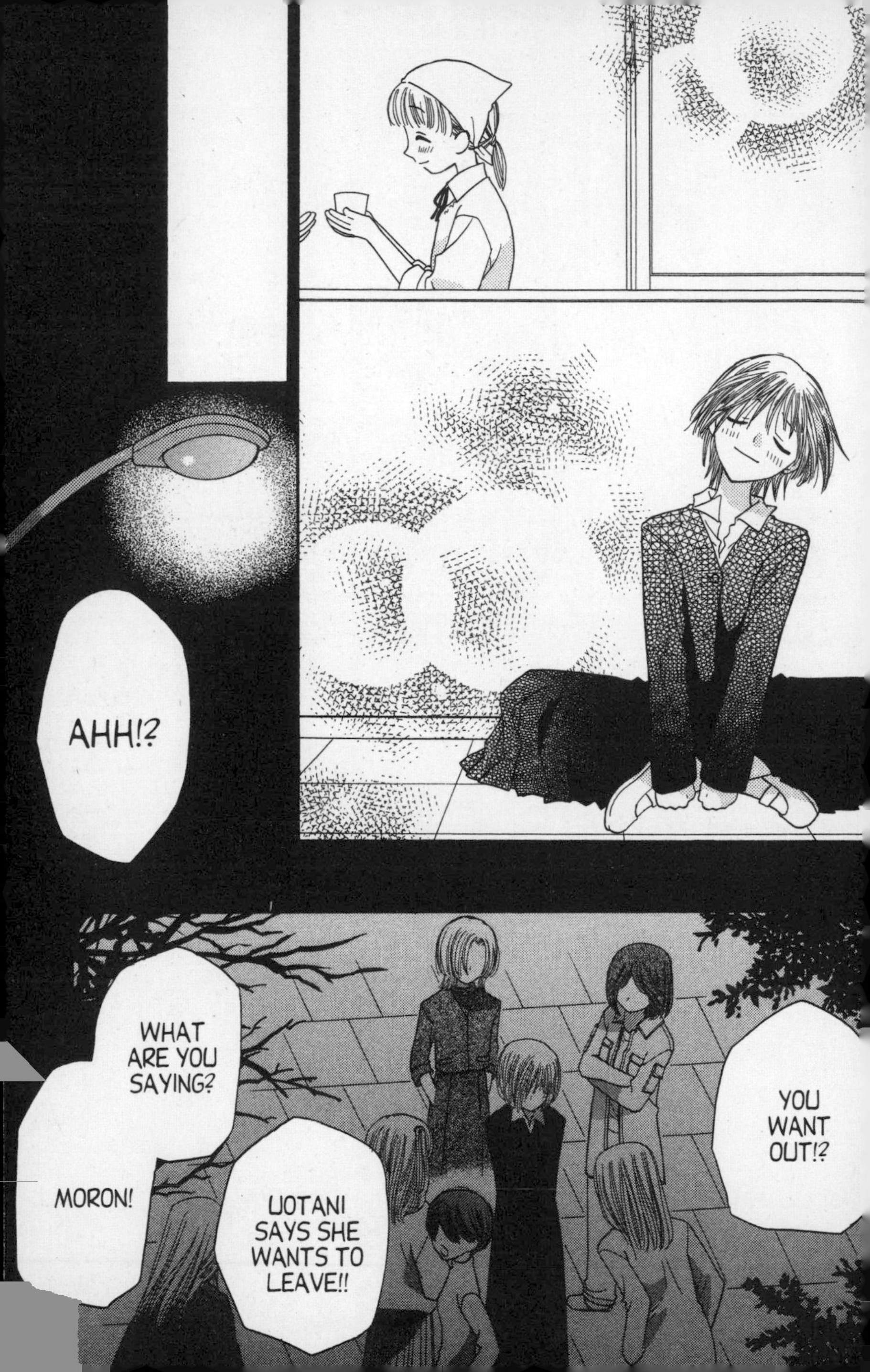
AHH!?
YOU WANT OUT!?
WHAT ARE YOU SAYING?
UOTANI SAYS SHE WANTS TO LEAVE!!
MORON!

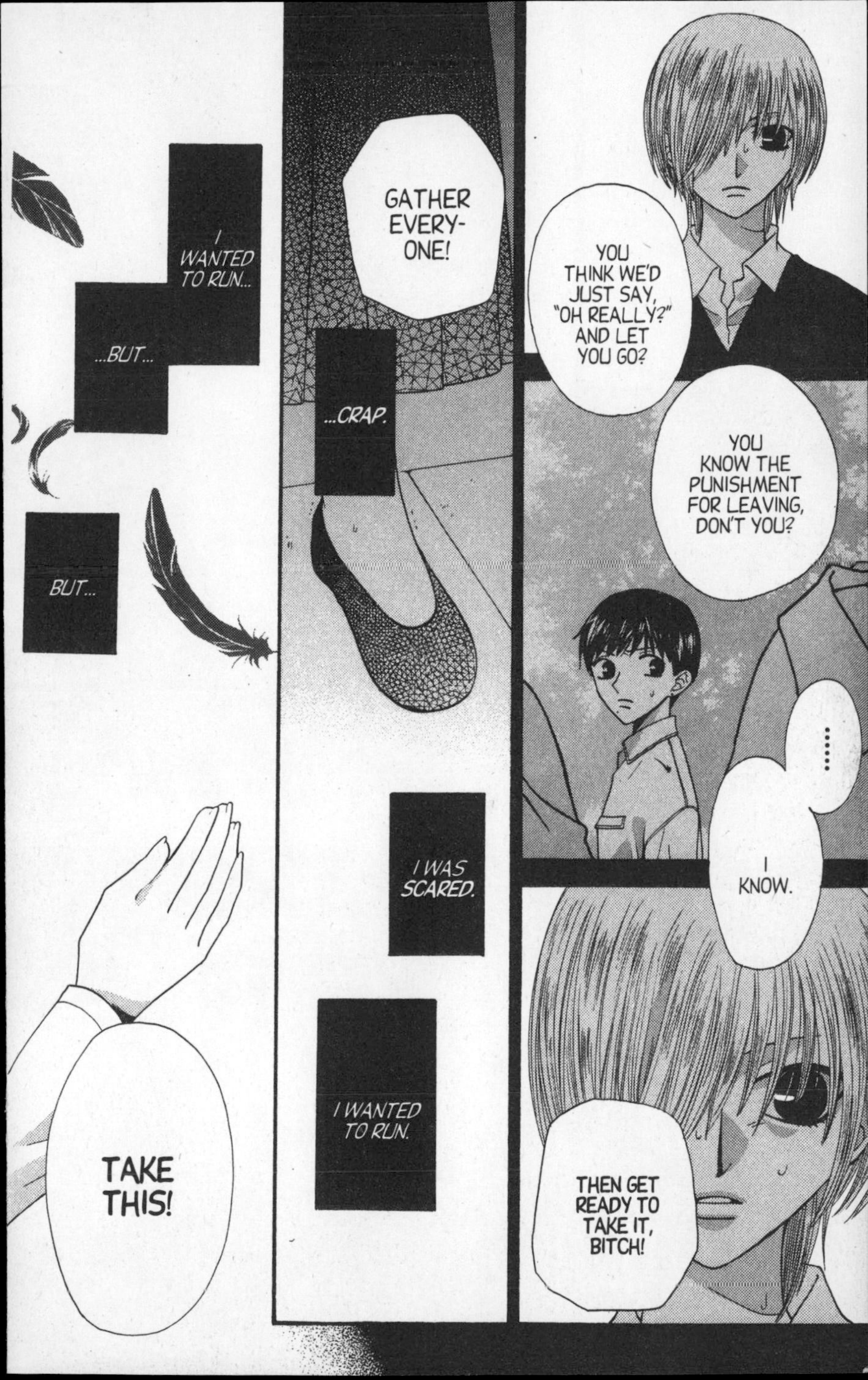
YOU THINK WE'D JUST SAY, "OH REALLY?" AND LET YOU GO?
YOU KNOW THE PUNISHMENT FOR LEAVING, DON'T YOU?
......
I KNOW.
THEN GET READY TO TAKE IT, BITCH!
GATHER EVERY-ONE!
...CRAP.
I WAS SCARED.
I WANTED TO RUN.
I WANTED TO RUN...
...BUT...
BUT...
TAKE THIS!

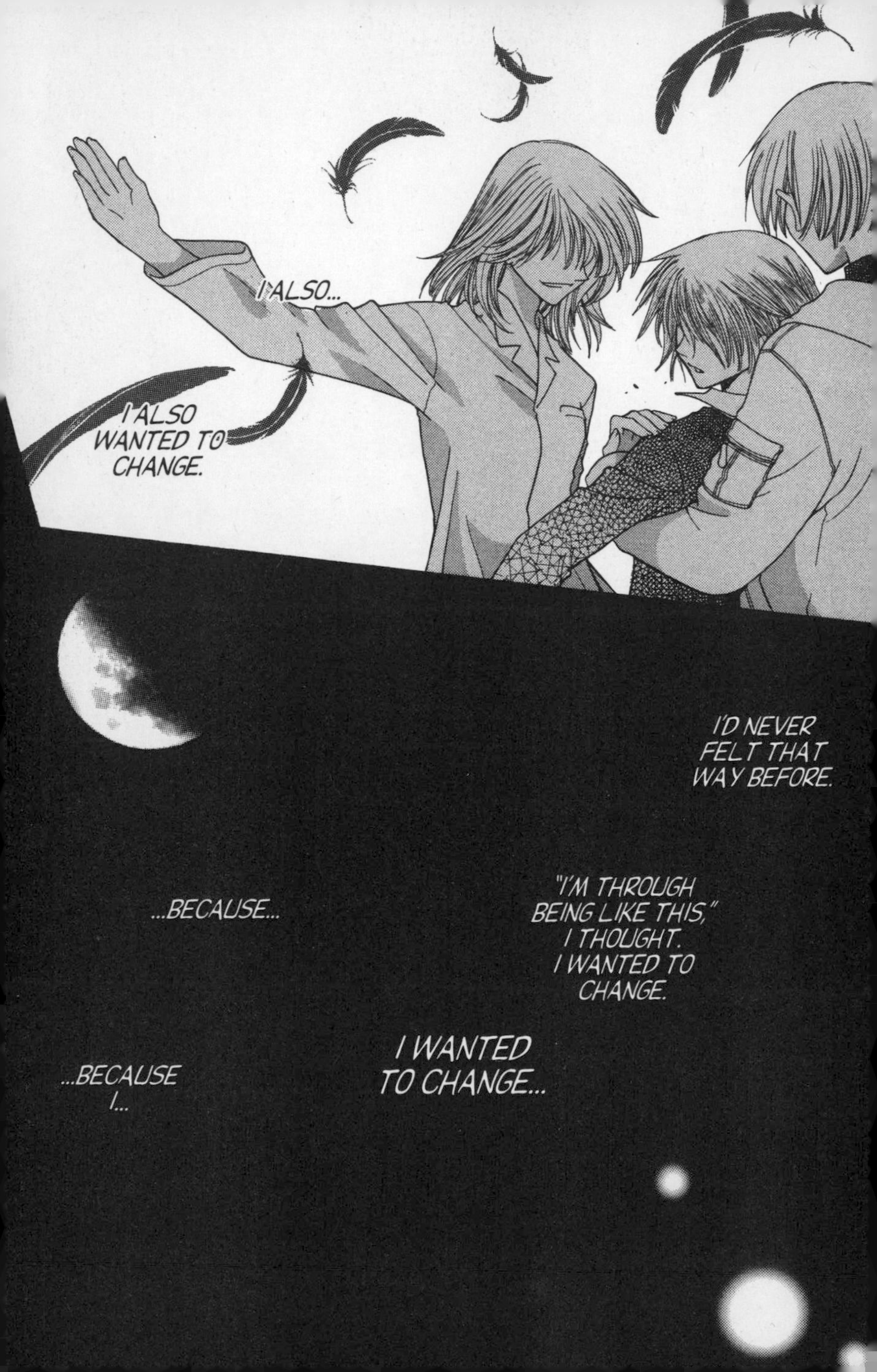
I ALSO...
I ALSO WANTED TO CHANGE.
I'D NEVER FELT THAT WAY BEFORE.
"I'M THROUGH BEING LIKE THIS," I THOUGHT. I WANTED TO CHANGE.
...BECAUSE...
I WANTED TO CHANGE...
...BECAUSE I...

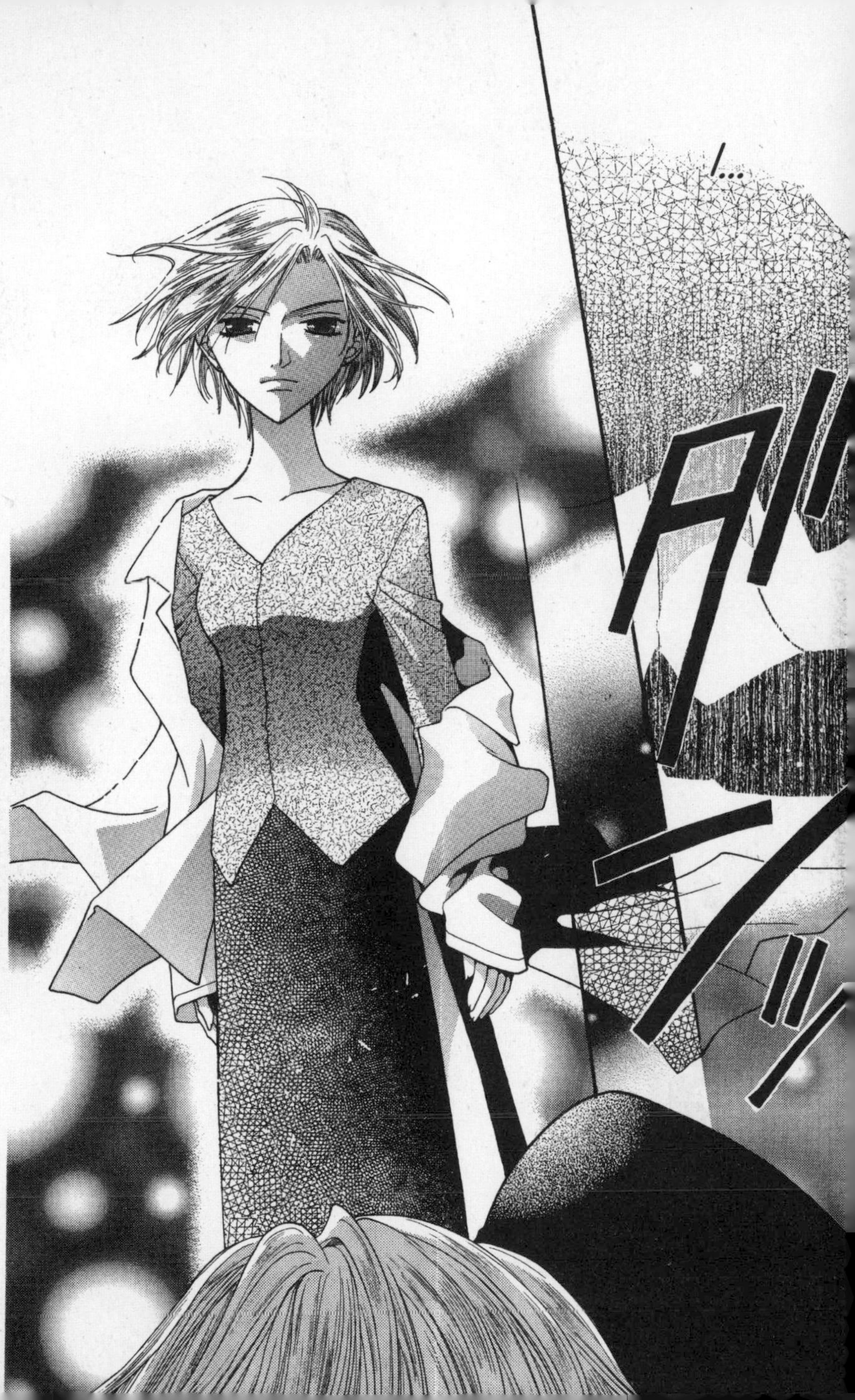
I...

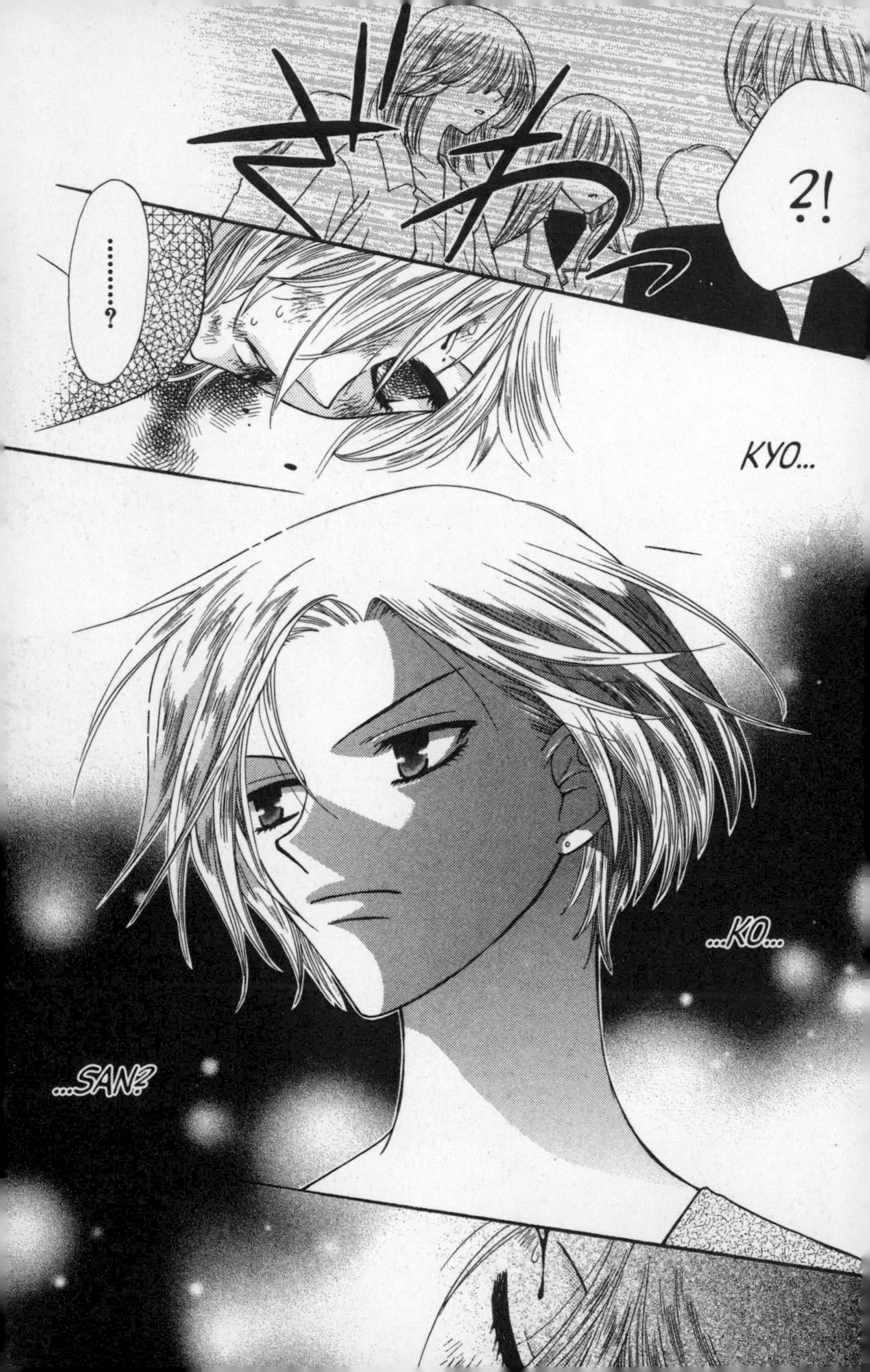
?!
......?
KYO...
...KO...
...SAN?

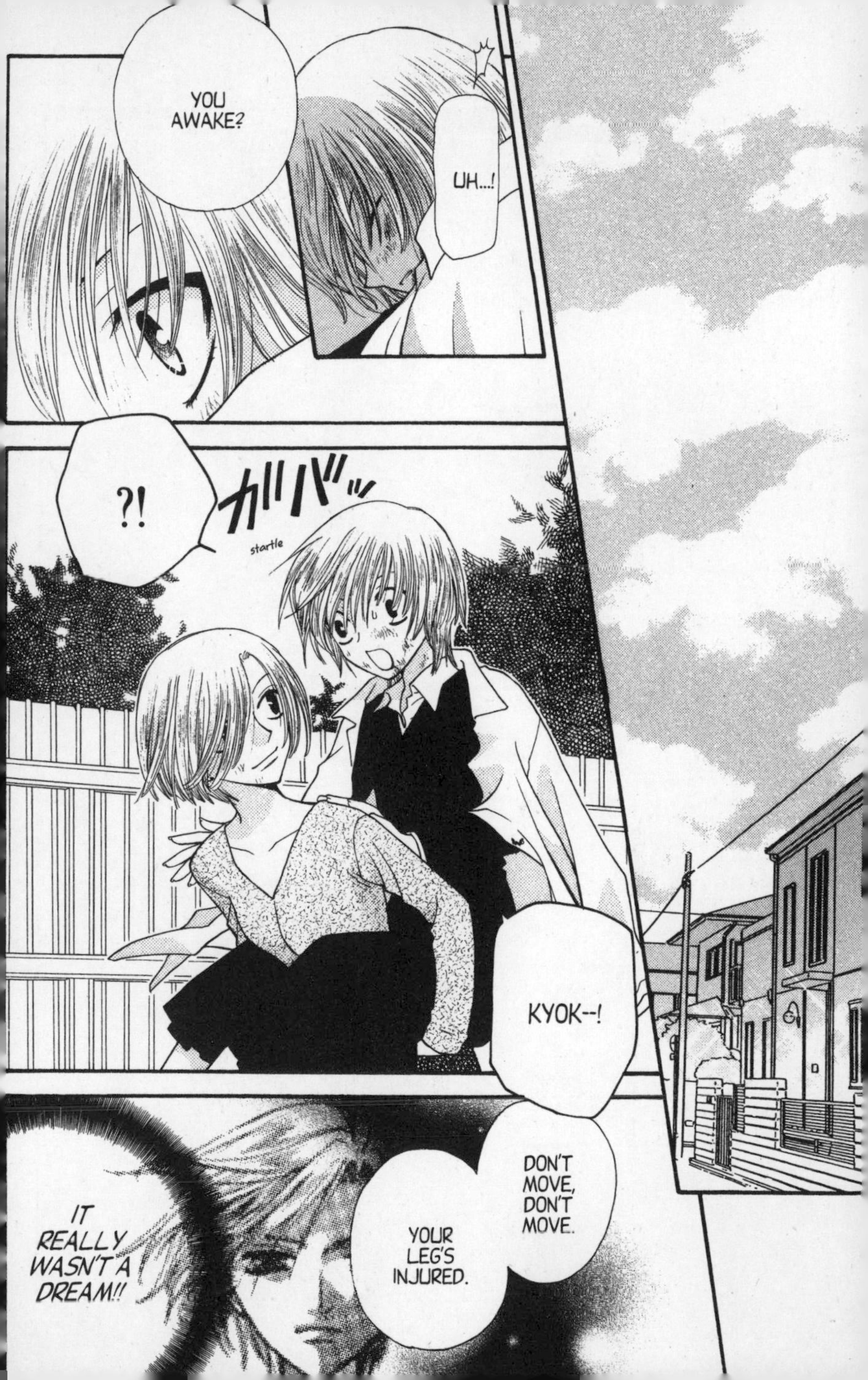
YOU AWAKE?
UH...!
?!
ガバッ
startle
KYOK--!
DON'T MOVE, DON'T MOVE.
YOUR LEG'S INJURED.
IT REALLY WASN'T A DREAM!!

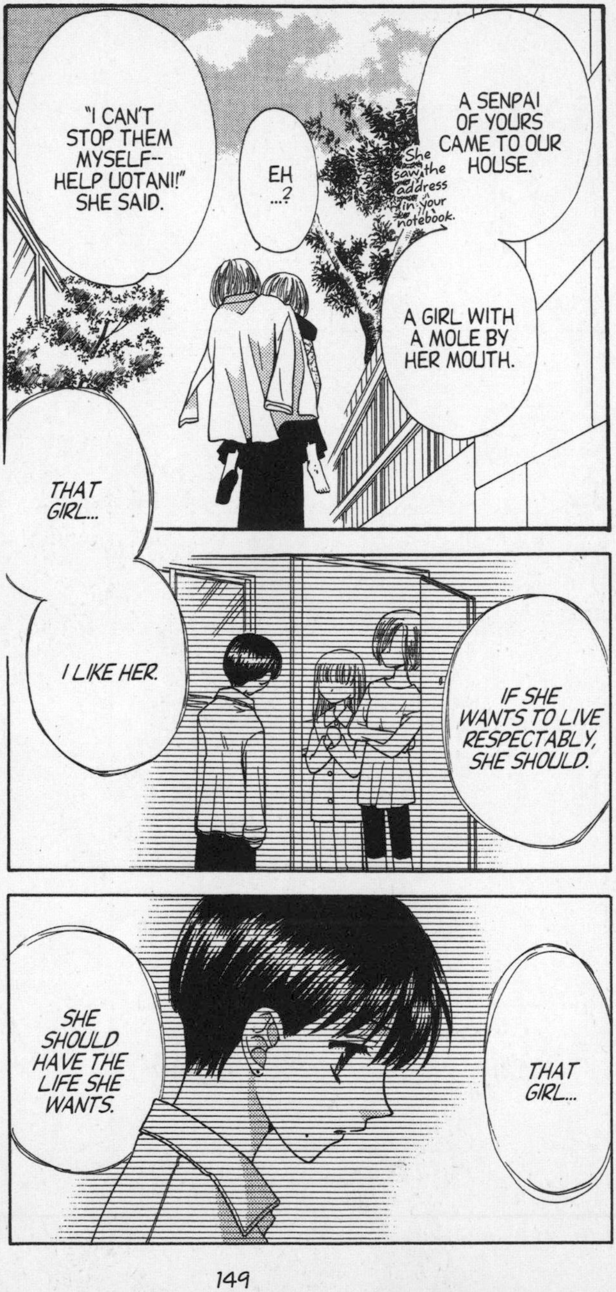

A SENPAI OF YOURS CAME TO OUR HOUSE.
She saw the address in your notebook.
A GIRL WITH A MOLE BY HER MOUTH.
EH ...?
"I CAN'T STOP THEM MYSELF--HELP UOTANI!" SHE SAID.
THAT GIRL...
IF SHE WANTS TO LIVE RESPECTABLY, SHE SHOULD.
I LIKE HER.
THAT GIRL...
SHE SHOULD HAVE THE LIFE SHE WANTS.

Fruits Basket 7: Part 5

Before I was hospitalized, I played video games, but since I couldn't use my left hand, I used my right hand... I mean I used only my right hand. And doing that I realized how much I love analog controllers! They really helped me out this time! I could use those even with my injured left hand.

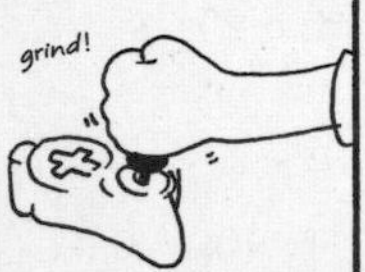

grind!

I can grind it with my fist.

I still have that habit, so when I have to use the directional pad, I feel inconvenienced.... Speaking of which, are they still making left-handed controllers? I want one.... A long time ago, when I was working part-time jobs, it seemed like all the office supplies were made for right-handed people. I cried... (laugh). I thought, "Why must I be left-handed?!"

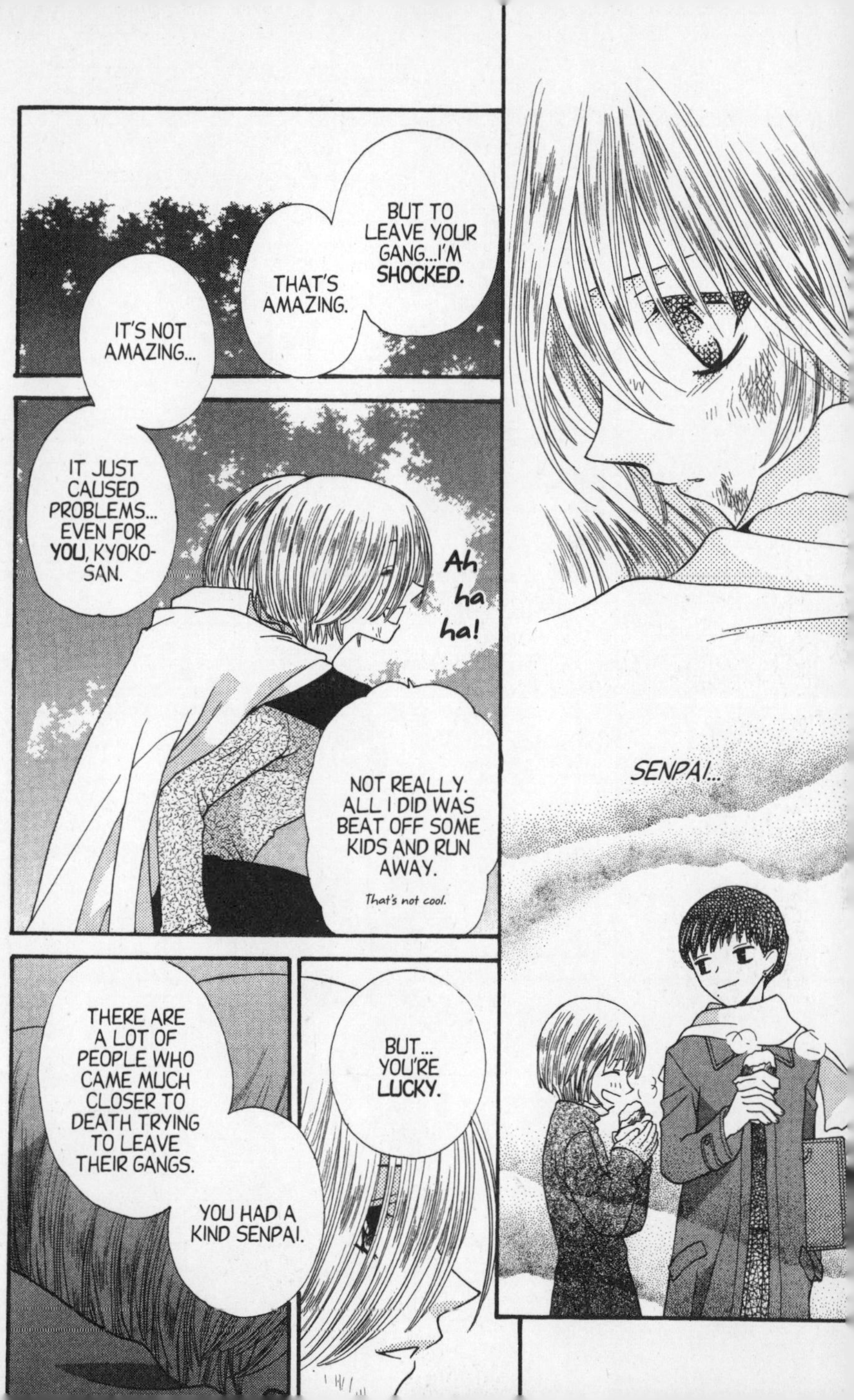
SENPAI...
BUT TO LEAVE YOUR GANG...I'M **SHOCKED**.
THAT'S AMAZING.
IT'S NOT AMAZING...
IT JUST CAUSED PROBLEMS... EVEN FOR **YOU**, KYOKO-SAN.
Ah ha ha!
NOT REALLY. ALL I DID WAS BEAT OFF SOME KIDS AND RUN AWAY.
That's not cool.
BUT... YOU'RE **LUCKY**.
THERE ARE A LOT OF PEOPLE WHO CAME MUCH CLOSER TO DEATH TRYING TO LEAVE THEIR GANGS.
YOU HAD A KIND SENPAI.

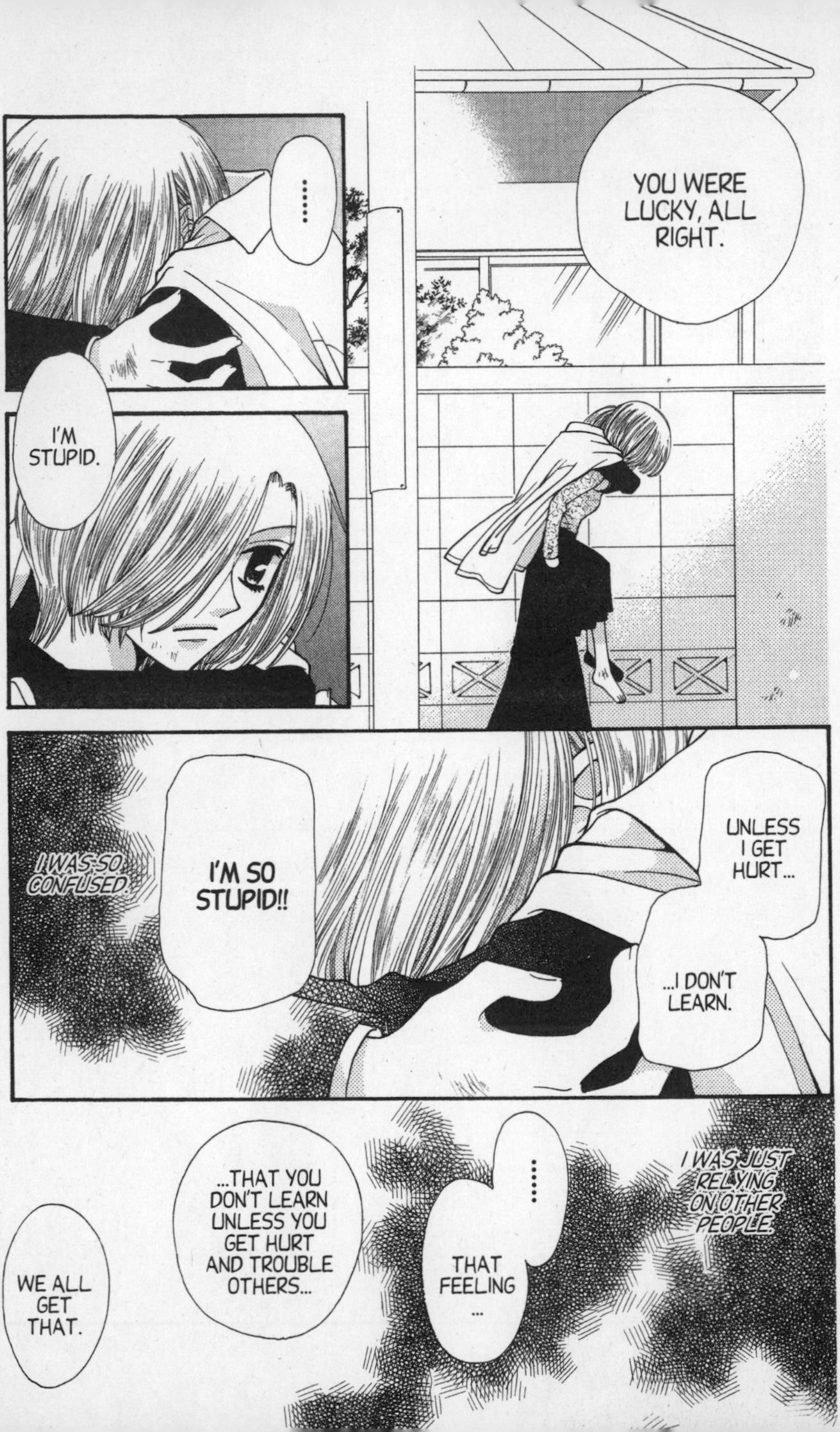
YOU WERE LUCKY, ALL RIGHT.
......
I'M STUPID.
UNLESS I GET HURT...
...I DON'T LEARN.
I'M SO STUPID!!
I WAS SO CONFUSED.
I WAS JUST RELYING ON OTHER PEOPLE.
......
THAT FEELING ...
...THAT YOU DON'T LEARN UNLESS YOU GET HURT AND TROUBLE OTHERS...
WE ALL GET THAT.

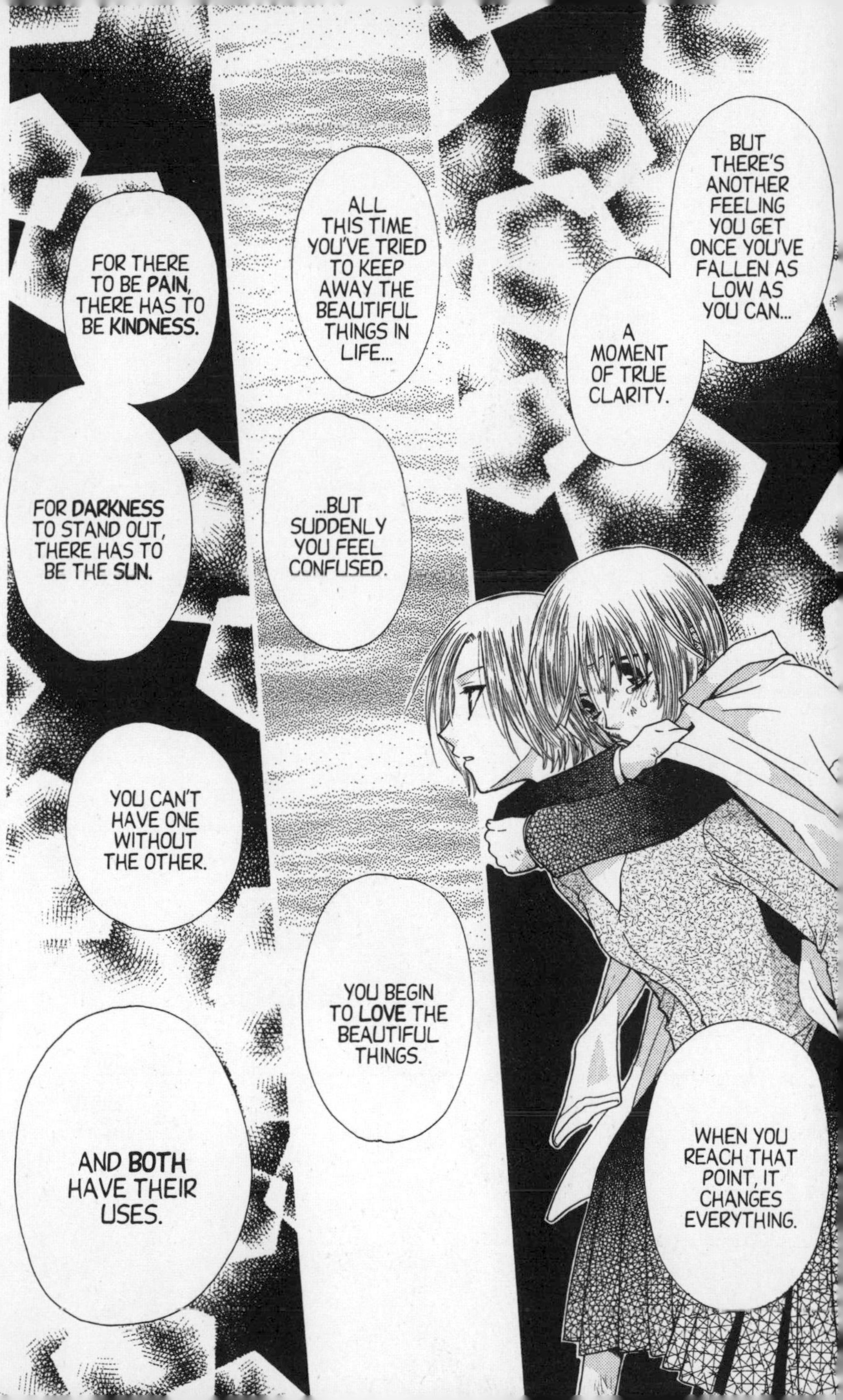
BUT THERE'S ANOTHER FEELING YOU GET ONCE YOU'VE FALLEN AS LOW AS YOU CAN...
A MOMENT OF TRUE CLARITY.
WHEN YOU REACH THAT POINT, IT CHANGES EVERYTHING.
ALL THIS TIME YOU'VE TRIED TO KEEP AWAY THE BEAUTIFUL THINGS IN LIFE...
...BUT SUDDENLY YOU FEEL CONFUSED.
YOU BEGIN TO LOVE THE BEAUTIFUL THINGS.
FOR THERE TO BE PAIN, THERE HAS TO BE KINDNESS.
FOR DARKNESS TO STAND OUT, THERE HAS TO BE THE SUN.
YOU CAN'T HAVE ONE WITHOUT THE OTHER.
AND BOTH HAVE THEIR USES.

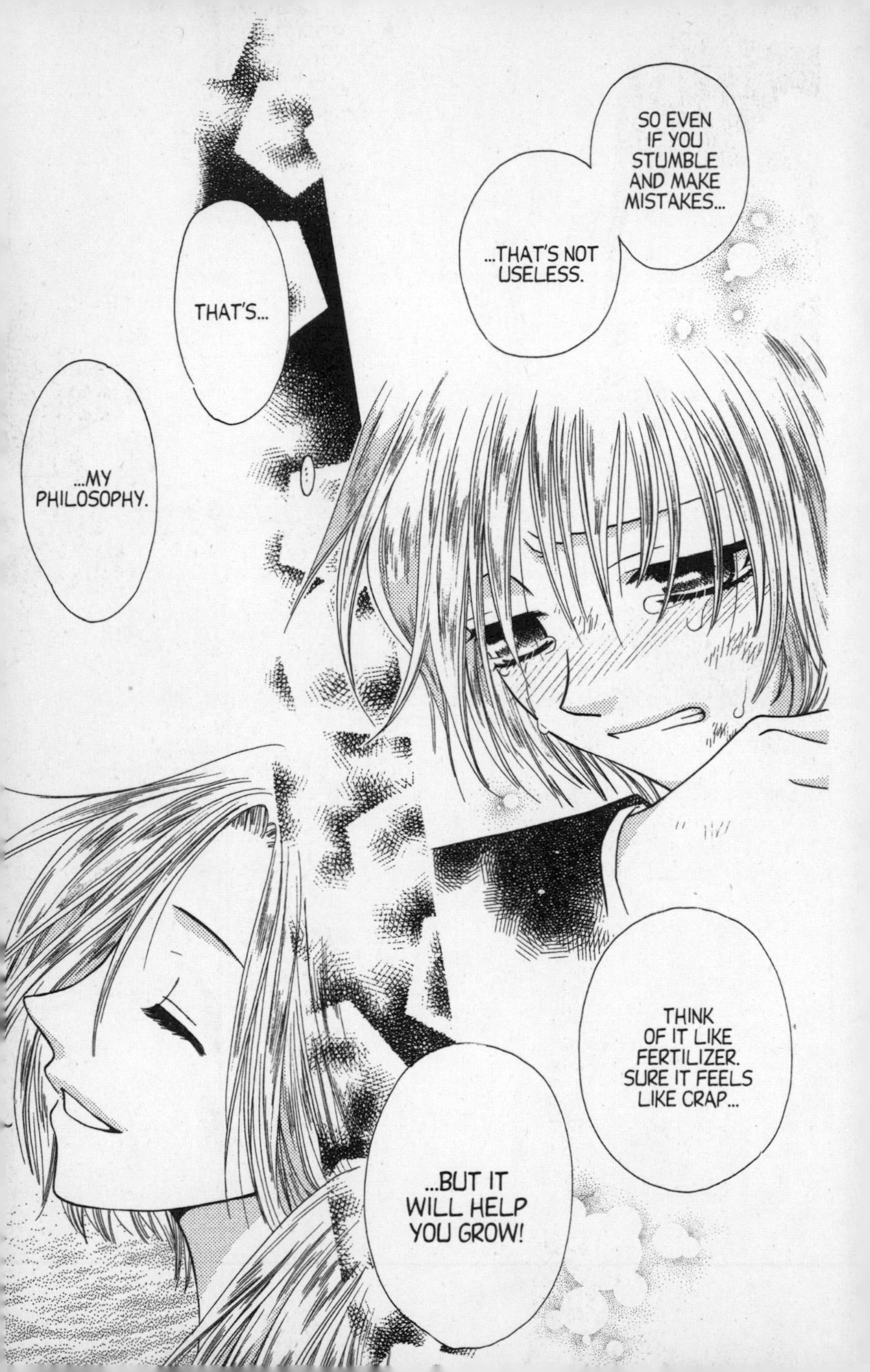
SO EVEN IF YOU STUMBLE AND MAKE MISTAKES...
...THAT'S NOT USELESS.
THAT'S...
...MY PHILOSOPHY.
THINK OF IT LIKE FERTILIZER. SURE IT FEELS LIKE CRAP...
...BUT IT WILL HELP YOU GROW!

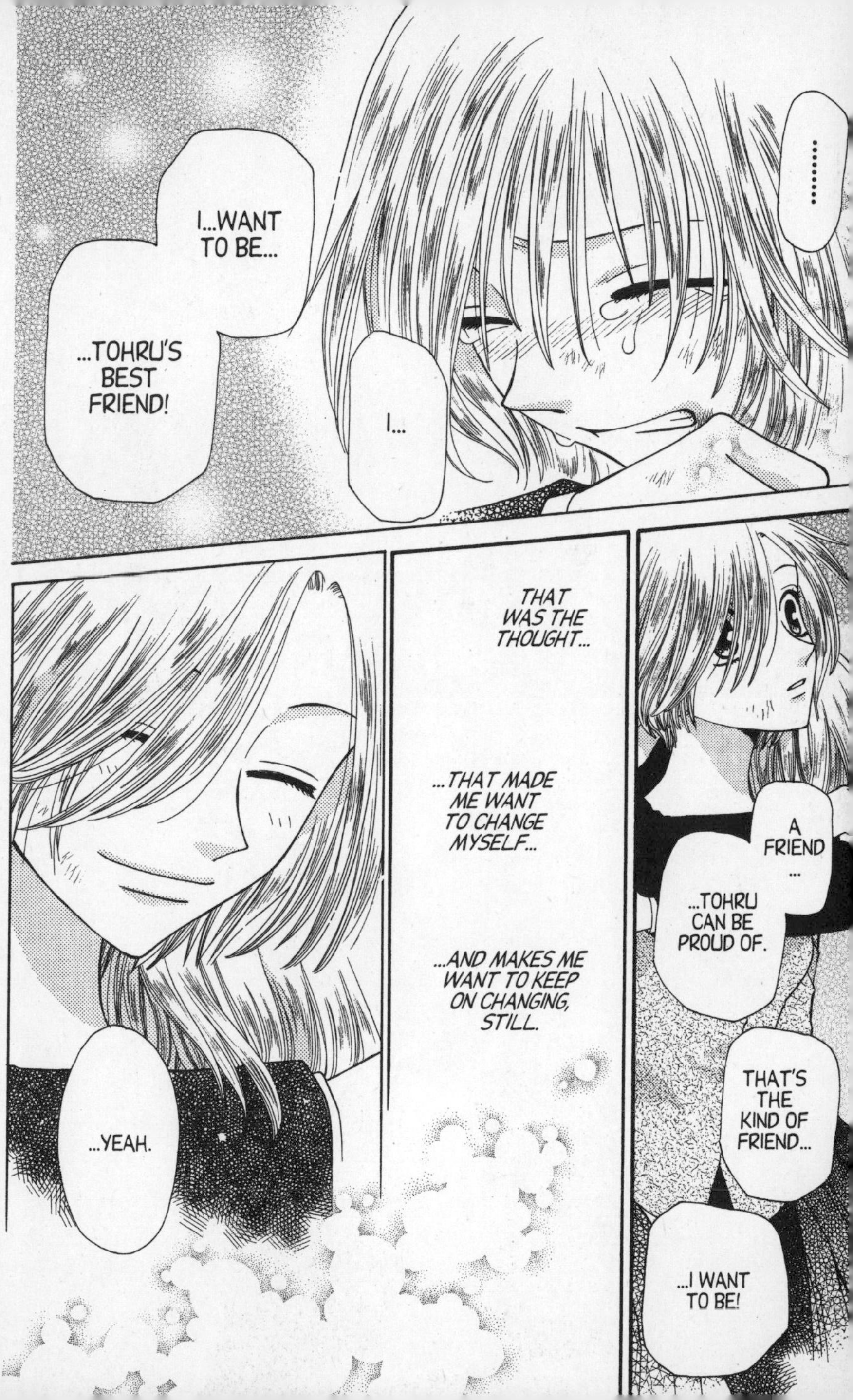
……
I...
I...WANT TO BE...
...TOHRU'S BEST FRIEND!
A FRIEND...
...TOHRU CAN BE PROUD OF.
THAT'S THE KIND OF FRIEND...
...I WANT TO BE!
THAT WAS THE THOUGHT...
...THAT MADE ME WANT TO CHANGE MYSELF...
...AND MAKES ME WANT TO KEEP ON CHANGING, STILL.
...YEAH.

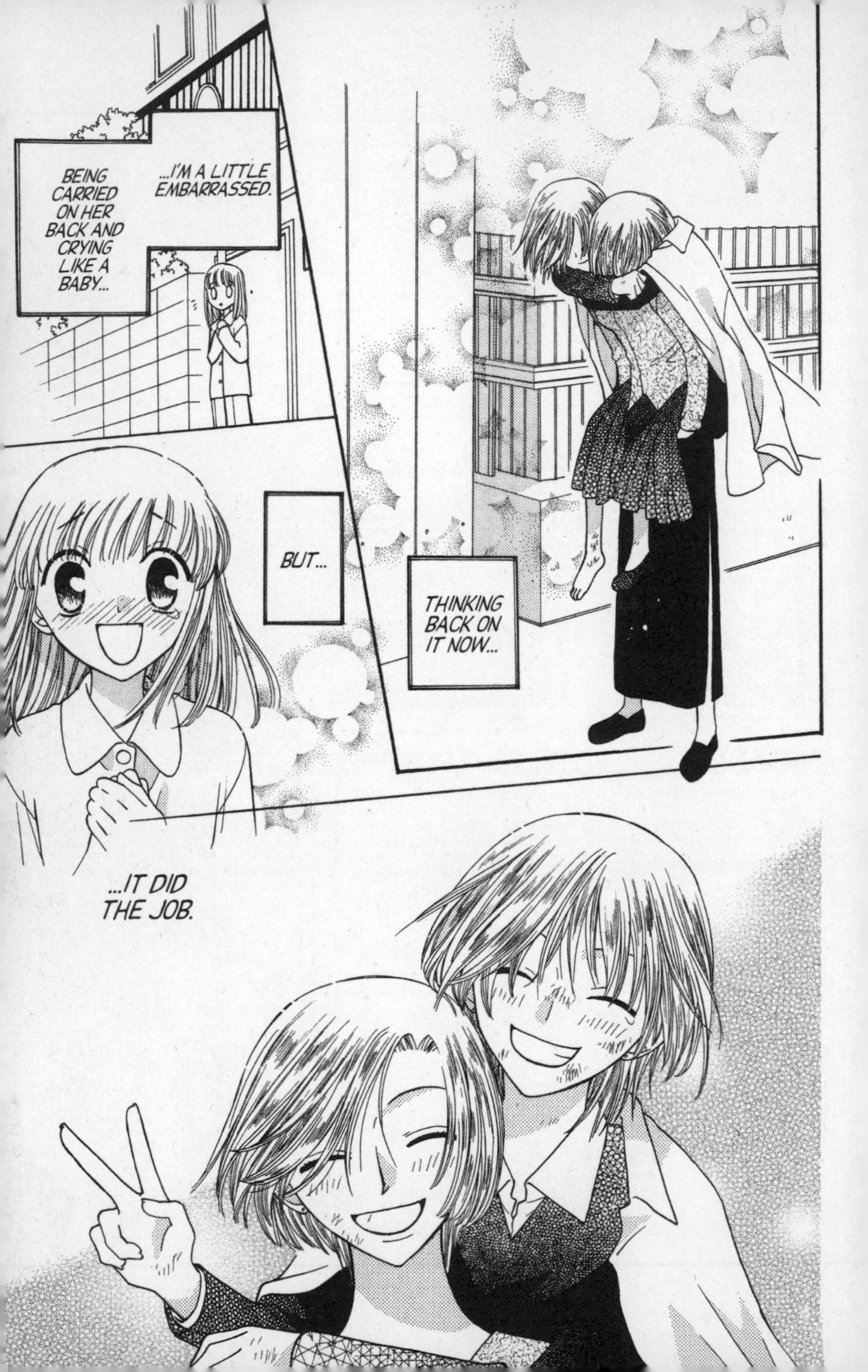
BEING CARRIED ON HER BACK AND CRYING LIKE A BABY...
...I'M A LITTLE EMBARRASSED.
BUT...
THINKING BACK ON IT NOW...
...IT DID THE JOB.

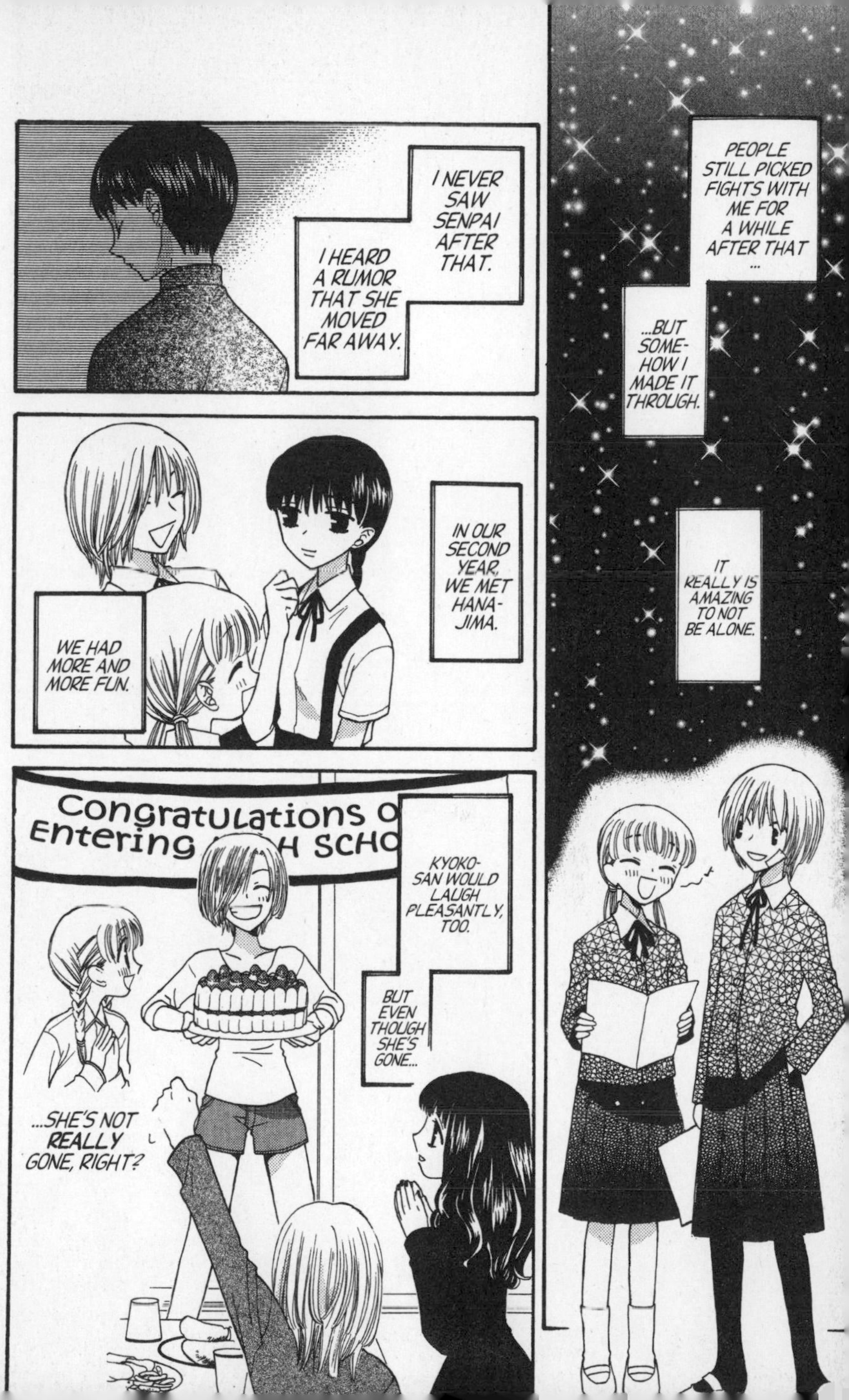
PEOPLE STILL PICKED FIGHTS WITH ME FOR A WHILE AFTER THAT ...
...BUT SOME-HOW I MADE IT THROUGH.
IT REALLY IS AMAZING TO NOT BE ALONE.
I NEVER SAW SENPAI AFTER THAT.
I HEARD A RUMOR THAT SHE MOVED FAR AWAY.
IN OUR SECOND YEAR, WE MET HANA-JIMA.
WE HAD MORE AND MORE FUN.
Congratulations O
Entering H SCHO
KYOKO-SAN WOULD LAUGH PLEASANTLY, TOO.
BUT EVEN THOUGH SHE'S GONE...
...SHE'S NOT REALLY GONE, RIGHT?

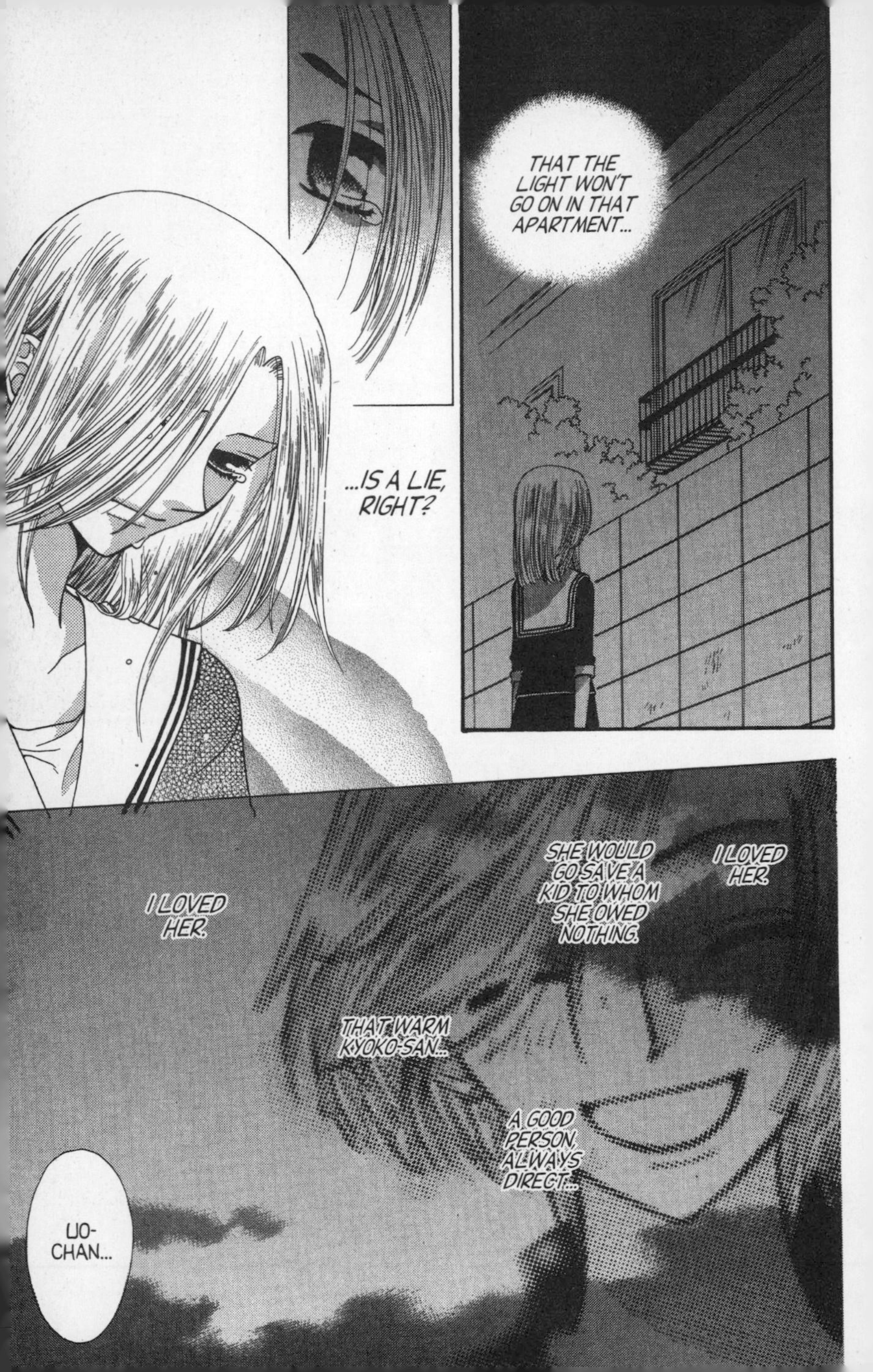
THAT THE LIGHT WON'T GO ON IN THAT APARTMENT...
...IS A LIE, RIGHT?
I LOVED HER.
SHE WOULD GO SAVE A KID TO WHOM SHE OWED NOTHING.
I LOVED HER.
THAT WARM KYOKO-SAN...
A GOOD PERSON, ALWAYS DIRECT...
UO-CHAN...

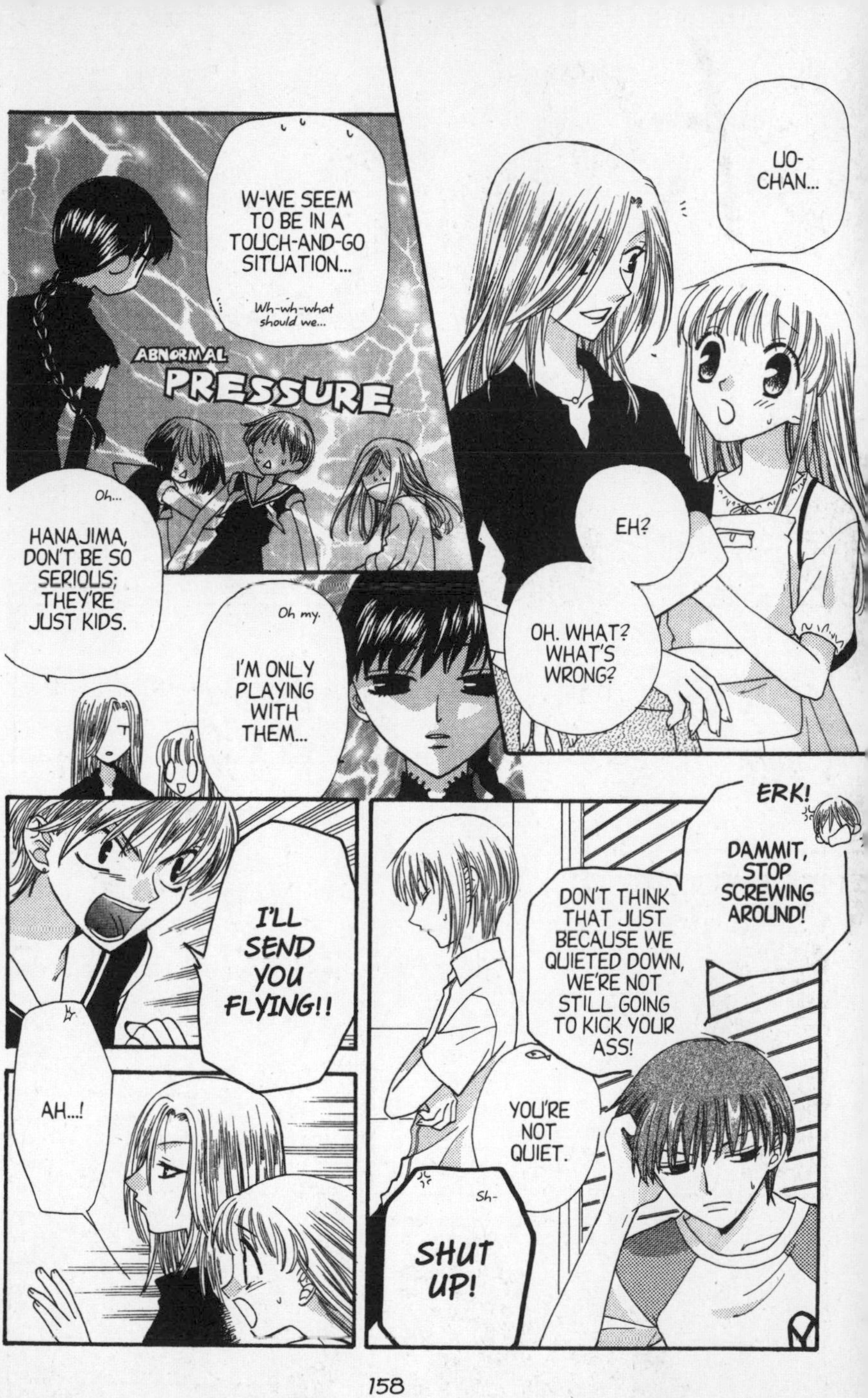
UO-CHAN...
EH?
OH. WHAT? WHAT'S WRONG?
W-WE SEEM TO BE IN A TOUCH-AND-GO SITUATION...
Wh-wh-what should we...
ABNORMAL PRESSURE
Oh... HANAJIMA, DON'T BE SO SERIOUS; THEY'RE JUST KIDS.
Oh my. I'M ONLY PLAYING WITH THEM...
ERK!
DAMMIT, STOP SCREWING AROUND!
DON'T THINK THAT JUST BECAUSE WE QUIETED DOWN, WE'RE NOT STILL GOING TO KICK YOUR ASS!
YOU'RE NOT QUIET.
Sh-
SHUT UP!
I'LL SEND YOU FLYING!!
AH...!

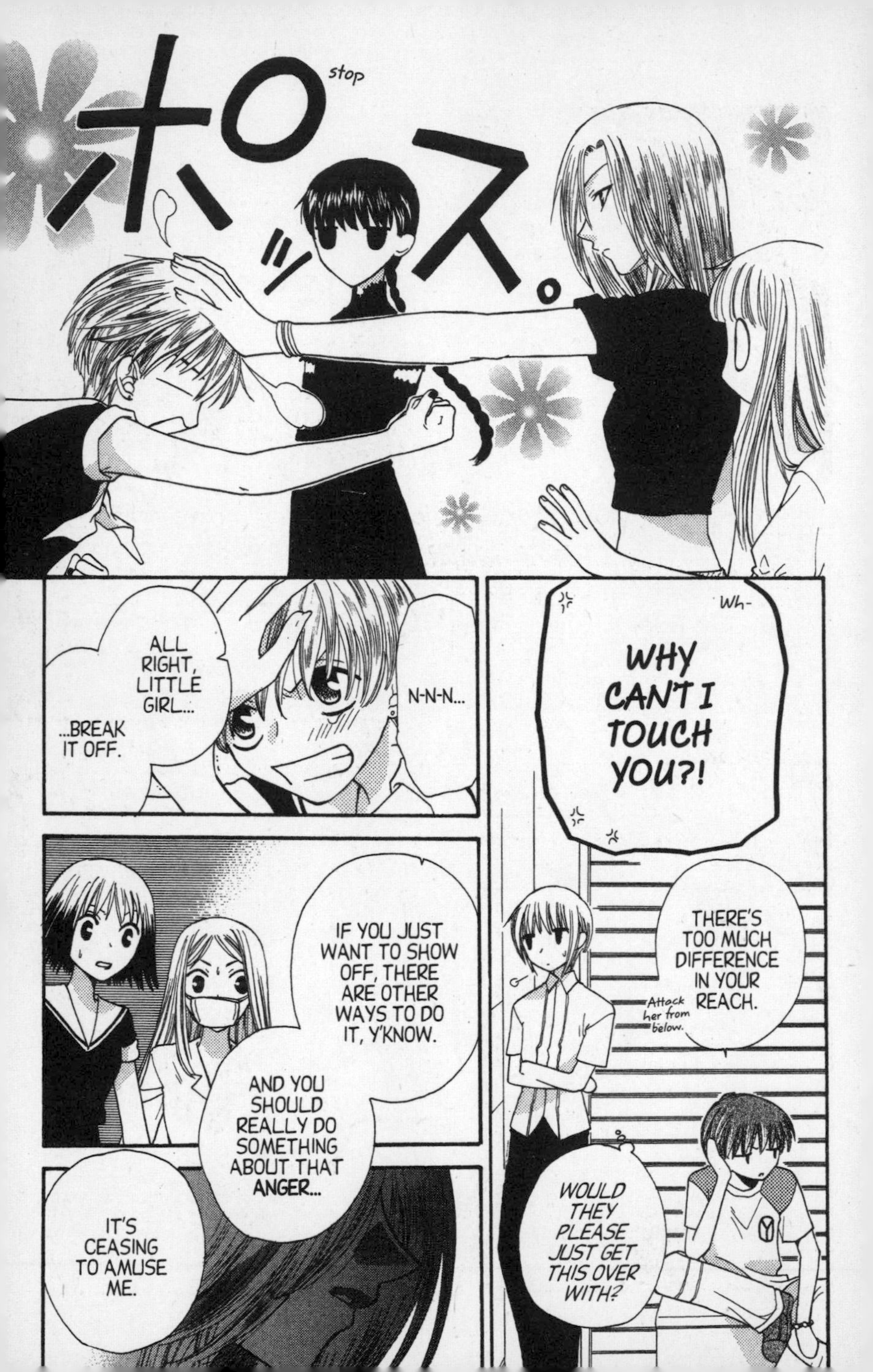
ホパッス。
stop
Wh-
WHY CAN'T I TOUCH YOU?!
N-N-N...
ALL RIGHT, LITTLE GIRL...
...BREAK IT OFF.
THERE'S TOO MUCH DIFFERENCE IN YOUR REACH.
Attack her from below.
WOULD THEY PLEASE JUST GET THIS OVER WITH?
IF YOU JUST WANT TO SHOW OFF, THERE ARE OTHER WAYS TO DO IT, Y'KNOW.
AND YOU SHOULD REALLY DO SOMETHING ABOUT THAT ANGER...
IT'S CEASING TO AMUSE ME.

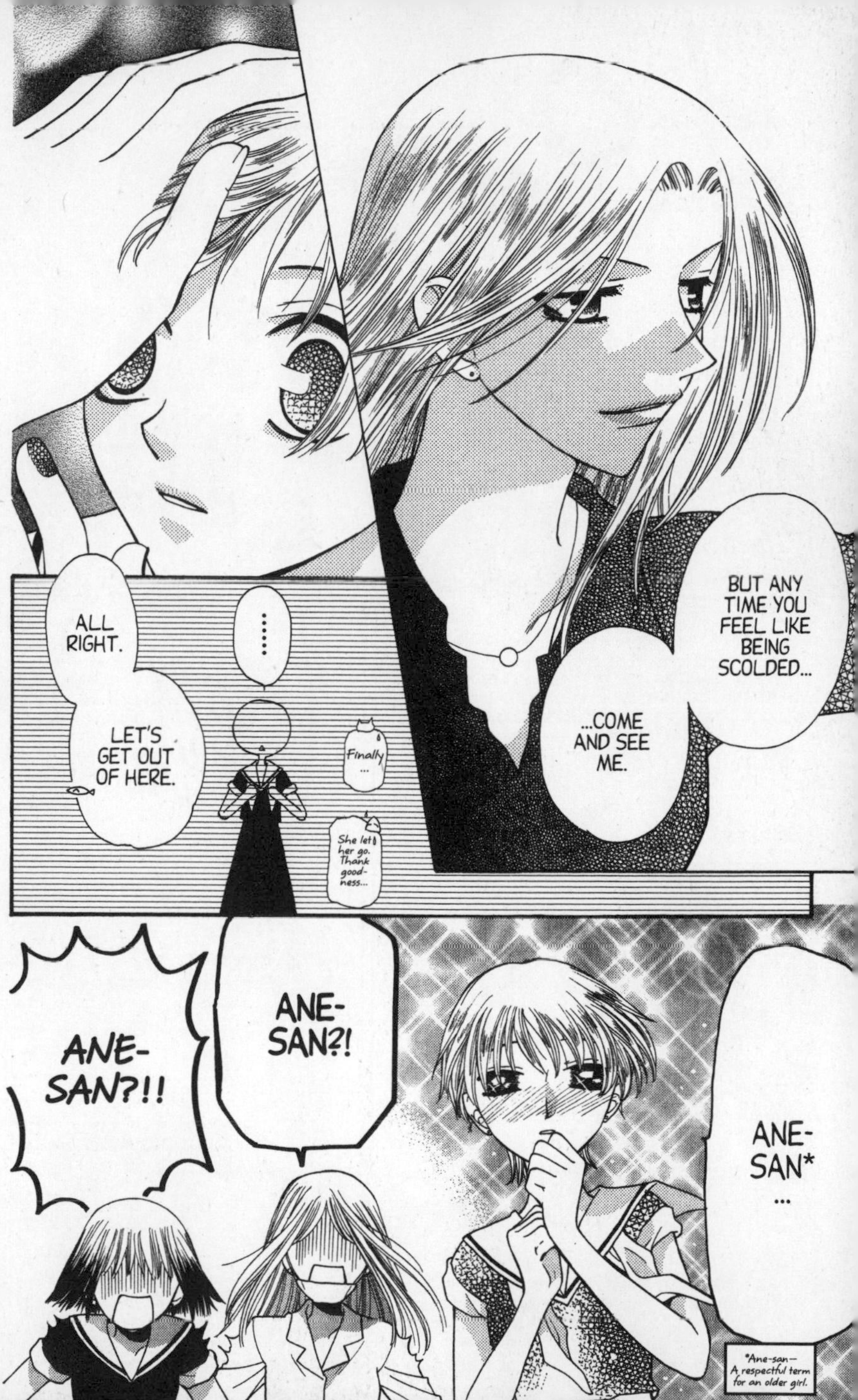
BUT ANY TIME YOU FEEL LIKE BEING SCOLDED...
...COME AND SEE ME.
......
ALL RIGHT.
LET'S GET OUT OF HERE.
Finally...
She let her go. Thank goodness...
ANE-SAN* ...
ANE-SAN?!
ANE-SAN?!!

*Ane-san— A respectful term for an older girl.

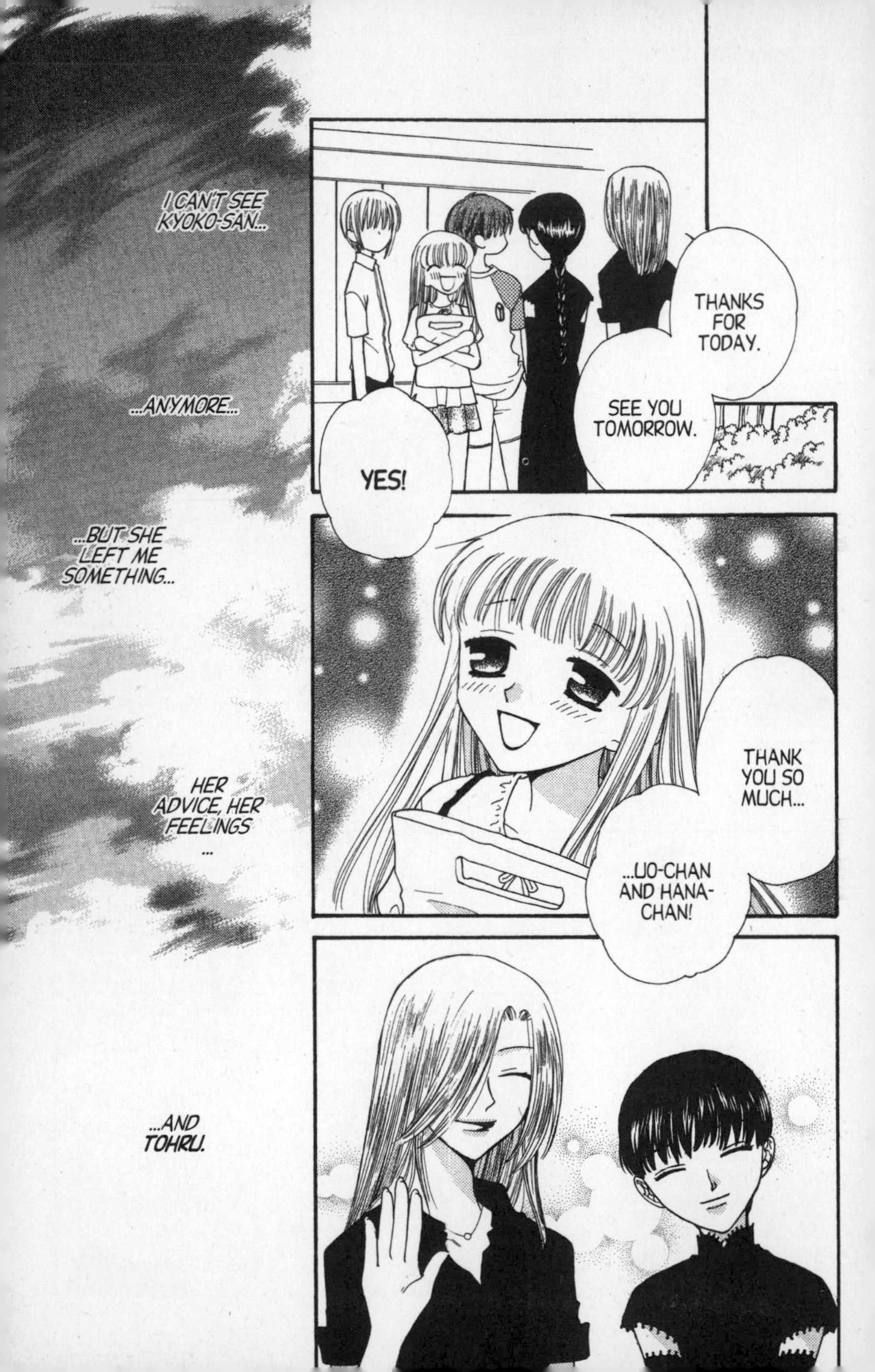
THANKS FOR TODAY.
SEE YOU TOMORROW.
YES!
THANK YOU SO MUCH...
...UO-CHAN AND HANA-CHAN!
I CAN'T SEE KYOKO-SAN...
...ANYMORE...
...BUT SHE LEFT ME SOMETHING...
HER ADVICE, HER FEELINGS ...
...AND TOHRU.

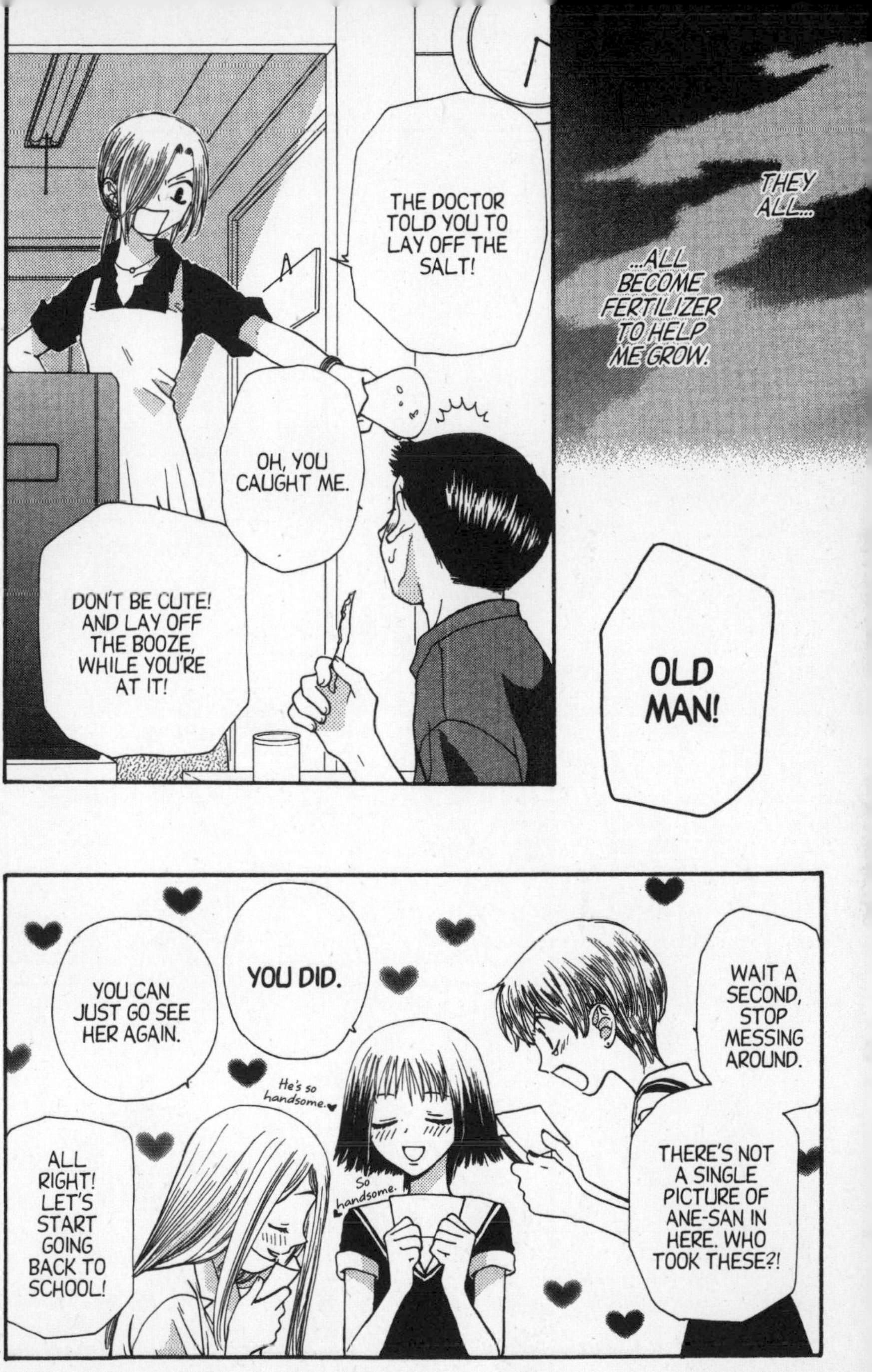

THEY ALL...
...ALL BECOME FERTILIZER TO HELP ME GROW.
OLD MAN!
THE DOCTOR TOLD YOU TO LAY OFF THE SALT!
OH, YOU CAUGHT ME.
DON'T BE CUTE! AND LAY OFF THE BOOZE, WHILE YOU'RE AT IT!
WAIT A SECOND, STOP MESSING AROUND.
THERE'S NOT A SINGLE PICTURE OF ANE-SAN IN HERE. WHO TOOK THESE?!
He's so handsome.
So handsome.
YOU DID.
YOU CAN JUST GO SEE HER AGAIN.
ALL RIGHT! LET'S START GOING BACK TO SCHOOL!

Chapter 42

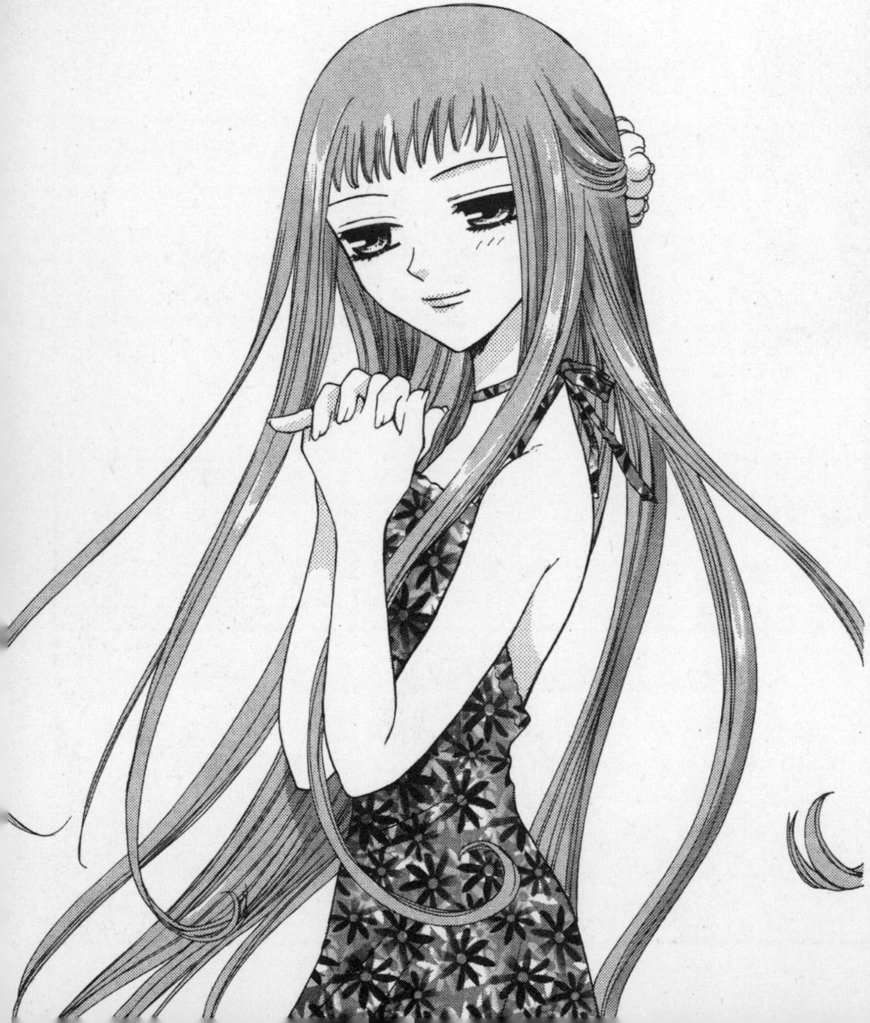

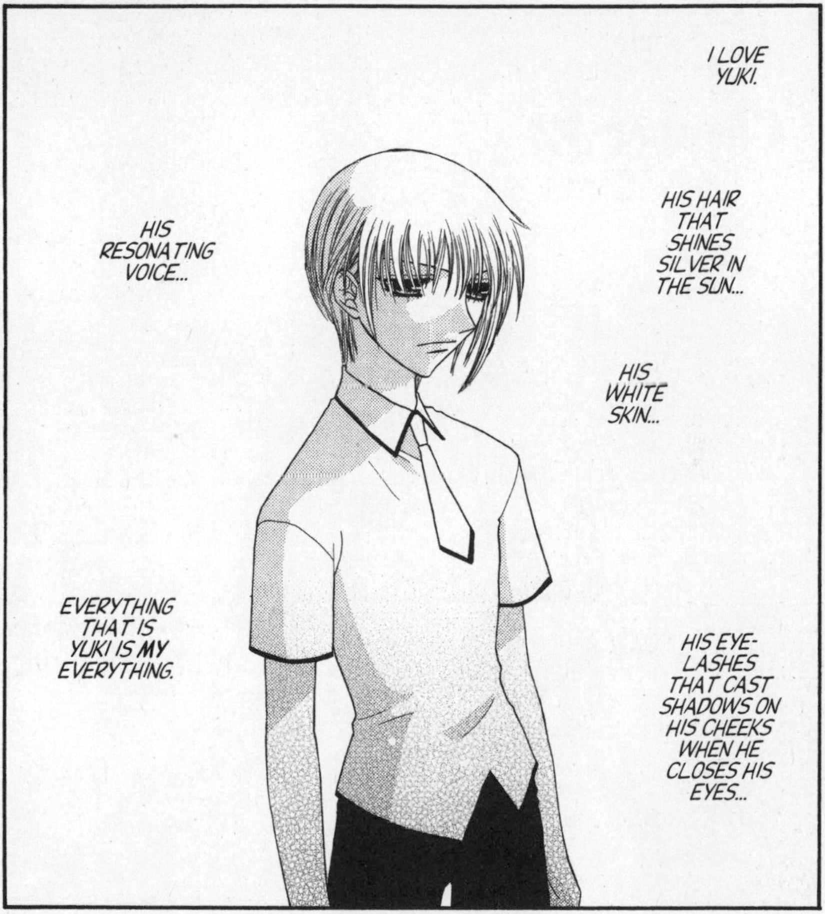
I LOVE YUKI.
HIS HAIR THAT SHINES SILVER IN THE SUN...
HIS RESONATING VOICE...
HIS WHITE SKIN...
HIS EYELASHES THAT CAST SHADOWS ON HIS CHEEKS WHEN HE CLOSES HIS EYES...
EVERYTHING THAT IS YUKI IS MY EVERYTHING.

ULTRA-SPECIAL BLAH, BLAH, BLAH 6

Seeing the form of a cheerful girl reminds me the earth is still spinning and all is right in the world...but... When Mio (the Yuki-Club first year rep) becomes president, Yuki will have already graduated... Or so someone reminded me...and they were absolutely correct (laugh). I was wrong. So careless. But that is, it's...okay...or isn't it? (laugh)

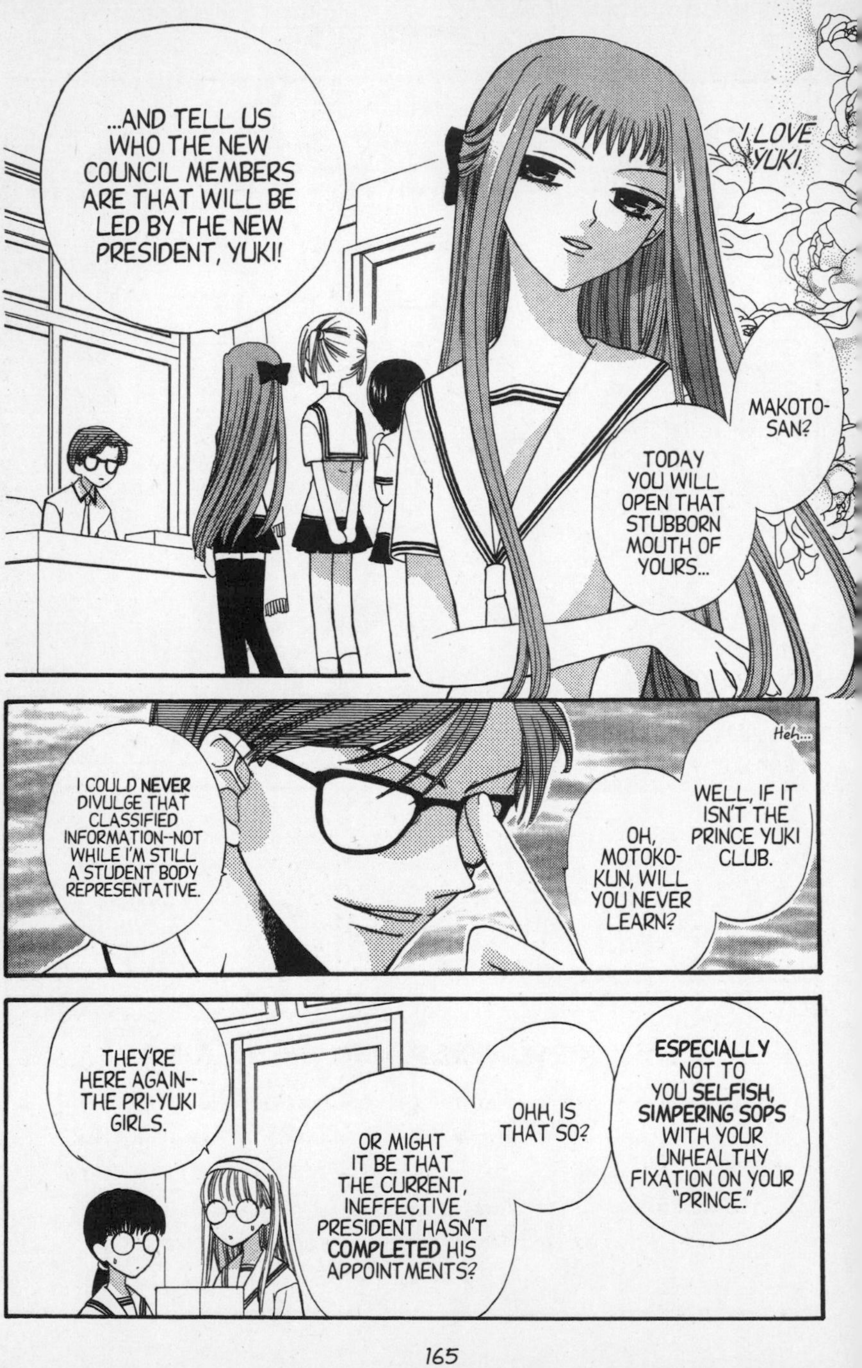
I LOVE YUKI.
MAKOTO-SAN?
TODAY YOU WILL OPEN THAT STUBBORN MOUTH OF YOURS...
...AND TELL US WHO THE NEW COUNCIL MEMBERS ARE THAT WILL BE LED BY THE NEW PRESIDENT, YUKI!
Heh...
WELL, IF IT ISN'T THE PRINCE YUKI CLUB.
OH, MOTOKO-KUN, WILL YOU NEVER LEARN?
I COULD NEVER DIVULGE THAT CLASSIFIED INFORMATION--NOT WHILE I'M STILL A STUDENT BODY REPRESENTATIVE.
ESPECIALLY NOT TO YOU SELFISH, SIMPERING SOPS WITH YOUR UNHEALTHY FIXATION ON YOUR "PRINCE."
OHH, IS THAT SO?
OR MIGHT IT BE THAT THE CURRENT, INEFFECTIVE PRESIDENT HASN'T COMPLETED HIS APPOINTMENTS?
THEY'RE HERE AGAIN-- THE PRI-YUKI GIRLS.

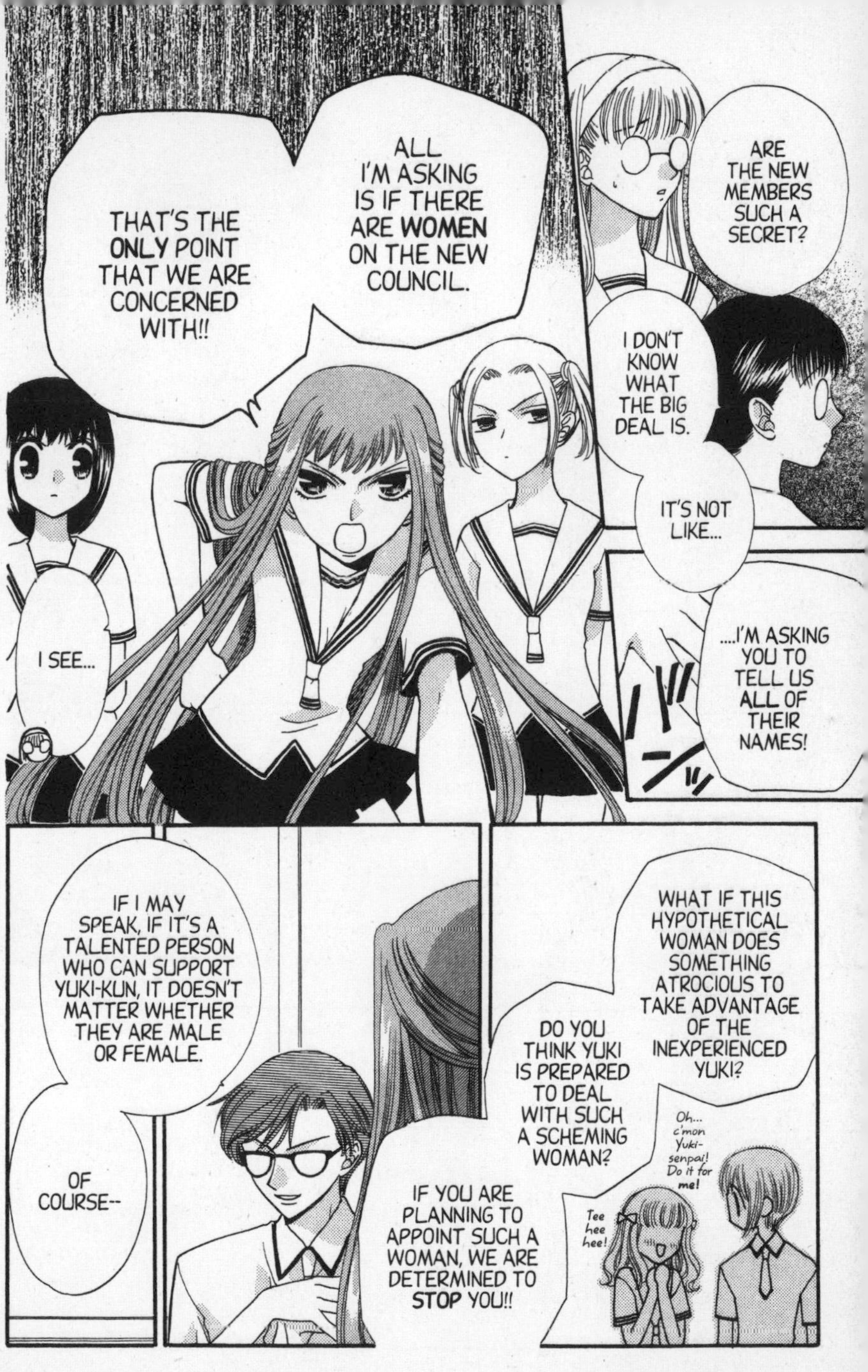
ARE THE NEW MEMBERS SUCH A SECRET?
I DON'T KNOW WHAT THE BIG DEAL IS.
IT'S NOT LIKE...
....I'M ASKING YOU TO TELL US **ALL** OF THEIR NAMES!
ALL I'M ASKING IS IF THERE ARE **WOMEN** ON THE NEW COUNCIL.
THAT'S THE **ONLY** POINT THAT WE ARE CONCERNED WITH!!
I SEE...
WHAT IF THIS HYPOTHETICAL WOMAN DOES SOMETHING ATROCIOUS TO TAKE ADVANTAGE OF THE INEXPERIENCED YUKI?
DO YOU THINK YUKI IS PREPARED TO DEAL WITH SUCH A SCHEMING WOMAN?
Oh... c'mon Yuki-senpai! Do it for **me!**
Tee hee hee!
IF I MAY SPEAK, IF IT'S A TALENTED PERSON WHO CAN SUPPORT YUKI-KUN, IT DOESN'T MATTER WHETHER THEY ARE MALE OR FEMALE.
OF COURSE--
IF YOU ARE PLANNING TO APPOINT SUCH A WOMAN, WE ARE DETERMINED TO **STOP** YOU!!

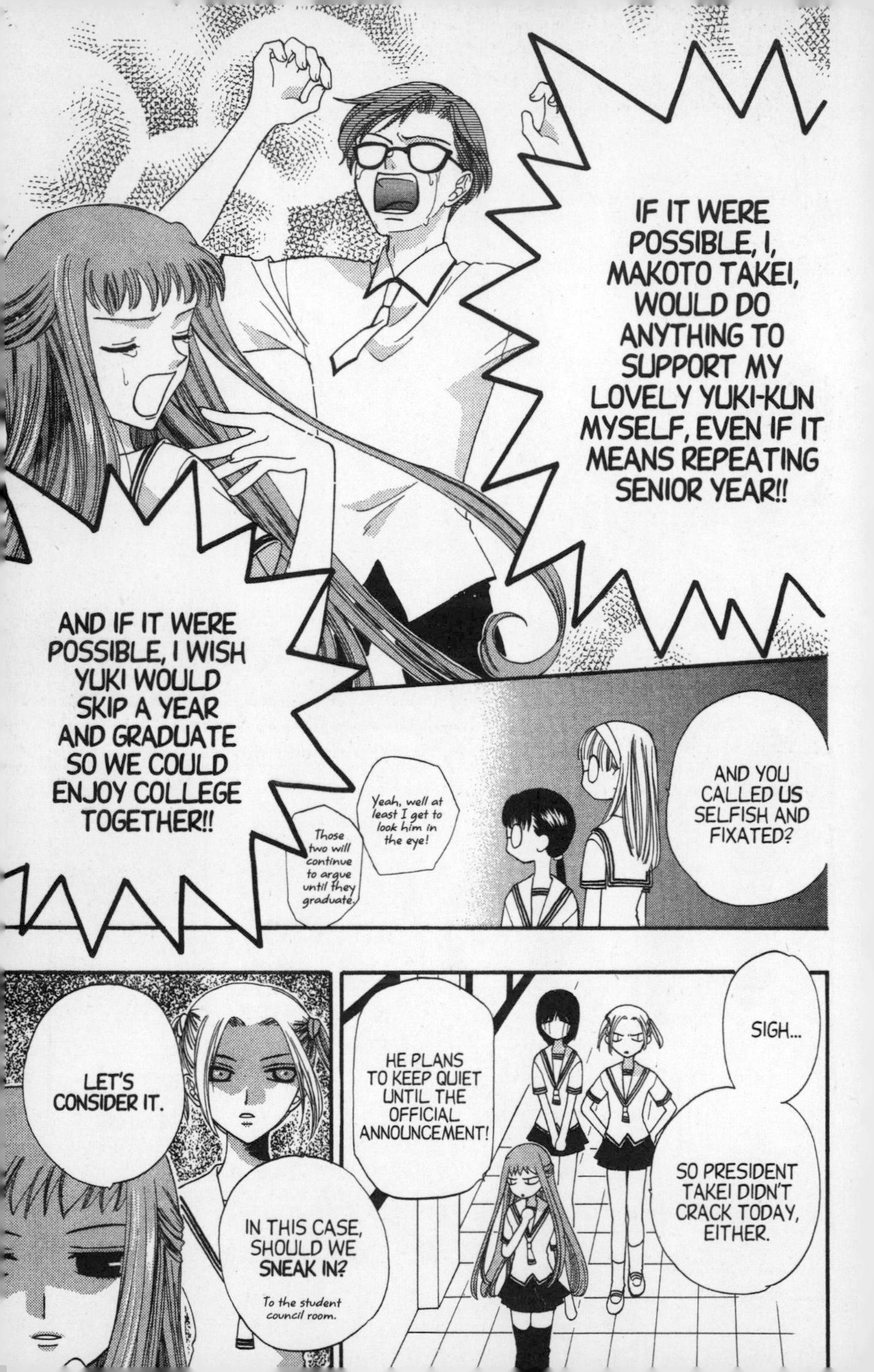
IF IT WERE POSSIBLE, I, MAKOTO TAKEI, WOULD DO ANYTHING TO SUPPORT MY LOVELY YUKI-KUN MYSELF, EVEN IF IT MEANS REPEATING SENIOR YEAR!!
AND IF IT WERE POSSIBLE, I WISH YUKI WOULD SKIP A YEAR AND GRADUATE SO WE COULD ENJOY COLLEGE TOGETHER!!
AND YOU CALLED US SELFISH AND FIXATED?
Yeah, well at least I get to look him in the eye!
Those two will continue to argue until they graduate.
SIGH...
SO PRESIDENT TAKEI DIDN'T CRACK TODAY, EITHER.
HE PLANS TO KEEP QUIET UNTIL THE OFFICIAL ANNOUNCEMENT!
IN THIS CASE, SHOULD WE SNEAK IN?
To the student council room.
LET'S CONSIDER IT.

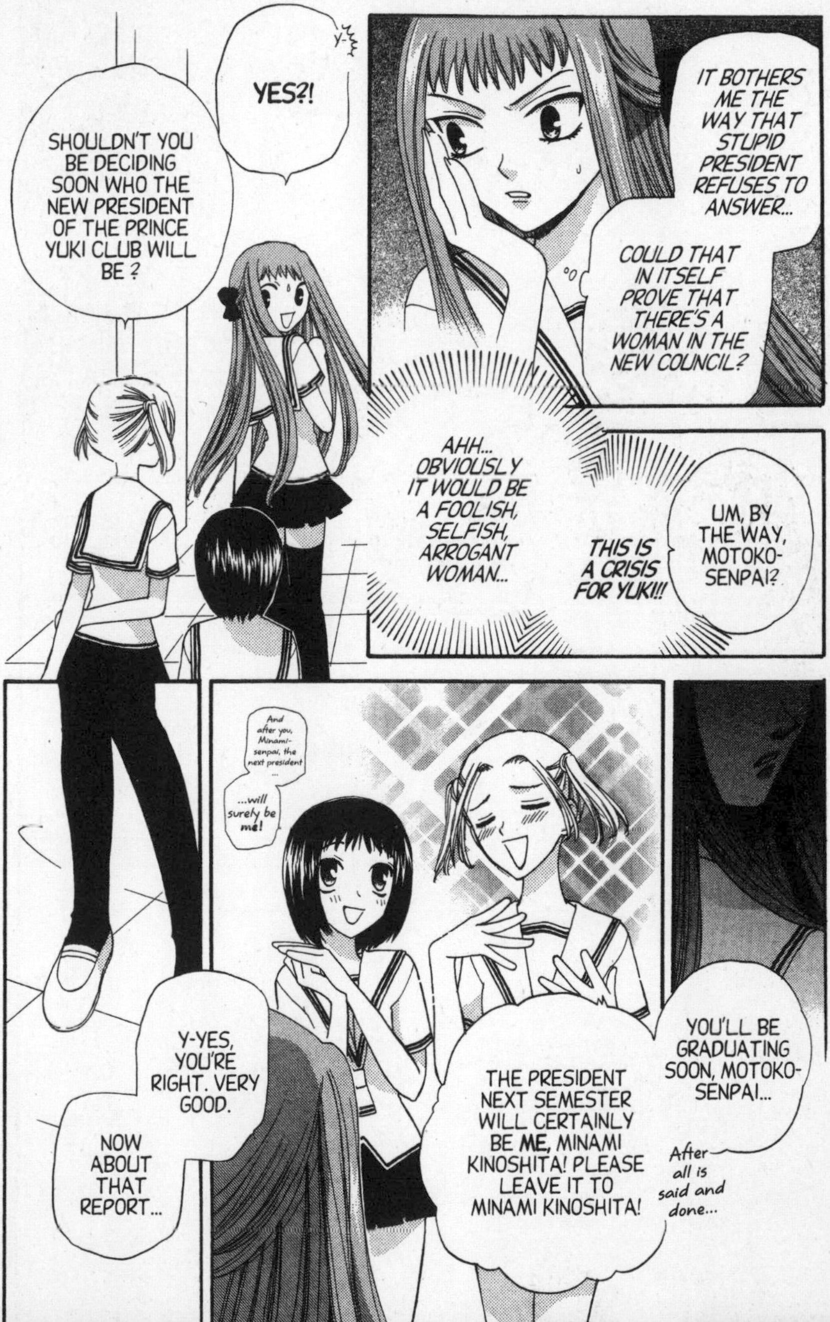
IT BOTHERS ME THE WAY THAT STUPID PRESIDENT REFUSES TO ANSWER...
COULD THAT IN ITSELF PROVE THAT THERE'S A WOMAN IN THE NEW COUNCIL?
AHH... OBVIOUSLY IT WOULD BE A FOOLISH, SELFISH, ARROGANT WOMAN...
THIS IS A CRISIS FOR YUKI!!
UM, BY THE WAY, MOTOKO-SENPAI?
YES?!
SHOULDN'T YOU BE DECIDING SOON WHO THE NEW PRESIDENT OF THE PRINCE YUKI CLUB WILL BE?
YOU'LL BE GRADUATING SOON, MOTOKO-SENPAI...
After all is said and done...
THE PRESIDENT NEXT SEMESTER WILL CERTAINLY BE ME, MINAMI KINOSHITA! PLEASE LEAVE IT TO MINAMI KINOSHITA!
And after you, Minami-senpai, the next president ...
...will surely be me!
Y-YES, YOU'RE RIGHT. VERY GOOD.
NOW ABOUT THAT REPORT...

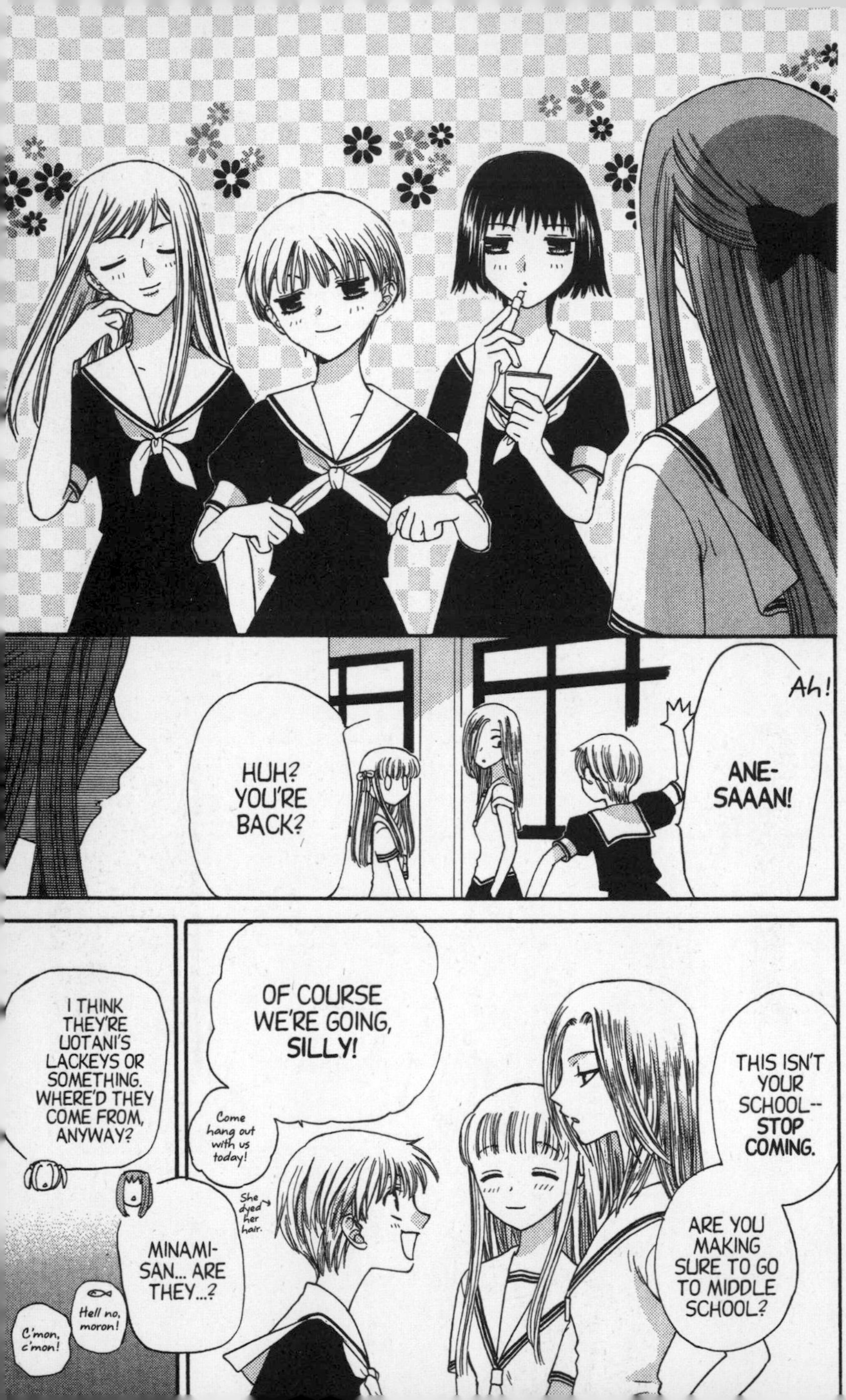

Ah!
ANE-SAAAN!
HUH? YOU'RE BACK?
THIS ISN'T YOUR SCHOOL-- STOP COMING.
ARE YOU MAKING SURE TO GO TO MIDDLE SCHOOL?
OF COURSE WE'RE GOING, SILLY!
Come hang out with us today!
She dyed her hair.
MINAMI-SAN... ARE THEY...?
Hell no, moron!
C'mon, c'mon!
I THINK THEY'RE UOTANI'S LACKEYS OR SOMETHING. WHERE'D THEY COME FROM, ANYWAY?

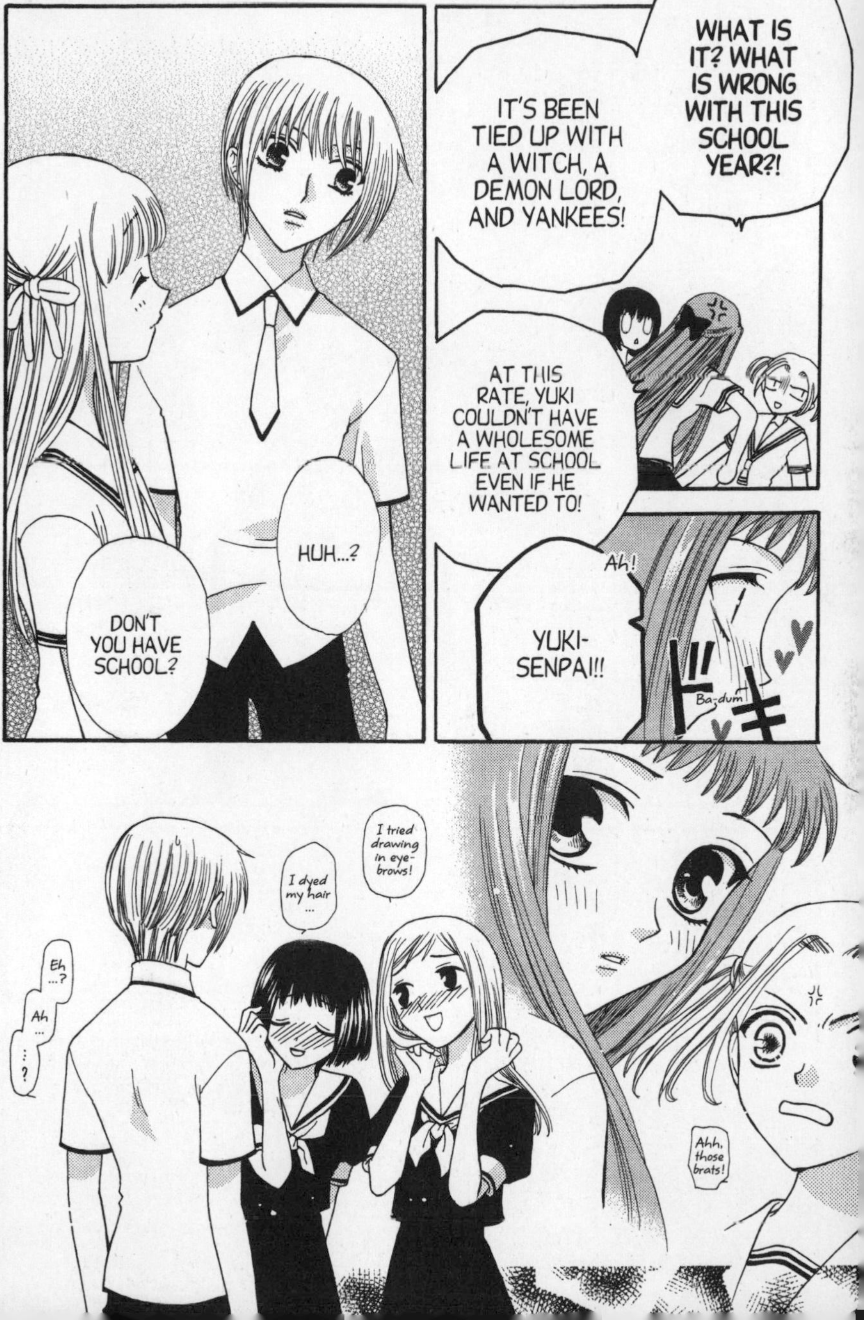
WHAT IS IT? WHAT IS WRONG WITH THIS SCHOOL YEAR?!
IT'S BEEN TIED UP WITH A WITCH, A DEMON LORD, AND YANKEES!
AT THIS RATE, YUKI COULDN'T HAVE A WHOLESOME LIFE AT SCHOOL EVEN IF HE WANTED TO!
Ah!
YUKI-SENPAI!!
Ba-dum
HUH...?
DON'T YOU HAVE SCHOOL?
Ahh, those brats!
I tried drawing in eye-brows!
I dyed my hair ...
Eh ...?
Ah ...
...?

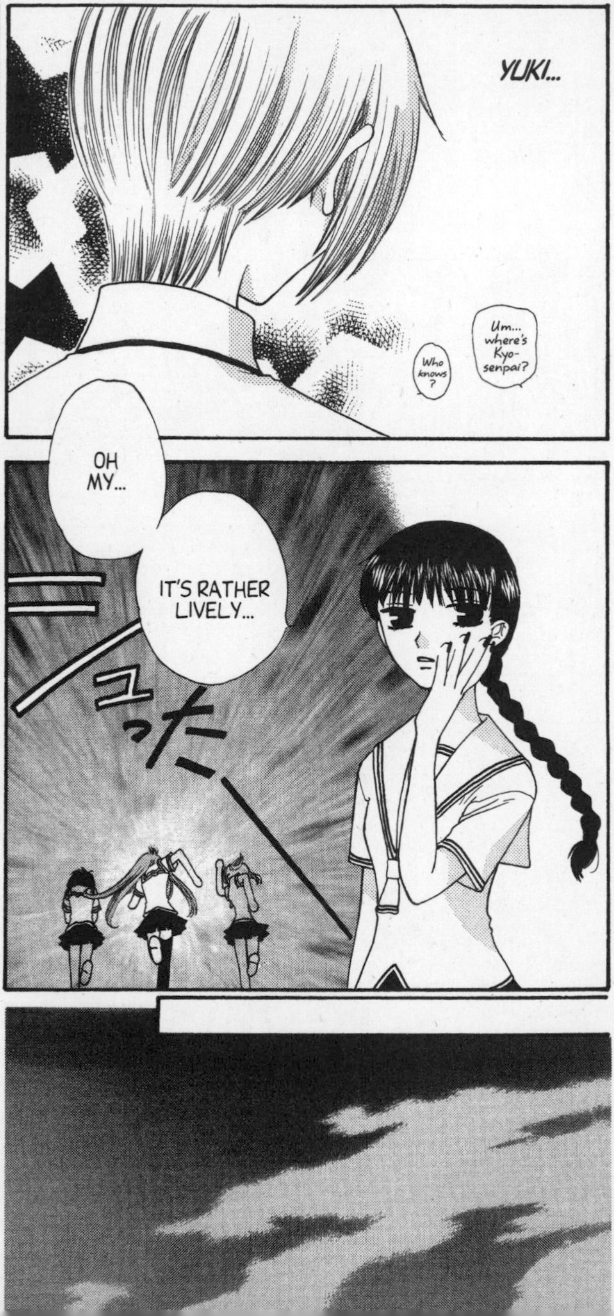
YUKI...
Um... where's Kyo-senpai?
Who knows?
OH MY...
IT'S RATHER LIVELY...

Fruits Basket 7: Part 6

Anyway... Anyway, I wanted to draw again, so I continued to do my best. I think it's good that I did. The possibility of it happening again isn't zero, so I might scare myself and the people around me, but I was so happy that I recovered. I'm praying that I can draw Furuba to the end, and I will keep doing my best. To all you readers who encouraged me, thank you very much. All I can ask is that you to please enjoy *Fruits Basket*. Well then, see you again soon!

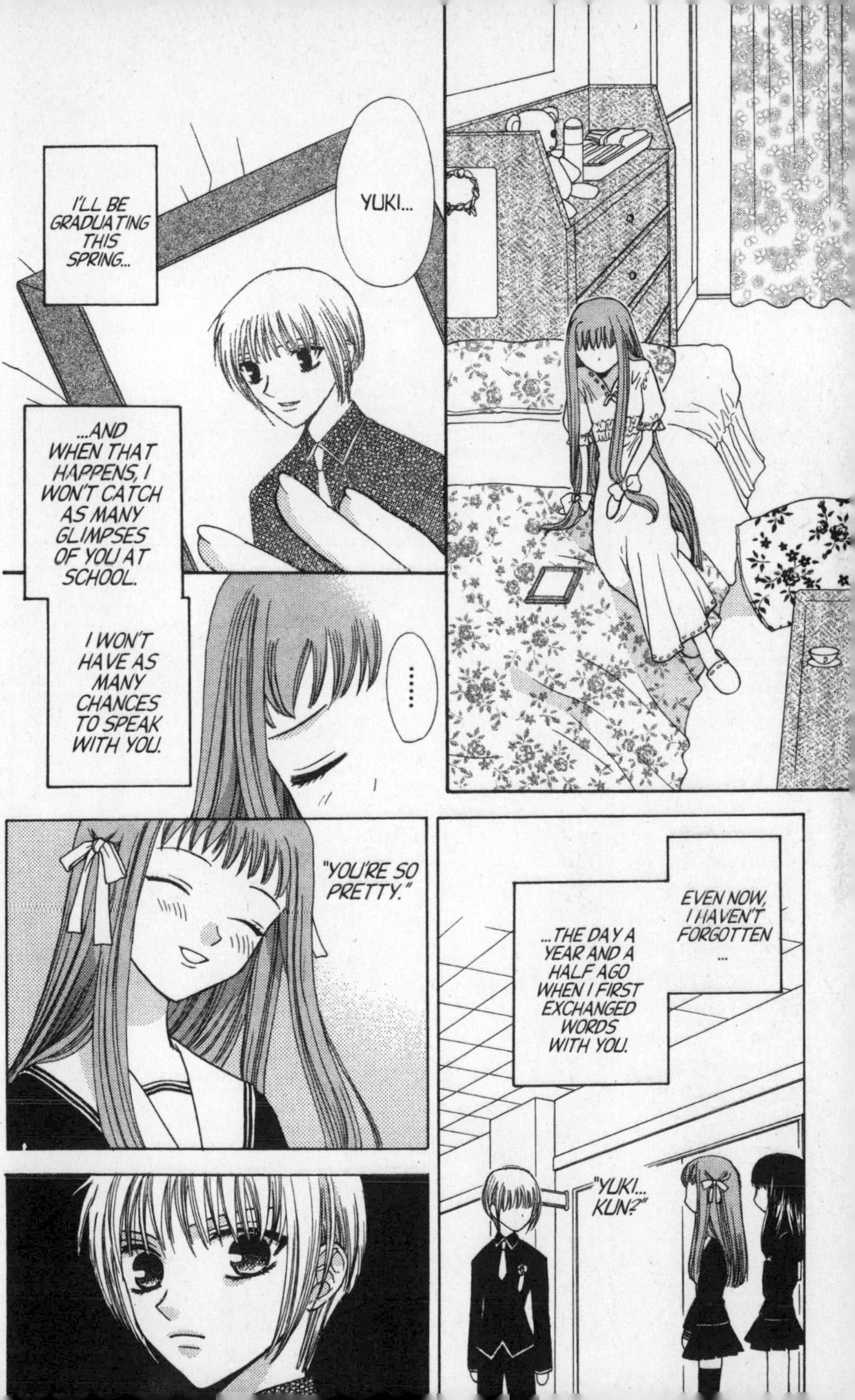
YUKI...
I'LL BE GRADUATING THIS SPRING...
...AND WHEN THAT HAPPENS, I WON'T CATCH AS MANY GLIMPSES OF YOU AT SCHOOL.
......
I WON'T HAVE AS MANY CHANCES TO SPEAK WITH YOU.
EVEN NOW, I HAVEN'T FORGOTTEN ...
...THE DAY A YEAR AND A HALF AGO WHEN I FIRST EXCHANGED WORDS WITH YOU.
"YUKI... KUN?"
"YOU'RE SO PRETTY."

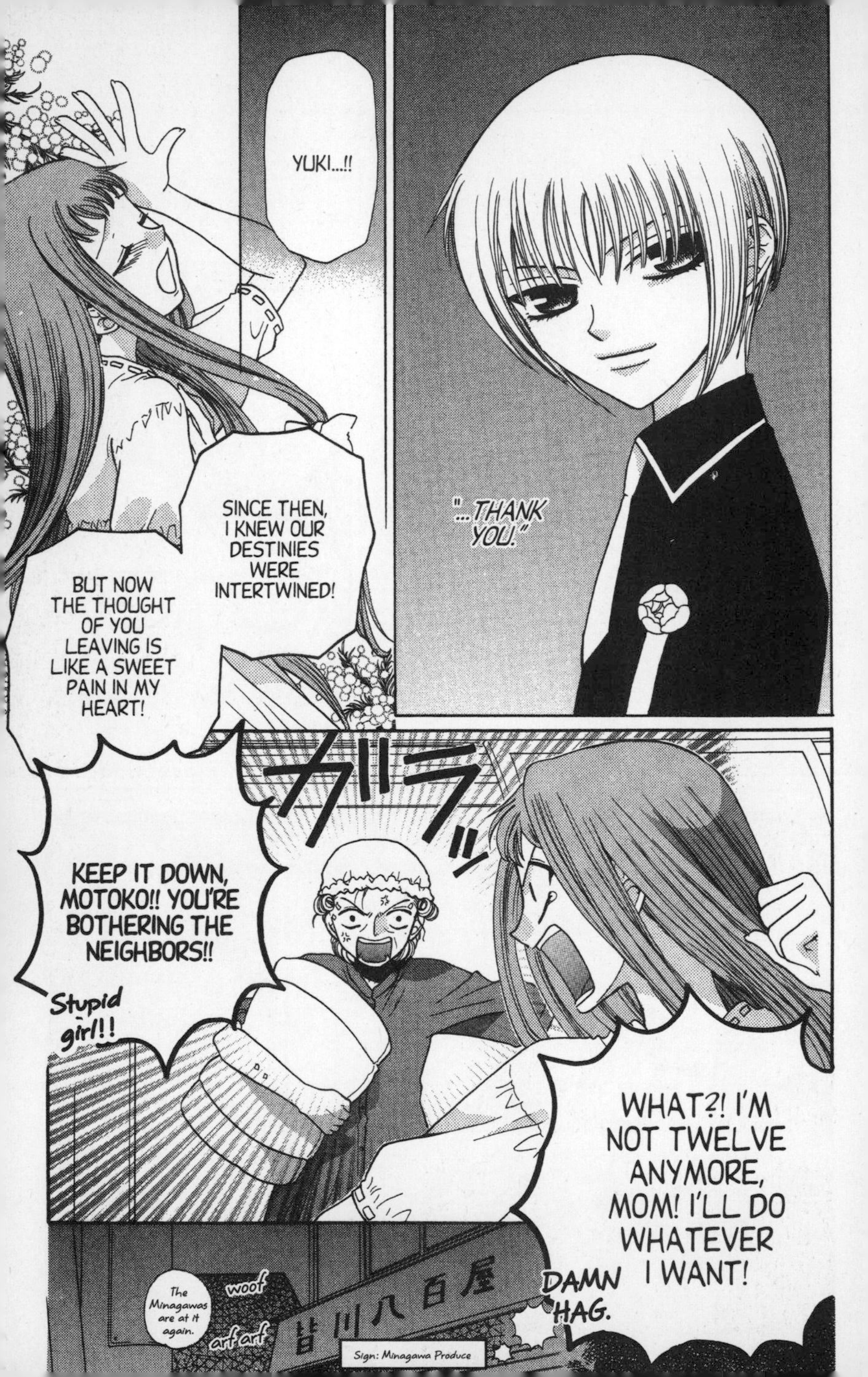
"...THANK YOU."
YUKI...!!
SINCE THEN, I KNEW OUR DESTINIES WERE INTERTWINED!
BUT NOW THE THOUGHT OF YOU LEAVING IS LIKE A SWEET PAIN IN MY HEART!
カラッ
KEEP IT DOWN, MOTOKO!! YOU'RE BOTHERING THE NEIGHBORS!!
Stupid girl!!
WHAT?! I'M NOT TWELVE ANYMORE, MOM! I'LL DO WHATEVER I WANT!
DAMN HAG.
皆川八百屋
woof
arf arf
The Minagawas are at it again.
Sign: Minagawa Produce

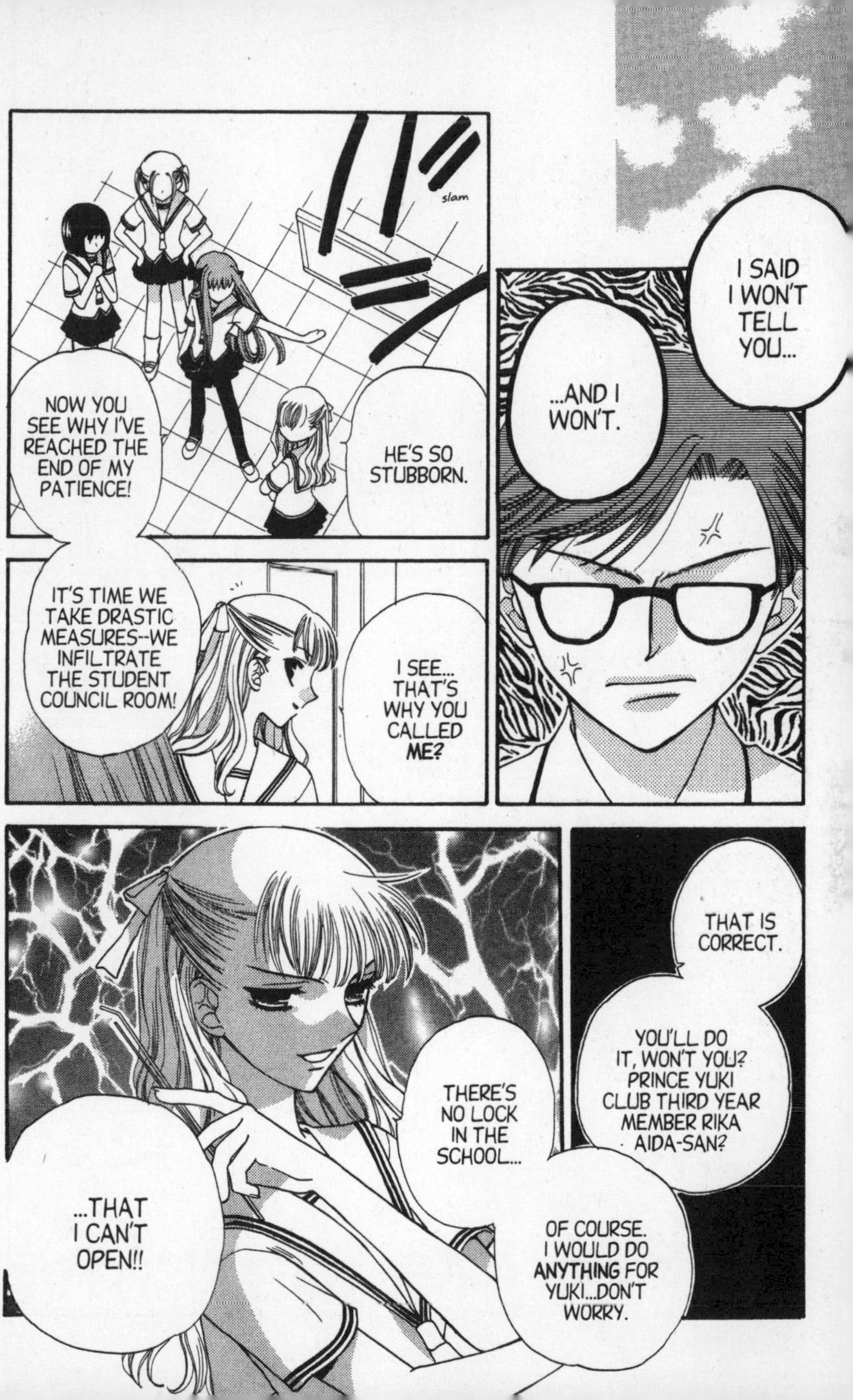
I SAID I WON'T TELL YOU...
...AND I WON'T.
slam
HE'S SO STUBBORN.
NOW YOU SEE WHY I'VE REACHED THE END OF MY PATIENCE!
IT'S TIME WE TAKE DRASTIC MEASURES--WE INFILTRATE THE STUDENT COUNCIL ROOM!
I SEE... THAT'S WHY YOU CALLED **ME?**
THAT IS CORRECT.
YOU'LL DO IT, WON'T YOU? PRINCE YUKI CLUB THIRD YEAR MEMBER RIKA AIDA-SAN?
OF COURSE. I WOULD DO **ANYTHING** FOR YUKI...DON'T WORRY.
THERE'S NO LOCK IN THE SCHOOL...
...THAT I CAN'T OPEN!!

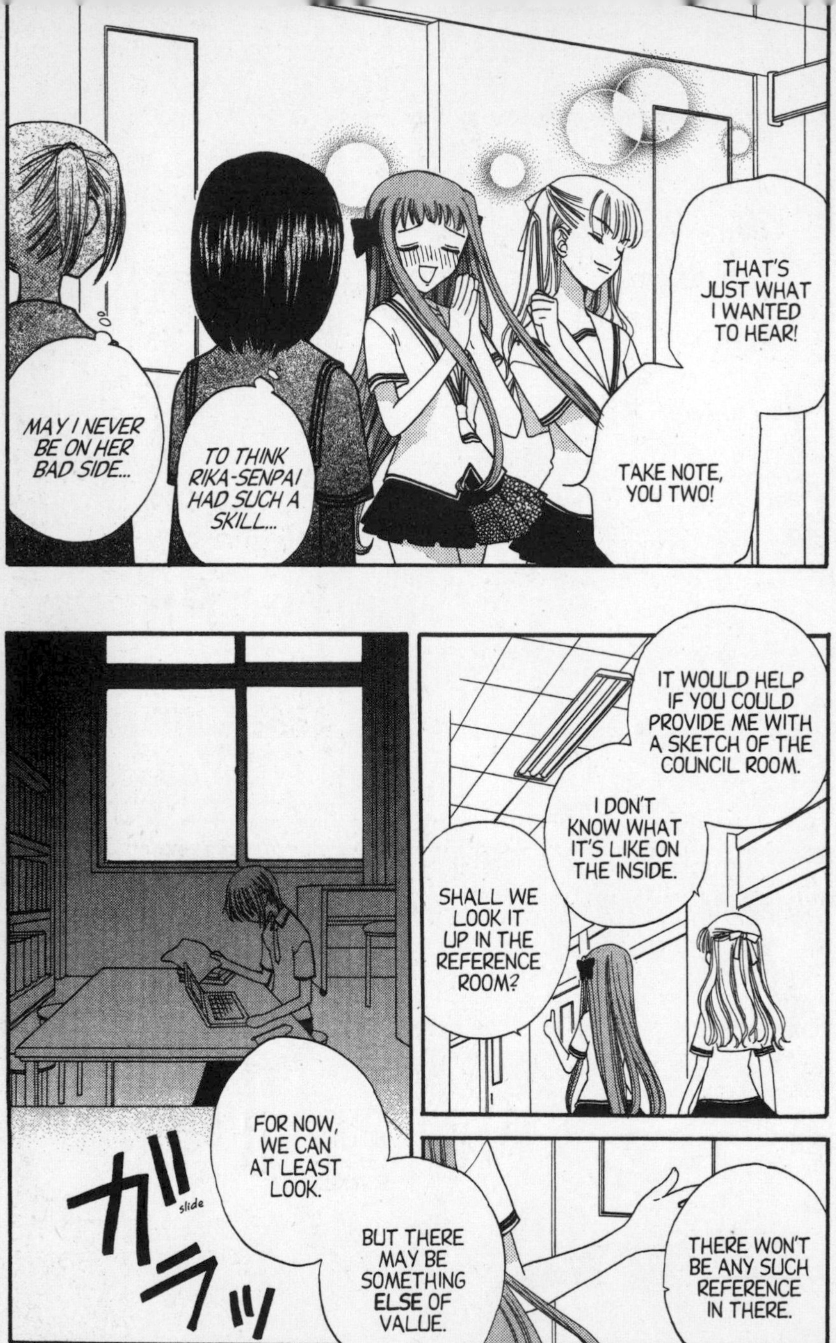
THAT'S JUST WHAT I WANTED TO HEAR!
TAKE NOTE, YOU TWO!
TO THINK RIKA-SENPAI HAD SUCH A SKILL...
MAY I NEVER BE ON HER BAD SIDE...
IT WOULD HELP IF YOU COULD PROVIDE ME WITH A SKETCH OF THE COUNCIL ROOM.
I DON'T KNOW WHAT IT'S LIKE ON THE INSIDE.
SHALL WE LOOK IT UP IN THE REFERENCE ROOM?
THERE WON'T BE ANY SUCH REFERENCE IN THERE.
FOR NOW, WE CAN AT LEAST LOOK.
BUT THERE MAY BE SOMETHING ELSE OF VALUE.
ガラッ
slide

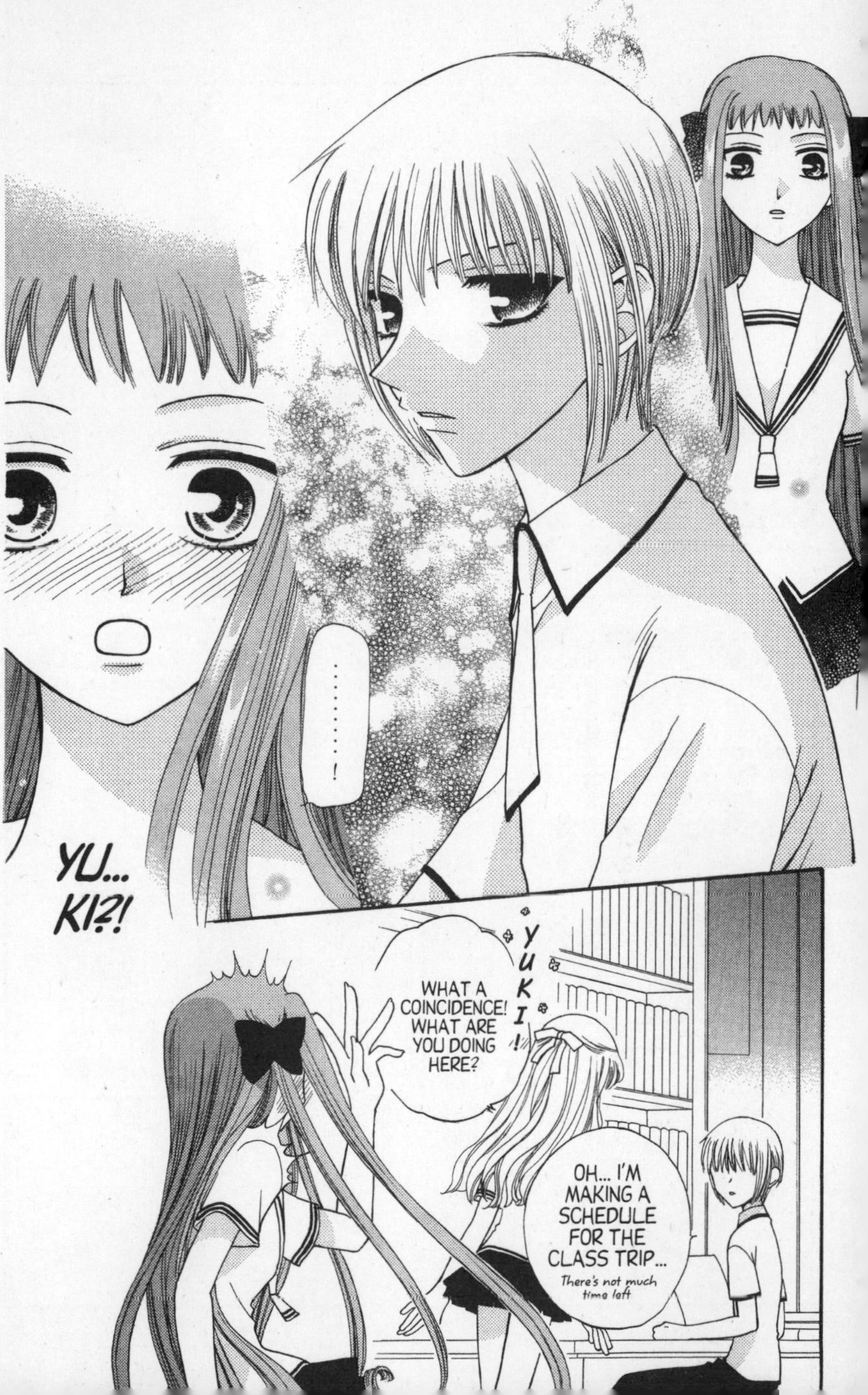
......!
YU... KI?!
YUKI!
WHAT A COINCIDENCE! WHAT ARE YOU DOING HERE?
OH... I'M MAKING A SCHEDULE FOR THE CLASS TRIP...
There's not much time left

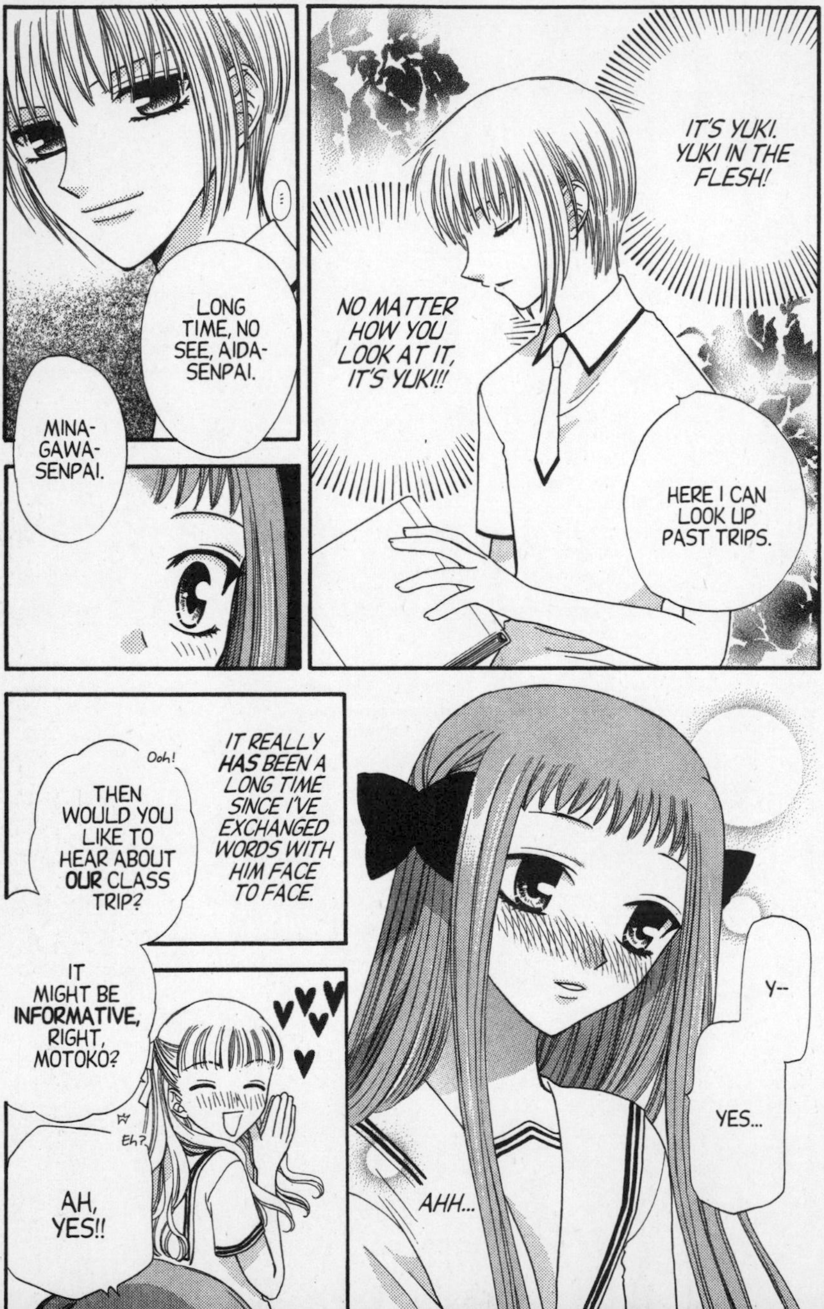
IT'S YUKI. YUKI IN THE FLESH!
NO MATTER HOW YOU LOOK AT IT, IT'S YUKI!!!
HERE I CAN LOOK UP PAST TRIPS.
...
LONG TIME, NO SEE, AIDA-SENPAI.
MINA-GAWA-SENPAI.
Y--
YES...
AHH...
IT REALLY HAS BEEN A LONG TIME SINCE I'VE EXCHANGED WORDS WITH HIM FACE TO FACE.
Ooh!
THEN WOULD YOU LIKE TO HEAR ABOUT OUR CLASS TRIP?
IT MIGHT BE INFORMATIVE, RIGHT, MOTOKO?
Eh?
AH, YES!!

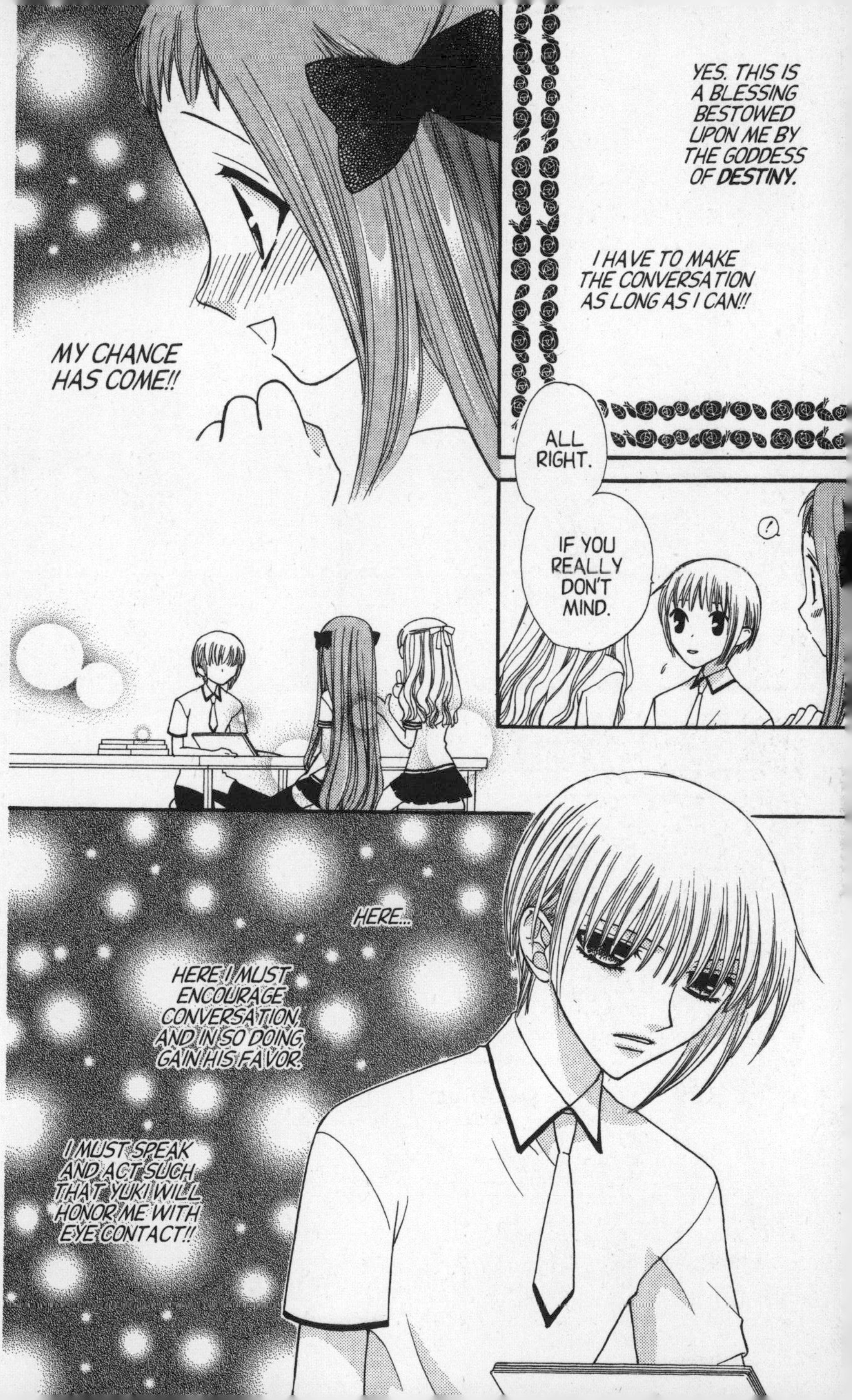
YES. THIS IS A BLESSING BESTOWED UPON ME BY THE GODDESS OF **DESTINY.**
I HAVE TO MAKE THE CONVERSATION AS LONG AS I CAN!!
ALL RIGHT.
IF YOU REALLY DON'T MIND.
!
MY CHANCE HAS COME!!
HERE...
HERE I MUST ENCOURAGE CONVERSATION, AND IN SO DOING, GAIN HIS FAVOR.
I MUST SPEAK AND ACT SUCH THAT YUKI WILL HONOR ME WITH EYE CONTACT!!

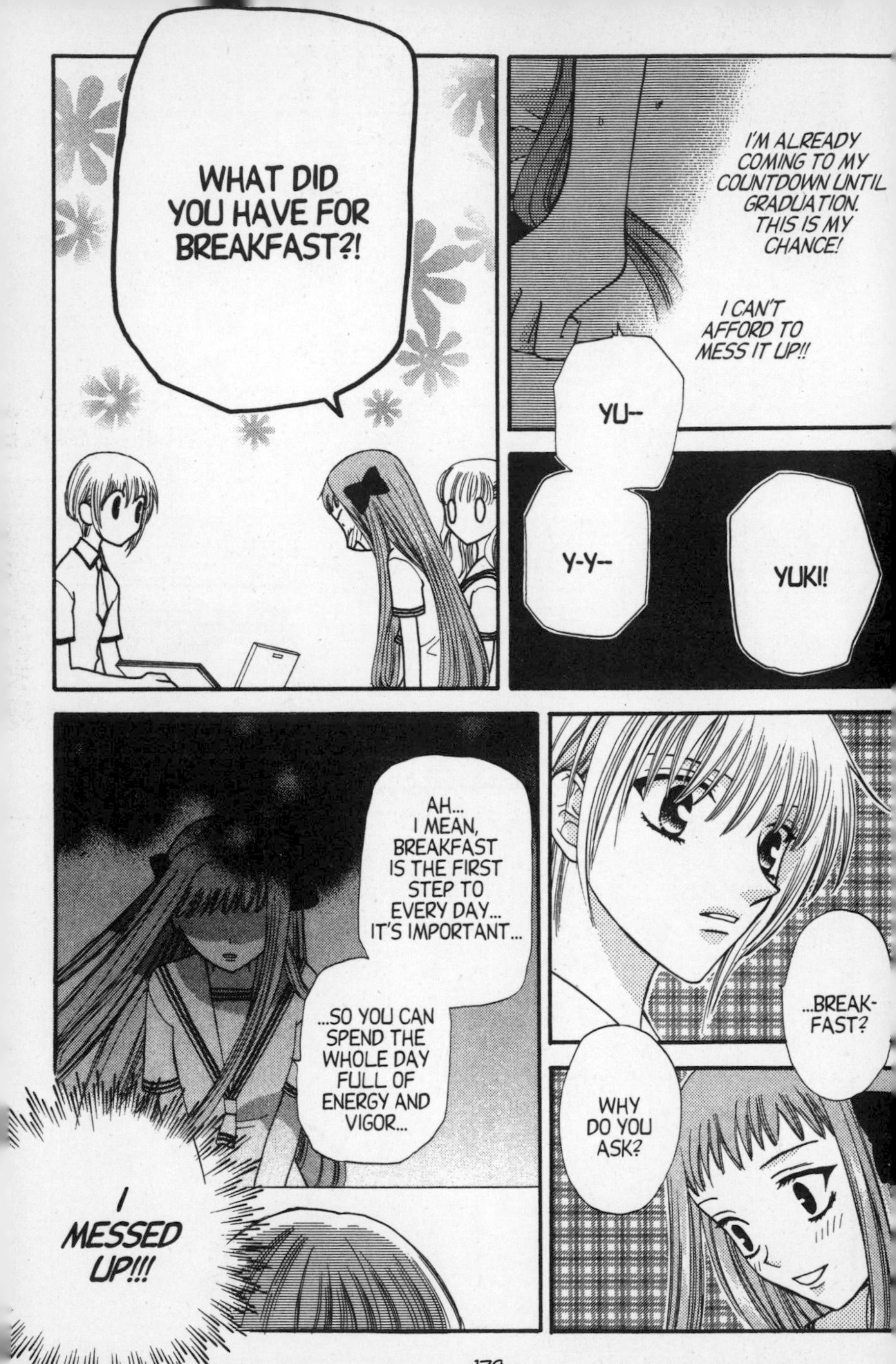

I'M ALREADY COMING TO MY COUNTDOWN UNTIL GRADUATION. THIS IS MY CHANCE!
I CAN'T AFFORD TO MESS IT UP!!
YU--
Y-Y--
YUKI!
WHAT DID YOU HAVE FOR BREAKFAST?!
...BREAK-FAST?
WHY DO YOU ASK?
AH... I MEAN, BREAKFAST IS THE FIRST STEP TO EVERY DAY... IT'S IMPORTANT...
...SO YOU CAN SPEND THE WHOLE DAY FULL OF ENERGY AND VIGOR...
I MESSED UP!!!

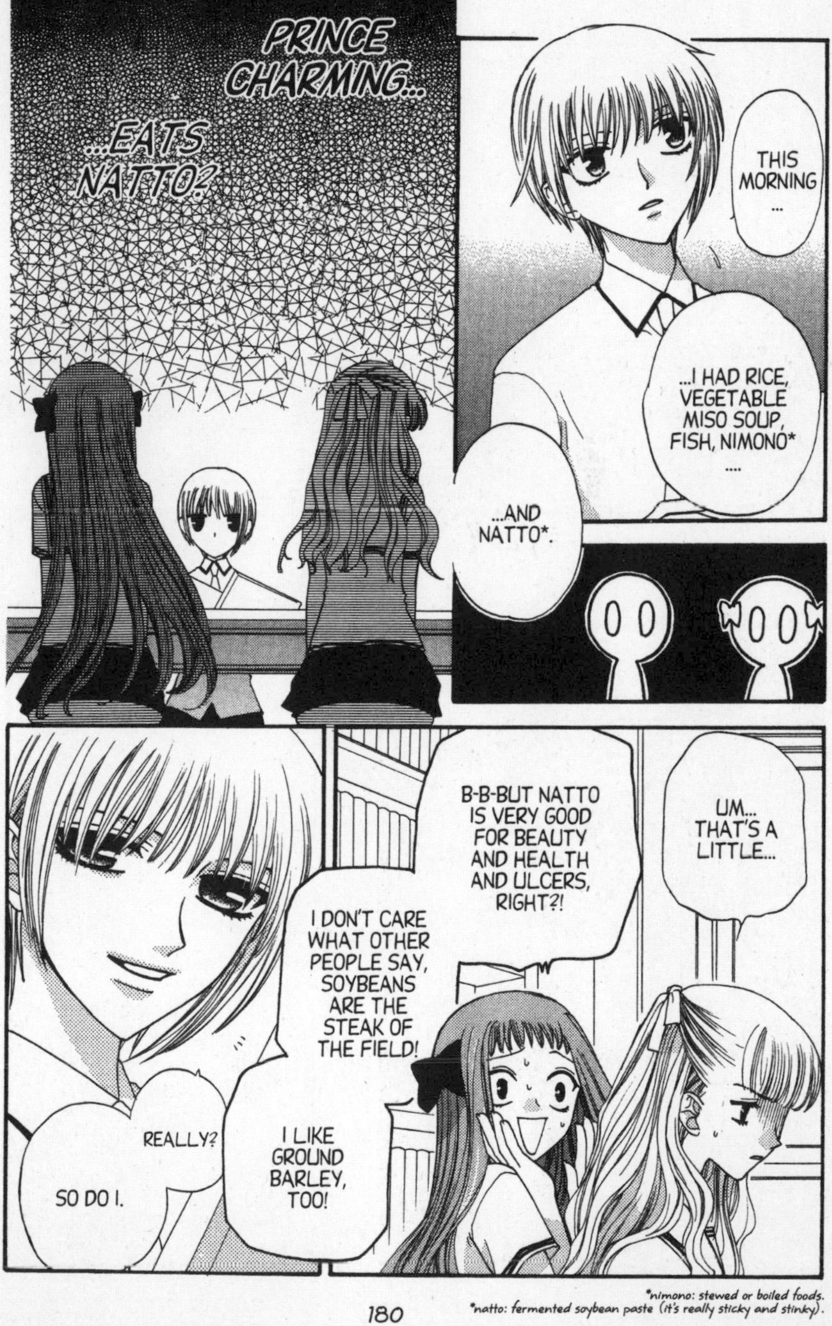
THIS MORNING ...
...I HAD RICE, VEGETABLE MISO SOUP, FISH, NIMONO* ....
...AND NATTO*.
PRINCE CHARMING...
...EATS NATTO?
UM... THAT'S A LITTLE...
B-B-BUT NATTO IS VERY GOOD FOR BEAUTY AND HEALTH AND ULCERS, RIGHT?!
I DON'T CARE WHAT OTHER PEOPLE SAY, SOYBEANS ARE THE STEAK OF THE FIELD!
I LIKE GROUND BARLEY, TOO!
REALLY?
SO DO I.

*nimono: stewed or boiled foods.
*natto: fermented soybean paste (it's really sticky and stinky).

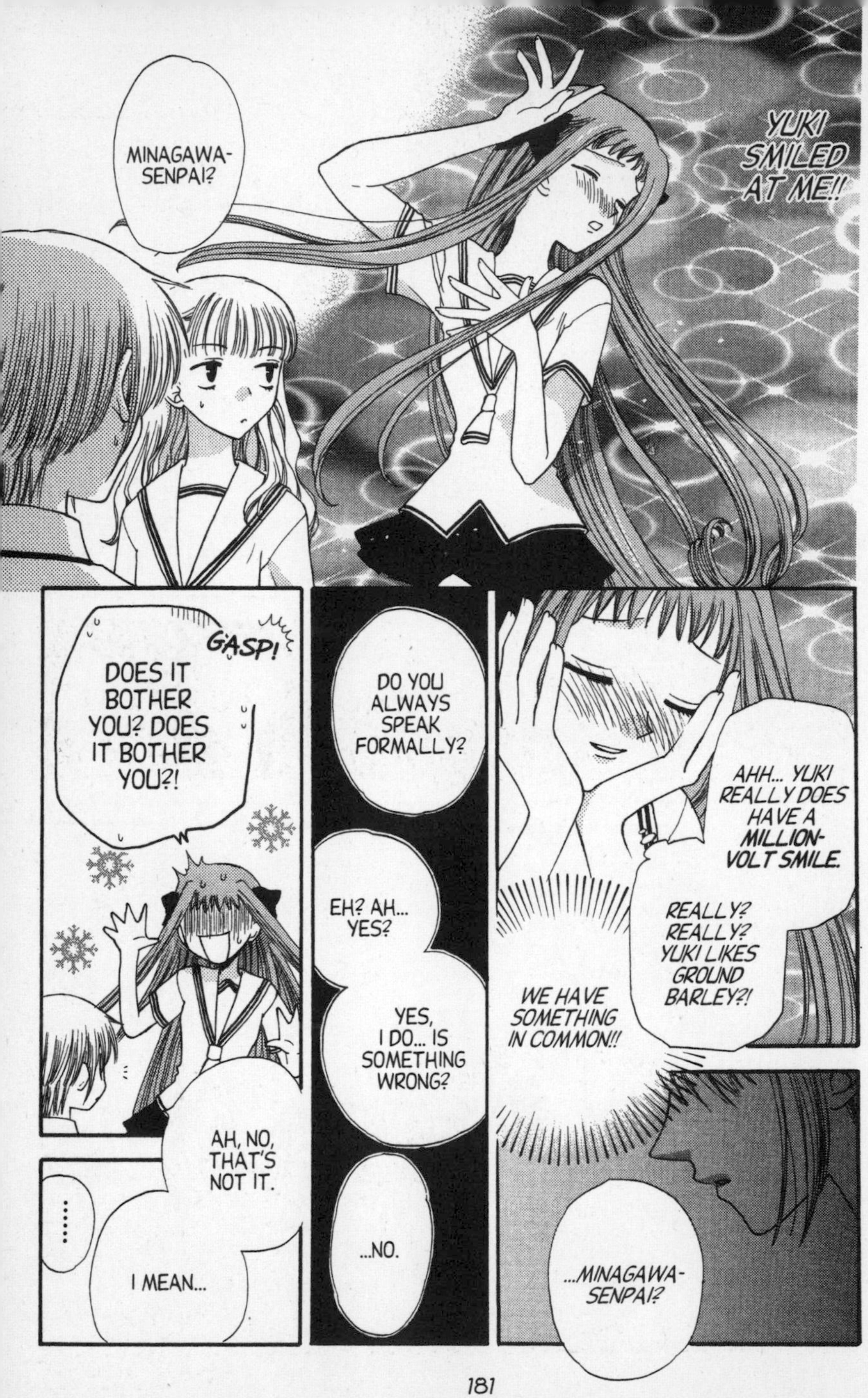
YUKI SMILED AT ME!!
MINAGAWA-SENPAI?
AHH... YUKI REALLY DOES HAVE A MILLION-VOLT SMILE.
REALLY? REALLY? YUKI LIKES GROUND BARLEY?!
WE HAVE SOMETHING IN COMMON!!
...MINAGAWA-SENPAI?
DO YOU ALWAYS SPEAK FORMALLY?
EH? AH... YES?
YES, I DO... IS SOMETHING WRONG?
...NO.
GASP!
DOES IT BOTHER YOU? DOES IT BOTHER YOU?!
AH, NO, THAT'S NOT IT.
......
I MEAN...

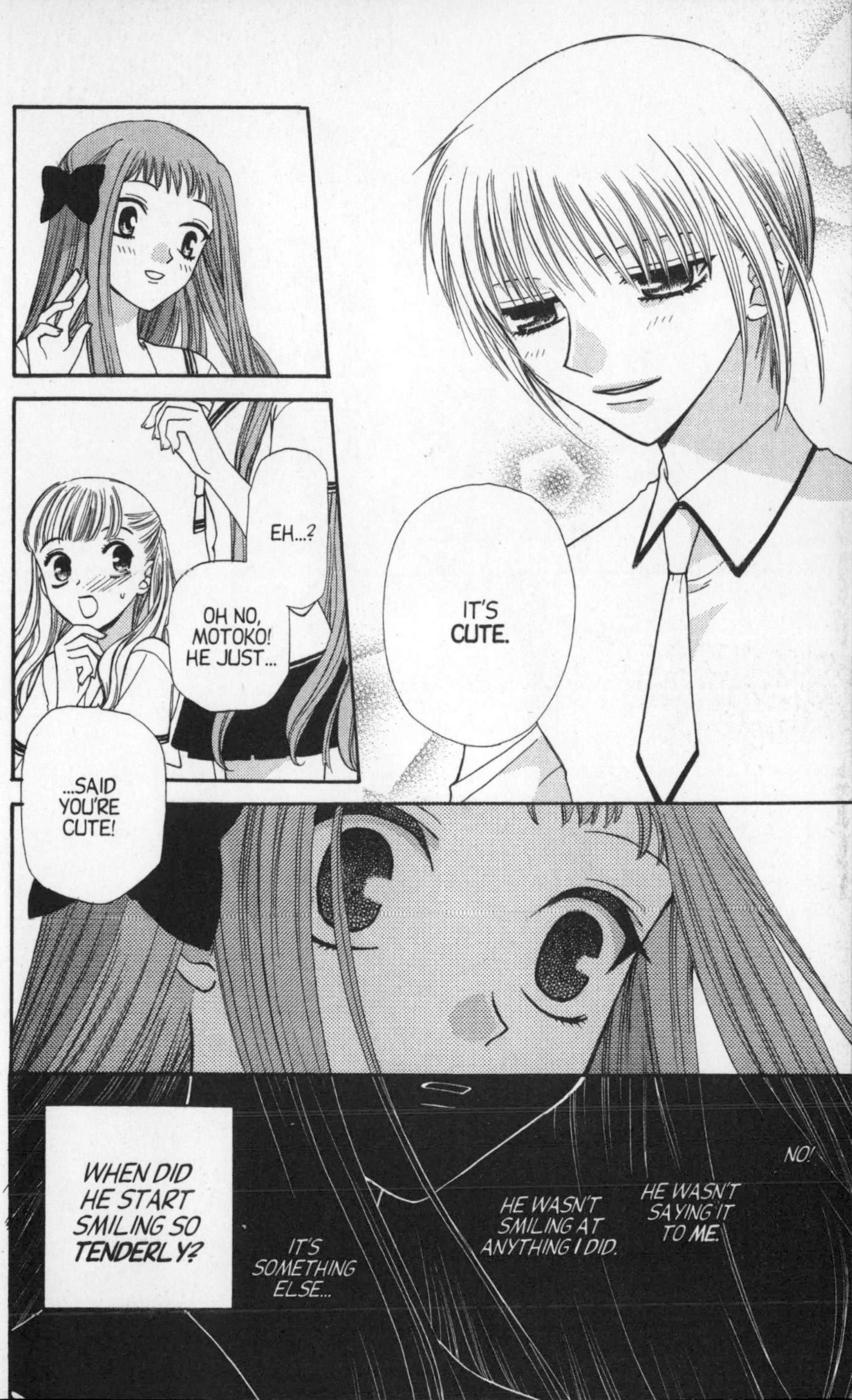
IT'S CUTE.
EH...?
OH NO, MOTOKO! HE JUST...
...SAID YOU'RE CUTE!
NO!
HE WASN'T SAYING IT TO ME.
HE WASN'T SMILING AT ANYTHING I DID.
IT'S SOMETHING ELSE...
WHEN DID HE START SMILING SO TENDERLY?

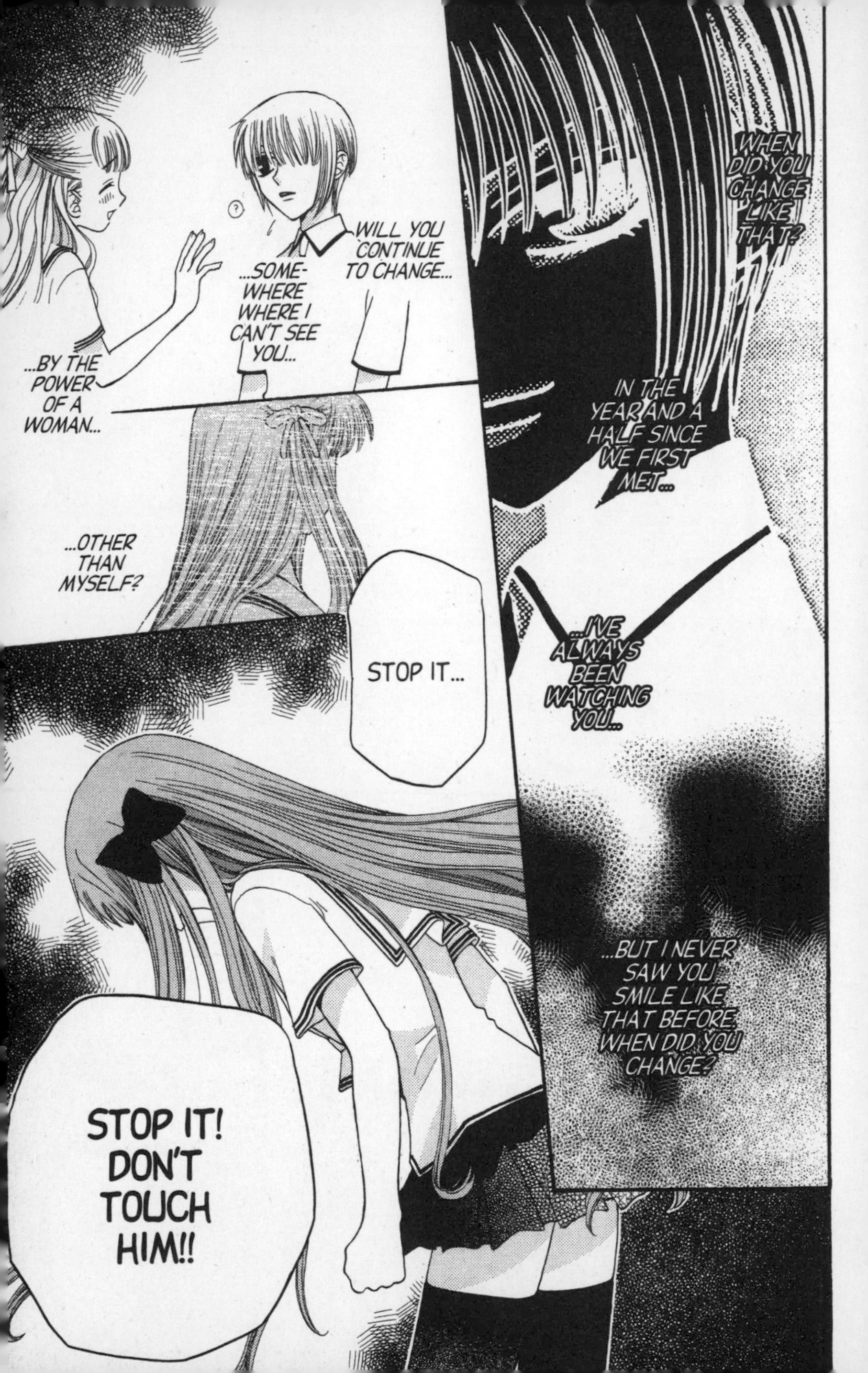
WHEN DID YOU CHANGE LIKE THAT?
IN THE YEAR AND A HALF SINCE WE FIRST MET...
...I'VE ALWAYS BEEN WATCHING YOU...
...BUT I NEVER SAW YOU SMILE LIKE THAT BEFORE. WHEN DID YOU CHANGE?
WILL YOU CONTINUE TO CHANGE...
...SOME-WHERE WHERE I CAN'T SEE YOU...
?
...BY THE POWER OF A WOMAN...
...OTHER THAN MYSELF?
STOP IT...
STOP IT! DON'T TOUCH HIM!!

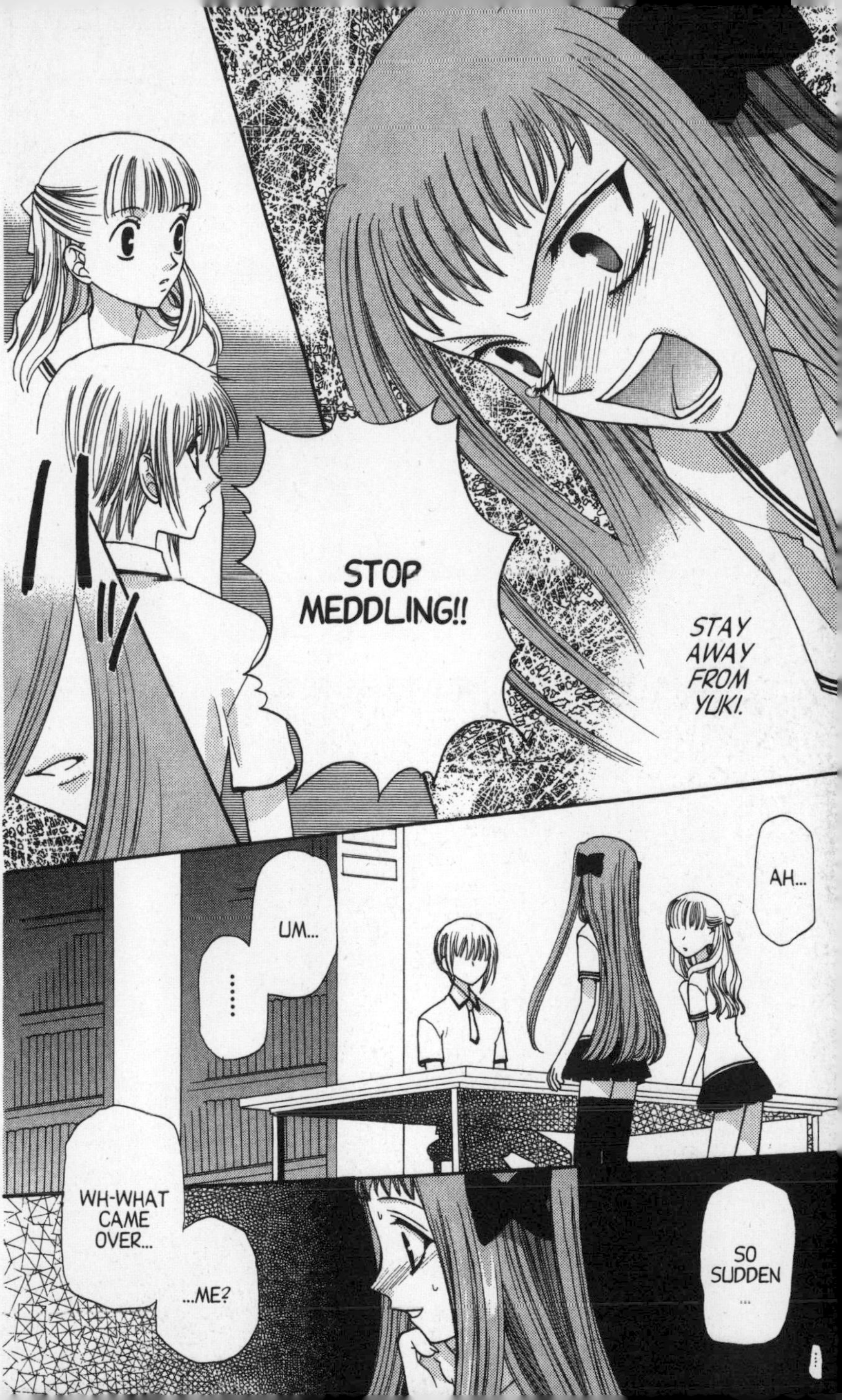
STAY AWAY FROM YUKI.
STOP MEDDLING!!
AH...
UM...
......
SO SUDDEN ...
WH-WHAT CAME OVER...
...ME?

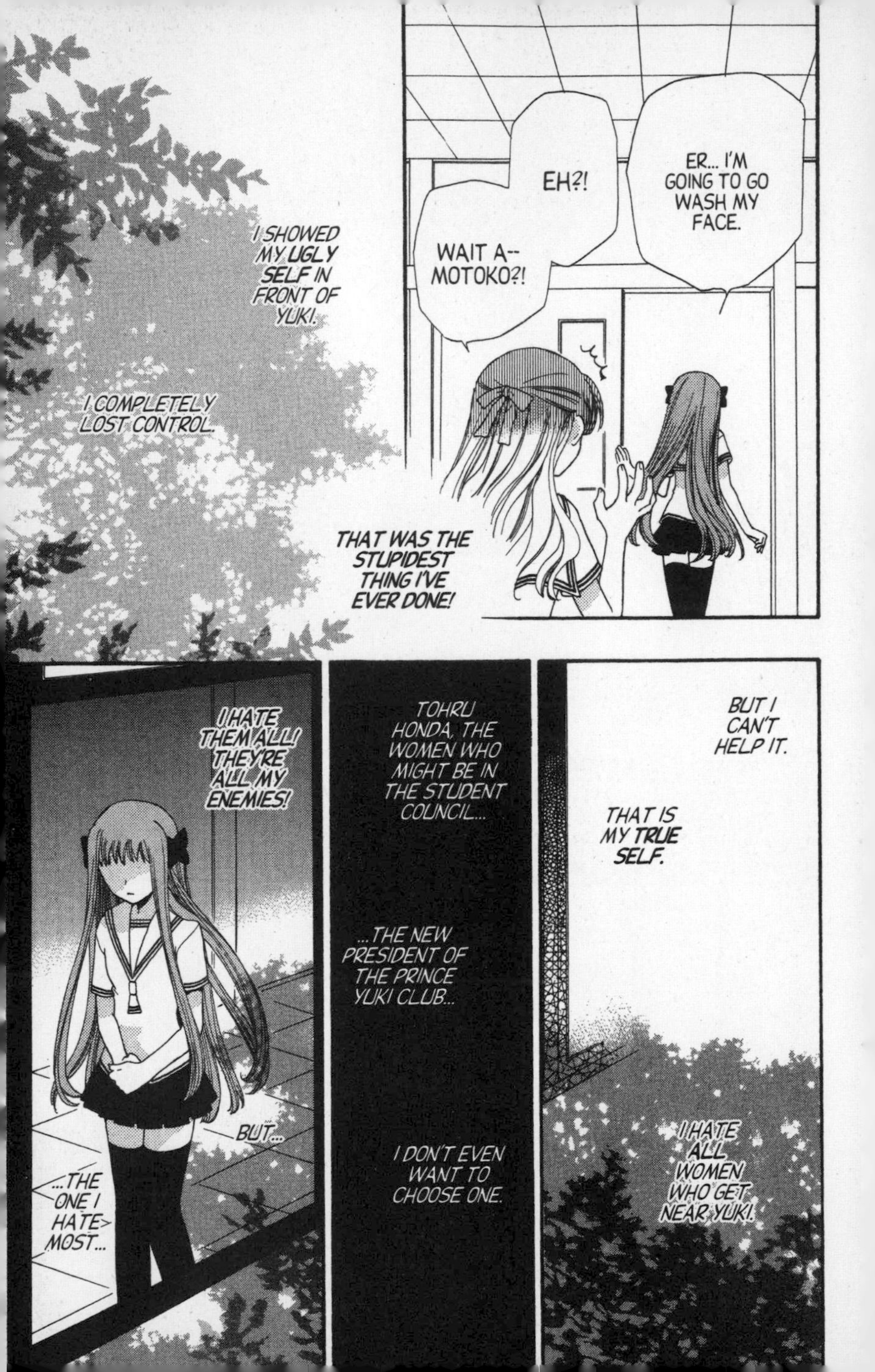
ER... I'M GOING TO GO WASH MY FACE.
EH?!
WAIT A-- MOTOKO?!
I SHOWED MY UGLY SELF IN FRONT OF YUKI.
I COMPLETELY LOST CONTROL.
THAT WAS THE STUPIDEST THING I'VE EVER DONE!
BUT I CAN'T HELP IT.
THAT IS MY TRUE SELF.
I HATE ALL WOMEN WHO GET NEAR YUKI.
TOHRU HONDA, THE WOMEN WHO MIGHT BE IN THE STUDENT COUNCIL...
...THE NEW PRESIDENT OF THE PRINCE YUKI CLUB...
I DON'T EVEN WANT TO CHOOSE ONE.
I HATE THEM ALL! THEY'RE ALL MY ENEMIES!
BUT...
...THE ONE I HATE MOST...

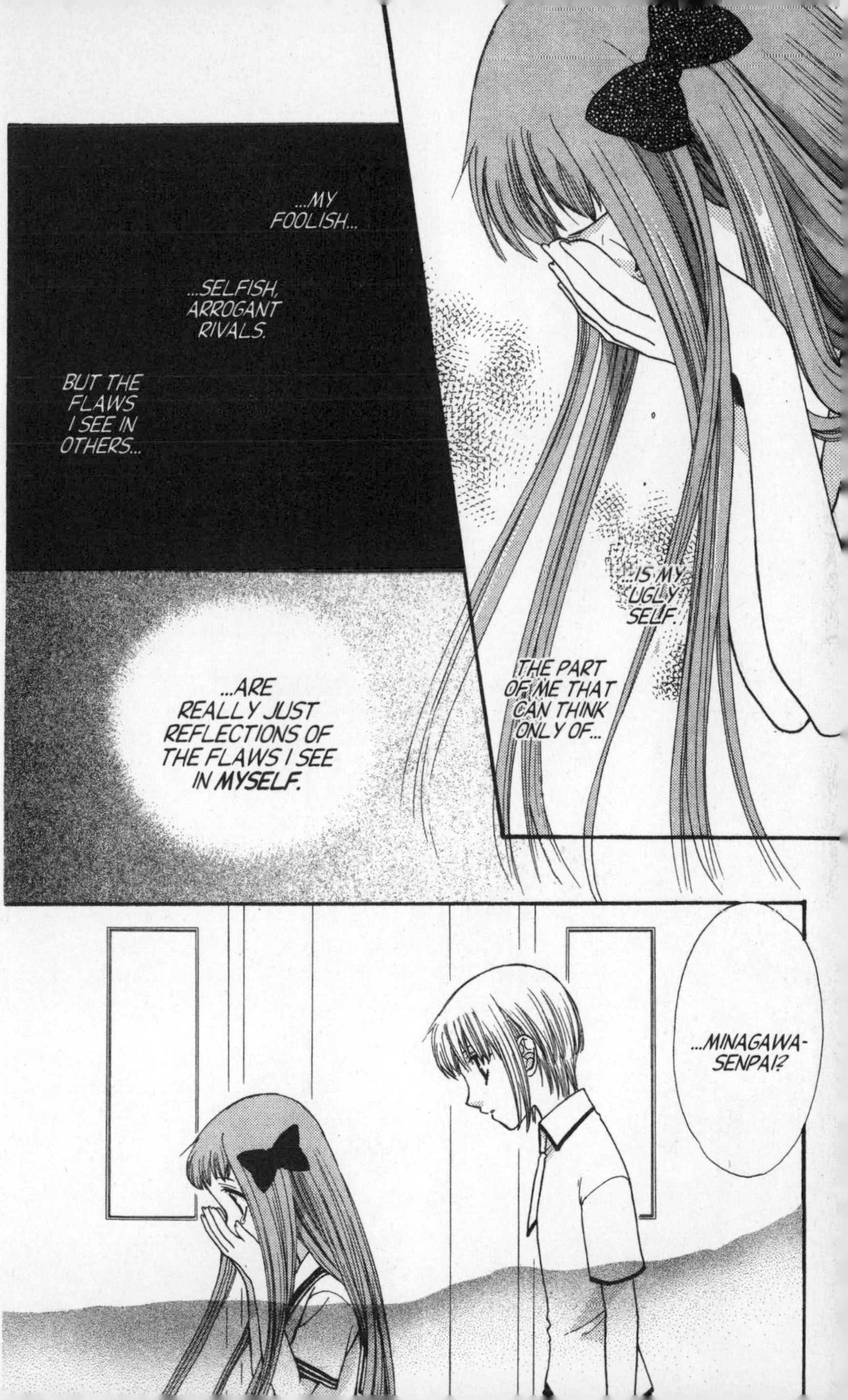
...IS MY UGLY SELF.
THE PART OF ME THAT CAN THINK ONLY OF...
...MY FOOLISH...
...SELFISH, ARROGANT RIVALS.
BUT THE FLAWS I SEE IN OTHERS...
...ARE REALLY JUST REFLECTIONS OF THE FLAWS I SEE IN MYSELF.
...MINAGAWA-SENPAI?

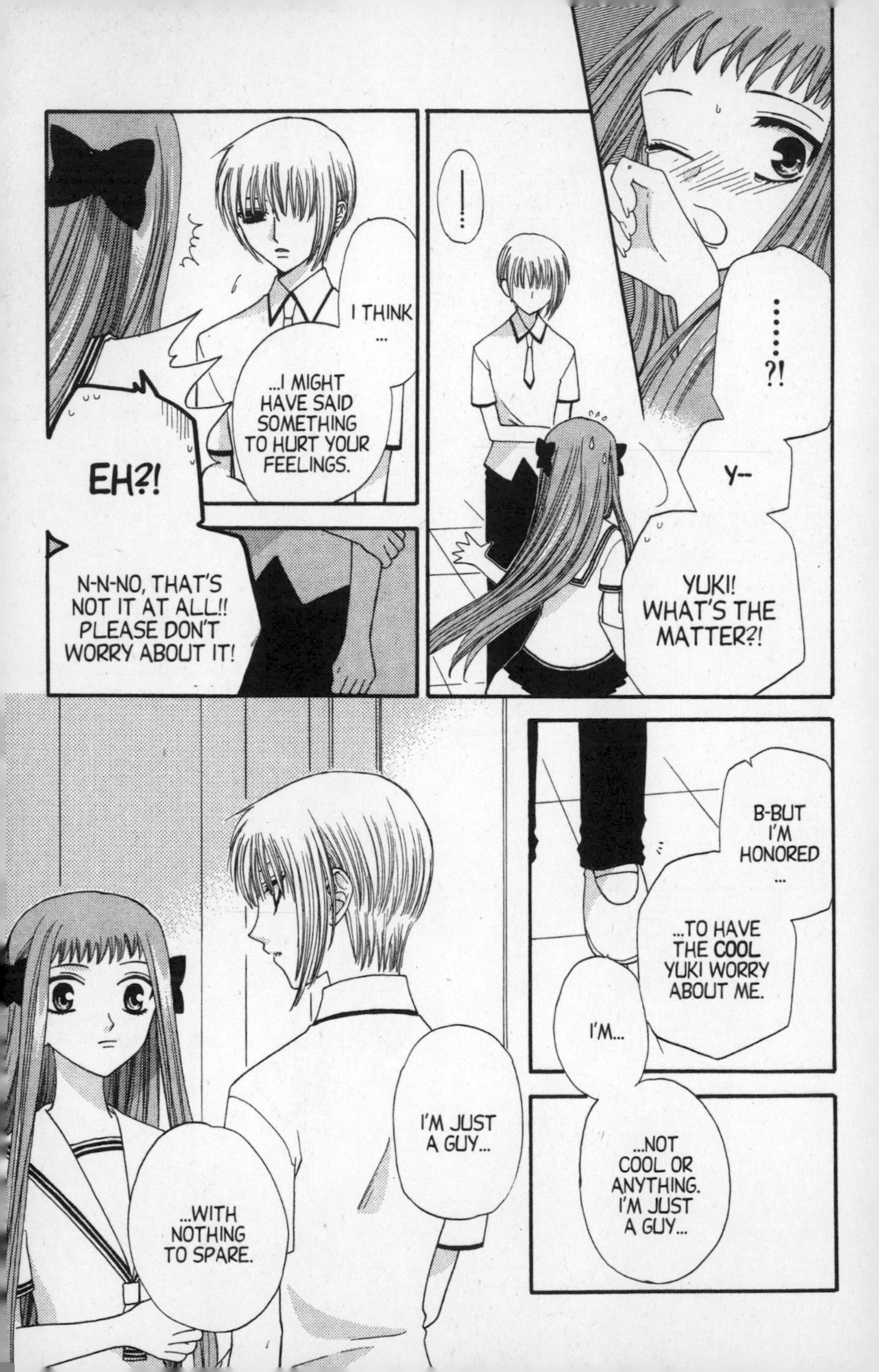
......?!
Y--
YUKI! WHAT'S THE MATTER?!
!......
I THINK...
...I MIGHT HAVE SAID SOMETHING TO HURT YOUR FEELINGS.
EH?!
N-N-NO, THAT'S NOT IT AT ALL!! PLEASE DON'T WORRY ABOUT IT!
B-BUT I'M HONORED...
...TO HAVE THE COOL YUKI WORRY ABOUT ME.
I'M...
...NOT COOL OR ANYTHING. I'M JUST A GUY...
I'M JUST A GUY...
...WITH NOTHING TO SPARE.

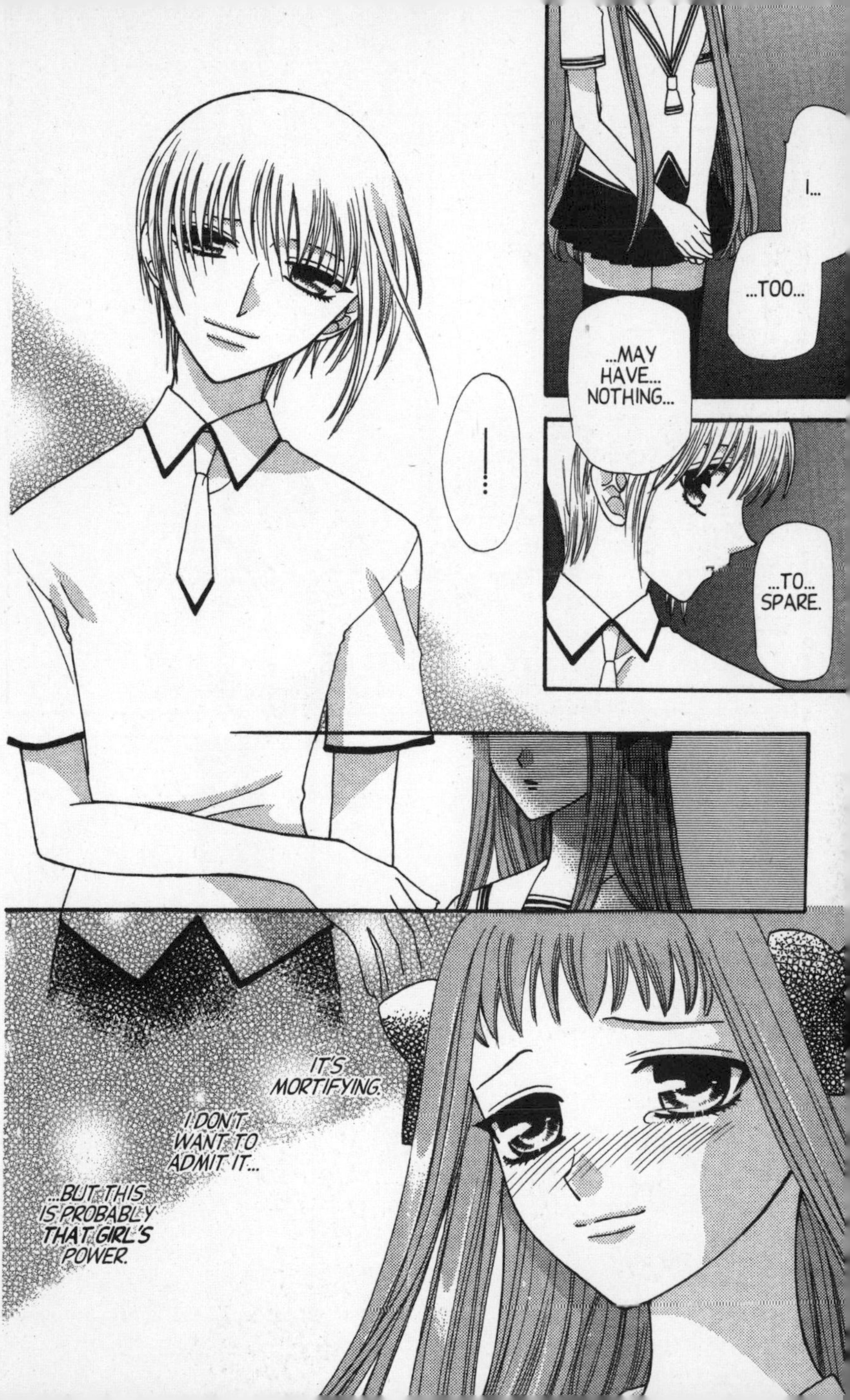
I...
...TOO...
...MAY HAVE... NOTHING...
...TO... SPARE.
!...
IT'S MORTIFYING.
I DON'T WANT TO ADMIT IT...
...BUT THIS IS PROBABLY THAT GIRL'S POWER.

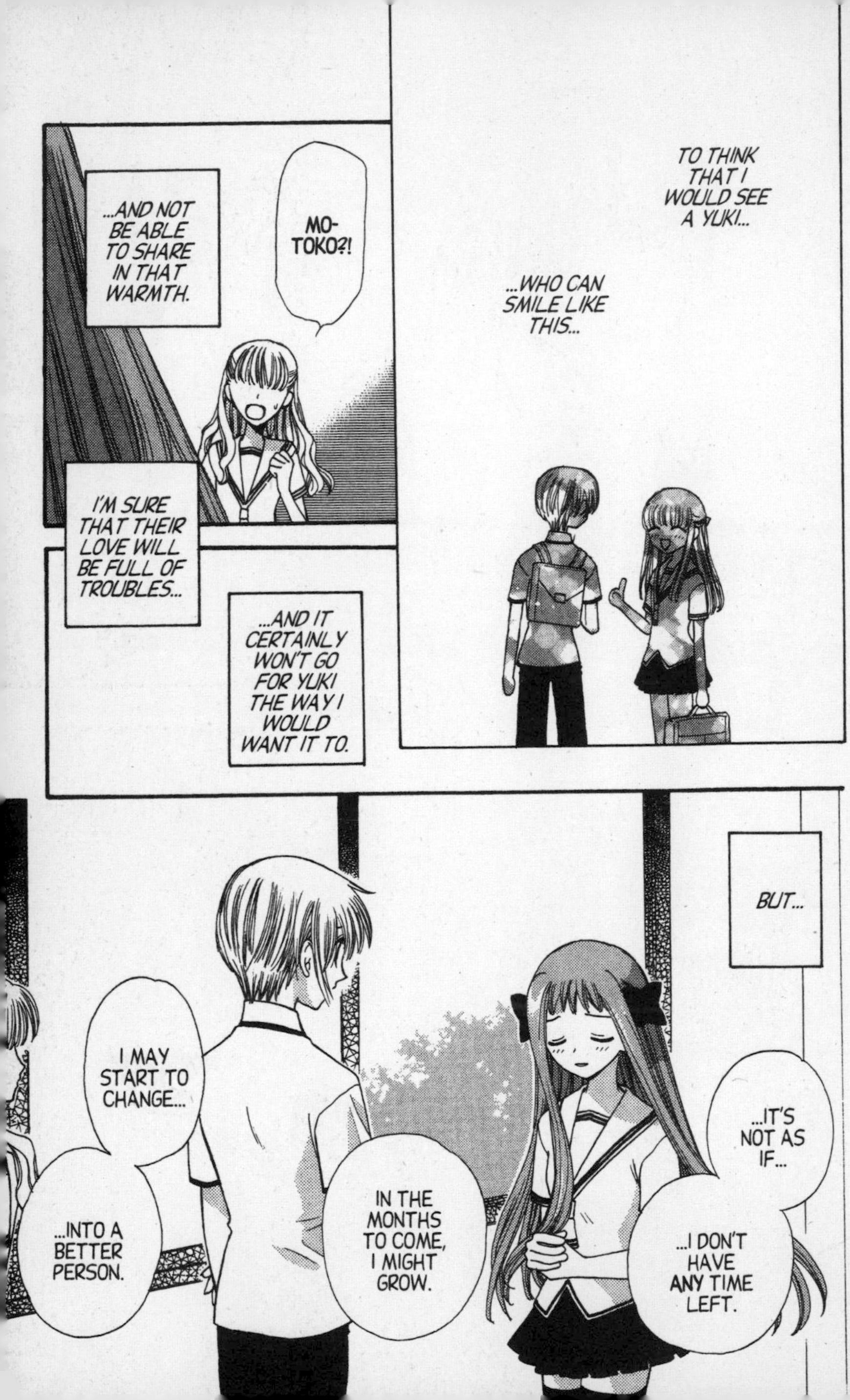
TO THINK THAT I WOULD SEE A YUKI...
...WHO CAN SMILE LIKE THIS...
...AND NOT BE ABLE TO SHARE IN THAT WARMTH.
MO-TOKO?!
I'M SURE THAT THEIR LOVE WILL BE FULL OF TROUBLES...
...AND IT CERTAINLY WON'T GO FOR YUKI THE WAY I WOULD WANT IT TO.
BUT...
...IT'S NOT AS IF...
...I DON'T HAVE ANY TIME LEFT.
IN THE MONTHS TO COME, I MIGHT GROW.
I MAY START TO CHANGE...
...INTO A BETTER PERSON.

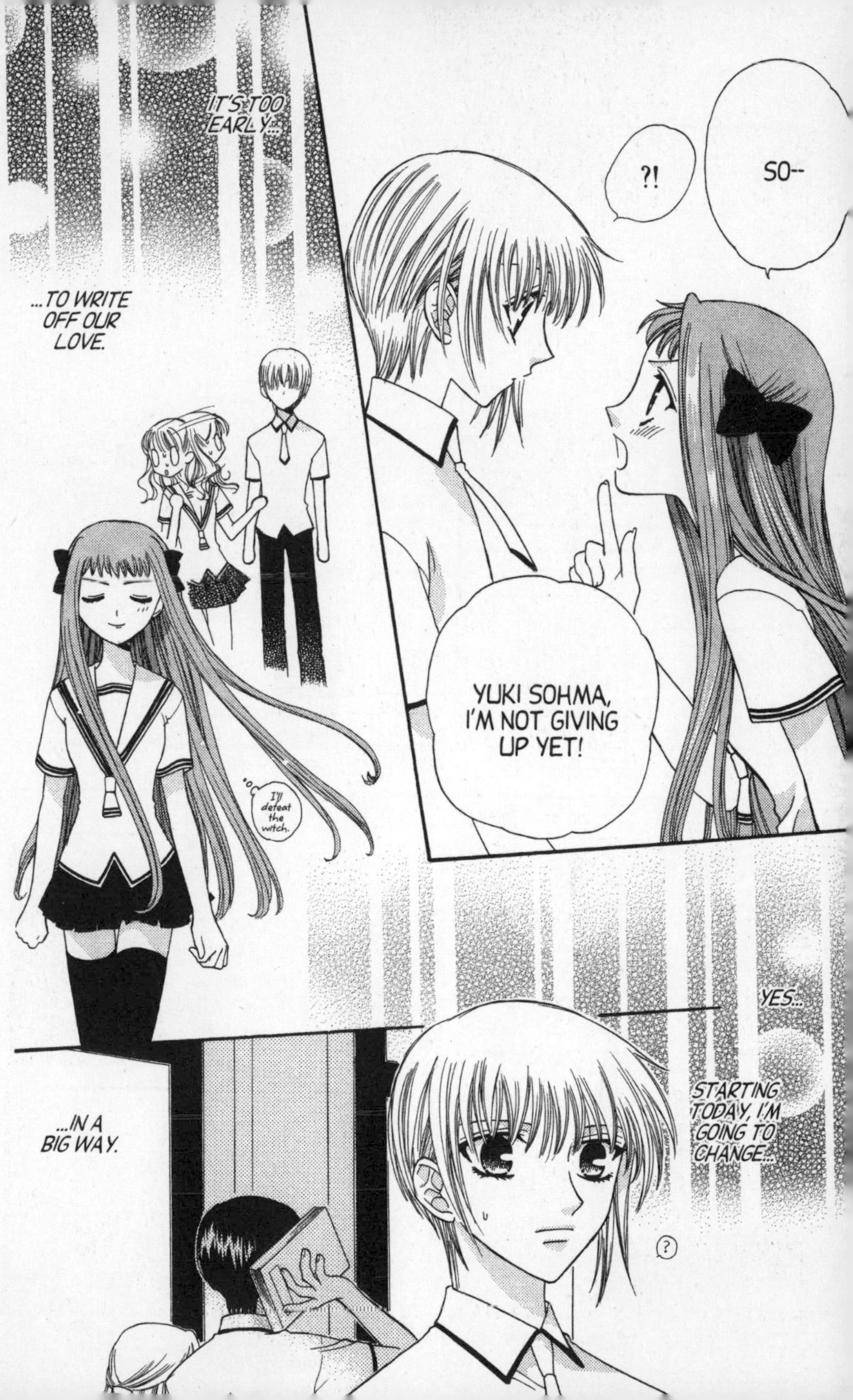
SO--
?!
YUKI SOHMA, I'M NOT GIVING UP YET!
IT'S TOO EARLY...
...TO WRITE OFF OUR LOVE.
I'll defeat the witch.
YES...
STARTING TODAY, I'M GOING TO CHANGE...
?
...IN A BIG WAY.

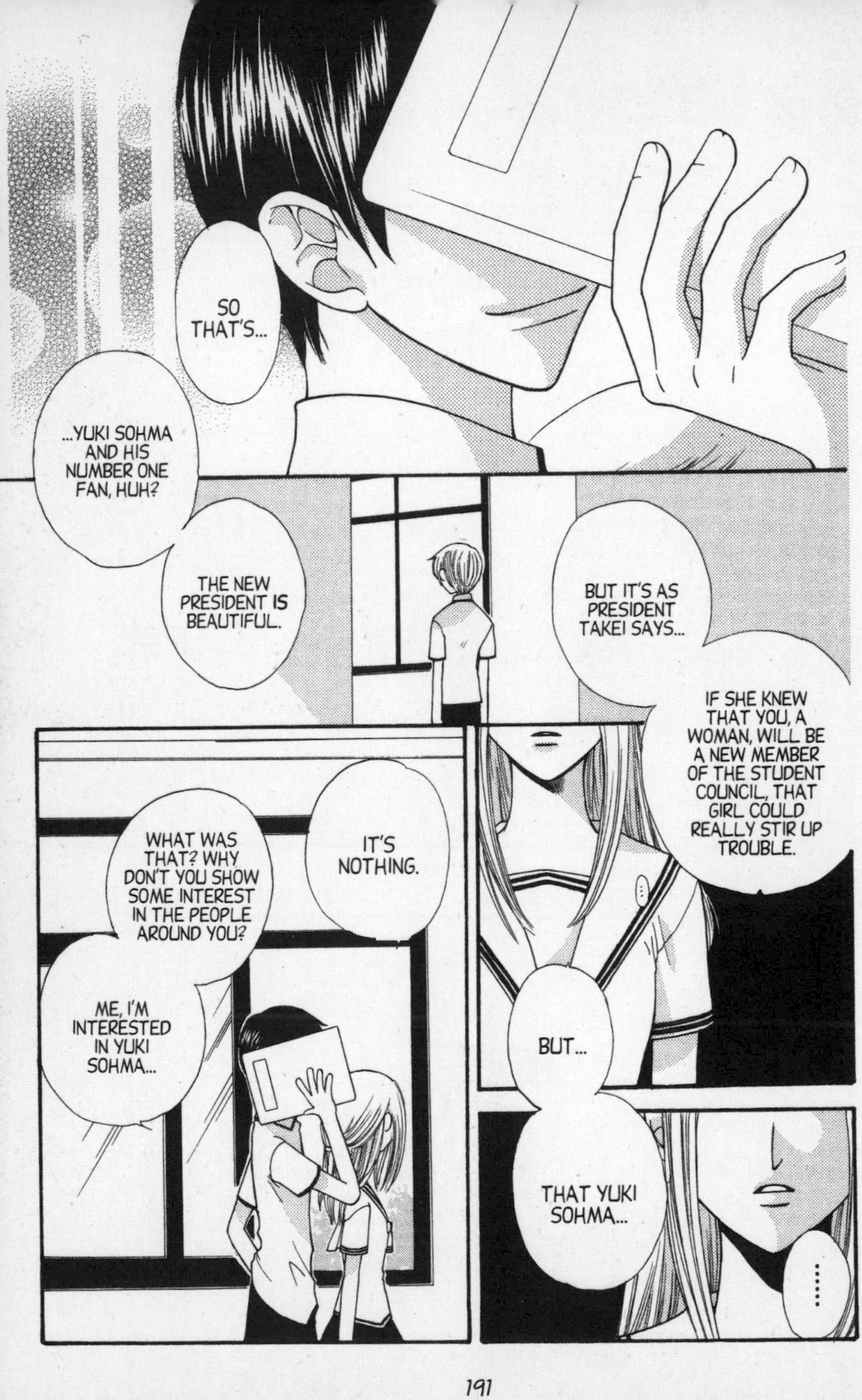
SO THAT'S...
...YUKI SOHMA AND HIS NUMBER ONE FAN, HUH?
BUT IT'S AS PRESIDENT TAKEI SAYS...
IF SHE KNEW THAT YOU, A WOMAN, WILL BE A NEW MEMBER OF THE STUDENT COUNCIL, THAT GIRL COULD REALLY STIR UP TROUBLE.
THE NEW PRESIDENT IS BEAUTIFUL.
...
BUT...
THAT YUKI SOHMA...
......
IT'S NOTHING.
WHAT WAS THAT? WHY DON'T YOU SHOW SOME INTEREST IN THE PEOPLE AROUND YOU?
ME, I'M INTERESTED IN YUKI SOHMA...

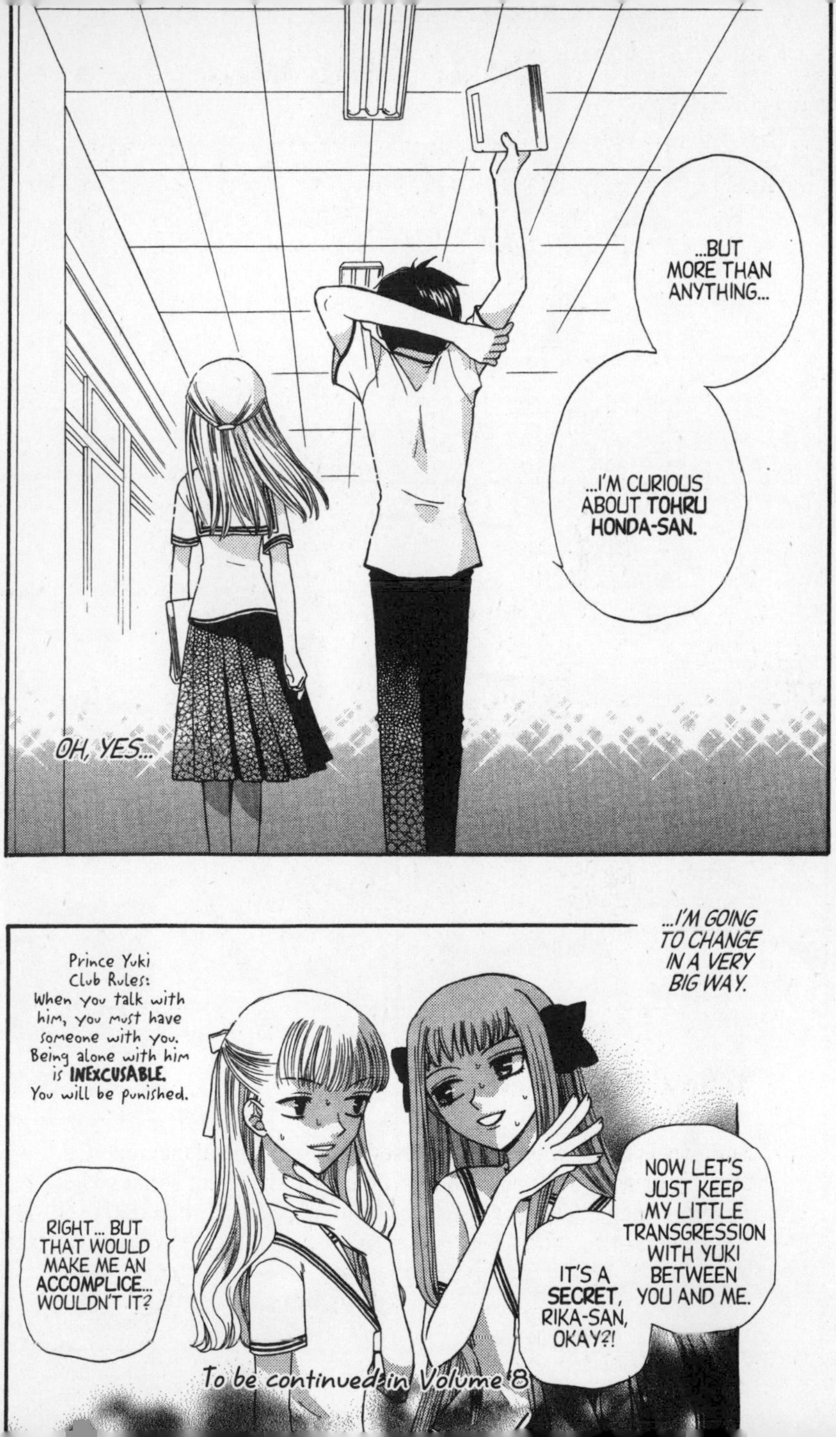
...BUT MORE THAN ANYTHING...
...I'M CURIOUS ABOUT TOHRU HONDA-SAN.
OH, YES...
...I'M GOING TO CHANGE IN A VERY BIG WAY.
Prince Yuki Club Rules: When you talk with him, you must have someone with you. Being alone with him is INEXCUSABLE. You will be punished.
NOW LET'S JUST KEEP MY LITTLE TRANSGRESSION WITH YUKI BETWEEN YOU AND ME.
IT'S A SECRET, RIKA-SAN, OKAY?!
RIGHT... BUT THAT WOULD MAKE ME AN ACCOMPLICE... WOULDN'T IT?
To be continued in Volume 8

Next time in...

Fruits Basket
TOKYOPOP
The #1 selling shojo manga in America!
8
Natsuki Takaya

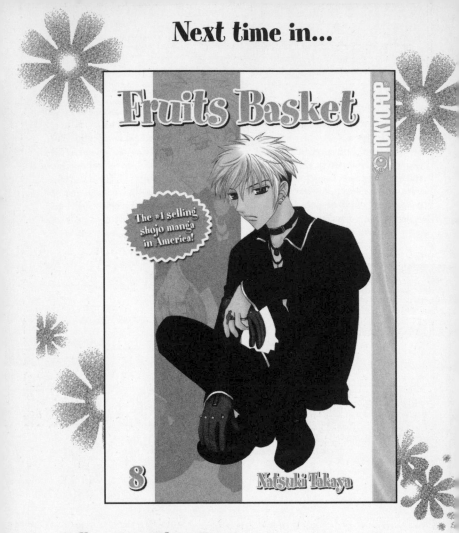

Yellow Sun, Black Haru...

Summer is on its way, so of course Tohru and friends are excited about the upcoming vacation and field trip. But what's that sound? It's Haru going beserk in the classroom...again! Black Haru is full of more rage than usual, so what will happen when Yuki intervenes? And then there's Ritsu Sohma, whose mom Tohru met at the hot spring; what's wrong with this kimono-wearing beauty?!

Fruits Basket Volume 8
Available April 2005

Fans Basket

As the new editor of "Fruits Basket," I have been utterly amazed at the amount of fan mail this book receives from its devoted readers. Seriously. You guys are drowning me in an ocean of letters and art. I have a giant sack under my desk that is continually expanding, like a sun about to go super nova. Trust me, you don't want to be around when that baby explodes. My hands are shredded with paper cuts, all from your brightly colored envelopes and spiffy pictures. I'm not even kidding, you guys. Legally, I am sure this is some form of abuse. But I won't press charges. I guess I'm some kind of masochist, because I am still encouraging you to keep flooding me with your touching words and adorable drawings. Despite the pain I've endured (my back is shot from lifting that sack), I take great joy in reading your mail, and I only wish I could publish every piece of art you send.

- Paul Morrissey, Editor

Chii
Age 14
Killeen, TX

A Hug how cute!
Total violation!!
9-10-04 Chii

I love Tohru's nonexistent skirt--but not as much as the perverted Shigure. I'm pretty sure that's more than just a hug!

Rachel B.
Age 16
Powder Springs, GA

Ich heiße Momiji!

This is simultaneously precious and disturbing. "I am called Momiji," indeed! Even though Momiji's half-German, I'm never quite ready see him in lederhosen!

Chelsea M.
Age 13
Milford, CT

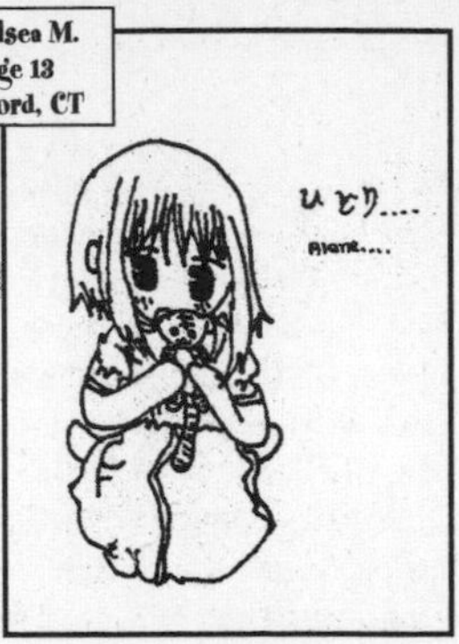
ひとり....
Alone....

Awwww, how adorably sad. Thanks for subtitling the Japanese.

Melissa C.
Age 13
Olathe, KS

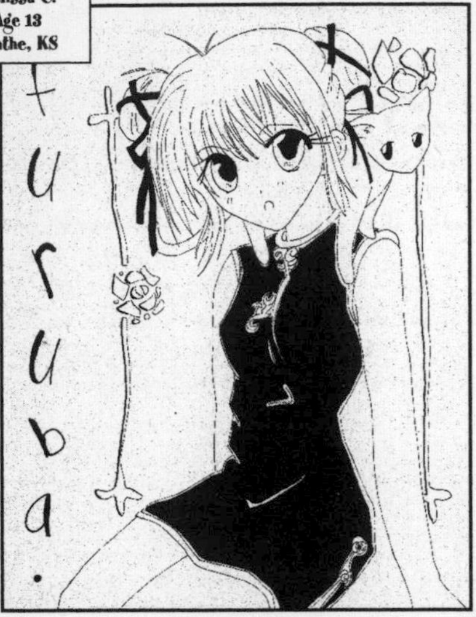
furuba.

Very nice! Love those thin lines. Makes for an interesting look! The dress looks awesome, too!

Liz W.
Age 13
Wilmington, DE

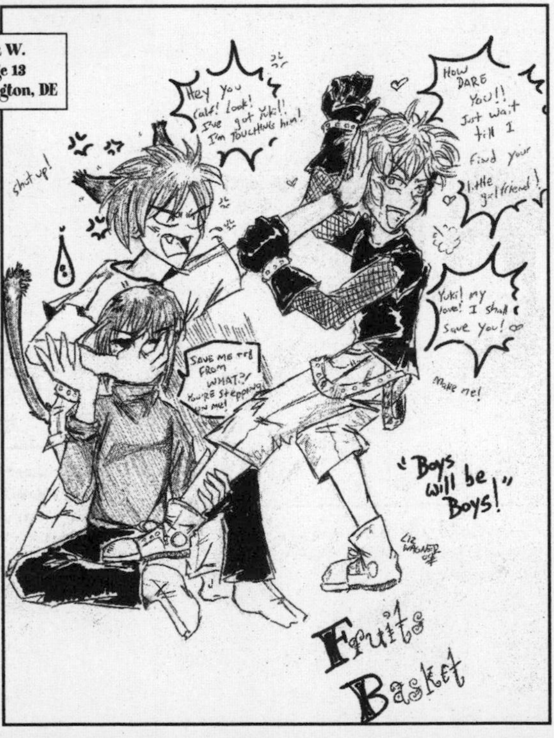
HOW DARE YOU!! Just wait till I find your little girlfriend!
Hey you calf! Look! I've got Yuki!! I'm TOUCHING him!
Yuki! my love! I shall save you!
Make me!
Shut up!
SAVE ME FROM WHAT?! YOU'RE STEPPING ON ME!
"Boys will be Boys!"
LIZ WAGNER
Fruits Basket

Hilarious! Thanks for making me laugh, Liz!

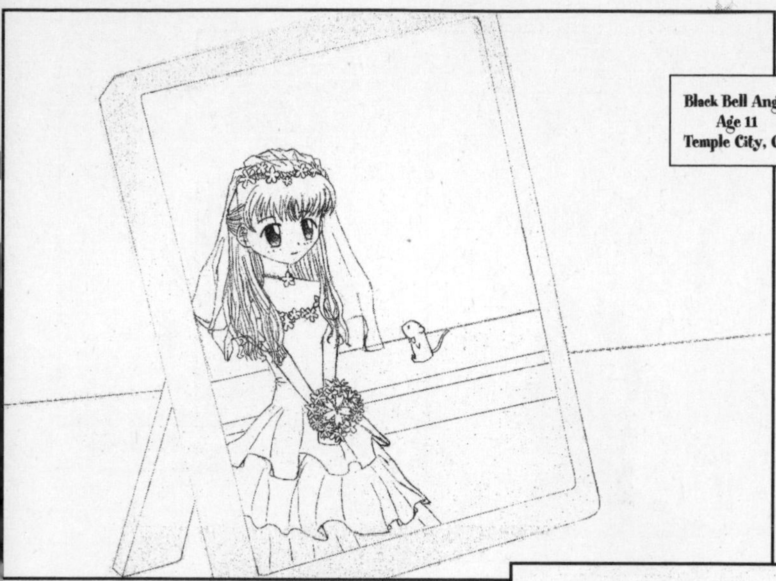

Black Bell Angel
Age 11
Temple City, CA

Wow! Look at that wedding photo! That's brilliant! What a gorgeous gown! And Yuki looks so handsome in his bowtie, but I bet he couldn't find a tux small enough to fit!

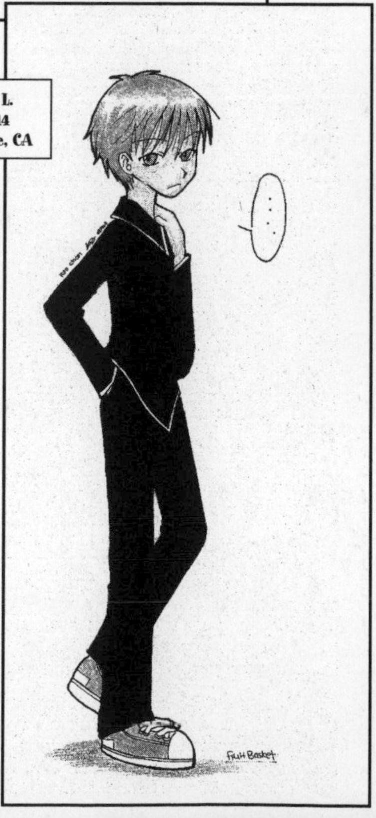
...
Fruit Basket

Jaera L.
Age 14
Torrance, CA

What a great sketch of Kyo! It's a shame we couldn't print it in color, though. I just loved his bright orange mop of hair.

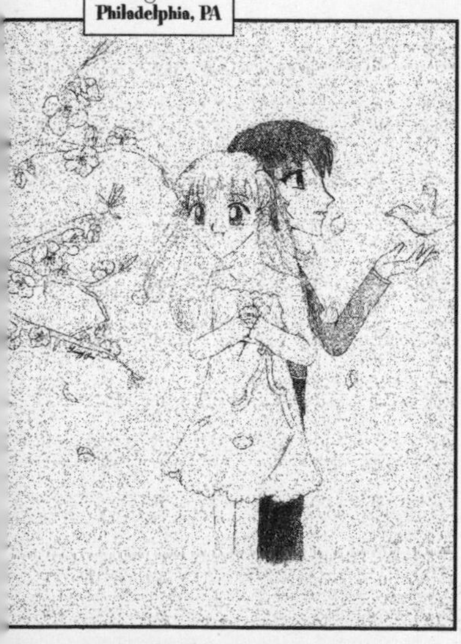

Tracey L.
Age 12
Philadelphia, PA

Awww, how romantic! Right under the cherry blossoms! I thought the bird was a nice touch, too!

♥ Fruits Basket ♥

Elizabeth J. D.
Age 17
Mustang, OK

Those Zodiac
symbols look
wonderful! Excellent
job!

Daniele S. Age ?
(She's under 18, though!)
Campbell, CA

わたしの
きょくん!

Fruits
Basket

ダニエレ・ミース

Long legs look totally
cool! Funky style. A lot
of nice little touches,
too--like the fruit in
Yuki's hands and the
Japanese characters!

Lindsay M.
Age 15
Modesto, CA

Tohru Honda

Sohma

SHIGURE SOHMA

MOMIJI SOHMA~

F U R U B A

I love seeing the
whole cast of
characters here. I
particularly liked
Shigure and his dog
biscuits!

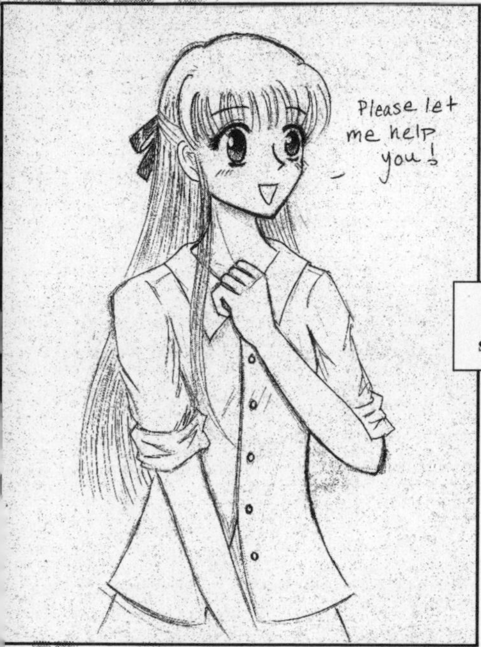
Please let me help you!

Kat T.
Age 14
San Jose, CA

A terrifically drawn picture of Tohru that captures her earnestness, her optimism and her generosity.

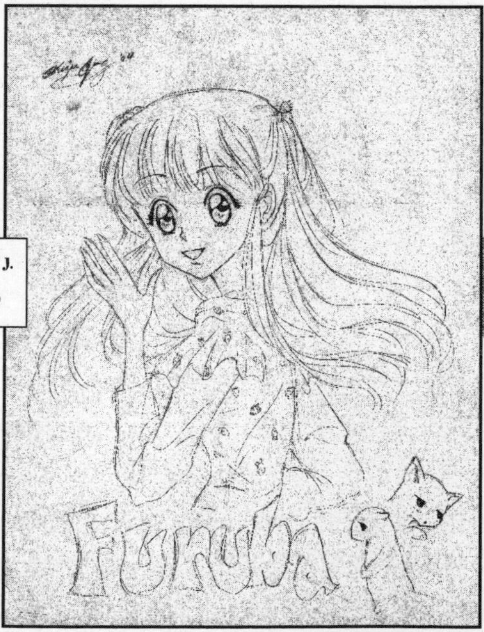
Furuba

Shichu "Suzie" J.
Age 13
Cheshire, CT

Sooooooo cute! I love the eyes and--of course--the strawberries! Nicely done, Suzie!

Do you want to share your love for *Fruits Basket* with fans around the world? "Fans Basket" is taking submissions of fan art, poetry, cosplay photos, or any other Furuba fun you'd like to share!

How to submit:

1) Send your work via regular mail (NOT e-mail) to:

"Fans Basket"
c/o TOKYOPOP
5900 Wilshire Blvd.
Suite 2000
Los Angeles, CA 90036

2) All work should be in black-and-white and no larger than 8.5" x 11". (And try not to fold it too many times!)

3) Anything you send will not be returned. If you want to keep your original, it's fine to send us a copy.

4) Please include your full name, age, city and state for us to print with your work. If you'd rather us use a pen name, please include that, too.

5) IMPORTANT: If you're under the age of 18, you must have your parent's permission in order for us to print your work. Any submissions without a signed note of parental consent cannot be used.

6) For full details, please check out our website: http://www.tokyopop.com/aboutus/fanart.php

Disclaimer: Anything you send to us becomes the exclusive property of TOKYOPOP Inc. and, as we said before, will not be returned to you. We will have the right to print, reproduce, distribute, or modify the artwork for use in future volumes of Fruits Basket or on the web royalty-free.

Hannah E.
Age 14
Mechanicsville, VA

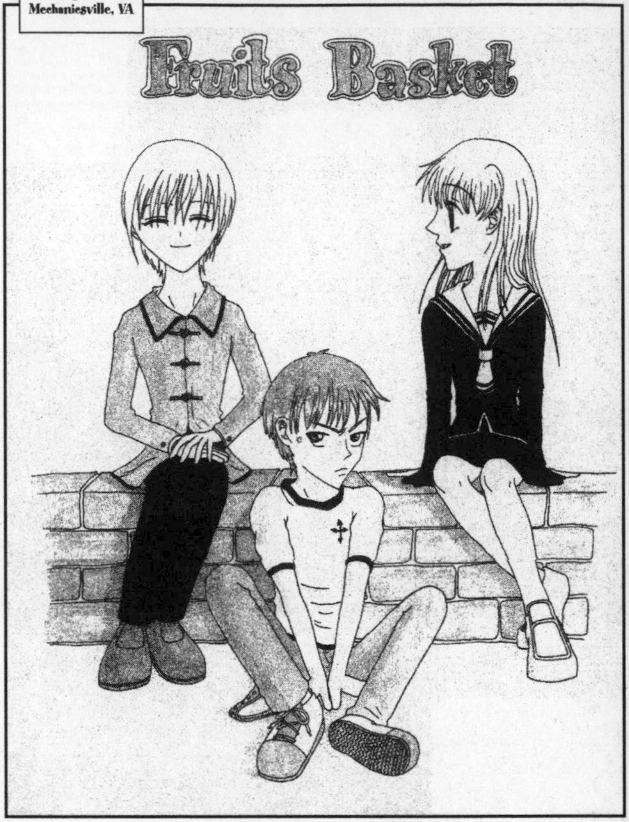
Fruits Basket

Ah. What great expressions! Not only do you get a sense of who these characters are, but you also get an idea of how they feel about each other!

Wendy Z.
Age 17
Toronto, Canada

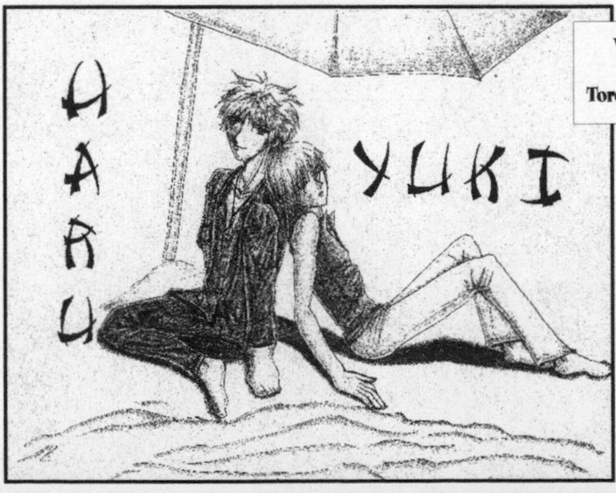
HARU
YUKI

Lovely, lovely! I really like the calligraphy. They don't really seem dressed for the beach, though! I guess that's just their style.

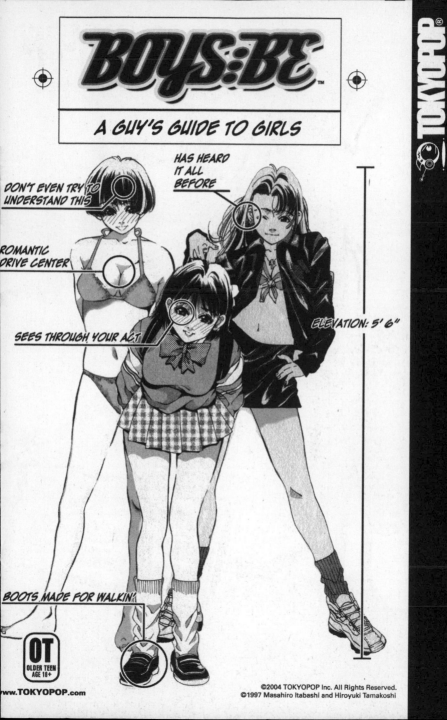

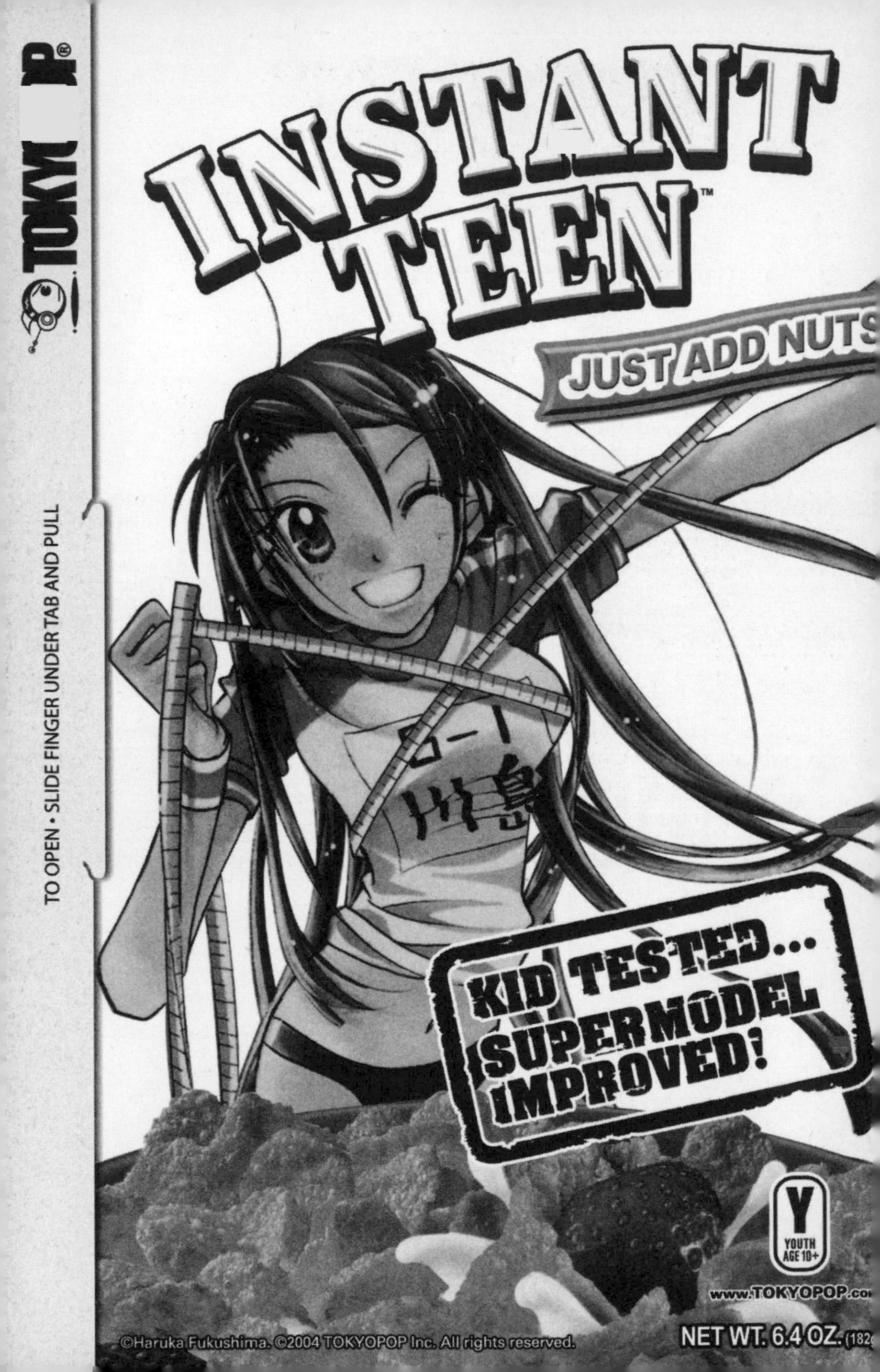
TO OPEN • SLIDE FINGER UNDER TAB AND PULL
INSTANT TEEN™
JUST ADD NUTS
KID TESTED...
SUPERMODEL IMPROVED!
Y
YOUTH AGE 10+
www.TOKYOPOP.co
NET WT. 6.4 OZ. (182
©Haruka Fukushima. ©2004 TOKYOPOP Inc. All rights reserved.

LEGAL DRUG™

When no ordinary prescription will do...

FROM THE CREATORS OF CHOBITS & TOKYO BABYLON

TOKYOPOP®

OT
OLDER TEEN
AGE 16+

©2001 by CLAMP. ©2004 TOKYOPOP Inc. All Rights Reserved.

www.TOKYOPOP.com

The Tarot Café © 2002 by Park Sang Sun. All rights reserved. First published in Korea in 2002 by SIGONGSA Co., Ltd.
English translation rights aranged by SIGONGSA Co., Ltd. through Shinwon Agency Co. All rights reserved.

www.TOKYOPOP.com

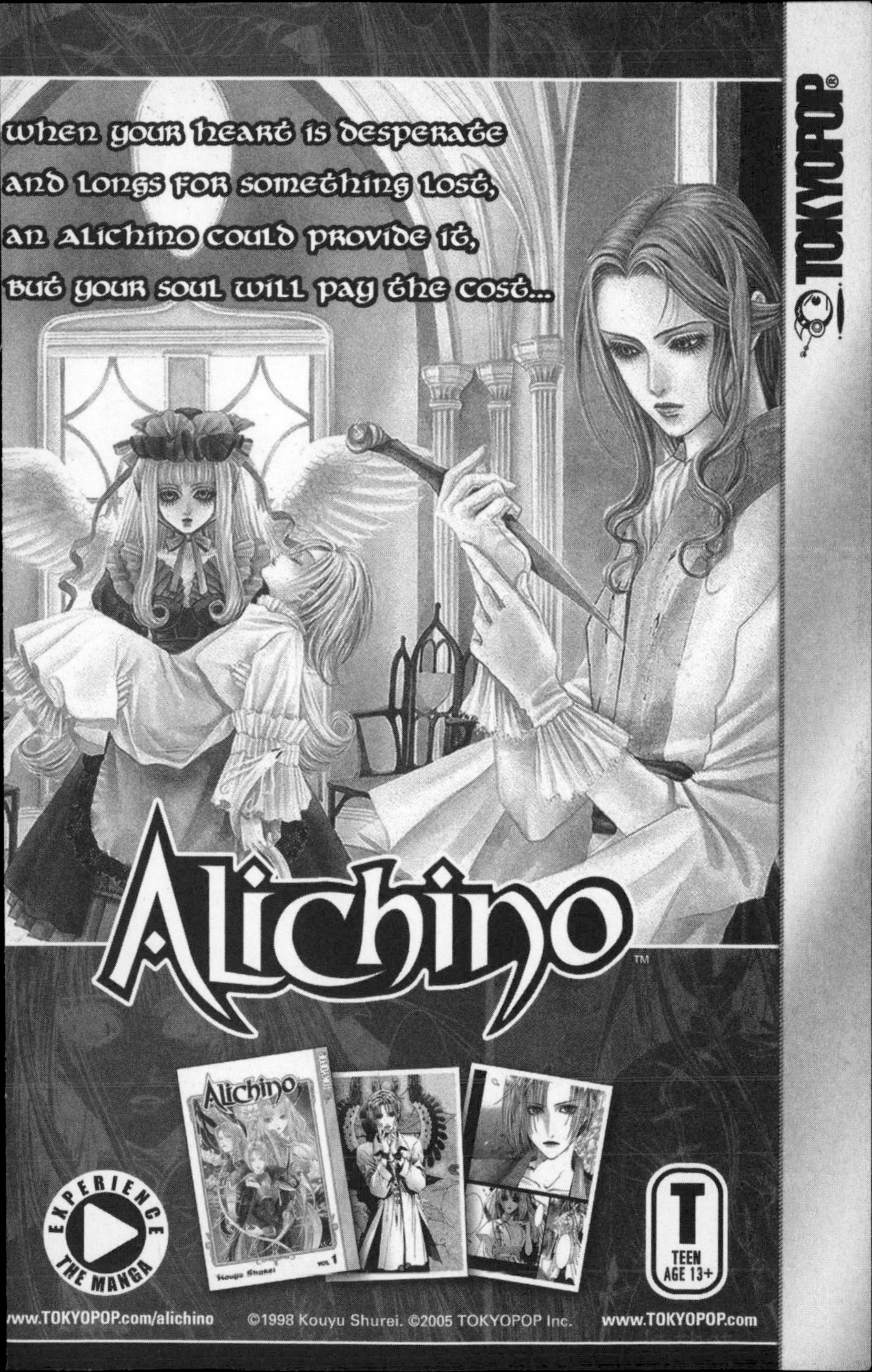
TOKYOPOP®
When your heart is desperate
and longs for something lost,
an Alichino could provide it,
but your soul will pay the cost...
Alichino™
Alichino
Kouyu Shurei
Vol. 1
EXPERIENCE THE MANGA
T
TEEN
AGE 13+
www.TOKYOPOP.com/alichino
©1998 Kouyu Shurei. ©2005 TOKYOPOP Inc.
www.TOKYOPOP.com

ALSO AVAILABLE FROM ◉ TOKYOPOP®

PLANETES
PRESIDENT DAD
PRIEST
PRINCESS AI
PSYCHIC ACADEMY
QUEEN'S KNIGHT, THE
RAGNAROK
RAVE MASTER
REALITY CHECK
REBIRTH
REBOUND
REMOTE
RISING STARS OF MANGA™, THE
SABER MARIONETTE J
SAILOR MOON
SAINT TAIL
SAIYUKI
SAMURAI DEEPER KYO
SAMURAI GIRL™ REAL BOUT HIGH SCHOOL
SCRYED
SEIKAI TRILOGY, THE
SGT. FROG
SHAOLIN SISTERS
SHIRAHIME-SYO: SNOW GODDESS TALES
SHUTTERBOX
SKULL MAN, THE
SNOW DROP
SORCERER HUNTERS
SOUL TO SEOUL
STONE
SUIKODEN III
SUKI
TAROT CAFÉ, THE
THREADS OF TIME
TOKYO BABYLON
TOKYO MEW MEW
TOKYO TRIBES
TRAMPS LIKE US
UNDER THE GLASS MOON
VAMPIRE GAME
VISION OF ESCAFLOWNE, THE
WARCRAFT
WARRIORS OF TAO
WILD ACT
WISH
WORLD OF HARTZ
X-DAY
ZODIAC P.I.

NOVELS

CLAMP SCHOOL PARANORMAL INVESTIGATORS
SAILOR MOON
SLAYERS

ART BOOKS

ART OF CARDCAPTOR SAKURA
ART OF MAGIC KNIGHT RAYEARTH, THE
PEACH: MIWA UEDA ILLUSTRATIONS
CLAMP NORTH SIDE
CLAMP SOUTH SIDE

ANIME GUIDES

COWBOY BEBOP
GUNDAM TECHNICAL MANUALS
SAILOR MOON SCOUT GUIDES

TOKYOPOP KIDS

STRAY SHEEP

CINE-MANGA®

ALADDIN
CARDCAPTORS
DUEL MASTERS
FAIRLY ODDPARENTS, THE
FAMILY GUY
FINDING NEMO
G.I. JOE SPY TROOPS
GREATEST STARS OF THE NBA
JACKIE CHAN ADVENTURES
JIMMY NEUTRON: BOY GENIUS, THE ADVENTURES OF
KIM POSSIBLE
LILO & STITCH: THE SERIES
LIZZIE MCGUIRE
LIZZIE MCGUIRE MOVIE, THE
MALCOLM IN THE MIDDLE
POWER RANGERS: DINO THUNDER
POWER RANGERS: NINJA STORM
PRINCESS DIARIES 2, THE
RAVE MASTER
SHREK 2
SIMPLE LIFE, THE
SPONGEBOB SQUAREPANTS
SPY KIDS 2
SPY KIDS 3-D: GAME OVER
TEENAGE MUTANT NINJA TURTLES
THAT'S SO RAVEN
TOTALLY SPIES
TRANSFORMERS: ARMADA
TRANSFORMERS: ENERGON

You want it? We got it!
A full range of TOKYOPOP
products are available now at:
www.TOKYOPOP.com/shop

10.19.04T

ALSO AVAILABLE FROM 🐸TOKYOPOP®

MANGA

.HACK//LEGEND OF THE TWILIGHT
@LARGE
ABENOBASHI: MAGICAL SHOPPING ARCADE
A.I. LOVE YOU
AI YORI AOSHI
ALICHINO
ANGELIC LAYER
ARM OF KANNON
BABY BIRTH
BATTLE ROYALE
BATTLE VIXENS
BOYS BE...
BRAIN POWERED
BRIGADOON
B'TX
CANDIDATE FOR GODDESS, THE
CARDCAPTOR SAKURA
CARDCAPTOR SAKURA - MASTER OF THE CLOW
CHOBITS
CHRONICLES OF THE CURSED SWORD
CLAMP SCHOOL DETECTIVES
CLOVER
COMIC PARTY
CONFIDENTIAL CONFESSIONS
CORRECTOR YUI
COWBOY BEBOP
COWBOY BEBOP: SHOOTING STAR
CRAZY LOVE STORY
CRESCENT MOON
CROSS
CULDCEPT
CYBORG 009
D•N•ANGEL
DEARS
DEMON DIARY
DEMON ORORON, THE
DEUS VITAE
DIABOLO
DIGIMON
DIGIMON TAMERS
DIGIMON ZERO TWO
DOLL
DRAGON HUNTER
DRAGON KNIGHTS
DRAGON VOICE
DREAM SAGA
DUKLYON: CLAMP SCHOOL DEFENDERS
EERIE QUEERIE!
ERICA SAKURAZAWA: COLLECTED WORKS
ET CETERA
ETERNITY
EVIL'S RETURN
FAERIES' LANDING
FAKE
FLCL
FLOWER OF THE DEEP SLEEP
FORBIDDEN DANCE
FRUITS BASKET
G GUNDAM
GATEKEEPERS
GETBACKERS

GIRL GOT GAME
GRAVITATION
GTO
GUNDAM SEED ASTRAY
GUNDAM SEED ASTRAY R
GUNDAM WING
GUNDAM WING: BATTLEFIELD OF PACIFISTS
GUNDAM WING: ENDLESS WALTZ
GUNDAM WING: THE LAST OUTPOST (G-UNIT)
HANDS OFF!
HAPPY MANIA
HARLEM BEAT
HYPER POLICE
HYPER RUNE
I.N.V.U.
IMMORTAL RAIN
INITIAL D
INSTANT TEEN: JUST ADD NUTS
ISLAND
JING: KING OF BANDITS
JING: KING OF BANDITS - TWILIGHT TALES
JULINE
KARE KANO
KILL ME, KISS ME
KINDAICHI CASE FILES, THE
KING OF HELL
KODOCHA: SANA'S STAGE
LAGOON ENGINE
LAMENT OF THE LAMB
LEGAL DRUG
LEGEND OF CHUN HYANG, THE
LES BIJOUX
LILING-PO
LOVE HINA
LOVE OR MONEY
LUPIN III
LUPIN III: WORLD'S MOST WANTED
MAGIC KNIGHT RAYEARTH I
MAGIC KNIGHT RAYEARTH II
MAHOROMATIC: AUTOMATIC MAIDEN
MAN OF MANY FACES
MARMALADE BOY
MARS
MARS: HORSE WITH NO NAME
MINK
MIRACLE GIRLS
MIYUKI-CHAN IN WONDERLAND
MODEL
MOURYOU KIDEN: LEGEND OF THE NYMPH
NECK AND NECK
ONE
ONE I LOVE, THE
PARADISE KISS
PARASYTE
PASSION FRUIT
PEACH FUZZ
PEACH GIRL
PEACH GIRL: CHANGE OF HEART
PET SHOP OF HORRORS
PHD: PHANTASY DEGREE
PITA-TEN
PLANET BLOOD
PLANET LADDER

10.19.04

STOP!

This is the back of the book.
You wouldn't want to spoil a great ending!

This book is printed "manga-style," in the authentic Japanese right-to-left format. Since none of the artwork has been flipped or altered, readers get to experience the story just as the creator intended. You've been asking for it, so TOKYOPOP® delivered: authentic, hot-off-the-press, and far more fun!

DIRECTIONS

If this is your first time reading manga-style, here's a quick guide to help you understand how it works.

It's easy... just start in the top right panel and follow the numbers. Have fun, and look for more 100% authentic manga from TOKYOPOP®!

100% AUTHENTIC MANGA